OVERCOMING
T H E
WORLD MISSIONS
CRISIS

OVERCOMING

T H E

WORLD MISSIONS
CRISIS

THINKING STRATEGICALLY TO REACH THE WORLD

RUSSELL L. PENNEY
GENERAL EDITOR

kregel
PUBLICATIONS

Grand Rapids, MI 49501

Overcoming the World Missions Crisis: Thinking Strategically to Reach the World

© 2001 by Russell L. Penney

Published by Kregel Publications, a division of Kregel, Inc., P.O. Box 2607, Grand Rapids, MI 49501. For more information about Kregel Publications, visit our Web site: www.kregel.com.

ISBN 0-8254-3466-1

Printed in the United States of America

1 2 3 4 5 / 05 04 03 02 01

To the memory of James (Jimmy) Swindoll, former missionary with the Baptist Missionary Association of America. Jimmy and his wife, Mary, gave ten years of faithful service in Bolivia before he went home to be with his Lord in November 2000.

And to Kenneth Hanna, former department chairman and professor of World Missions at Moody Bible Institute. Ken spent twenty-five years as a missionary in Mexico and Central America with CAM International. He went home to be with his Lord in September 1999.

CONTENTS

CONTRIBUTORS

J. Ronald Blue, Th.M., Ph.D., is former chairman of the World Missions Department of Dallas Theological Seminary and president of CAM (Central American Mission) International. He is currently coordinator, Spanish Doctor of Ministries, Dallas Theological Seminary, and mobilizer for Latin Missions with CAM International.

Jennifer Collins, M.A.R., is adjunct professor of Biblical Studies and Missions at Taylor University, Upland, Indiana, and director of Lighthouse, Taylor's short-term missions program.

John F. Hart, Th.M., Th.D., is professor of Bible at Moody Bible Institute, Chicago, Illinois.

George Hilgeman, Th.M., Th.D., is a veteran missionary of more than forty years and former director of Seminario Teologico Hebron, Santa Cruz de la Sierra, Bolivia. He is now retired and resides in Dallas, Texas.

Steven McAvoy, Th.M., Th.D., is director of the Institute of Biblical Studies, Lake Oswego, Oregon.

Russell L. Penney, M.A., D.Sc., Th.D., is a missionary with Gospel Missionary Union and director of postgraduate studies at Seminario Teologico Hebron, Santa Cruz de la Sierra, Bolivia.

Albert T. Platt, Th.M., Th.D., is president emeritus, CAM International.

Michael Pocock, Th.M., Ph.D., is chairman and professor of the World Missions Department, Dallas Theological Seminary, Dallas, Texas.

Chuck Sutton, M.Div., Ph.D., is chairman and professor of the Missions Department, Philadelphia College of Bible, Langhorne, Pennsylvania. He is currently director, Member Care for World Team, a nondenominational missions agency, Warrington, Pennsylvania.

PREFACE

IN 1995, MY WIFE AND I returned from serving the Lord in Bulgaria. Formerly, my education had been in the area of systematic theology, but through my experiences in Bulgaria the Lord had given me a greater understanding of missions. It soon developed into a passion. I had traveled throughout Eastern Europe and in parts of Western Europe as well. Wherever I went, I became aware of people's tremendous spiritual needs.

On our return to Tyndale Theological Seminary, my alma mater, we began to develop a fledgling missions program. As I researched textbooks and curricula, I was alarmed at some of the strange ideas that were being hailed as "cutting edge"—ideas that had no foundation in the Word of God. Together, they represented a basic lack of attention to the doctrines and missionary patterns given in Scripture and a fundamental lack of belief in the sufficiency of God's Word for missions strategy. Many of these concepts are addressed in this volume.

But this was not all. During my time on the mission field, I had become increasingly alarmed at the lack of theological conviction of many of the other missionaries there. While it is true that missionaries will eventually form their own circles of fellowship and that these circles will be larger for some than for others, nevertheless, I could see that capitulating to the least-common-denominator syndrome was the surest way to hinder missions work. Unfortunately, this practice is becoming more and more prevalent. The words "just believe in Jesus" sound good, but I don't see undeveloped theology such as this evidenced by the early church—nor by Paul, our premier missionary. Why not? Because oversimplistic thinking naturally leads the church into apostasy.

In developing the program at Tyndale, I spent a great deal of time studying how missions institutions, sending churches, missionaries themselves, and

receiving churches or people groups could best work together. I found that
the Word of God has sufficient information to form the framework for our
practice. This book is an attempt to set forth a biblically and theologically
sound presentation in all these areas. If it proves helpful to the church of
Jesus Christ, this is due to the prayer, support, encouragement, and
contribution of many saints. I first want to thank my family—Joann, Joseph,
Hannah, and Micah—for giving me the many hours it took to write my part
of the book and to edit, edit, and reedit the book as a whole. I am very
grateful to Dr. Mal Couch, my spiritual father and mentor, for encouraging
me when this work was a mere idea. Many thanks to Dennis Hillman and
Steve Barclift at Kregel, both for their patience as I moved to my present
ministry in Bolivia and for giving this spiritual pygmy a chance to work with
the giants who comprise the other contributors—to whom I also give thanks.
I owe a debt of gratitude to Dr. George Peters, Dr. Harold Lindsell, Dr.
David J. Hesselgrave, Roland Allen, Dr. Harold R. Cook, and Dr. J. Herbert
Kane, who taught me so much through their writings. Finally, and most
importantly, I give thanks to our Lord Jesus Christ. May we not rest until all
the earth has heard of Christ's love!

A PLEA TO RETURN TO A BIBLICAL MODEL

RUSSELL L. PENNEY

A PLEA FOR PRAYERFUL EVALUATION

We can evaluate someone and then guess their motives, but only God knows what's in a person's heart. And the intent of this book is not to question the motives of any brother or sister in Christ who may disagree on the doctrinal matters discussed. What is questioned, however, is the position that evangelicals take on certain doctrinal issues in light of the teaching of God's Word. To those who claim to be evangelical—whether at the lectern, behind the pulpit, or in the pew—this book calls you to reexamine what you think about missions.

As we enter a new millennium, our starting point in doing the Lord's work must—*must*—be a belief in the Bible as the inerrant and fully inspired Word of God. Both internal and external evidence offers overwhelming proof that the Bible is what it claims to be. Absolute truth *does* exist in the Bible and, interpreted literally, the Bible can be trusted as our guide to faith and practice. The Author of the universe has said so, and He *is* Truth. He is the only standard in the universe against which truth and morals can be measured. Truth can be known, and the Truth in written form is God's Word.

Francis Schaeffer stated, more than fifteen years ago,

> "But if we truly believe this [that the text is inspired of God and fully inerrant], then something must be considered. *Truth carries with it confrontation.* Truth demands confrontation; loving confrontation, but confrontation nevertheless. If our reflex action is always accommodation regardless of the centrality of the truth involved, there is something wrong." (italics his)[1]

The same is true about the major doctrines discussed in this volume. Evangelicals must lovingly confront others in areas of doctrine where errant teaching is gaining acceptance—even at the cost of possible schism.

Evangelicals, too, must reevaluate their approach to making disciples. Hesselgrave writes, "At the procedural level . . . the Bible contains more than a divine message, it constitutes a divine method of delivering that message."[2] The basic strategies and procedures that Paul and his companions used are as applicable today as they were nearly two thousand years ago. Their example is God's divine pattern for success in our mission. This model does not rule out individual thoughts and plans on how to apply biblical strategies in each unique culture. But individual plans must agree with and complement the scriptural pattern, not conflict with it.

As individual believers, we must reevaluate our priorities in light of Scripture. Consider first that, we are not of this world (John 17:16). This world is not our home—we are just passing through. Because, therefore, we are "fellow-citizens with the saints, and are of God's household" (Eph. 2:19), we should concentrate on our Father's business in this life. We should constantly be examining our lives in the light of Paul's prohibition against conforming to this world (i.e., the thinking, actions, and speech of the world). Let us also, as often as possible, study God's Word carefully as a safeguard against complying with our godless culture. And let us remind ourselves that the culture we live in is the way it is because it follows the god of this world (1 Cor. 4:4). As Christians, we should not be like the culture around us.

Finally, let us all ask ourselves these questions:

- How does God want me to be involved in the mission of the church?
- Am I willing to say, "Here am I Lord, send me"?
- Am I willing to spend time on my knees and to invest a portion of my earnings—even give up some of my pleasures—to assist frontline missionaries at home and abroad in reaching the world for Christ?
- Am I willing—in order to further the missionary work at home or abroad—to commit some of my vacation time to using the gifts, talents, and educational expertise that God has given me?
- Am I willing to expose my children to missionary biographies and to missionaries who are on furlough in order to help them develop a missionary passion?
- Am I willing to support my children if they should some day decide to go to the mission field?

WHAT IS AT STAKE?

Because doctrinal purity is often neglected, compromise can occur at the highest levels (and it has). Doctrinal compromise will in turn lead to a re-definition of what it means to be a Christian. Far from bringing unity, compromise will lead to massive disunity among true believers. The whole idea of a nondoctrinal unity—or a unity based on the lowest common denominator of doctrine—is a myth, a lie propagated by the father of lies (John 8:44). The Bible teaches that unity develops around commonly held truths derived from Scripture and faithfully taught by pastor-teachers (John 14–17; Eph. 4:11–16).

If the church continues to buy into the cultural relativism of the age, we are going to have churches full of people who are unwilling to stand for anything at all. The Bible is a book that presents a specific way to approach God and to maintain a relationship with Him. It presents a specific and uncompromising moral standard. Culture, as we know it, provides none of this. Rather, it offers a satanic smorgasbord of deviant behaviors and thousands of ways of relating to God, all of which ultimately lead to the worship of Satan (Isa. 14:14; 2 Thess. 2:4; Rev. 13.4). Unless the church stands up against postmodernism, it will lose its savor and light (Matt. 5:16; Eph. 5:8) and become an impotent caricature of what it once was. Further, the modern missions movement will lose its worldwide impact and will melt away into apostasy.

The very gospel of Jesus Christ is at stake. In order to redefine what the term *Christian* means, the gospel itself would have to be compromised. And because the threefold mission of the church includes the propagation of this gospel, its perversion would mean the death blow to evangelical missions.

A PASSION FOR PRIORITIES

If visitors attended your local church for a reasonable amount of time, what would they say was the passion of its people? What would they think the church held dear? Would it be the teaching of God's Word? Would it be the desire to reach the world for Christ? Would it be the worship of God through prayer and service?

It is hoped the visitors would soon be aware of all these aspirations. All are of ultimate importance for they all constitute the mission of the church. Let us return to these passions and thereby bring the crisis in missions to an end. May God give us the strength and wisdom to do so.

PART 1

THE CRISIS DEFINED

CHAPTER 1

THE CRISIS IN MISSIONS

RUSSELL L. PENNEY

DOES A CRISIS EXIST IN evangelical missions? The contributors to this book believe that the answer is yes. This response is based on what we see today and also on what we see as trends for tomorrow. These trends indicate a philosophical shift in our culture and, more importantly, in the church. Thomas Ice writes,

> Sometime in the 1980's, American culture shifted from "What do you think . . . ?" to "How do you feel about . . . ?" Since then, the evangelical church has been drifting right along with the secular tide. This transformation of the culture is usually known as the shift from modernism to postmodernism. The postmodern mentality is having a huge impact upon American evangelicalism.[1]

This shift toward postmodernism affects evangelical missions in several ways. From the budding missionary to the seasoned veteran, from the Bible school student to the theologian, and from the missions major to the missiologist—evangelicals are shifting from the rational, objective, and textual approach to doctrine and practice to the mystical, subjective, and experiential.

EVIDENCE OF THE SHIFT

Doctrinal Deterioration of the Church

Seminaries impact the theological passion and depth of a denomination. When a seminary or Bible school embraces liberalism or errant doctrine, its denomination usually follows. Changes such as these eventually kill missions. True, missionaries might continue going to points unknown to "reach" the heathen, but the "mission" is skewed toward social enrichment rather than proclamation of the power of God (Rom. 1:16).

The tendency in our society toward subjectivism, and thus mysticism, has resulted in a shift of focus—away from God and toward self as the object of worship. And because "great worship experience" has become so important to people, a pragmatic approach to ministry has crept into the American church. Seminaries and Bible schools are now emphasizing administration and "spiritual" counseling (i.e., the modern phenomenon of "Christian counseling") rather than theology. Wells states,

> The quest for contemporary practicality has transformed the nature of the Christian ministry, the work of the seminaries, and the inner workings in denominational headquarters, and in each case the transformation has sounded the death knell of theology. In today's seminaries, Edward Farly observed, the "theological student neither studies divinity nor obtains scholarly expertise in theological sciences, but trains for professional activities." In other words, the old divinity has largely died, as has its importance for the Church, and so seminary training increasingly is about inculcating a kind of public demeanor and etiquette, along with know-how in the soul-caring business, to lay paths to successful careers for students. Seminary students are not blind to the fact that the big churches and the big salaries often go to those who are un-theological or even anti-theological. They know what kind of training they need: they need to become managers who have the status of professionals, not scholars, thinkers, or theologians.[2]

Missionaries coming out of these institutions are often ill-prepared for the theological confrontations they will face on foreign fields. They have not developed staunch theological convictions through careful study and prayer, nor have they learned technical skills in biblical languages and hermeneutics that might enable them to discern biblical error if it is introduced into the churches they plant or into the schools where they teach. Some have been influenced by the compromise of erring evangelical leaders such as those who signed the "Evangelicals and Catholics Together: The Christian Mission in the Third Millennium" statement (see "An Antibiblical and False Unity" below). An influence of this kind might easily lead to a deterioration of belief in the gospel itself. For instance, according to Wells, more than a third of seminary students surveyed reported that theology had a small influence on their lives. They also expressed doubts about the value of historic church doctrine for knowing religious truth. Wells's conclusion was that "[Seminary students] have little confidence that the church's 'long-standing' doctrines are the 'surest guide for knowing ultimate religious truth.'"[3]

Wells, a seminary professor, also observed, "Students now enter seminary with less biblical literacy than they used to have, often with less moral literacy, and with a considerable indebtedness to modernity for their self-understanding and for the values by which they live."[4]

The shifts in modern culture, philosophy, ministry approach, seminary training, and mission objectives are alarming and, unless they are reversed, the likelihood of Christians boldly confronting their neighbors or coworkers about the truth of the gospel—much less forsaking all and going to foreign fields—will decrease. It might also be expected that the American church's interest in missions will decrease as well. This trend has already begun.

Jennifer Collins, with regard to short-term missions, points out in chapter 16 of this book, "A survey of Southern Baptist congregations found that foreign missions ranked as least important among seven suggested ministry areas." Of the Christian baby boomers Engel and Jones surveyed, more than 75 percent believed the need for missionaries was greater in the United States than overseas. Engel and Jones concluded that the baby boomer generation will not provide either the personnel or the money for traditional world missions in the future. This being the case, they encourage mission agencies to offer short-term assignments as a way to turn matters around.[5]

Doctrinal deterioration inevitably douses enthusiasm for missions. The church is losing its way doctrinally, with a corresponding loss of passion for the souls abroad who are on a direct course to an eternity in the lake of fire (Rev. 20:15).

An Antibiblical and False Unity

The move to a more subjective approach to studying Scripture has led to a de-emphasis on objective doctrinal truth, and this, when combined with a desire for Christian unity, has led to doctrinal compromise. With doctrine compromised, unity centers solely on moral and social issues. There is more of a desire to "save our *Christian* society" than to save the sinners from their lost state and a future of eternal damnation. This desire manifested itself most clearly on March 29, 1994, when key Catholic and evangelical leaders signed a heretical document entitled "Evangelicals and Catholics Together: The

Christian Mission in the Third Millennium" (ETC). As one writer states, "The document, in effect, overturned the Reformation and will unquestionably have far-reaching repercussions throughout the Christian world for years to come."[6]

High-profile evangelicals—including the head of a missionary organization, a theologian, and representatives from a home mission board—signed this agreement.[7] The document they signed contains at least two deceptions that, if accepted, would deal a fatal blow to evangelical missions and their attempt to carry the gospel to key areas of the world. First, the document insinuates—if it does not outright state—that the mission of the Catholic Church and that of evangelicals are the same. Second, it claims that Catholics and evangelicals are brothers and sisters in Christ: "All who accept Christ as Lord and Savior are brothers and sisters in Christ. Evangelicals and Catholics are brothers and sisters in Christ" (par. 22, fifth draft).

If these claims are true, the proclamation of the gospel in areas such as Mexico and Central and South America is senseless, because most people in these areas claim to be Catholics, having been baptized into the Roman Catholic Church. But official Catholic doctrine holds that the simple acceptance of Christ as Savior and Lord is not enough. The Council of Trent, in fact, states,

> If anyone says that after the reception of the grace of justification the guilt is so remitted and the debt of eternal punishment so blotted out to every repentant sinner that no debt of temporal punishment remains to be discharged either in this world or in purgatory before the gates of heaven can be opened, let him be anathema.[8]

And,

> If anyone says that in order to obtain the remission of sins it is necessary . . . to believe with certainty and without hesitation . . . that his sins are forgiven him, let him be anathema. (Council of Trent, Six, XVI, 13)[9]

And again,

> If anyone says that he will for certain . . . have that great gift of perseverance even to the end [eternal security] . . . let him be anathema. (Council of Trent, Six, XVI, 16)[10]

But Scripture states,

> "Sirs, what must I do to be saved?" And they [Paul and Silas] said,
> "*Believe* in the Lord Jesus, and you *shall be saved,* you and your house-
> hold." (Acts 16:30–31 NASB, italics added)

And,

> He who believes in the Son *has eternal life;* but he who does not
> obey the Son shall not see life, but the wrath of God abides on him.
> (John 3:36 NASB, italics added)

And again,

> The one who believes in the Son of God has the witness in himself;
> the one who does not believe God has made Him a liar, because he
> has not believed in the witness that God has borne concerning His
> Son. And the witness is this, that God has given us eternal life, and
> this life is in His Son. He who has the Son *has the life;* he who does
> not have the Son of God does not have the life. These things I have
> written to you who believe in the name of the Son of God, in order
> *that you may know* that you have eternal life. (1 John 5:10–13 NASB)

Thus, Scripture and the statements of the Council of Trent cannot be
reconciled. If Catholics believe that salvation comes through faith in Christ
plus baptism *plus* membership in the Roman Catholic Church *plus* the sacraments, then they are not our brothers and sisters in Christ. They are lost
men and women, still in need of a Savior and still under God's wrath (John
3:36). As evangelicals, we hold that Scripture is correct when it states,
"Abraham believed God, and it was *reckoned* to him as righteousness" (Rom.
4:3 NASB, italics added). Here the verb is ἐλογίσθη (from λογίζομαι) meaning "to reckon to one's account," which, in Paul's day, was an accounting
term.[11] Notice that the crediting of righteousness took place in response to
simple belief, not as a result of Abraham's works. Paul goes on to state,

> Now, to a workman wages are not credited as a favor but as an obli-
> gation; while to the person who has not worked by Law, but whose
> faith rests on Him who makes the ungodly righteous, to him *faith*

[not works, sacraments, baptism, and church membership] is accounted for righteousness. (Romans 4:4–5, Berkeley)

Yet Vatican II states,

Preaching the gospel [is to help all men] attain to salvation through faith, baptism and the observance of the commandments.[12]

This is a different gospel—a works-based gospel—and Paul states that those who preach such a gospel should be "anathema"—eternally condemned (Gal. 1:8–9). The above citations and Scripture passages make it evident that, unless Catholics are justified by faith through grace alone as Scripture states, they are not brothers and sisters to evangelicals. And if, indeed, some Catholics are our brothers and sisters, they have not become so through the "gospel" of the Catholic Church. Roman Catholicism, because it preaches a gospel at variance with Scripture, is an apostate church and does not in any way share the same mission as evangelicals. As Christians, evangelicals are commanded to go into all the world (even the Catholic world) and proclaim the gospel to the lost (Matt. 28:18–20).

The ECT document also states,

. . . the shameful reality is that, in many places around the world, the scandal of conflict between Christians [the term *Christians* is used loosely here to refer to Orthodox, evangelicals, and Catholics] obscures the scandal of the cross, thus crippling the one mission of the one Christ. (ECT, fifth draft, par. 13)

But because Catholic and Orthodox "Christians" have a different gospel from evangelicals, their missions are not in accord with those of evangelicals nor with the commands of Christ.

The range of this chapter does not allow for a detailed analysis of the ECT document. Many excellent critiques have already been written, and all evangelicals and Catholics alike should read them. Yet, even our very brief comparison of Scripture and the ECT document demonstrates that the latter contains false doctrine. If that false doctrine and the false gospel it spawns are tolerated, nurtured even, by evangelicals, the mission of the church is in danger.

Departure from Objective Truth

In the modern era, Satan's goal has been to convince us that the Bible is not true. That strategy has dealt a deathblow to many of the mainline denominations. The fundamentalist movement preserved conservative Christianity and pushed us to prepare a stronger defense against attacks on Scripture (i.e., historical criticism). Now, in the postmodern era, Satan has gone a step further. He is tempting us to believe that the Bible is not true and, moreover, that truth itself cannot be known. To the postmodernist, truth is always relative or, more precisely, there is no such thing as absolute truth.

Satan's strategy is having an effect. Steven McAvoy, commenting on postmodernism in chapter 8 of this book, relates, "In 1991, the Barna Research Group reported that 28% of Americans agree strongly, and an additional 39% agree somewhat (for a total of 67%), that there is no such thing as absolute truth; different people can define truth in conflicting ways and still be correct."[13] Even more alarming, the survey found that 53 percent of born-again Christians and 53 percent of adults associated with evangelical churches held a relativistic view of truth. When polled again in 1994, "a staggering 72 percent of American adults—almost three out of four—affirmed some kind of relativism."[14]

If 53 percent of adults in evangelical churches hold to a relativistic view, the next generation of evangelicals can be expected to embrace not only the views of their parents but also the relativistic outlook of their culture. They will probably attend an "evangelical" church that does not hear strong doctrinal exposition from the pulpit or in Bible study. Few of these young people will be likely to, as Steven Curtis Chapman terms it, "abandon it all for the sake of the call." One wonders if these same young people will even understand that "there is salvation in no one else; for there is no other name under heaven that has been given among men, by which we must be saved" (Acts 4:12 NASB).

If the church continues in its surrender to relativism and its distaste for sound doctrine, then the future of evangelical missions is in grave danger. The purpose of this book is to help stem the tide.

LAYOUT OF THIS BOOK

Intertwined with and building upon the doctrinal and biblical examinations of missions in this book are many practical suggestions for missionaries. It is hoped that these suggestions will help to prepare them for the field and enable them to follow biblical procedure once they are there.

The book is arranged in three parts. The first part, "The Crisis Defined," lays the foundation for the rest of the book by defending the sufficiency of Scripture to validate missions and showing the proper place of missions in systematic theology. The second part, "Key Theological Concerns: Enduring and Contemporary," deals with the major doctrinal and theological concerns prevalent in missions today. The third part, "Practical Matters in Missions," offers help in such practical areas as support raising and spells out the special responsibilities of missionaries, churches, and mission agencies in the missionary endeavor. Part 3 also includes a chapter on short-term missions, which has been and continues to be a very important part of world missions.

A CLARION CALL

It is not the purpose of this book to add to existing biblical scholarship, although the Word of God is on our side in the doctrinal matters that we discuss. Rather, this book is a clarion call for the evangelical church to return to the Word of God, to a passion for saving souls, and to being a church that does not desire simply to have its ears tickled (1 Tim. 4:3) but desires to be reproved, rebuked, and exhorted (2 Tim. 4:2). We must, once again, be the pure and holy witnesses to the world that Christ called us to be so that we can go to all nations, carrying the pure gospel of Jesus Christ (1 Cor. 15:3–4), which is the power of God unto salvation to everyone who believes (Rom. 1:16).

May God be glorified through our efforts, and may He use this book to inspire many to go into all of the world and make disciples (Matt. 28:18–20).

CHAPTER 2

THE SUFFICIENCY OF SCRIPTURE AS A FOUNDATION FOR MISSIONS THEOLOGY AND PRACTICE

RUSSELL L. PENNEY

THE FINAL AUTHORITY FOR doctrinal truth is the Bible as penned in the original autographs. Scripture is God breathed and, thus, inerrant (verbal, plenary inspiration). Its theology and the basic strategy for missions as observed in the earliest missionaries—most specifically Paul and his colleagues—constitute our basic pattern for missions today.

SCRIPTURE AS FINAL AUTHORITY

At one time in history, inherent in the title *evangelical* was a commitment to Scripture as the final authority of faith and practice. Evangelicals have historically held that ministry principles and practices should be based on the theological foundations presented in God's Word. Thus, older evangelicals might be amazed to learn that the issue of biblical authority even needs to be touched on in a book on evangelical missions. But, in truth, the title *evangelical* does not mean that a person necessarily believes in a fully inspired, fully inerrant, and fully authoritative biblical text. One leading missiologist, for example, speaking of himself and a colleague, writes,

> [We] are just two traditional evangelicals and former cessationists among rapidly increasing numbers of others who believe that a valid source of divine knowledge comes through what some would call "extrabiblical revelation." I daresay that the standard-brand evangelical doctrine of "*logos* only" that we were taught might now find a place on an "endangered doctrines" list, about to become extinct. As always, I would

not fail to reemphasize that any purported extrabiblical revelation that contradicts or violates the written Word of God *ipso facto* must be rejected by faithful Christians. The Bible remains the only final and authoritative litmus test for divine revelation. The 66 books of the Bible constitute a closed canon.[1]

By adding the last couple of sentences, the author tries to soften his first two statements. But the result of such a view, nonetheless, is that Scripture is interpreted in light of experience and not the other way round. People's interpretations of their experiences become the greater authority; thus, the interpreters, not the Word of God, become the final power. This is evident in the following statement by the same missiologist as he discusses the epistemology of his spiritual warfare practices: "One fundamental thesis will control this discussion—the thesis that ministry precedes and produces theology, not the reverse."[2] It is not surprising, then, that his "theology" of spiritual warfare is man-made and at odds with Scripture.[3] It is hard to understand how someone arrives at such a contradiction in logic—that one can believe in a "closed canon" and yet believe in continuing divine revelation.

Any ministry that produces theology, rather than the reverse, leads away from the biblical—and, thus, the most effective approach—to spiritual warfare in missions. Missions-minded saints are led astray by the teachings of strategic-level spiritual warfare, as promoted by the above-quoted missiologist, and spend their time praying against demons by name instead of praying for their missionary "that utterance may be given to [him] in the opening of [his] mouth, to make known with boldness the mystery of the gospel, . . . [and] that in proclaiming it [he] might speak boldly, as [he] ought to speak" (Eph. 6:19–20 NASB), or praying that ". . . the word of the Lord may spread rapidly and be glorified" (2 Thess. 3:1 NASB). Paul realized that prayer could not be neglected as an ingredient in successfully reaching the nations, but he neither prayed against demons nor encouraged those with whom he corresponded to do so.

People's abandonment of belief in Scripture as the final authority and their dependence on subjective experiences spell disaster for future evangelical missions. And the belief that subjective experience "produces theology" is even more frightening when one considers the degree of departure from Scripture that is possible with such an epistemology.

LITERAL OR NORMAL INTERPRETATION

The belief in the inspiration, inerrancy, and authority of Scripture commits one to a careful exegesis of the text in determining *its* meaning. Thus, the only approach that allows the Word of God to speak for itself is a *literal* or normal interpretation. As Ramm states, *"[Literal]* means interpretation that gives to every word the same meaning it would have in normal usage, whether employed in writing, speaking, or thinking."[4] A literal approach, then, accepts that "each biblical writing—that is, each word, sentence, and book—was recorded in a written language and followed normal, grammatical meanings, including figurative language."[5] Many people claim that they employ a normal interpretation, but *literal* here refers to a *consistent* application of a literal hermeneutic.

Ryrie has stated,

> If God is the originator of language and if the chief purpose of originating it was to convey His message to humanity, then it must follow that He, being all-wise and all-loving, originated sufficient language to convey all that was in His heart to tell mankind. He would use language and expect people to understand it in its literal, normal, and plain sense. The Scriptures, then, cannot be regarded as an illustration of some special use of language so that in the interpretation of these Scriptures some deeper meaning of the words must be sought. If language is the creation of God for the purpose of conveying His message, then a theist must view that language as sufficient in scope and normative in use to accomplish that purpose for which God originated it.[6]

Applying a consistent literal hermeneutic to the Scriptures is justified by the literal fulfillment of the prophecies concerning the first coming of Christ. Further, if a normal hermeneutic is not correct, then all objectivity in interpretation is lost. As Ryrie states, "What check would there be on the variety of interpretations that man's imagination could produce if there were not an objective standard, which the literal provides. . . . Literalism is a logical rationale."[7] Those who are involved in missions must be guided by an inerrant, inspired, authoritative text that is interpreted literally, or they risk wandering in the maze of human wisdom in the quest to reach the world for our Lord.

THE SUFFICIENCY OF SCRIPTURE:
A FIRM FOUNDATION FOR THEOLOGY

We have been given a commission—the Great Commission—to make disciples by baptizing and teaching. A positive by-product of believing in biblical authority is the acceptance of biblical principles—derived from a careful study of Scripture by using literal interpretation—as a sufficient foundation for carrying out the commission. In fact, to hold that God did not reveal everything that we need in the areas of theology and basic missiological principles in His Word is to deny the sufficiency of Scripture.

But, indeed, all we need in order to make disciples, baptize, and teach can be found in the Word of God. To start the process of disciple-making, the gospel must be proclaimed (Matt. 28:19; Mark 16:15; Acts 1:8; 2 Cor. 5:20; 1 Tim. 3:15); in other words, we cannot be disciples without first being saved. We are called to make disciples of the converts by baptizing them and teaching them, in both word and deed, the doctrinal truths of the Word of God (Eph. 4:11–16; 1 Thess. 5:11; 2 Tim. 2:2; 3:16–17; 4:2–3). The process of proclaiming the gospel, baptizing, and teaching the Word of God results in the planting of indigenous churches that then continue the same process in their own cultures. During this process, Christ has promised to be with us "even to the end of the age" (Matt. 28:20 NASB).

A Firm Foundation for the Mission of the Church

Much time, energy, and prayer is wasted when the mission of the church is uncertain. The church, especially the liberal element, spends a lot of time meeting temporal needs, yet it has neglected caring for the weightier matters that have eternal implications. Certainly, medical missions and Christian orphanages have a place in facilitating the spread of the gospel of Jesus Christ—but only if they are a means to an end. That end is the eternal salvation of souls through the proclamation of the gospel and "the equipping of the saints for the work of service" (Mark 16:15; Eph. 4:11–16 NASB). Thus, we know from inspired text that any missions endeavor that does not place salvation at its center has lost its focus.

A Firm Foundation for Our View of God's Sovereignty

Probably no doctrine in all of Scripture so grates against our self-centered and pride-ridden sin nature as that of God's sovereignty. Yet, a great amount of mystery is connected to this doctrine. It is impossible for us, with our limited human minds, fully to understand God's sovereignty in salvation.

We tend, therefore, to respond to it in one of two ways: We either deny and explain it away, creating a theory of a human-orchestrated salvation, or we become ultra-Calvinistic, diminishing or denying any human responsibility in salvation or world evangelism and having little or no zeal at all for missions. The same Holy Writ that says, "You did not choose Me but I chose you" (John 15:16 NASB), also says, "Go therefore and make disciples" (Matt. 20:18 NASB). We have no excuse for de-emphasizing one and emphasizing the other. God has sovereignly chosen some people to be His children (Eph. 1:4), and He has also sovereignly chosen to use humans as instruments in proclaiming the gospel—to which His elect will respond.

God is sovereign in salvation and in all other things. Paul states,

> The God who made the world and all things in it, since He is Lord of heaven and earth, does not dwell in temples made with hands; neither is He served by human hands, as though He needed anything, since He Himself gives to all life and breath and all things; and He made from one, every nation of mankind to live on all the face of the earth, having determined their appointed times, and the boundaries of their habitation, . . . for in Him we live and move and exist. (Acts 17:24–26, 28 NASB)

God is sovereign and so, in order to be faithful to His message, we must carry out the commission with which we have been charged and trust Him for results. Prayer and proclamation are our responsibilities; conviction and conversion are His. Culturally adjusting the methods we use to convey the message is one thing, but culturally conforming the message is another. Human wisdom that compels us to tamper with the gospel disgraces Scripture and diminishes God's sovereignty. Scripture gives us a pure gospel and shows us a sovereign God who uses His Word and the power of His Spirit to bring in the elect (Acts 13:48; 16:14).

A Firm Foundation for Our Gospel

If Satan can subvert the gospel, he has won the victory. For this reason, Paul states, "But even though we, or an angel from heaven, should preach to you a gospel contrary to that which we have preached to you, let him be accursed" (Gal. 1:8 NASB). A false gospel is like a poisoned stream—all who drink of it perish. The message of the death, burial, and resurrection of Jesus Christ (1 Cor. 15:3–4) is distasteful to many people. That Christ's blood served as a propitiation (satisfaction) for the righteous wrath of God and was due payment for the penalty of humankind's sins sounds pagan to some (Rom. 3:24–26). Yet, the doctrine of salvation comprises a large portion of the New Testament. The Scriptures are also clear on the doctrine of hell and eternal punishment, even though some evangelicals are now departing from this orthodox doctrine and taking an annihilationist position.[8] Regardless of the compromises made in order to accommodate those who are uncomfortable with what the Bible teaches, Scripture is nonetheless the final authority for the gospel message.

A Firm Foundation for Our Message of Exclusivity

The Bible clearly states that salvation and reconciliation to God can come only through Jesus Christ and through the proclamation of the gospel of Jesus Christ—the gospel of justification through faith in Christ alone. Acts 4:12 says it succinctly: "And there is salvation in no one else; for there is no other name under heaven that has been given among men, by which we must be saved." Yet, as George Barna states,

> In the spirit of cultural diversity, more and more teens are allowing
> that all religious faiths have value, offer equally valid solutions and
> ought to be given a fair hearing before they make a choice. The foundation for this open-mindedness among teenagers is their stand on
> moral truth. By an overwhelming margin, teens reject the notion of
> absolute moral truth in favor of a relative view of right and wrong. . . .
> From a spiritual point of view, the all-roads-lead-to-heaven mind-set
> is widely ingrained. Half of all teenagers state unapologetically that
> it doesn't matter what faith you embrace since they all teach similar
> lessons.[9]

As the trend of inclusion continues, a new generation of missionaries becomes more unlikely. One cannot help but wonder if young people such as this would give up comfort, ease, the pleasures of home, and the possibility of lucrative careers to tell the heathen that they are assured of an eternity in hell if they do not place their faith in Jesus Christ alone.

Regardless of the pluralistic view of religion, God's Word states that there is only one way to salvation. Narrow? Yes. The Truth? Yes. That's what God says in His Word—our final foundation for doctrine and practice.

A Firm Foundation for Truth

It's alarming enough that some evangelicals are uncertain about the truths of heaven, hell, and the gospel of Jesus Christ. Even more alarming is the fact that so many evangelicals are uncertain about whether truth can be known at all. As mentioned in chapter 1, "In 1991, the Barna Research Group reported that 28% of Americans agree strongly, and an additional 39% agree somewhat (for a total of 67%), that there is no such thing as absolute truth; different people can define truth in conflicting ways and still be correct."[10] Further, 53 percent of "born-again" Christians and 53 percent of adults associated with evangelical churches held a relativistic view of truth. In a succeeding poll in 1994, "a staggering 72 percent of American adults—almost three out of four—affirmed some kind of relativism."[11] With relativism's increasing influence on our American culture, the numbers have surely grown. Such a trend will spell the death not only of the church as we know it but also of evangelical missions.

The truth of Word of God is the unequivocal claim of Jesus Christ: "Thy Word is truth" (John 8:31–59). And John declares the apostolic word to be "the spirit of truth" as opposed to "the spirit of error" (1 John 4:6). When God speaks, His words are true, because He is true. It is impossible for God to speak falsehoods (Titus 1:2; Heb. 6:18; 2 Sam. 7:28). Whether He speaks directly (Exod. 34:6), or through Jesus (Matt. 22:16; Luke 9:27; John 8:45; Rom. 15:8), or by the prophets and apostles (Deut. 18:18; 1 Kings 17:24; Isa. 66:1; Jer. 1:1–4; Acts 26:25; 2 Tim. 3:16; 1 Peter 1:11–12; 2 Peter 1:21), His Word is reliable because it is rooted in and ruled by the divine absolute. His Word corresponds to reality, because reality is measured by God, the ultimate reality.[12]

A Firm Foundation for Missionary Preparedness

Scripture provides a pattern for the preparation of missionaries. Those who are chosen must have a sound theological and doctrinal grounding. Only then are they in a position to be appointed and sent out to preach the gospel and plant churches. A cursory look at Paul's missionary endeavors proves not only that the initial pattern of the church was to send theologically trained individuals to the field (Acts 13:1–3) but also that Paul's experience, subsequent to his being sent out, confirmed the wisdom of God in doing so (13:2: "*the Holy Spirit said,* 'Set apart for Me Barnabas and Saul for the work to which I have called them'").

Paul and his associates constantly confronted false religions and aberrant worldviews. And Paul's epistles show that his missionary activities included instruction, the provision of theological insight to equip converts, and the correction of error and heresy that arose in the congregations—all of which required an in-depth theological understanding. What the Word of God shows to be the pattern, logic necessarily dictates for frontline missionaries.

A Firm Foundation for Our Demonology

As already noted, the Bible teaches that God is sovereign. Neither Satan nor his minions can do anything to prevent a person coming to God if the sovereign God so desires it. Scripture also teaches that Satan can do nothing to one of God's children unless he is sovereignly allowed to do so by God Himself (Job 1–2; 2 Cor. 12:7–9).

Thus, the key to fulfilling the Great Commission is not "strategic-level spiritual warfare" but bold proclamation of the gospel. The power of God provides for the salvation of all those who believe (Rom. 1:16), and no power is greater than our sovereign God (1 Sam. 2:6–8; Isaiah 14; 26–27). When the gospel is proclaimed, it is accompanied by His power through His Spirit, and the result is that His elect—those whom He has chosen from the foundation of the world (John 15:16; Rom. 9:21–23; Eph. 1:4; 2 Thess. 2:13; 2 Tim. 1:9)—respond and are saved (Acts 13:48; 16:14). No demon or group of demons—not even Satan himself—can thwart God's purpose.

A Firm Foundation for God's Design for the Sexes

Because of the cultural context of the United States and much of Western society, any demonstration of biblically dictated roles for the sexes causes a stirring of emotions. Controversy often arises over the role of women in the local church, in mission agencies, and on the mission field because of cultural influences (Rom. 12:1 NASB: "do not be conformed to this world").

Scripture says some definite things about the design of the sexes and the roles men and women have in the family, in society, and in the church. And because missions are an outreach of the local church, the principles that apply in the church also apply in them. The Word of God, not culture, is, in doctrine and practice, our guide for the roles of the sexes.

A Firm Foundation for All Doctrine

The preceding doctrinal truths certainly are not exhaustive, but they are the ones most often attacked, twisted, and deserted today in evangelical circles.

However, the Word of God—the Bible—is the only certain source of theological truth. Ministry does not produce theology, as the aforementioned missiologist has theorized. This would be a fatal blow to biblical evangelicalism. John Hart, in a critique of missiologist Peter Wagner's book *Confronting the Powers,* writes,

> Traditionally, Evangelicals have argued that experience and ministry ought to flow out of theology and Scripture. Wagner offers us a paradigm shift: Theology must flow out of ministry (à la experience in exorcisms and healings)! Correspondingly, emphasis is placed on subjective experience over the objective Word of God. Personal experience becomes the veritable proof of new doctrines about the spirit world. Theology is defined as "a human attempt to explain God's Word and God's works in a reasonable and systematic way." . . . In light of this, the charge of theological relativism does not seem to be an unfair assessment.[13]

As evangelicals, we must flee from Wagner's approach and return to our sure foundation—God's inspired, inerrant Word—for faith and practice. Subjective case study is not a reliable method for testing new approaches to the task of world evangelism. Rather, new approaches should be scrutinized in light of a literal interpretation of the inerrant text.

THE SUFFICIENCY OF SCRIPTURE: A FIRM FOUNDATION FOR OUR MISSIONS PRACTICE

Missions Practice Defined

Missions practice is not so much defined by "strategy" *per se* (although some overlap might occur in a discussion of "practice" as opposed to "strategy") but by the pattern of missionary activity as seen in the book of Acts and by those activities logically and transculturally applied in any missions setting. Practices are either directly tied to biblical doctrine or they logically proceed from it, but all are worth careful consideration and emulation simply because they derive from the divine text. As Hesselgrave states, "At the procedural level we would maintain that the Bible contains more than a divine message, it constitutes a divine method of delivering that message."[14]

Tucker, speaking from a historical perspective in her book *From Jerusalem to Irian Jaya,* writes,

Paul's extraordinary accomplishments in the field of missions have prompted a number of missiologists to argue that his methods should be closely, if not precisely, emulated today. . . . It is difficult to over-emphasize the significance of the apostle Paul in laying a pattern for effectively reaching the lost, and *to a degree the successes or failures of missionary work since can be attributed in part to the adherence to or deviation from his own personal example and the general guidelines that he set forth.* (italics added)[15]

What, then, were the missionary practices of Paul and his companions?

Who Will Go for Us?

Not long after the stoning of Stephen, some of the scattered believers made their way to Antioch (Acts 11:19), where a large church was established. There the apostles spent time becoming grounded in the faith (vv. 20–26). The Antioch church became the first "sending church," dispersing Christian missionaries.

Paul's missionary activity began when God chose him, along with Barnabas, and the leadership of the Antiochan church set them apart (Acts 13:2). Thus, the first principle for missionary practice is that the *leadership* recognizes those whom God had chosen to be sent out. Second, note that those who were sent were not among the *least* qualified from the church but two of the *most* qualified. Paul and Barnabas undoubtedly exhibited spiritual maturity, a necessity for missionaries representing Christ on the field. Sending highly qualified individuals makes sense, considering that the main task of the missionary is to baptize, teach, and develop leadership in planting new churches.

Even in the most complex of modern missions, a place certainly exists for theologically untrained support workers. Anyone who has a heart for missions, from a mechanic to a computer programmer, can benefit the frontline missionary as a support worker. But frontline missionaries themselves, who are to reach the unreached and plant churches, must be as Paul was, trained and qualified.

Where Will He Go and What Will He Do?

A third principle to learn from Paul and his helpers has to do with strategy. When they planned the evangelization of an area, they primarily considered the province rather than the city. Roland Allen writes,

Both St. Luke and St. Paul speak constantly of the provinces rather than the cities. Thus St. Paul was forbidden to preach the word in Asia [Acts 16:6], he was called from Troas not to Philippi, or to Thessalonica, but to Macedonia [Acts 16:9, 10, cf. Acts 18:5, 19:22; 2 Cor. 1:16, 2:13, 7:5, Phil. 4:15, etc.]. Speaking of the collection for the saints at Jerusalem St. Paul says that he boasted that Achaia was ready a year ago [2 Cor. 9:2]. The suggestion is that in St. Paul's view the *unit* was the province rather than the city. (italics added)[16]

Today, of course, few countries have *no* Christian influence at all. Cities in some countries may have a significant Christian presence, and others may have very little. Yet, the basic strategy still holds. The area—whether country, state, or region—should be examined strategically and approached as a unit. This is not as much a rule as it is a logical approach. The reason lies in the fourth principle, which is set forth by Allen:

St. Paul's theory of evangelizing a province was not to preach in every place in it himself, but to establish centres of Christian life in two or three important places from which the knowledge might spread into the country round. . . . [Thus Paul] intended his congregation to become at once a centre of light.[17]

Paul's strategy was to evangelize a province by first evangelizing the cities, which were centers of commerce and trade. "Through some of [those cities] the commerce of the world passed. They were the great marts where the *material* and *intellectual* wealth of the world was exchanged" (italics added).[18]

Although, today, evangelizing cities is an important aim, it is not an end in itself. Allen notes that this strategy has failed in the past because of the neglect of the fifth principle: The gospel must be proclaimed in such a way that the ones who receive it not only understand it but also want to proclaim it themselves, knowing *that it is entrusted to them for that purpose*. It is for this reason, as stated earlier, that "Concentrated missions, at strategic centres, if they are to win the province, must be centres of evangelistic life."[19]

It is necessary for missionaries to create centers of evangelism where people native to the culture can become equipped to further spread the gospel. Cultural differences and language barriers tend to limit the effectiveness of outsiders. William Carey recognized these difficulties. Davis, quoting Robinson, writes,

The distinguishing characteristic of Carey's work was his adoption of the principle of concentration. . . . To a far greater degree than any of his predecessors he realized the comparative futility of diffused missions, and the impossibility of converting India by European evangelists. By concentrating the greater part of his activities within a narrow circle and by spending his time upon the education and training of Indian teachers he inaugurated a new method of missionary work the importance of which it is impossible to exaggerate.[20]

Carey himself wrote, "It is only by means of native preachers that we can hope for the universal spread of the Gospel throughout this immense continent [referring to India]."[21]

As we will see in subsequent chapters, Paul proclaimed a consistent gospel—the death, burial, and resurrection of Christ as the propitiation of God's wrath and the payment for our sin (Acts 13:28–30, 38; Rom. 3:25–26; 1 Cor. 15:3–4). He also proclaimed that individuals must place their trust in Christ alone, through faith alone (Rom. 3:22; 4:3; Gal. 2:15–16). Paul was an exclusivist, believing that the pagans were totally depraved and that, without faith in the gospel of Jesus Christ, they were condemned to *eternal* destruction (Rom. 2:5–16; 3:1–3; 2 Thess. 1:7–9). Although demonic activity confronted Paul on several occasions, he never prayed against demons, nor did he ask those to whom he wrote to pray against them. He knew that the Holy Spirit, through the proclamation of the gospel, was the power of God unto salvation.

The sixth principle for missionary practice is that the converts must be taught. Recall the command in the Great Commission: ". . . and teaching them to observe all that I commanded you." Christ's disciples were not only to teach new converts all that Christ had taught them but also they were "to observe" all these things. The Greek term (τηρεῖν), translated here "to observe," can also be translated "to guard" or "to keep."[22] Thus, the intent of the command was to make disciples and teach them by word and deed both. This is the pattern that Christ left to us in the Gospels through His interactions with His own disciples. Leadership, relationship, and moral conduct are all communicated best by our actions; therefore, the missionary must take seriously the command, "You shall be holy, for I am holy" (1 Peter 1:16 NASB).

If sound doctrine is imparted to converts, a doctrinally sound church will be established. For this reason, follow-up is a necessity not an option. The

New Testament epistles show the depth of teaching that missionaries, who seek to establish indigenous churches, must confer on converts. The converts, out of whom God will raise leaders, must know right doctrine and be able to study Scripture for themselves. A philosophy of diffusion—that is, reaching as many people as possible but without the "teaching" required to fulfill the Great Commission—spells disaster. It imparts little knowledge of the faith and creates a fertile field in which cults may deceive converts. J. Hudson Taylor's China Inland Mission (now Overseas Missionary Fellowship) applied the philosophy of diffusion with unfortunate results. Tucker, as a missions historian, makes the following evaluation:

> That Taylor sought to reach all of China with the gospel was certainly a lofty ambition, but that very goal may have been the decisive weakness of the CIM. In its effort to reach all of China the policy of diffusion (as opposed to concentration) was implemented. According to the great missions historian, Kenneth Scott Latourette, "The main purpose of the China Inland Mission was not to win converts or to build a Chinese church, but to spread a knowledge of the Christian Gospel throughout the empire as quickly as might be. . . . Nor, although Chinese assistants were employed, did it stress the recruiting and training of a Chinese ministry." Such a policy was unwise. The hostility of the Boxer Rebellion, and the Communist takeover some decades later glaringly illustrate the inherent weakness of a policy that did not make the building of a strong local ministry and church its number one priority.[23]

As Hesselgrave states, "Actually, the central missionary undertaking is to win men to Christ and establish churches in new areas."[24] If this undertaking is kept in mind, the pitfalls of diffusion will be avoided. The goal is to establish indigenous churches that are self-governing, self-supporting, and self-propagating.

A stern warning must be given here, for it is here that many efforts fail: Missionaries must impart truth by teaching converts through word and deed, and encouraging them slowly to take responsibility for their own ministry. Allen comments:

> St. Paul did not go about as a missionary preacher merely to convert individuals: he went to establish churches from which the light might

radiate throughout the whole country round. The secret of success in this work lies in beginning at the very beginning. *It is the training of the first convert which sets the type for the future.* If the first converts are taught to depend upon the missionary, if all work, evangelistic, educational, social is concentrated in his hands, the infant community learns to rest passively upon the man from whom they receive their first insight into the Gospel. Their faith, having no sphere for its growth and development, lies dormant. A tradition very rapidly grows up that nothing can be done without the authority and guidance of the missionary. The people wait for him to move, and the longer they do so, the more incapable they become of any independent action. Thus the leader is confirmed in the habit of gathering all authority in to his hands, and of despising the powers of his people, until he makes their activity an excuse for denying their capacity. (italics added)[25]

Paul, on his first missionary journey, enabled the elders of newly established churches to care for their congregations, to evangelize, and to teach others in their provinces (Acts 14:23). This goal was accomplished in some cases, according to Ramsey, in only five to six months.[26]

In many of these congregations, Paul's involvement after that point was to send letters containing further instructions and addressing specific problems that had come up in the churches. Paul's methods were, in his own estimation, so effective that "ten years after his first start from Antioch, he told the Romans that he had 'fully preached the Gospel of Christ from Jerusalem and round about Illyricum,' and that he had 'no more place in these parts.'"[27]

Out of the principle of teaching converts comes the missionary phrase "working ourselves out of a job." Having this aim in mind from the very beginning will prevent missionaries from holding on to the work too long and making those whom they reach for Christ dependent on them. David Sitton endorses this approach:

My ambition is to establish mature vibrant churches. These are congregations that are growing in grace, knowledge and Christian experience—assemblies where disciples are increasingly responsible for themselves before the Lord.[28]

If this spiritual weaning process is followed, churches will be able to make a transition to independence that is less painful and more natural.

Summary of Principles

1. The leadership must recognize those whom God has chosen to be sent.
2. Those who are sent should not be among the *least* qualified from the church but among the *most* qualified.
3. Like Paul and those with him, missionaries must consider the province rather than the city in their approach to the evangelization of an area.
4. Missionaries should evangelize a province (i.e., state, region, and so on) by first establishing centers of Christian life in two or three important places from which knowledge might spread into the surrounding country (preferably by the native peoples of the province, who will be more effective).
5. The gospel must be proclaimed in such a way that those who receive it not only understand it but want to proclaim it themselves, knowing that *it is entrusted to them for that purpose.* "Concentrated missions, at strategic centres, if they are to win the province, must be centres of evangelistic life."[29]
6. Missionaries must make disciples of the converts, not by keeping them dependent but by equipping them and then turning the responsibility for evangelizing and teaching over to them early; thus, the converts become a light that radiates throughout the whole country. Their dependence should be on Christ, not on the missionaries.

A RETURN TO ABSOLUTES

These six principles are only the rudiments. Conservative missiologists have refined and expanded these ideas. But because these basic biblical missionary foundations have been departed from in preference to human wisdom or "extrabiblical" revelation, it is appropriate that we restate the biblical pattern that God has established.

To be faithful to God is to honor His Word in doing His work. Honoring His Word means interpreting it literally. Thus, the only logical, God-honoring position is what Lindsell has termed the *absolutist* position. In his volume, *An Evangelical Theology of Missions,* he states,

The absolutist position of the Christian when thinking about missions is that we have a sound and solid foundation on which that enterprise rests. That foundation is the Word of God. Any enterprise and all aspects of such an enterprise must be conducted along lines which are constant with the revelation of the Word. The message must be directly derived from the Word; the methods must be in full accord with the Word; the aims of missions must jibe with the Word; and the theology of missions with regard to its view of man, and the world or any other doctrine must be able to meet the same test. The unalterable test is agreement with that written Word either directly or by reason of any logical and reasonable derivation therefrom. The Word is the only adequate standard of reference, the measuring rod by which all tests are to be made. In itself it is not subject to an antecedent or subsequent test. It is the basic a priori assumption from which all other decisions are derived. Its understanding comes through faith as the Holy Spirit works in the hearts of men.[30]

The absolutist position may not be in vogue, but neither the theologically perverted and relativistic culture nor the "academically minded" theologian must be allowed to distract missions from their purpose or make missions conform to their viewpoints. The work of missions must remain faithful to the living, preaching, and teaching of His Word.

CHAPTER 3

THE PROPER PLACE OF THE STUDY OF MISSIONS IN SYSTEMATIC THEOLOGY

ALBERT T. PLATT

BECAUSE IT IS THE SCIENCE AND ART of going and making disciples of all nations, missions draws from and depends upon the entire scope of systematic theology for its message, method, purpose, and power. In the biblical "timeline," however, the program for disseminating the gospel message of the grace of God begins between the truths of John 1:11 and John 1:12. Thus, the New Testament character of this specific message, method, purpose, and power places missions as the unique responsibility of the members of the equally unique body of Christ. The biblical doctrine of missions—the going and making of disciples—properly belongs to that division of systematic theology known as ecclesiology—the doctrine of the church. As stated above, missions depends upon and draws from the other major divisions of theology but is not to be confused with other parts of God's program.

THEOLOGY IS . . .

Over the years, and from friend and foe alike, the term *theology* has endured the addition of a seemingly endless number of expanding or contracting qualifiers: ascetic, biblical, dogmatic, ethnic, geographic, moral, natural, period and historic, polemic, proponent's proper name, psychological, racial, rational, relational, religious origin, sociological, speculative, systematic, and, thankfully, revealed. Nor is the preceding list of qualifiers exhaustive. Certainly, listing them does not lend them all validity. The word *theology* has, in fact, often been employed to legitimize pet schemes. Granted, words do change meaning through usage; and although usage might make a term familiar, it has dealt *theology* an unfortunate demotion.

Simply stated, *theology* is "the study of God and the relations between God and the universe."[1]

THEOLOGY MUST HAVE . . .

The following characteristics constitute the *sine qua non* of true theology.

1. True theology is *theocentric*. It must deal with the Person and works of God.
2. True theology must be *drawn from a trustworthy source*. The only source that speaks authoritatively on the subject is the Bible. Thus the "qualifier" that counts in the aforementioned list is *revealed*.
3. True theology will, therefore, *have universal application, being supracultural*—an extremely important point in the biblical doctrine of missions. Note that the contextualizing of theology does not equal theology itself.
4. True theology *sees God at the beginning, in the course of, and at the end of history*. It understands God to be personal and provident, Creator and Conserver, Savior and Sovereign.

So-called theology that does not embrace these characteristics could properly be called speculative and is therefore without authority.

THEOLOGY DEPENDS UPON . . .

"Systematic theology correlates the data of biblical revelation as a whole in order to exhibit systematically the total picture of God's self-revelation."[2] Systematic theology is itself, however, dependent upon that branch of theological science (the correct principles) and art (the knowledge of those principles and the skill with which they are applied) known as biblical theology.[3] Foundational to both systematic and biblical theology is biblical (the "authoritative source") exegesis, which is made possible only with sound hermeneutical principles, that is, a grammatical-historical or consistently literal hermeneutic.[4] Only this particular method of exegesis enables the interpreter to distinguish the specific place of missions in the overall biblio-theological scheme. Proper exegesis also distinguishes from true revelation that which is merely another "new" message with another "new" responsibility for another "new" entity.

GOD'S CHARACTER IS UNCHANGING

Neither *another* nor *new* are words appropriate to the character of the God of the Bible. What has been consistently revealed about Him throughout the pages of Scripture has remained and will always remain unchanged. "Who *is* like unto thee, O LORD, among the gods? who *is* like thee, glorious in holiness, fearful *in* praises, doing wonders?" (Exod. 15:11 KJV); "Who *is* like unto the LORD our God, who dwelleth on high" (Ps. 113:5); "Remember the former things of old: for I *am* God, and *there is* none else; *I am* God, and *there is* none like me, Declaring the end from the beginning, and from ancient times *the things* that are not *yet* done, saying, My counsel shall stand, and I will do all my pleasure" (Isa. 46:9–10); "For I *am* the LORD, I change not; therefore ye sons of Jacob are not consumed" (Mal. 3:6).[5]

GOD'S PURPOSE IS UNCHANGING

Note, too, that careful study of the Scriptures likewise reveals God's consistent and noble purpose, unchanged and unchanging. Whereas many people are properly convinced that the chief end of humankind is to glorify God, some people have tried to make people and their salvation the chief aim of God. Without question, the cord of redemption—blood red in color—runs throughout the Bible, and "soteriology, the doctrine of salvation, must be the grandest theme in the Scriptures. It embraces all of time as well as eternity past and future. It relates it one way or another to all mankind without exceptions."[6] Nevertheless, one must avoid the error of making humanity and its salvation the supreme focus of God. It is entirely within the circumference of humankind's high opinion of itself to wish that this were so, but that thought finds no biblical support. The real focus of God is God. Regarding God's purpose, Showers writes,

Although the redemption of elect human beings is a very important part of God's purpose for history, it is only one part of that purpose. During the course of history, God not only has a program for the elect but also a program for the nonelect (Rom. 9:10–23). In addition, God has different programs for nations (Job 12:23; Isa. 14:24–27; Jer. 10:7; Dan. 2:36–45), rulers (Isa. 44:28–45:7; Dan. 4:17), Satan (John 12:31; Rom. 16:20; Rev. 12:7–10; 20:1–3), and nature (Matt. 19:28; Acts 3:19–21; Rom. 8:19–22). Since God has many different programs which He is operating during the course of history, all of them must be contributing something to His ultimate purpose for history. *Thus, the ultimate goal of history has to be large enough to incorporate all of God's programs, not just one of them.* (italics added)[7]

THE STATED PURPOSE

The qualifying God-ordained aim of history and beyond is the glorification and exaltation of His name in time and eternity.[8] Because all that God does reflects all that He is, His programs are the products of His own perfections: eternal wisdom, righteousness, love, omnipotence, and sovereignty. Those planned programs move inexorably to the final glorification of His name.

Be still, and know that I *am* God: I will be exalted among the heathen, I will be exalted in the earth. (Psalm 46:10)

Then Moses said unto Aaron, This *is it* that the LORD spake, saying, I will be sanctified in them that come nigh me, and before all the people I will be glorified. (Leviticus 10:3)

And say, Thus saith the Lord GOD; Behold, I *am* against thee, O Zidon; and I will be glorified in the midst of thee: and they shall know that I *am* the LORD, when I shall have executed judgments in her, and shall be sanctified in her. (Ezekiel 28:22)

Father, glorify thy name. Then came there a voice from heaven, *saying,* I have both glorified *it,* and will glorify *it* again. (John 12:28)

I have glorified thee on the earth: I have finished the work which thou gavest me to do. And now, O Father, glorify thou me with thine own self with the glory which I had with thee before the world was. (John 17:4–5)

THE PURPOSE IN ACTION: ADAM AND NOAH

The creation of the race is traceable to God's great purpose, namely, the glorification of His name. But our ancestors failed in that end.

Because that, when they knew God, they glorified *him* not as God, neither were thankful; but became vain in their imaginations, and their foolish heart was darkened. Professing themselves to be wise, they became fools, And changed the glory of the uncorruptible God into an image made like to corruptible man, and to birds, and fourfooted beasts, and creeping things. Wherefore God also gave them up to uncleanness through the lusts of their own hearts, to dishonour their own bodies between themselves. (Romans 1:21-25)

The same is true for those upon the earth in the time of Noah, who with his family were preserved from among those who were corrupt: "For all flesh had corrupted his way upon the earth . . . for the earth is filled with violence through them; and, behold, I will destroy them with the earth" (Gen. 6:12-13). The sinful attitude that prompted Noah's descendants to build the tower in Shinar was yet another eruption of flagrant disobedience and nonconformity to the will of God. It, too, ended in punishment (Gen. 11).

THE FIRST MANDATE . . . AND THE REPEAT

It is interesting to note that, in the cases of both Adam and Noah, a mandate was issued. To Adam and Eve God said, "Be fruitful, and multiply, and replenish the earth, and subdue it: and have dominion over the fish of the sea, and over the fowl of the air, and over every living thing that moveth upon the earth" (Gen. 1:28). After the Flood, the same mandate was given to Noah: "Be fruitful, and multiply, and replenish the earth" (9:1). Peters summarizes the Genesis mandate as "populate, subjugate, dominate, cultivate and preserve."[9] In neither case is this mandate to be confused with what the New Testament sets forth as the mandate of going and making disciples. Peters adds,

Neither do I find anywhere in the New Testament that the church of Jesus Christ as a church is charged with the mission of special cultural contributions, though every member as a member of mankind has a contribution to make. . . . I do not find anywhere in the Bible that the first mandate comes under the biblical category of missions. It is man's assignment as man and is to be fulfilled on the human level. It is not implied in the Great Commission of our Lord to His disciples, nor do any of the spiritual gifts *(charismata)* as presented in Scriptures relate to it. It is therefore unscriptural to confuse these two mandates and speak of them on equal terms as missions and church ministries.[10]

THE PURPOSE IN ACTION: ABRAHAM AND THE ELECT NATION

At a postnoahic juncture, God's eternal purpose to glorify His name inaugurated another totally different program, one involving dealings that cover millennia of this world's history and the vast majority of Holy Writ. God chose Abraham and his descendants—known as Israel—establishing them in the unique position as an elect nation to accomplish His ends. Beginning with the unconditional covenant that God made with Abraham (Gen. 12:1–3, 7; 15:7–21; 17), confirmed to Isaac (26:3–5, 23–25), and then to Jacob (28:3–4, 10–22), and finally "to their seed after them" (Deut. 4:37), this human vehicle—blessed above all contemporaries, privileged beyond them all, and thus responsible far beyond them—moved across the stage of history to what might charitably be called mixed reviews. It is true that great prophets, faithful priests, and good kings appeared in the nation's history, but God Himself allowed the people to be called "rebellious" (Deut. 9:24; Isa. 30:9) and "stiffnecked" (Exod. 32:9; Deut. 9:13).

WHY ISRAEL?

On various occasions, God presented the reasons for electing a nation and for electing the nation of Israel in particular.[11] A primary reason is that anything and everything that God does must be attributed to *all* that God is. Thus, one does not err in saying that He *sovereignly* chose Israel. A number of biblical references, however, provide more details.

1. *His love:* "And because he loved thy fathers, therefore he chose their seed after them" (Deut. 4:37). "The Lord did not set his love upon you, nor choose you, because ye were more in number than any people; for ye were the fewest of all people. But because the Lord loved you, and because he would keep the oath which he had sworn unto your fathers, hath the Lord brought you out with a mighty hand, and redeemed you out of the house of bondmen, from the hand of Pharaoh, king of Egypt" (Deut. 7:7–8).
2. *Their spiritual responsibility* (a) *Godward:* "And thou shalt love the Lord thy God with all thine heart, and with all thy soul, and with all thy might" (Deut 6:5). (b) *Humanward:* "And ye shall be unto me a kingdom of priests, and an holy nation" (Exod. 19:6).
3. *To receive, record, and constantly review His revelation:* "And these words, which I command thee this day, shall be in thine heart: And thou shalt teach them diligently unto thy children, and shalt talk of

them when thou sittest in thine house, and when thou walkest by the way, and when thou liest down, and when thou risest up. And thou shalt bind them for a sign upon thine hand, and they shall be as frontlets between thine eyes, and thou shalt write them upon the posts of thy house, and on thy gates" (Deut. 6:6–9).

4. *To be the nation/race of the Messiah:* "Who are Israelites; to whom *pertaineth* the adoption, and the glory, and the covenants, and the giving of the law, and the service *of God,* and the promises; Whose are the fathers, and of whom, as concerning the flesh, Christ *came,* who is over all, God blessed for ever. Amen." (Rom. 9:4–5).[12]

Whereas many privileges and many responsibilities existed for Israel because of their status as a chosen nation, the overriding reason for their election was to glorify God. The program, however, did *not* call for Jewish missionaries to go into all parts of the world and convert its inhabitants to Judaism, although Israel was to demonstrate the character of God. Nothing in biblical Judaism corresponds to or parallels the New Testament "going to make disciples."[13]

APPROPRIATING SALVATION IN ANY AGE

In each phase of history, God made known the elements of His soteriological plan, which would allow members of the race to come into a right relationship with Him, all in precisely the same way (i.e., by faith, believing what God said). The point is illustrated in the case of Abraham, of whom it was said, "Even as Abraham believed God, and it was accounted to him for righteousness" (Gal. 3:6). Taking God at His Word has ever been the means by which the race has participated in God's soteriological plan.

Revelation has been progressive, of course, and other stages of history have not had the light that is available now through the completed written revelation. Nor was there some mystical gnostic communication to the ancients granting them the full details and results of Christ's death on the cross. People came into right relationship with God by faith, by taking Him at His word, by believing what He said. We now know that in God's eyes all such relationships and their benefits were obtained in anticipation of the efficacious sacrifice that Christ would make at Calvary, even as the relationship and benefits today look back to that event. In this age, much of the world is blessed with the written Word, which contains all that God wants humanity to know about Him and His plan of salvation.

ELECTION SURE, PROMISES SECURE,
"BUT HIS OWN RECEIVED HIM NOT"

Judaism many times and in many ways failed to glorify God. None of this failure—by His mercy and grace and based upon His unconditional covenant— abrogated the guarantee of their status as elect nation. But the sinful rejection of their God, His norms, His commands, and finally the Messiah brought a postponement of the promised and greatly anticipated messianic blessing. The turning point in God's plan came when "He came unto his own, and his own received him not" (John 1:11).

Israel's rejection of the Messiah introduced a totally new divine program, different from any activated before. The messianic Jewishness of the Lord Jesus Christ's early ministry, the evidences of growing rejection during the public ministry period, and the change in message and emphasis that this rejection brought about are elements clearly delineated in the gospel accounts.

God's "elect nation" program called for our Lord Jesus Christ's early identification with John the baptizer's message—"Repent for the kingdom of heaven is at hand" (Matt. 3:2; 4:17)—a message summarized as "the gospel of the kingdom" (4:23; 9:35; 24:14). The exegete must examine carefully just what this message meant, beginning with a consideration of the varied kingdoms described in Scripture.

Four "kingdoms" are mentioned: (1) the universal kingdom of God, referring to the right of the Creator to rule over everything in His creation (Pss. 103:19; 145:13); (2) the spiritual kingdom of God, which is His rule over all moral creatures who willingly submit to His authority (i.e., true believers) and in which kingdom there is no mere profession of allegiance; (3) the promised messianic kingdom, when Christ will reign on earth in Jerusalem from David's throne (2 Sam. 7:12–16; Isa. 9; 11; Dan. 7; Matt. 24:29–30; 25:31, 34); (4) the mystery form of the kingdom, so called because it was not revealed in the Old Testament. It has its termini in the two advents of the Lord Jesus Christ. Pictured in Matthew 13, the form of the kingdom includes both the saved and the unsaved.[14]

RECEIVED HIM NOT . . . RECEIVED HIM

Which of these several kingdoms would the first-century Jewish listeners to John the baptizer have understood he was referring to? Obviously, their high hopes were for the coming of the Messiah and the promised kingdom that He would bring. Granted, the hopes of most people were political rather than spiritual; therefore, they were unwilling to accept the spiritual requirements for the rule of heaven. The "good news" (the gospel of the kingdom) that the anticipated messianic kingdom was at hand was based on the presence of its King, but spiritual responsibilities first had to be faced in order to take advantage of the Messiah's legitimate offer.

The "sending out" in Matthew 10 was a Jewish preaching mission to Jews, the message being the good news of the King's presence, and the exhortation being to meet the spiritual requirements of a change of mind, heart, and life. This "good news," or "gospel," was not that which later was called "the gospel of the grace of God" (Acts 20:24); the gospel of the kingdom in Matthew 10 did not refer to the substitutionary death of Christ; it was not available to Gentiles and, although it was a "sending," it had nothing to do with "world missions."[15] Furthermore, this offer of the gospel of the kingdom should not be associated with the gospel of Christ of Romans 1:16, as though the kingdom offer were the offering of the gospel of the grace of God to the "Jew first"; the gospel of the kingdom was a totally different message.

DIFFERENT PROGRAMS, DIFFERENT MESSAGES

Good reasons exists for the marked contrast between our Lord's mandate to His Jewish disciples in Matthew 10 and His commission in Matthew 28.

> Go not into the way of the Gentiles, and into *any* city of the Samaritans enter ye not: But go rather to the lost sheep of the house of Israel. And as ye go, preach, saying, The kingdom of heaven is at hand. (Matthew 10:5–7)

> All power is given unto me in heaven and in earth. Go ye therefore, and teach all nations, baptizing them in the name of the Father, and of the Son, and of the Holy Ghost: Teaching them to observe all things whatsoever I have commanded you: and, lo, I am with you alway, *even* unto the end of the world. (Matthew 28:18–20)

In the Matthew 28 passage, another program in God's design is on the threshold. A new commission accompanies a new program, and neither the program nor the commission is like anything that has preceded them. Much of the latter part of our Lord's ministry on this earth was devoted to preparing His disciples to be foundational in the new program that God was ordaining (Eph. 2:20). The plan was eternal, but temporal events marked the change. The forerunner was incarcerated and soon lost his life (Matt. 11:2; 14:10). Woes were pronounced on cities that had been favored with the message but had rejected it (11:20-24); Christ rebuked the Jewish religious leaders (scribes, Pharisees, and Sadducees, chapters 15; 22; 23); indications of our Lord's coming suffering began to appear (12:39-40; 16:21; 17:12; 20:18-19). Then, in the very heart of Matthew's gospel, Christ states, "I will build my church; and the gates of hell shall not prevail against it" (16:18).[16] There it was: this new program was to be His church, which was described later as His body (Eph. 1:22-23; Col. 1:18).

NEW PROGRAM, NEW MANDATE

In God's sovereign, all-wise, and eternal plan, the period of flagrant and progressive rejection of the Messiah became the backdrop of our Lord's promise to build His church and of His preparation of those who would be foundational to that process (John 13-17; Eph. 2:19-21). Precisely at the end of this preparation period for God's new program, the Gospel accounts and the book of Acts record the new program's unique mandate, what has come to be recognized as the Great Commission.

Peters comments, "The Great Commission does not make Christianity a missionary religion. The latter is such because of its source, nature and total design. The apostles became missionaries not because of a commission but because Christianity is what it is and because of the indwelling Holy Spirit who is an outgoing and witnessing Spirit."[17] It is true, however, that the content and structure of the new program lay an unmistakable imperative on the believer.

The message in the church program deals with, among other things, (1) the universal need—"all have sinned, and come short of the glory of God" (Rom. 3:23); (2) the fatal consequences—"The wages of sin is death" (6:23a); (3) the unique remedy—"but the gift of God is eternal life through Jesus Christ our Lord" (v. 23b); "Christ died for our sins" (1 Cor. 15:3); (4) how humankind acquires the remedy—"believe on the Lord Jesus Christ, and thou shalt be saved" (Acts 16:31); "He that hath the Son hath life; and he that hath not the Son of God hath not life" (1 John 5:12); "He that believeth on him is not condemned: but he that believeth not is condemned already, because he hath not believed in the name of the only begotten Son of God" (John 3:18); (5) the life of a believer—"walk worthy of the vocation wherewith ye are called" (Eph. 4:1); (6) the glorious destiny of the saved—"And if I go and prepare a place for you, I will come again, and receive you unto myself; that where I am, there ye may be also" (John 14:3); "and so shall we ever be with the Lord" (1 Thess. 4:17).

PRIORITY OF THE MANDATE

It is incumbent upon the exegete to note that the unique mandate—the Great Commission as recorded in the Scriptures—was given at the threshold of the formation of the church. The mandate actually antecedes the communication of virtually all of the details of the truths that are contained in the new program message, given in the above list. In other words, the apostles heard the mandate before they received the full-blown, progressive revelation of God's mind regarding the church, certainly before they understood church doctrine and even before the Day of Pentecost.

It is apparent that our Lord thought it sufficiently important to give the mandate to his followers before He left—ascended—and before they received more advanced teaching about the new program. He thereby emphasized its centrifugal nature. Note that the mandate, as it appears in the Gospels and Acts 1, is given to individuals who, on the Day of Pentecost, would become members of the church "which is his body" (Eph. 1:23). Taking for granted that the commission was given before Christ's ascent, the later revealed doctrinal details—although less explicit in terms of a specific mandate to the organized church—build the case theologically, morally, and logically that the commission was indeed intended to be a mandate to the church.[18]

NEW AND VERY DIFFERENT

Much has been written on the distinctiveness of this new program—that is, the church.[19] So, although the church is extremely important to the equally distinctive commission that she received, only a summary of her distinctions will be given here.[20]

1. Promised in Matthew 16 but not in the Old Testament, the church belongs to that period between the two advents of the Lord Jesus Christ. Each advent was foreseen by the Old Testament prophets, but often the first was virtually superimposed upon the second, a fact more readily understood from later revelation. The church simply was not the subject of Old Testament prophecy.
2. The New Testament never combined, confused, or compromised the terms *Israel* and *church*.[21]

3. Certain elements had to be in place to start the church: *(a)* the
    death of Christ was a prerequisite (Eph. 2:13-16); *(b)* the Resur-
    rection and Ascension were also prerequisites (Eph. 1:20-21); *(c)*
    the apostles and New Testament prophets had to be in place, since
    Ephesians 2:19-21—following the building analogy—calls them
    foundational; *(d)* spiritual gifts (and therefore gifted men so
    important to the ministry of the church) were given in conjunction
    with the ascension of our Lord (Eph. 4:8, 11-12); *(e)* the advent
    of the Holy Spirit, by whom the believer is regenerated (Titus 3:5),
    had to first be placed into the body of Christ (1 Cor. 12:13) and
    then sealed (Eph. 4:30).

THE GREAT COMMISSION IS "CHURCH PROPERTY"

The Great Commission belongs to this new program, which was unan-
nounced in the Old Testament, is not to be confused with Israel, and was
designed neither to replace the elect nation nor to abrogate her promises.

Although the message of the church program is still based on the only
biblical requirement in either testament for a right relationship with God—
that of faith—the message is nonetheless different from that of other divine
programs. I reiterate, the new message, being the gospel of grace, is not
different in providing a means of salvation other than by faith; it is different
by reason of the rejection of the Messiah by Israel and the finished work of
Christ on the cross. This gospel of the grace of God is offered to all, Gentile
and Jew alike. True, like other messages, it is called "good news," but this
specific good news is then defined.

> Paul gives us the precise definition of the Gospel we preach today in
> 1 Corinthians 15:3-8. The Gospel is the good news about the death
> and resurrection of Christ. He died and He lives—this is the content
> of the Gospel. The fact of Christ's burial proves the reality of His
> death. He did not merely swoon only to be revived later. He actu-
> ally died and died for our sins. The inclusion of a list of witnesses
> proves the reality of His resurrection. He died for our sins and was
> buried (proof of His death); He arose and was seen by many wit-
> nesses, the majority of whom were still alive when Paul wrote
> 1 Corinthians (the proof of His resurrection). The same twofold con-
> tent of the good news appears again in Romans 4:25: He "was
> delivered up . . . and was raised." Everyone who believes in that good

news is saved, for that truth and that alone, is the Gospel of the grace of God (1 Cor. 15:2).[22]

THE PROPER PLACE OF MISSIONS IN SYSTEMATIC THEOLOGY

The Great Commission is peculiarly the responsibility of believers in this age, does not copy any other mandate, and does not need to strive for some Old Testament identity to establish its validity. The New Testament mandate and the theme "missions" is simply not, as some missiologists try to establish, to be found under every rock in the Old Testament. Indeed, when by some sort of "complimentary hermeneutics" missions is read back into the Old Testament Scripture, it is more than just a disservice to Bible study; it is eisegesis. There is absolutely no need to support the New Testament mandate by means of a contrived Old Testament basis. And no need exists to establish, through Genesis 3:15—the Abrahamic covenant—or the Jonah incident, that our God has always been a "missionary God."[23]

On the other hand, to say that our God is and always has been a God of mercy *and* justice is quite proper. New Testament missions is certainly no departure from that or any other revealed divine characteristic, but the message and the program are exclusively New Testament in character. The new program draws on all of what the Scriptures teach about God, but it enjoys a specific and distinct place in progressive revelation, theology, and history.

The proper place of missions in the total scheme of systematic theology is first that of total dependence upon what the Scriptures teach about God. Second, the biblical theology of missions—it draws from and teaches about theology proper, Christology, pneumatology, biblical anthropology, soteriology, and eschatology—is placed solidly in the area of that which is uniquely New Testament—ecclesiology.

PART 2

KEY THEOLOGICAL CONCERNS

Enduring and Contemporary

CHAPTER 4

THE MISSION OF THE CHURCH

Russell L. Penney

WHAT IS THE MISSION OF THE CHURCH? Is it simply the evangelization of the lost? Is it the betterment of humankind through meeting the nutritional, medical, and educational needs of less-developed countries? Is it the battle for social equality among the persecuted minority groups of the world?

Some people would say *yes* to all these suggestions. But, as with any other divine endeavor, we must first check the divine plan—that is, the inspired text—to determine the primary mission of the church.

THE MISSION OF GOD

To understand the mission of God for the church, we must first understand the "mission" of God in history. John Piper demonstrates that the ultimate goal of God in history, and therefore in the church, is worship of Him. In other words, God's ultimate mission through all that He does is to bring glory to Himself. Piper writes,

> Missions is not the ultimate goal of the church. Worship is. Missions exists because worship doesn't. Worship is ultimate, not missions, because God is ultimate, not man. When this age is over, and the countless millions of the redeemed fall on their faces before the throne of God, missions will be no more. It is a temporary necessity. But worship abides forever.[1]

Piper adds that it is the chief end of God to glorify Himself and enjoy Himself forever. Note Isaiah 48:9–11:

For the sake of My name I delay My wrath, And *for My praise* I restrain it for you, In order not to cut you off. Behold, I have refined you, but not as silver; I have tested you in the furnace of affliction. *For My own sake, for My own sake,* I will act; For how can My name be profaned? And *My glory I will not give to another.* (italics added)

God's chief end is also confirmed repeatedly in the church age. In Paul's treatise on the nature of the church of Jesus Christ, he writes,

Blessed be the God and Father of our Lord Jesus Christ, who has blessed us with every spiritual blessing in the heavenly places in Christ, just as He chose us in Him before the foundation of the world, that we should be holy and blameless before Him. In love He predestined us to adoption as sons through Jesus Christ to Himself, according to the kind intention of His will, *to the praise of the glory of His grace,* which He freely bestowed on us in the Beloved. (Ephesians 1:3-6, italics added)

Bringing in the elect from all nations of the earth through the proclamation of the gospel is to fulfill the ultimate goal of bringing praise to God. Thus, any definition of the mission of the church must include the exaltation of God. Because this is God's mission, His exaltation will be reflected as well in the mission of the church, Christ's body.

THE MISSION OF GOD THROUGH THE CHURCH

To clarify and further expand the definition of the mission of the church, it is necessary to understand the nature of humanity. God's holiness and justice seen against the sinful state of humankind sets the stage for understanding God's redemptive work through the sacrifice of His Son. Thus, the proclamation of the finished work of Christ on the cross is the message of missions.

Because God is holy, He cannot have a relationship with sinful humanity unless sin is first dealt with. Thus, for God to bring in His elect in a way that is consistent with His nature, He had first to deal with the lack of holiness inherent in humanity since the Fall. That provision was made through the sacrifice of His Son (Rom. 3:24-25).

Several passages clarify God's view of humanity, but Romans 1:18-3:8 is probably the most succinct in the New Testament. There, Paul shows the need of the whole human race by condemning, in order, the Gentile (1:18–32), the moralist (2:1–16), and even the Jew (2:17–3:8). Then comes the ultimate condemnation of all humankind:

> As it is written, "There is *none righteous, not even one;* There is none who understands, There is *none who seeks for God;* All have turned aside, together they have become useless; There is *none who does good,* There is not even one." "Their throat is an open grave, With their tongues they keep deceiving," "The poison of asps is under their lips;" "Whose mouth is full of cursing and bitterness;" "Their feet are swift to shed blood, Destruction and misery are in their paths, And the path of peace have they not known." "There is *no fear of God before their eyes.*" (Romans 3:10–18, italics added)

This passage makes clear the depravity of all humanity. What this means is that, as a result of the Fall (Gen. 1–3), "corruption has extended to all aspects of man's nature, to his entire being; and total depravity means that because of that corruption there is nothing man can do to merit saving favor with God."[2] When Adam fell spiritually in the garden, he plunged the entire human race into sin: "Therefore, just as through one man sin entered into the world, and death through sin, and so death spread to all men, *because all sinned*" (Rom. 5:12, italics added).

Paul's assessment of unregenerate humankind is the same assessment found in the entirety of Holy Writ. Warburton concludes,

> They are apostates from the womb, and as soon as they are born go astray, speaking lies (Ps. 58:3); they are even shapen in iniquity, and conceived in sin (Ps. 51:5). The propensity of their heart is evil from their youth (Gen. 8:21), and it is out of the heart that all the issues of life proceed (Prov. 4:23; 20:11). Acts of sin are therefore but the expression of the natural heart, which is deceitful above all things and exceedingly corrupt (Jer. 17:9).[3]

Warburton emphasizes that all of humankind is born in a sin condition (Ps. 51:5). Thus, not only do we commit sins, but we are sinners by nature. "Sin *(hamartia)* is defined as missing the mark: It is an athletic term that indicates whether the javelin struck the target or not. God has a target (or standard of morality or rightness) for man to live up to, though no one does, nor ever has, nor ever will."[4] Martin Luther stated, "We are not sinners because we commit sins—now this one, now that one—but we commit these acts because we are sinners before we do so: that is, a bad tree and bad seed produce bad fruit, and from an evil root nothing but an evil tree can grow."[5] Once we understand that God demands perfect righteousness in order for us to have a relationship with Him (Hab. 1:13), we see our need for a Savior.

We must also understand these doctrines—the depravity of humanity and the holiness of God—before we can understand missions. Peters writes,

> Christian missions make sense only in the light of an existing abnormality or emergency and in the conviction that an answer to and remedy for such a malady is available. . . . The emergency is the fact of *sin* in the world which has overpowered and infected the human race and which threatens the very existence of mankind. There would be no need for Christian missions if sin were not a serious reality. Neither would the doctrine of soteriology make sense without the presence and awfulness of sin. Sin made salvation necessary and sin makes Christian missions necessary.[6]

In light of this depravity, God provided, from the foundation of the world, His Son as a substitute for the sins of the world (Acts 2:23; John 3:16). Although the plan of God was conceived outside of time, its fruition occurred in time.

Humankind has always been saved on the basis of the shed blood of Christ and has had some limited understanding of the Redeemer, but it was not until the Crucifixion that this truth became the unique content of faith. Until then, human beings were saved by grace on the basis of their faith in God and were credited with righteousness on the basis of the death of Christ (e.g., Abraham [Gen. 15:6]). It was only after the death, burial, and resurrection of Christ that salvation by grace became the central content of the gospel message (1 Cor. 15:3-4).

Thus, another aspect of the mission of the church is to proclaim the gospel of the death, burial, and resurrection of Jesus Christ, God's Son, until He returns. This part of the church's mission is set forth most clearly in the various recordings of the Great Commission in both the Gospels and the book of Acts.

WHOSE IS THE GREAT COMMISSION?

Some dispensationalists have argued that, since the church did not begin until the coming of the Holy Spirit in Acts 2, the Great Commission—which was given in the Gospels (Matt. 28:18-20; Mark 16:15; Luke 24:44-49)—is not given to the church. Most dispensationalists agree that the birth of the church did not come until the advent of the Holy Spirit. This was confirmed by the Holy Spirit's ministry of "baptizing"—that is, placing each member in Christ's body, which is the church (1 Cor. 12:13). It is also true that since this ministry of Spirit baptism did not begin until the coming of the Holy Spirit at Pentecost (Acts 1:5; 2:1-4; 11:15-16), the church was not formed until Acts 2.

Still, although technically the dispensation of grace (or the church) had not yet begun before this time, the program of God had already changed focus from the nation of Israel to the nations as a whole. This change of focus is made evident by contrasting Christ's previous commission to the disciples in Matthew 5:5-7 with the Great Commission as given in Matthew 28:18-20; Mark 16:15; Luke 24:44-49; John 21:15-17; and Acts 1:8. In the former passage, the content of the gospel concerned preparing for the kingdom by recognizing Christ as the King, and the limit of the proclamation was the nation of Israel; in the latter passages, the disciples are to take the message of the gospel of the death, burial, and resurrection of Christ (1 Cor. 15:3-4) to *all of the world*.

The period between Christ's resurrection and Pentecost, then, was a transitional period leading from the dispensation of the Law to the dispensation of grace. Christ was appearing to His disciples and giving them needed encouragement and instruction for their tremendous task of proclaiming His gospel to the world. As has been seen, the twelve apostles were first given the commission to take the gospel of the kingdom to the nation of Israel (Matt. 5:5-7). Then, when Israel rejected the kingdom and their King (chap. 21; the Triumphal Entry; esp. 21:43; also 23:37-39), the apostles became the foundation of the church (Eph. 2:20).

Thus, Enns, a dispensationalist, writes,

> The foundational command for evangelism in the world is Matthew 28:18-20. The work of the church in the world is to make disciples (learners), baptize them, and bring them into the fellowship of believers. The ministry of evangelism was not carried on by a select few but by ordinary believers as well (Acts 8:4). The central message

the early Church proclaimed was Christ (Acts 8:5, 12, 35; 9:20; 11:20); moreover, they took the message beyond the Jewish boundary, crossing previously rigid cultural barriers (Acts 2:41; 4:4; 5:14; 6:1; 8:12; 10:48; 11:24; 13:48; 14:1, 21).[7]

And Lightner, another dispensationalist, states,

> In broad outline Christ's great commission sets forth the answer to the question, Why does the church exist? The evangelization of the lost is a major responsibility of the church (Matt. 28:19). "Go ye therefore and teach all nations" [KJV] is better translated, "Go therefore and make disciples of all nations" [NASB]. This is the evangelization command of the commission. The edification command is in the baptizing and teaching which follow. The church exists as a gathered community of believers to edify or build up those who are a part of it. The emphasis throughout the New Testament is evenly distributed between these two responsibilities.[8]

Thus, the Great Commission is directed to the church of Jesus Christ. An exegesis of Matthew 28:18–20 and references to other recordings of the commission as well as other scriptural instructions—will yield the fullest biblical understanding of the mission of the church.

THE GREAT COMMISSION (MATT. 28:18–20)

The Authority of the Commission (Matt. 28:18)

Jesus stated, "All authority has been given to Me in heaven and on earth" (28:18). At this point, some of the disciples were still "doubtful" (28:17). Thus, the statement that preceded Christ's commission in verse 18 was important. This statement would help Christ's followers realize that their resurrected Messiah, who was the Head of the church, was sovereign in the universe. Nothing would thwart His hand. All whom His Father had chosen from the foundation of the earth to be part of Christ's body—the church—would come to Him in this age.

Our responsibility is to proclaim the gospel, which is the power of God unto salvation (1 Cor. 15:3–4; Rom. 1:16); our sovereign Lord's responsibility is to bring in His elect (Acts 13:48; 16:14). The authority of the commission assures the success of that mission, success being that all of the elect whom God wants to call to Himself during the dispensation of the church will be preached to and regenerated. Christ's own assurance should be an encouragement to us.

The Imperatives of the Commission: Go and Make Disciples (28:19a)

Christ's command is, "*Go* therefore and *make disciples* of *all the nations,* baptizing them in the name of the Father and the Son and the Holy Spirit, teaching them to observe all that I commanded you. . . ." Christ's first command is to "go." Although Matthew uses an aorist participle here instead of an imperative, many Greek grammarians believe that this is a rare case of the use of a participle to issue a command.[9] Christ meant for His church to be an aggressive, outgoing organism that perceived as its goal the proclamation of the gospel "to the remotest part of the earth" (Acts 1:8).

We should note, however, that the main verb in the commission is *to make* disciples. The verb in Greek is *mathēteuō* and the noun form is *mathētēs,* which in the New Testament can be translated "disciple," "learner," or "adherent."[10] Bauer indicates that the verb means "to make a disciple of, or [to] teach [someone]."[11]

In Luke 15:25–35, Christ gives the following three conditions for discipleship:

1. The disciple's relationship with God has a priority over all other relationships (v. 26).
2. The disciple must be willing to submit to the lordship (authority) of Christ (v. 27).
3. The disciple must hold loosely to earthly possessions and simply be a steward of God's possessions (v. 33).

Peters describes the Christian disciple this way:

> The biblical concept of Christian discipleship must always be interpreted to involve humble following, constant fellowship, sanctified openmindedness, undisputed obedience, ready submission, heroic faith, arduous labor, unselfish service, self-renunciation, patient suffering, painful sacrifice, and cross-bearing. It is the bringing of all of life under the lordship of Christ. This is not only the purpose of salvation but the fullness of salvation—redemption from self and devotion to the Lord. And to this *every* Christian is called. (italics added)[12]

He continues,

> Discipleship is a perpetual school which may lead from one degree
> to another but does not graduate its scholars. . . . Discipleship is a
> unique and continuous experience, a growth in grace and in the
> knowledge of the Lord Jesus Christ.[13]

Thus, Christ's existing disciples were commanded to go and make other
disciples, and in doing so they were to go to "all nations." Until this time,
God had chosen to work primarily through His chosen people, Israel. They
were to be a kingdom of priests and a holy nation whose righteous behavior
would draw nations to them and to their God. But Israel had failed miser-
ably. In fact, they had even rejected their Messiah and, thus, had been set
aside for a time in God's divine program (Rom. 11:25).

Now Christ was sending out his servants to proclaim the good news of
His death, burial, and resurrection to all nations—that is, to *the Gentiles*. Paul
explained God's new program in the following terms:

> Therefore remember [Gentiles] . . . that you were at that time [be-
> fore this commission was given] separate from Christ, excluded from
> the commonwealth of Israel, and strangers to the covenants of prom-
> ise, having no hope and without God in the world. But now in Christ
> Jesus you who formerly were far off have been brought near by the
> blood of Christ. For He Himself is our peace, who made both groups
> into one, and broke down the barrier of the dividing wall. (Ephesians
> 2:11–14)

So it is that the field in which we are to make disciples is the world—"all
nations." The inclusion of the whole world as a mission field is confirmed
by the other writers of Scripture as well (see Mark 16:15; Luke 24:46–49;
Acts 1:7–8).

The Manner of Fulfilling the Commission (28:19b–20a)

Baptizing Them

Christ made clear how to fulfill the task. He followed the imperative "make
disciples" with two modal participles (sometimes referred to as "participles
of manner"). A modal participle "signif[ies] the manner in which the action

of the main verb is accomplished."[14] Thus, the making of disciples involves "baptizing" and "teaching." Barbieri writes,

> They were to make disciples by proclaiming the truth concerning Jesus. Their field was to include all nations, not just Israel. They were to make disciples by proclaiming the truth concerning Jesus. Their hearers were to be evangelized and enlisted in Jesus' followers. Those who believed were to be baptized in water in the name of the Father and of the Son and of the Holy Spirit. Such an act would associate a believer with the person of Jesus Christ and with the Triune God. . . . Those who respond are also to be taught the truths Jesus had specifically communicated to the Eleven.[15]

Although the commission recorded in Matthew does not mention proclamation, Mark's gospel does. Mark writes, "And He said to them, 'Go into all the world and preach the gospel to all creation'" (Mark 16:15). Mark contributed the method of missions to our understanding of the commission—the method being the oral proclamation of the gospel of Jesus Christ.

To clarify, the gospel is the proclamation of the death, burial, and resurrection of Jesus Christ as payment for our sins (1 Cor. 15:3–4; Acts 13–39), and that salvation can come only through Him (John 14:6; Acts 4:12). The Bible teaches that general revelation is enough to condemn pagans yet not enough to save them (Rom. 1:16–32); thus, they need the revelation of the gospel of Jesus Christ to be saved (see chap. 6: "The Destiny of the Unevangelized"). In this age, only the gospel of Jesus Christ is the power of God to salvation; "missions" is not "missions" unless the gospel is preached. That was the pattern of Peter, Paul, and all true disciples in the early church.

Missiologist David Hesselgrave is correct when he states, "Converts are to be baptized *into [eis]* the name of the Father, and the Son, and the Holy Spirit. This implies that they come into ownership of the Triune God."[16] But this in no way implies baptismal regeneration. The pattern that we see in Acts is proclamation of the message, faith in the message, and then water baptism by immersion (2:41; 4:4; 5:14; 8:12; 8:36–37; 10:43–48; etc.), which is a public identification with the Father, Son, and Holy Spirit.

Based on the missionary accounts in Acts, a normal pattern for baptism was for it to occur shortly after the converts had placed their faith in the gospel message. In Philippi, for instance, Lydia, her household (Acts 16:14–15), and the jailer (vv. 31–34) placed their faith in Christ and, within hours, were baptized without extensive instruction. Water baptism symbolizes the baptismal work of the Spirit. And since that work has already been accomplished in response to the convert's faith (Rom. 6:1–4; 1 Cor. 12:12–13), it makes sense that no long period should exist between conversion and baptism. Clearly, Paul would have given the converts some instruction as to the meaning of water baptism. Thus, converts can and should receive brief instructions about the meaning and importance of water baptism before the baptism actually takes place.

Teaching Them

The Content of Teaching

Christ stated that the content of teaching was to be all that He commanded them. Some people believe that Christ's command did not include teaching new disciples the truths contained in the completed canon. It is believed, for instance, that subjects relating to future events are too complex for new converts and that they should not be confused with such things. It is amazing to see, however, the depth and content of Paul's teaching to new converts, and his is the pattern we must follow. He taught almost all of his fledgling churches about eschatological matters (e.g., 1 Thess. 4:13–18; 1 Cor. 15:50–58).

Some doctrines are, of course, more important than others. Since the completion of the scriptural canon, the content of a convert's initial instruction in a church planting situation should be selected from that completed canon. A course of study that gives new converts a good foundation includes the following topics:

Primary Teachings	Secondary Teachings
1. Salvation	1. Inspiration and inerrancy
2. Assurance	2. Bible interpretation
3. Daily time with God	3. The Trinity
4. Prayer life	4. The Deity of Christ
5. Personal Bible study	5. Salvation (deeper understanding)
6. Scripture memorization	6. Sanctification
7. Confession of sin	7. Satan and demons
8. Dealing with temptation	8. The Christian life and future events
9. The Spirit-filled life	9. Systematized Bible knowledge
10. Obedience	10. Evidences for the Christian faith
11. God's discipline	11. Biblical family roles
12. Developing godly habits of living	12. The man: husband and father

13. Knowing God's will
14. Stewardship
15. The church[17]

13. The woman: wife and mother
14. The child

Missionaries must evaluate individual converts, going more slowly with some than with others. Early on, they should spend extra time with those converts who show leadership capabilities and quick minds in grasping and communicating the truths of Scripture. These people should soon take on limited and guided responsibilities to teach and lead the assembly. Culley writes,

> Special attention needs to be given to the spiritual growth of those whom God raises up as leaders of each local church. Paul's word to Timothy is sharply pointed in directing that what he has learned he must in turn commit "to faithful men, who shall be able to teach others also" (II Tim. 2:2).[18]

Again, the gradual transfer of responsibilities will prevent converts from becoming overly dependent on the missionary.

Converts must do more than just go to church and learn facts about the Bible. They must also be encouraged to learn the truths of Scripture and confront the world with those truths through evangelism and further church planting. The method is best learned by example; the message is best learned by formal instruction.

The Logical Necessity of the Teaching

Paul, in his masterful treatise on the nature of the church, writes of the ascended Christ,

> And he gave some as apostles, and some as prophets, and some as evangelists, and some as pastors and teachers, for the equipping of the saints for the work of service, to the building up of the body of Christ; until we all attain to the unity of the faith, and of the knowledge of the Son of God, to a mature man, to the measure of the stature which belongs to the fulness of Christ. (Ephesians 4:11–13)

The ascended Christ gifted men and gave them to the body "for the equipping of the saints" (v. 12). This equipping was—and still is—to be carried out by gifted men of the church. In the local church, this equipping is to be done by pastor-teachers or elders. On the mission field, missionaries are to equip the first converts and then train and appoint leaders to continue the work (Acts 14:21-23). The term *missionary* is, in the present context, an anglicized Latin term that translates the Greek *apostolos*. Although the term was used officially to refer to certain individuals who met specific qualifications and, along with the New Testament prophets, were the foundation of the church, the term also was used generally for such men as Barnabas (Acts 14:4, 14), James (Gal. 1:19), Andronicus and Junias (Rom. 16:7), and Epaphroditus (Phil. 2:25). [19]

Paul teaches that this equipping is for "building up the body of Christ" (Eph. 4:12), and the goal of this "building up" is fourfold:

1.   the unity of the faith
2.   the knowledge of Christ
3.   spiritual maturity
4.   Christlikeness (v. 13)

None of these goals can be attained, however, without sound doctrinal instruction.

Paul then gives the result of this kind of "building up": the church is now doctrinally literate and stable in her beliefs (v. 14). She is no longer easily swayed from the pure doctrine of Christ, but her members are able to defend the truth and growing up into Christ. As each member matures and draws from the Head for sustenance, the body grows and is built up in love (vv. 15-16).

During the growth process, Christians are laying "aside the old self" and putting "on the new self, which in the likeness of God is "created in righteousness and holiness of truth" (vv. 22, 24). Putting on the new self results in Christians becoming "imitators of God, as beloved children," and "walking in love" (5:1-2).

Converts can accomplish all these goals only if they have been thoroughly taught by word and deed. Paul, in his twilight hours on this earth, told Timothy,

All Scripture is inspired by God and *profitable for teaching, for reproof, for correction, for training in righteousness;* that the man of God may be adequate, equipped for every good work. (2 Timothy 3:16-17, italics added)

And,

> preach the word; be ready in season and out of season; *reprove, rebuke, exhort, with great patience and instruction.* For the time will come when they will not endure sound doctrine; but wanting to have their ears tickled, they will accumulate for themselves teachers in accordance to their own desires. (2 Timothy 4:2-3, italics added)

Christ has not commissioned us merely to preach the gospel and then leave converts to fend for themselves. To do so would be nothing less than child abandonment on a spiritual level. We are commanded by Christ to proclaim the gospel and baptize converts, but we are also commanded to teach them. Nowhere did Christ commission us merely to lead people to Christ; our commission is to *make disciples.* Christ's goal is the formation of a mature church, and this goal can only be accomplished by *disciples.*

The Support of the Commission (28:20b)

We are to make disciples, then, by proclaiming the gospel message—which God uses to convict and convert—and by baptizing them and teaching them to observe sound doctrinal truth. The disciples who first received the commission may well have thought, "How can a tiny band of followers have any hope of fulfilling such an overwhelming task?" Christ said, "And lo *[idou]*, I am with you always, even to the end of the age." In light of the disciples' doubts, Christ assured them that He would be with them. The Greek particle *idou,* translated "lo" in the *New American Standard Bible,* is a demonstrative particle that has no exact English equivalent. It is often used to "emphasize the size or importance of something."[20] An appropriate English translation of the phrase above might be "And *take notice,* I am with you every day, until the completion of the age!" This statement would have assured Christ's disciples that they were not alone in their endeavor, but the One who has all authority in heaven and on earth (28:18) would be walking with them every day until the completion of the age—and the completion of their task (v. 20). We have that same promise. He is with us always.

OTHER STATEMENTS OF THE COMMAND TO EVANGELIZE THE WORLD

Scripture records other statements that refer to evangelizing the world and help to clarify our task. Luke 24:46-49, for instance, says,

And He said to them, "Thus, it is written, that the Christ should suffer and rise again from the dead the third day; and that repentance for forgiveness of sin should be proclaimed in His name to all the nations, beginning from Jerusalem. You are witnesses of these things. And behold, I am sending forth the promise of My Father upon you; but you are to stay in the city until you are clothed with power from on high."

Peters outlines Luke's record of the commission as follows:

1. the revelational foundation of the gospel—the Scriptures, the Law of Moses, the Prophets, the Psalms
2. the content of the gospel—the death and resurrection of Christ
3. the charge of the gospel—repentance and remission of sins
4. the scope of the gospel—among the nations
5. the instruments of the gospel—you are witnesses
6. the dynamic of the gospel—the promise of the Father and the Holy Spirit[21]

Luke's record makes several contributions to this current study of the Great Commission. It shows, for instance, that the Old Testament is the foundation of the gospel and highlights the progress of revelation. In recent years, New Tribes Mission and others have used chronological Bible teaching very effectively, showing the continuity of God's program and giving a fuller context for understanding the nature of the gospel.[22]

Luke's record also confirms that the death, burial, and resurrection of Christ and the remission of sins on the basis of His work is the content of the gospel, and that this gospel is to be proclaimed (preached, vv. 46-47) to all nations. John's gospel records that Christ's disciples were the instruments for proclaiming the gospel to the ends of the earth: "Jesus therefore said to them again, 'Peace be with you; as the Father has sent me, I also send you'" (John 20:21). Thus, the Father sent the Son to proclaim the gospel, and the Son has sent us. Although God could have brought in the elect some other way—through the ministry of angels, through general revelation, or even through a talking donkey (Num. 22:28-30)—He chose to give us the privilege and responsibility of bearing the Good News. God "reconciled us to Himself through Christ, and gave *us* the ministry of reconciliation, namely, that God was in Christ reconciling the world to Himself, not counting their trespasses against them, and He has committed to *us* the word of reconciliation. *Therefore, we are ambassadors for Christ, as though God were entreating through us"* (2 Cor. 5:18–20a, italics added).

The last point to be discussed in regard to the commission as recorded in Luke concerns what Peters has termed the *dynamic of the gospel,* that is, the promise of the Holy Spirit. The importance of the Holy Spirit is also emphasized in Acts 1:8 through the restatement of the commission Jesus gave us: "But you shall receive power when the Holy Spirit has come upon you; and you shall be My witnesses both in Jerusalem, and in all Judea and Samaria, and even to the remotest part of the earth." Because the Holy Spirit plays such an integral role in the book of Acts, it has been suggested that Acts could be titled the "Acts of the Holy Spirit through the Apostles."

In a special way, the Holy Spirit has taken up residence in each member of the body of Christ (John 14:17; Eph. 1:13; 4:30), and through the power of the Holy Spirit we, as ambassadors, are able to bear witness for Christ (John 15:26) and His work to the ends of the earth. In and of ourselves—no matter how gifted, talented, and educated—we are incapable of converting a single soul. God does the work of missions through us in the power of the Holy Spirit. Longenecker states,

> Luke's stress on the importance of the Spirit . . . in the mission of the church can readily . . . be seen by noting the comparative frequency of pneuma (*pneuma*, "spirit") in . . . Acts: . . . [it occurs] seventy times in Acts—though, admittedly, a few of these occurrences refer to the human spirit (e.g., Acts 17:16) or even to unclean spirits (e.g., Luke 4:33; 6:18).[23]

The servant of Christ, without the power and work of the Spirit of God (see Acts 13:48; 16:14), is powerless, too, against the wiles of the Devil and the depraved heart of the unregenerate. In this age, then, the Holy Spirit accomplishes the missionary purposes of God, calling out the elect by working in and through the disciples of Christ. Hesselgrave writes, "After the Holy Spirit came, they [the disciples] discovered experientially that the *Holy* Spirit is also the '*Missionary* Spirit.' *He* obeyed the Commission in and through them."[24]

WHAT IS THE MISSION OF THE CHURCH?

Since the mission of God is His glorification, all that He does is related to that goal. Thus, the aim of the church—confirmed in Ephesians 1:3–6 (see also John 4:23–24; Phil. 3:3)—is first to glorify God. Second, we are called to proclaim the gospel to "all the nations" (Matt. 28:19; Mark 16:15; Acts 1:8; 2 Cor. 5:20; 1 Tim. 3:15). And third, we are called to make disciples of the converts by baptizing them and teaching them through both word and deed the doctrinal truth of the Word of God (Eph. 4:11–16; 1 Thess. 5:11; 2 Tim. 2:2; 3:16–17; 4:2–3).

Missiologist George Peters writes,

> From the teaching of the New Testament it is easily perceived that the church operates in three relationships: *upward* to God in worship and glorification; *inward* to herself in edification, purification, education and discipline; *outward* to world evangelization and service ministries.[25]

Dr. Robert Lightner, a systematic theologian, writes, "[I] not only believe strongly in this threefold mission and purpose of the local church, but I also believe they should be stressed in the order given."[26] According to Lightner, this threefold mission includes the following aspects:

> (1) *The Exaltation of God.* This is what worship is (John 4:23–24; Phil. 3:3). (2) *The education, edification, and equipping of the saints in and through the Word of God* (Eph. 4:11–16; 1 Thess. 5:11). Both the written Word of God and living Son of God need to be central in every facet of the local church's ministry. To be Bible centered and Christ centered is to be true to the Scriptures. The local church ought to be the place where God's people can be built up in the most holy faith. Here they also ought to be encouraged to be involved in personal Bible study and a consistent walk with God. The local church . . . is where we are instructed in God's Word, edified or built up in the most holy faith and equipped to go out into the world as salt and light. (3) *The evangelization of the lost* (Matt. 28:19–20; Acts 1:8; 2 Cor. 5:20; 1 Tim. 3:15). This should be done both in the church and outside it. Members of the church need to be instructed and encouraged on how to share the good news of salvation with the lost. They need to know God expects them to do this with their lives and their lips.[27]

Hesselgrave, commenting on the Great Commission in John, writes,

> In sum, the Johannine statement of the Great Commission does not change the direction of the statements in the Synoptic Gospels. Rather, it underscores the authority behind our mission to disciple the nations by preaching, baptizing, and reaching. To allow any understanding of mission to obscure the proclamatory, sacramental, and didactic responsibility of the Church is to put the knife to the heart of the Christian mission. To substitute other activities for those distinctly specified by our Lord is to attempt a "heart transplant—one that sooner or later certainly will be rejected.[28]

If evangelicals decide to work toward social and cultural goals instead of saving souls, they will be, as Hesselgrave states, attempting a "heart transplant." Our focus must return to the mission of the church—the mission with which Christ commissioned us. Otherwise, our evangelical endeavor, as we know it, will die on the operating table.

CHAPTER 5

THE SOVEREIGNTY OF GOD IN MISSIONS

Michael Pocock

WHY WOULD ANYONE REFUSE GOD'S gift of love and grace? It is a mystery to those of us who have experienced the forgiveness of sin and the joy of salvation that anyone would reject these gifts. We want others to share our experience. Yet, the gospel is frequently met with resistance by those of other cultures, by neighbors across the street, and even by members of our own families. The question is: What is the reason for this resistance?

I'm reminded of a marvelous film that probably launched a generation of fly fishers. *A River Runs Through It* told the story of a clergyman and his wife who raised their two sons with large doses of love, fishing, and the Westminster Catechism. They lived along the banks of the Blackfoot River in Montana. In spite of their efforts, prayers, and dreams, one son became "Mr. Responsible" and the other "Mr. Hell Raiser." The former followed, in large measure, his father's hopes, but the latter went his own way—to destruction. In his later years the old clergyman, saddened by the death of the son who had rejected all counsel to mend his ways, asked his congregation, "What is it about those we love? Don't we have what they need? Or is it just that they won't take what we offer?"

The answers to that clergyman's questions are elusive. So, too, are the reasons why some people resist the gospel and others respond. "Lord," we might say, "we know that you so loved the whole world and that you gave your only son for our redemption. We have accepted your challenge to make disciples of all nations. We believe that we have been given the presence and power of your Spirit to reach them, and we've tried to reach as many as we could. So why are so many people as yet unreached? And why are so many resistant to the gospel?"

SHOULD WE BE SURPRISED BY RESISTANCE?

After two thousand years of missionary endeavor, there is hardly a nation where the gospel has not been proclaimed, though many within those nations may not have heard it. All cultures are wonderfully originated by God (Gen. 11:1-9; Acts 17:24-27) but fatally flawed by sin. We can be sure that the easiest cases have already responded to the cure the gospel offers, leaving the most resistant for our own day. And unfortunately, those that have been repeatedly exposed to the cure may have become even more entrenched.

In 1972, David Liao, writing about the Hakka of Taiwan, showed that, although most missionaries considered this group resistant to the gospel, there had in fact been periods of great response among them—especially on the mainland of China. But Liao demonstrated statistically that, especially after 1950, proportionately less outreach, resources, and personnel had been targeted toward the Hakka than toward other groups in Taiwan. He concluded that the Hakka were not more resistant than others but were simply neglected.[1] The lesson here is simple. Sometimes we may be in danger of using the idea of resistance to excuse ourselves from engaging with unreached peoples, when in reality we simply don't know what their disposition toward the gospel might be.

WHAT IS MEANT BY *Resistant?*

The *resistant* are those who have had the opportunity to hear the gospel in a meaningful way but, over time, have not responded positively. *Unreached* in modern missiological parlance does not mean "unengaged by mission efforts." Rather, it means that "there is no indigenous community of believing Christians with adequate numbers and resources to evangelize the group to its margins."[2] So some groups, although they have a mission outreach among them, may nevertheless be both resistant and unreached.

WHY PEOPLE GROUPS ARE RESISTANT TO THE GOSPEL

Martin Luther believed that resistance to the gospel was akin to "spiritual madness." "Demented, mad, irrational" people, when offered a cure by a competent doctor, may rant, be abusive, and reject it. Such a response to the Good News, he thought, could only be attributed to madness.[3]

Other people, speaking more temperately, have suggested that, when the gospel is rejected, communication might have been flawed, that the culture might not have been respected, or that adaptations might not have been made. The church has failed, in some cases, because it has locked the Bible into a single language, such as Latin in the case of the Roman Catholics and Greek in the case of the Orthodox.[4] Missionaries like Methodius and Cyril (ninth century) took the trouble to develop a Slavonic alphabet and liturgy, and they achieved a breakthrough among the people of Bulgaria. The ministry of these two men actually set the stage for the Christianization of all Slavic peoples in Eastern Europe and Russia.[5]

Donald McGavran observed, in what has now been termed the homogeneous principle, that "people everywhere like to become Christians without crossing barriers of race, language, and class."[6] He maintained that resistance has often resulted when one culture is forced to give up its identity and merge with another in order to come to Christ. Instead, it should be possible for all people to respond to the gospel while remaining true to their own culture. In Acts 15, the early church began to admit Gentiles without forcing them to become Jews first. The apostles determined not to lay obligations on Gentiles that they themselves had been unable to keep. This decision was greeted with joy and Gentiles continued to swell the ranks of the church (Acts 15:31; 16:4-5).

Peter Lundell, writing about presenting the gospel in Japan, argues that resistance is met as a result of *Nihonkyo*—the concept of Japanism—which even Japanese pastors believe inhibits church growth among their people. *Nihonkyo* is "a pervasive glue permeating every sector of life."[7] It is not simply national pride or ethnocentrism but a pervasive integration of core worldview assumptions.[8] It is interesting that *Nihonkyo* developed from the 1600s in marked contrast to the openness found originally in Japan when Catholic missions first began to work there. Like the Hakka of Taiwan, the Japanese did have a receptive period, after which their responsiveness was greatly reduced. Lundell argues that churches and leaders in Japan should abandon trying to accommodate *Nihonkyo* and focus on New Testament principles, which are at variance with that concept.

The reasons for both resistance and the failure to target a people are many. Repkin adds the following reasons to those already mentioned:

- a mentality that fails to see that the mandate is to share the gospel broadly, regardless of whether there is a harvest or not. When harvest is the bottom line, missionaries often stop proclaiming prematurely.
- a monocultural view of what churches should be like
- the lack of safety among people with limited access

- a fear of persecution. Believers are often badly treated, even more so than those who go to share the gospel.
- prejudice and ignorance toward Christianity on the part of nonbelievers
- expensive and weak support systems for those in dangerous or trying circumstances[9]

Samuel Zwemer (who had a lifetime of experience) argued that, although Muslims were winnable, the chief deterrent to their conversion was the Islamic law against apostasy. He wrote an entire book on the subject.[10]

More recently, a great deal has been made of Satanic opposition—and surely this view needs no refutation.[11] Scripture tells us that Satan blinds the eyes of people so that they will not believe the gospel of the Lord Jesus Christ (2 Cor. 4:4). The Evangelical Missiological Society has considered the matter of satanic opposition and territorial spirits at previous conferences (1995 and 1996), and more can, will, and should be said. What has not been discussed, however, is evidence that God Himself can sometimes be the author of resistance.

WHAT IS THE ROLE OF GOD IN RESISTANCE?

Both Scripture and experience demonstrate that the development of resistance, resulting from a multiplicity of dynamics, is a complex and interactive phenomenon. Everyone who is involved the evangelistic encounter is fallen, sinful, and limited. The evangelists, as humans and sinners saved by grace, will do their work imperfectly. Their good motives and their dependence on the Spirit of God, whom they possess as agents of God (Acts 1:8), will ebb and flow. Their inevitable failures are one of the dynamics involved in the development of resistance. But unbelievers often resist the gospel because of their own stubborn desire to live on their own terms—a characteristic of all people since Adam. And God, as sovereign Lord, may cause initial resistance for His own reasons or, in response to rejection, cause continuing and growing hardness.

The passages relating the interaction between Moses, God, and Pharaoh in Exodus 7–14 illustrate the dual sources of resistance—or hardening—in an unregenerate Gentile: "But I will harden Pharaoh's heart, and though I multiply my miraculous signs and wonders in Egypt, he will not listen to you" (7:3–4 NIV). The confrontational chapters show that Pharaoh hardened his own heart seven times (7:13, 22; 8:15, 19, 32; 9:7, 34), and seven times the Lord is said to have hardened Pharaoh's heart (9:12; 10:1, 20, 27; 11:10; 14:4, 17). All of the passages regarding hardening are preceded by the promise of God to harden Pharaoh's heart, yet the passages regarding Pharaoh's self-hardening tend to precede the passages that indicate God was doing the hardening. The purpose of all this is mentioned several times (9:16; 10:1; 11:9; 14:4, 7): to show the glory and power of Yahweh in a display of miraculous signs that identify Him as the true God.

The great displays in the Exodus passages of resistance being overcome are not lost on later Scripture writers; time and again these writers refer to them. But in other narratives as well, the sovereign power and discretion of the Lord in the process of resistance—equivalent to hardening—is demonstrated. Thus, it is shown that both Gentiles and the Lord's people can harden their own hearts, but they also can have their hearts hardened by God. In Romans 1:21, 26, and 28, for instance, Paul states that God reveals Himself to humankind through general revelation, and humankind deliberately resists Him, leading in turn to greater hardness initiated by God. In Romans 9–11, too, Paul expounds on God's sovereign discretion and power. He refers to the raising up of Pharaoh to display God's own power (9:17) and concludes, "Therefore God has mercy on whom he wants to have mercy, and he hardens whom he wants to harden" (9:18 NIV). Thus, the elect obtain the promises of God, but others are hardened (11:7): "God gave them a spirit of stupor, eyes so that they could not see and ears so that they could not hear" (11:8 NIV, citing Isa. 29:10). In this case, God is the agent of hardening, but His hardening is also a response to man's resistant spirit. [11]

David Brickner, speaking of the issue of Jewish resistance to the gospel, shows that although a temporal, general resistance of the Jewish people does exist, they are not all resistant, and many Jews do respond to the gospel. This view squares with Paul's assessment that they experience a hardening in part "until the full number of the Gentiles has come in" (Rom. 11:25 NIV), after which all Israel will be saved.

Few people have, in such precise fashion, expounded the biblical teaching on the matter of the sovereignty of God in missions as has missionary, missiologist, and theologian J. Herbert Kane. In his chapter "The Sovereignty of God" (subtitled "God's Dealing with the Sinner"), he summarizes:

1. **The fate of the sinner is decided by a judicial act of God**. However difficult it may be for us to explain, the fact remains that God in His sovereignty opens the eyes of some (Matt. 13:14–17) and closes

the eyes of others (Rom. 11:8). The Scriptures tell us that God hard-ened Pharaoh's heart (Exod. 7:3) and opened Lydia's heart (Acts 16:4). The early church grew in strength and size, not because people decided to join the church, but because they were added to the church by an act of God (Acts 2:47). The only ones who believed were those who were "ordained to eternal life" (Acts 13:48 KJV).

2. Only those who are drawn by the Father will ever come to Christ. The teaching of Christ is clear on this point. He said, "No one can come to me unless the Father who sent me draws him" (John 6:44 NIV). Left to himself, the ungodly sinner will never for-sake his wicked way and seek after God (Rom. 3:10–18). There-fore God must take the initiative. Jesus Christ came into the world to seek and to save that which is lost (Luke 19:10). The Holy Spirit came to convince the world of sin, righteousness, and judgment (John 16:8). Without the seeking Shepherd the sheep would never be found. Without the convicting Spirit the sinner would never be saved.

3. The very faith by which a person believes is itself the gift of God. Paul is emphatic on this point. "For by grace you have been saved through faith, and this is not your own doing, it is the gift of God" (Eph. 2:8 NRSV).

We must never forget that it is God who saves. It is God who brings men and women under the sound of the gospel, and it is God who brings them to faith in Christ. . . . If we forget that only God can give faith, we shall start to think that the making of converts de-pends, in the last analysis, not on God but on us. [12]

If God of His own free will does not give this faith, man cannot by the independent exercise of His own intellect "believe" in Christ. He can give intellectual assent to certain historic facts concerning Christ, but saving faith is something else. The insight that enabled Peter to confess Jesus as the Son of God came as a revelation from God (Matt. 16:17). Paul informs us that no man can call Jesus "Lord" except by the Holy Spirit (1 Cor. 12:3).

4. Only persons united to Christ by the Holy Spirit remain steadfast in the faith; the others fall away. The way of God is through Jesus Christ (John 14:6). The way to Christ is through the Holy Spirit (John 16:13–14). He and He alone unites the soul to Christ (1 Cor. 12:13). Not all of Christ's disciples remained with Him to the end. In mid-career many of them left Him and went their way when they were introduced to "hard sayings" (John 6:60, 66). Only those whose faith was God-given (Matt. 16:17) and therefore genuine (John 6:69) remained with Him to the end (John 17:12).

The apostles were disturbed when the Pharisees took offense at the teachings of Christ. They feared that the "hard sayings" would alienate them, and so they expressed their fears to the Master. Jesus had no such fears. He replied, "Every plant which My heavenly Father has not planted will be uprooted" (Matt. 15:13 NKJV). Jesus had implicit faith in the sovereignty of God and refused to panic when the crowds began to dwindle. He believed that every soul "given" to Him by the Father would ultimately come to Him. None would be cast out (John 6:37), none would be uprooted (Matt. 15:13). If they took offense and went away, that was proof that they had never been "given" or "planted" by the Father. If their roots were not in God, sooner or later they were sure to be plucked up.[13]

We must be careful in our own strategic planning to recognize the hand of God in the matter of resistance. In some peoples, we might see what we consider resistance but what, in fact, is the result of their rejection of previously known truth. Always, however, a portion of those peoples are prepared by God to respond. It is to them, by addressing the whole culture broadly, that we are to announce the gospel.

Consider the confidence of earlier evangelists to Muslims. They felt certain about the possibility of response among that often-resistant people. Zwemer cites W. H. T. Gairdner, who says,

Those who care for Christ's Kingdom of God now know for certain that the evangelization of Moslems is possible . . . the talk (about the impossibility of Moslem conversion to Christianity) is utterly baseless and has been confuted by contrary fact in almost all countries again and again.[14]

When God wants Muslims to respond—or any other groups for that matter—they will!

THE WAX

The waxing and waning of resistance is a mystery. It would be an error to search solely for human, environmental, Satanic, or demonic causes while neglecting the sovereign purpose, plan, and timing of God. All matters are brought back, time and again, to the role of God in ordering history for His greater glory—to the glory of the Lord of the harvest, who both sends out the workers and delays or develops the harvest according to His wisdom. With regard to agricultural practices in the ancient Near East, Oded Borowski observed that farmers were able to harvest all of their crops—barley, wheat, grapes, and olives—only because those commodities ripened at different times.[15] In other words, distinct times of ripening make a comprehensive harvest possible; otherwise, the individual farmers would have been overwhelmed. That God is called "the Lord of the harvest" (Luke 10:2 NIV) means that He coordinates times of responsiveness. Note how Jesus indicated in Mark 4:26-29 that harvests ripen gradually, "first the stalk, then the head, then the full kernel in the head" (v. 28 NIV), all without any outside cause. When the crop is ripe, the farmer harvests it. So, although evangelists and missionaries must preach sow seeds—the actual harvest is not in their hands. "The Spirit gives life; the flesh counts for nothing" (John 6:63 NIV). The worker, then, is nothing more than the channel of the Holy Spirit's power (Acts 1:8)—and that power, let us remember, is held in earthen vessels that the glory may be of the Lord (2 Cor. 4:7).

THE OFFER

In *A River Runs Through It,* the clergyman asks of loved ones, "Don't we have what they need?" Yes, we do have what our loved ones—and the world—need. And we must offer it to them. But we cannot make them take it. That lies in God's power, timing, and grace.

CHAPTER 6

THE DESTINY OF THE UNEVANGELIZED

GEORGE HILGEMAN

IF GOD WANTS EVERYONE TO BE SAVED, why the need for the Great Commission? If God is "*not wanting anyone to perish,* but *everyone* to come to repentance" (2 Peter 3:9 NIV), why did Jesus command His disciples to, "Go into all the world and preach the good news to all creation" (Mark 16:15)?[1]

The question is not as contradictory as it sounds. Consider: Once the gospel is shared with unbelievers, those individuals become responsible either for receiving it or rejecting it. If unbelievers receive the Lord Jesus, they are saved. If they reject Him, they are lost and will suffer eternal damnation (unless, of course, individuals place their trust in Christ before they die). Would it not, then, have been better—*if one could be saved by ignorance*—for our Lord to have commanded His disciples, "Now let's keep this a secret. Don't tell a soul, and then everyone will be saved."

But He didn't say that. He said, "Go into all the world and preach the good news *to all creation*" (Mark 16:15). He reiterated it in Acts 1:8: "But you will receive power when the Holy Spirit comes on you; and you will be *my witnesses* in Jerusalem, and in all Judea and Samaria, and *to the ends of the earth*" (lit. "to the last part of the earth"). Why *everyone?* Because Jesus died for everyone, and all persons have a right to know that Christ died for them. If all but one person in all the earth heard the gospel, Jesus would not be content. If the gospel were preached to every part of the world but one, He would not be satisfied.

Considering that we are called to evangelize the world, it is natural that we should ask, "What is the destiny of the unevangelized or the unsaved?" Scripture indicates that it is a place called hell. But is hell a real place?

Just before Moses died, God instructed him to write a song for Israel that called to mind God's faithfulness: "He is the Rock, his works are perfect, and all his ways are just. A faithful God *who does no wrong, upright and just is he*" (Deut. 32:4). But God also reminds Israel of their sin: "You deserted the Rock, who fathered you; *you forgot the God* who gave you birth. . . . For a *fire* has been kindled by my wrath, *one that burns to the realm of death below*" (vv. 18 and 22).

The latter verse refers to God's judgment. The word *death* in verse 22 is *sheol*, which refers to either the grave or the place of departed spirits—both the saved and the lost—and is synonymous with the Greek word *hades* in the New Testament. *Sheol* is divided into two parts—the place of torment and the blessed side (paradise). The patriarch Abraham lived, died, and went to *sheol* in the Old Testament, but in Luke 16:23 we read, "In hell *[hades]*, where he [the rich man] was in torment, he looked up and saw *Abraham* [in paradise] far away, with Lazarus by his side." From Luke 16:19–31, then, we understand that in the days before Christ the destiny of the unsaved who died was the tormented side of *sheol*, or *hades*—whereas paradise was for the saved. Since the resurrection and ascension of Christ, however, the saved go directly to be with Christ (2 Cor. 5:8; Phil. 1:23), but the lost continue to go to the place of torment in *hades* (Rev. 20:13–14).

At the end of Old Testament times, instructions similar to those given to Moses in the above passage from Deuteronomy are given by God to the prophet Habakkuk: "Write down the revelation and make it plain on tablets. . . . The revelation awaits an *appointed time; it speaks of the end.* . . . Though it linger, wait for it; *it will certainly come and will not delay*" (Hab. 2:2, 3). The revelation first includes salvation, "The righteous will live by his faith" (v. 4). But the prophet warns the sinner, "He is as greedy as the grave *(sheol)* and like death is never satisfied" (v. 5). God's love is placed first, offering salvation: "He is . . . not wanting anyone to perish" (2 Peter 3:9). But His holiness follows in judgment for those who reject His provision. As salvation is eternal, so is the judgment. There is no annihilation, no purgatory and, although there will be degrees of punishment, no lessening of the suffering.

Luke 10:14 states, "It will be more bearable for Tyre and Sidon at the judgment than for you." The unbeliever who has died is in *hades*, the tormented side. *Hades* is similar to a prison where the convicted person awaits his final judgment, which will take place at the Great White Throne. There the unbelievers will be condemned eternally to the lake of fire, but to what degree the unbeliever will suffer in hell will depend on God's decision as to what that person was and what he or she did while alive on earth (Rev. 20:13).

How can a loving God send anyone to hell? To understand the answer, we must understand two of God's attributes—His holiness and His love. Tracing these attributes through Scripture leads to the "appointed time" mentioned in the Habakkuk passage above, when the inhabitants (unsaved only) of *hades* will be judged and cast into the lake of fire for eternity (v. 14).

GOD'S HOLINESS AND LOVE

The Garden of Eden

At the time of creation, God put the finishing touches on His handiwork by making humankind in His own image: "God saw all that he had made, and it was *very good*" (Gen. 1:31). No imperfection existed. But knowing of the danger of sin, God warned Adam and Eve of the consequences.

Then the serpent, Satan, entered the scene. He knew that he could not oppose God directly because he had already been cast out of heaven with his angels. Nor did he go straight to Adam. He would approach Eve, Adam's beloved wife. He recognized that what Adam might not do if approached directly he might do for his helpmate. "And Adam was not the one deceived; it was the woman who was deceived" (1 Tim. 2:14). Eve ate of the fruit of the knowledge of good and evil and then gave it to Adam. Thus, sin entered the human race. Adam and Eve brought forth offspring after *their* image, which now included their fallen nature. Every child born into the world since then inherits that same sinful nature (Gen. 5:3; Ps. 51:5; Rom. 5:12).

It looked as though Satan had won the battle. God must reject humankind just as He had rejected Lucifer—who became Satan—and his angels because of their sin. But Satan was in for a great surprise. When Lucifer (and his angels) sinned, God had judged them according to His holiness; a holy God must condemn sin and the sinner. God had to judge the sin of Adam and Eve as well.

But God is not only a God of holiness, He is also a God of love. What a shock it must have been for Satan to see God providing a sacrifice for sinful humankind. God had never done that for sinful angels! Total condemnation fell on Satan and his host because God is absolutely holy. It must be concluded, then, that God would have been completely holy and just to condemn eternally every human being without offering salvation.

But God demonstrated that He is simultaneously a holy God and a God of love. *His love, however, cannot contradict His holiness.* God promised Adam, "You must not eat from the tree of the knowledge of good and evil, for *when you eat of it you will surely die*" (Gen. 2:17). Adam did indeed die, but in the person of his substitute, Jesus Christ. In like manner, the apostle Paul would receive the same provision: "I have been crucified with Christ and I no longer live, but Christ lives in me" (Gal. 2:20). According to tradition, he was beheaded, but because of his faith in the Lord Jesus, God imputed Christ's death to Paul's account, and will do the same to the accounts of each of us who believe.

Still, in the days of Adam and Eve, God provided a temporary means of sacrifice that would meet the need of sinners. But He also promised that one day he would meet their need perfectly and completely: "And I will put enmity between you [Satan] and the woman, and between your offspring and hers; he will crush your head [mortal wound], and you will strike his heel" [only a temporary injury] (Gen. 3:15).

This verse referred to the Lord Jesus, God's Son, who would have to die for sinners because "the wages of sin is death" (Rom. 6:23). The most amazing thing about this prophecy is that it was made when there was *only one sin,* and that perhaps the least possible sin—at least in human eyes—that could be committed. Humanity had not yet sunk to the depths of degradation. The sin was not that of theft, as the tree actually belonged to Adam and Eve; nor was it adultery—there was only one man and one woman made for each other; nor murder; nor anything that humans now recognize as a depraved act. No, although practically every sin is against another person, Adam and Eve sinned with the hope that it would be to their advantage, to "be like God, knowing good and evil" (Gen. 3:5). Their sin was simply the sin of disobedience, doing what God had told them not to do.

In God's holiness, there is no such thing as a "mortal" or a "venial sin" (Roman Catholic theological terms). As small as this one sin might appear in our eyes, it was such a heinous offense before God that the only solution He—the omniscient God—could devise was the price of infinite love, that being the crucifixion of His only Son. The entrance of sin, however, opened the floodgates of iniquity in its grossest forms. May we see sin as God perceives it.

Cain and Abel

The writer of Hebrews states, "*By faith* Abel offered God a better sacrifice than Cain did" (Heb. 11:4); Abel brought his sacrifice by faith. Faith, during the time of Genesis, could come only by believing the spoken word of God. Cain, however, decided that he liked his own method of worship better than he liked God's. His sacrifice was rejected, and this set in motion Cain's murder of his brother. It is important to remember throughout this study that the God of the Old Testament is the same God whom we worship today.

Noah and His Family

The book of Genesis demonstrates that as sin increased, so did ignorance concerning God and His requirements. People, it seems, purposely put God out of their minds. God's holiness demanded the most severe punishment that we can imagine—the destruction by flood of the entire populated world. More than that, *hades* awaited those who perished. In love, God spared eight souls—Noah and his family. According to Hebrews 11:7, "By faith Noah, when warned about *things not yet seen,* in holy fear built an ark to save his family." The ark, then, was the only way of salvation. And as for Noah, he was saved not because he *built* the ark but because he was *in the ark*, a representation analogous of our salvation through our position *in Christ:* "For we were *all* baptized by one Spirit *into one body*—whether Jews or Greeks, slave or free—and we were *all* given the one Spirit to drink" (1 Cor. 12:13). "Now you are the body of Christ" (v. 27).

Notice in the preceding passage from 1 Corinthians the word *all.* There are no exceptions; *all* speaks only of believers. Unbelievers were not included, and that principle applied, too, in Noah's time. Noah though, in his role as preacher, had no radio, TV, or press to carry the message that destruction of unbelievers would come through a flood. Moreover, he was confined to the location of the ark's construction. Surely, though, the news spread rapidly by word of mouth concerning the strange building of such a large boat so far from the sea. Too, people had apparently never seen rain because "the Lord God had not sent rain on the earth . . . but streams came up from the earth and watered the whole surface of the ground" (Gen. 2:5–6). Surely if God could have overlooked the ignorance of those people, He would have done so.

Still, God demonstrated love. According to 2 Peter 2:5, Noah was a "preacher of righteousness." And over a period of at least one hundred twenty years, while building the ark, Noah warned the people of God's impending judgment, during which time God's patience was severely tried with that corrupt generation.

While Noah worked and shared God's warning of the approaching judgment, the people laughed and mocked him and his sons. When all of the animals had entered, then Noah, his wife, and his sons and their wives entered. God waited seven more days (Gen. 7:10), then "*the Lord* shut him in" (v. 16).

As the rain descended and the waters rose, I'm sure that people pounded on the door shouting, "Noah, we believe you. Let us in." But Noah was unable to open the door because God had shut it. Humankind had gone too far. Can we claim that the Almighty was unjustly punishing those who perished? They had at least one hundred and twenty years plus one week to repent. And those who perished not only suffered physical death but also continue in torment in *hades* even today. Although only unbelievers will be thrust into hell, none of the people there are unbelievers now. Within minutes, all of them became believers, but it was too late.

The judgment the Flood—fell equally upon the ark and the believers in it as it fell upon unbelievers. The unbelievers perished, however, while Noah and his family did not because they were *in the ark*. Believers are saved today because, by the baptism of the Holy Spirit, we have been placed in Christ, upon whom our judgment fell at Calvary: "*We all, like sheep, have gone astray, each* of us has turned to his own way; and the Lord has laid *on him,* the iniquity of *us all*" (Isa. 53:6). Jesus is our ark of safety.

Even after the Flood, however, God's love was not finished. As the earth became repopulated, all human beings (the eight who came out of the ark) knew God personally and believed His Word. Knowing God and knowing that God meant what He said—whether He spoke of blessing or of judgment—would humankind change in regard to their rebellion? God promised, "Never again will all life be cut off by the waters of a flood; never again will there be a flood to destroy the earth" (Gen. 9:11). This statement did not mean, though, that He would pass over sin as being of no consequence.

Tower of Babel

In the post-Flood period, sin again increased, with people joining together to build a tower "that reaches to the heavens" (Gen. 11:4). Some have suggested that the building of the tower demonstrated a lack of faith in God's promise to never again destroy the earth with a flood. The tower served as high ground to escape floodwaters.

The more likely explanation, however, is that the sin committed was that of immense pride. Following the deluge, God told Noah and his sons, "Be fruitful and multiply, and fill the earth" (Gen. 9:1b). In spite of this direct command to "fill the earth," verses 1-4 emphasize the idea of staying together. Verse 4 also states that they wanted to make a name for themselves. Pride led to their downfall. What they would not do in humble obedience, God did for them in judgment. He confused their language, scattered them throughout the whole earth, and their tower became an unfinished monstrosity.

Even today we experience the effects of this judgment on them. One of the greatest trials for a missionary is learning different languages.

Abraham

How would God now make known His will for man? He chose one man—Abraham—and promised him, "I will make you into a great nation and I will bless you; . . . and all peoples on earth will be blessed through you" (Gen. 12:2-3).

To fulfill His plan, He gave to Abraham and Sarah in their advanced age a son, Isaac. After the lad had grown, the Lord commanded Abraham, "Take your son, *your only son,* Isaac, whom you love, and go to the region of Moriah. Sacrifice him there as a burnt offering . . ." (22:2). Abraham's faith in God was great concerning His earlier promise, "It is through Isaac that your offspring will be reckoned." Abraham reasoned that God could raise the dead, and figuratively speaking, he did receive Isaac back from death (Heb. 11:18-19). Note that later, God the Father "*did not spare his own Son,* but gave him up for us all" (Rom. 8:32). The Scripture might well read, "He did not spare His own self." What love!

In fulfillment of His promise, God did make a new nation, a privileged nation, who among polytheistic nations bore testimony to the one God (Deut. 6:4) and to whom He sent prophets to speak against sin and to encourage faithfulness. The prophets also foretold that the coming Messiah would rule over the whole earth, bringing in a reign of righteousness. The fulfillment of God's promise to Abraham was unconditional and depended on God's faithfulness inasmuch as a promise is valid as long as the one who made the promise lives. Because Yahweh is eternal, His holiness demands an absolute fulfillment in spite of man's obedience or disobedience. What was Abraham's response? "Abram believed the Lord, and [God] credited it to him as righteousness" (Gen. 15:6).

God's covenant was repeated to Isaac and then to his son Jacob, despite Jacob being a deceiver who could hardly be called a believer until he returned to the land of Canaan. Even after God spoke to Jacob concerning the fulfillment of His covenant with Jacob's grandfather Abraham, even then Jacob's promise was only "*If* God will be with me and will watch over me on this journey I am taking and will give me food to eat and clothes to wear so that I return safely to my father's house, *then the Lord will be my God*" (Gen. 28:20–21).

The Lord's graciousness finally brought Jacob to fulfill the vow he had made to God. Jacob's sons became heads of the twelve tribes of Israel (the name God gave to Jacob, hence becoming the name of God's chosen people). God's love was evident, too, in His later allowing Jacob to live in Egypt with his son Joseph. The nation Israel became very comfortable under the kindness of Pharaoh; more than four centuries passed, and God's earthly people had no apparent desire to return to the land that God had promised to them. Thus, it was necessary to make them willing to go. Another Pharaoh came to the throne, and he feared this growing nation of Israel. The result was oppressive slavery for Israel until they cried out to the Lord for deliverance.

Moses

Egypt offended God's holiness by worshiping other gods and by repeatedly disobeying God's instruction to free Israel. The Lord then raised up a deliverer in the person of Moses, and through God's power, Moses delivered ten plagues upon Egypt and its people until Pharaoh himself had a change of heart (but did not repent toward the true God). "The ten plagues were designed as visitations on the Egyptians and their gods at the same time. . . . Thus the plague of darkness (10:21–23) was directed against the sun god *Ra,* the most prominent of the Egyptian deities."[2]

In spite of their liberation from slavery, however, Israel continually offended God's holiness by grumbling and complaining until they reached the border of Canaan. There, ten of the twelve spies sent to assess the land claimed that the women and the little ones would die at the hands of the Canaanites. God's judgment eventually fell upon all ten spies. Because of Israel's disobedience to enter the Promised Land, God led them for forty years through the desert. Yet, at the end of the forty years the Lord, in love, was merciful. Although the ten spies and the men of Israel's army (the strongest of the people) had all died, Joshua and Caleb—the two spies who remained obedient to God—and the children whom the other spies had claimed would die, entered the Promised Land under Joshua.

Although Moses was God's beloved and faithful prophet and leader of the people, he and Aaron were disobedient at the waters of Meribah. As a result, God's judgment did not permit Moses to reach the Promised Land:

"But the Lord said to Moses and Aaron, 'Because you did not trust in me enough to *honor me as holy* in the sight of the Israelites, you will not bring this community into the land I give them" (Num. 20:12). Moses, then, allowed only to view the Promised Land from the top of the mountain, could testify as to the importance of God's holiness.

Perhaps Moses' greatest accomplishment was giving God's Law to the people in written form. The Ten Commandments addressed humankind's rebellion and were condensed into ten areas of sin relating to both God and man. In recent years, a billboard along the highway depicts messages as if from God: "What part of 'Thou shalt not' don't you understand?"

In the days of Moses, God did not leave the revelation of His Laws to chance. Specific grievances were spelled out in Exodus through Deuteronomy— 614 prohibitions in all. Never again was man able to plead ignorance for not knowing God's will regarding sin. But humankind would indeed continue to sin. In fact, Moses recorded his prophecy concerning the Israelite's rebellion: "For I know that after my death you are sure to become utterly corrupt and to turn from the way I have commanded you. In days to come, disaster will fall upon you because you will do evil in the sight of the Lord and provoke him to anger by what your hands have made" (Deut. 31:29-30).

God offered Israel a choice—blessing for obedience (Deut. 28:1-14) or judgment (vv. 15-48) for disobedience. Verse 49 foretold that Israel, because of disobedience, would endure a siege of Jerusalem, which would bring a famine so great that the Israelites would actually eat their own children (vv. 53, 56-57), then Israel would be taken captive by another nation (Babylon under Nebuchadnezzar). Second Kings 6:28-29 records the fulfillment of this prophecy.

Yet when Israel did return to the Lord, He blessed them and gave them victory. As He was true to His Word in doing them good, He was just as faithful in fulfilling His judgments. And this pattern of disobedience, judgment, repentance, and restoration reappears throughout the rest of the Old Testament. Yet God sought to encourage Israel, looking far into the future when He will regather them from all of the nations to which they have been scattered and will bless them. Deuteronomy 30:1-5 promises, "When all these blessings and curses I have set before you come upon you and you take them to heart wherever the Lord your God disperses you among the nations, and when you and your children return to the Lord your God and obey him with all your heart and with all your soul according to everything I command you today, *then* the Lord your God will restore your fortunes and have compassion on you and gather you again *from all the nations where he scattered you. . . .* He will make you more prosperous and numerous than your fathers."

In spite of Israel's stubborn rebellion, which culminated in the crucifixion of their Messiah, God's love for them never changed. According to His holiness, He punished them. And they still continue to suffer in unspeakable ways. God will continue to plead with them in order to bring them back to Him. Their return will take place even though thousands of years will have passed since the event was first foretold. When Christ returns the second time to this earth in power and glory, this prophecy will come to pass. God must be true to His Word to Abraham, Isaac, and Jacob. "If we are faithless, he will remain faithful, for he cannot disown himself" (2 Tim. 2:13). Even if God loves Israel, Israelites who have died and will die in unbelief will suffer eternally. Neither His holiness nor His love ever changes.

In Old Testament times, God promised to honor those who by faith offered His prescribed sacrifices even when they did not understand their real significance. God said it; they believed it. But when people offered such sacrifices without faith, they gained no benefit. Isaiah writes, "Hear the word of the Lord, you rulers of Sodom; listen to the law of our God, you people of Gomorrah! 'The multitude of your sacrifices—what are they to me?' says the Lord. 'I have more than enough of burnt offerings, of rams and the fat of fattened animals; I have no pleasure in the blood of bulls and lambs and goats. When you come to appear before me, who has asked this of you, this trampling of my courts? Stop bringing meaningless offerings. Your New Moons, Sabbaths and convocations—I cannot bear your evil assemblies. Your New Moon festivals and your appointed feasts my soul hates. They have become a burden to me; I am weary of bearing them" (Isa. 1:10-14).

If this was true in Old Testament times, what is God's attitude today toward those who attend church, go through religious acts, use the name of the Lord, preach from the pulpit using the Bible as their text, seek to gain favor with God by good works, and go through other motions of religion? Trusting in "spiritual exercises" is all in vain when the heart is wrong, when individuals have not placed their trust for salvation in the death and resurrection of Christ. God cannot accept such a sham.

THE NEW TESTAMENT

After looking at the Old Testament and the severity of God, can it be hoped that the God of the New Testament will be more loving and merciful and not so unsparing?

The angel Gabriel came to the Virgin Mary with the announcement, "You will be with child and give birth to a son, and you are to give him the name Jesus. He will be great and will be called the Son of the Most High. The Lord God will give him the throne of his father David, and *he will reign over the house of Jacob forever; his kingdom will never end"* (Luke 1:31-33).

Joseph, Mary's espoused husband, hesitated to accept this report from Mary. A virgin birth had never before occurred. Joseph loved Mary, and a legal marriage contract had already been publicly made (Matt. 1:18). We can only imagine the tremendous conflict in his heart: "Because Joseph her husband was a righteous man and did not want to expose her to public disgrace, he had in mind to divorce her quietly" (v. 19).

What assurance did Joseph receive that Mary's child was truly the result of a miracle? "An angel of the Lord appeared to him in a dream and said, 'Joseph, son of David, do not be afraid to take Mary home as your wife, because what is conceived in her is from the Holy Spirit. She will give birth to a son, and you are to give him the name Jesus, because *he will save his people from their sins'"* (vv. 20-21). At last, after thousands of years, the first prophecy made in Genesis 3:15 was being fulfilled. How faithful is our God.

The apostle Paul later stated, "But God demonstrates his own love for *us* in this: While we were still sinners, Christ died for *us"* (Rom. 5:8). At the same time, His righteous judgment because of sin still continues: "But because of your stubbornness and your unrepentant heart, you are storing up wrath against yourself for the day of God's wrath, when his *righteous judgment* will be revealed. God will give to each person *according to what he has done"* (2:5-6). God is just as loving and holy now as He was in the past. He is eternally the same.

JESUS CHRIST

If anyone can speak definitively about salvation, it is Jesus Christ. And it is notable that in His ministry the Lord Jesus speaks more concerning eternal punishment than of heaven. Because most people, no doubt, want to go to heaven, they must be warned of the coming judgment if they refuse God's provision of salvation. Luke 16:19-31 offers perhaps the clearest example of the consequences of rejecting God in the story of a real man named Lazarus (parables do not name characters).

The time came when the beggar died and the angels carried him to Abraham's side. The rich man also died and was buried. In hell [*hades,*

the place of departed spirits with two compartments—one for the
saved, and the other for the lost], where he was in torment, he looked
up and saw Abraham far away, with Lazarus by his side. So he called
to him, "Father Abraham, have pity on me and send Lazarus to dip
the tip of his finger in water and cool my tongue, because *I am in
agony in this fire.*" But Abraham replied, "Son, *remember* [one of
the most terrible things about hell is memory]. . . . And besides all
this, between us and you a great chasm has been fixed, so that those
who want to go from here to you cannot, nor can anyone cross over
from there to us."

Notice that the rich man does not accuse God of being unjust, and Christ
Himself many times had compassion on those who were suffering. But no
mercy is shown here.

Then the rich man becomes "missionary minded" (far more so than many
Christians). "Then I beg you, father, send Lazarus to my father's house, for
I have five brothers. *Let him warn them,* so that they will not also come to
this place of torment" (16:27–28). Abraham further reminds Lazarus of the
Jews' privilege of having God's Word through Moses and the Prophets. "'No,
father Abraham' he said, 'but if someone from the dead goes to them, they
will repent.' [Abraham] said to him, 'If they do not listen to Moses and the
Prophets, they will not be convinced even if someone rises from the dead'"
(16:30–31).

When the Son of God Himself rose from the dead, the same religious
leaders who knew the prophesies about Messiah from Scripture yet nailed
Him to the cross bribed the soldiers to lie and say that Christ's disciples had
stolen the body. These religious leaders were responsible to God's Word regardless of whether they received it. Jesus Himself said, "There is a judge
for the one who rejects me and does not accept my words; that very word
which I spoke will condemn him *at the last day*" (John 12:48).

But in the days of Christ why was Abraham still in *hades,* albeit on the
comforted side? Approximately two thousand years had passed, and the patriarch still had *not* reached heaven. The clue is found in Hebrews 10:3–4,
wherein is a reminder of the infinite holiness of God: "But those [animal]
sacrifices are an annual reminder of sins, because it is *impossible for the blood
of bulls and goats to take away sins."* Animal sacrifices offered in obedience to
God's command were like a promissory note that God pledged to pay in the
future. On the basis of the promissory note He could forgive sins on the part

of the believer. "Blessed are they whose transgressions are forgiven, whose sins are *covered*," [but not taken away] (Rom. 4:7). When the time came and Jesus, the Lamb of God, shed His blood, the promissory note was paid in full. Until that time, those who died in faith were not permitted to enter God's holy presence in heaven because their sin was only "covered."

According to Ephesians 4:8, "When [Christ] ascended on high, he led captives in his train." That is, Christ took Abraham and all others in faith to the Father's presence. Until then, they had been captives, not of Satan but of their own sin, which still had to be taken away. When Christ paid the price, they at last were fit to enter God's holy presence. Since that time, when a believer dies, he or she goes immediately to be with the Lord: "As long as we are at home in the body we are away from the Lord. . . . We are confident, I say, and would prefer to be away from the body and at home with the Lord" (2 Cor. 5:6–8).

Let this passage remind those who believe that the Lord in His mercy will accept those who have never heard the Good News or for any other reason have not accepted the sacrifice of Christ as the only way to heaven—His infinite holiness has no other remedy for sin.

THE APOSTOLIC AGE

A Transition in God's Program

The Acts of the Apostles is a book of transition, especially in typology, because the type is replaced by the reality. Repeated blood sacrifices are superseded by the once-for-all death of the Lamb of God. In memory of the day of Christ's resurrection on the first day of the week, the Sabbath loses its significance in favor of the Lord's Day. The Aaronic priesthood gives way to the priesthood of our Great High Priest, the Lord Jesus. Instead of the temple in Jerusalem, the body of Christ made up of believers since Pentecost becomes the habitation of God (Eph. 2:19–22). Believers are not only the building blocks, "living stones," but also the priests who are to offer "spiritual sacrifices" (1 Peter 2:4–10).

Other changes take place; Israel became God's earthly people, but the church is His heavenly people, the "citizens" of heaven (Phil. 3:20). That the church now comprises the kingdom of heaven indicates the changes that took place through the redemptive work of Christ when He ascended. Isaiah foretold concerning Israel, "I, the Lord, have called you in righteousness; I will take hold of your hand. I will keep you and will make you to be a covenant for the people *and a light for the Gentiles,* to open eyes that are blind, to free captives from prison and to release from the dungeon those who sit in darkness" (42:6–7). Israel, however, was not concerned with reaching out to the Gentiles. Even Jonah sought to escape his responsibility to preach to the dwellers of Nineveh. But God loved the Gentiles as He loved Abraham's descendants. In God's righteousness, then, a change had taken place: "I do not want you to be ignorant of this mystery, brothers, so that you may not be conceited: Israel has experienced a hardening *in part until the full number of the Gentiles has come in*" (Rom. 11:25).

The tables are turned. God now reaches out especially to the Gentiles in these days, although the door is still opened to the small number of Israelites who are saved. God's love is still for all who will put their trust in His Son. As the tormented side of *hades* was the portion of neglected Gentiles who in ages past never heard of God's provision, so it is today when Israelites or Gentiles reject Him.

The Gospel and the Spirit

Perhaps the most distinguishing change wrought by the death and resurrection of Christ was the work of the Holy Spirit. On that last night with His disciples before His betrayal, Jesus promised, "I will ask the Father, and he will give you another Counselor *to be with you forever*—the Spirit of Truth. The world cannot accept [receive] him, because it neither sees him nor knows him. But you know him, for he lives with you and will be *in you*" (John 14:16–17). The fulfillment of Jesus' promise came on the Day of Pentecost.

Faith now depends on two actual events. Paul explains in 1 Corinthians 15:1–4, "Now, brothers, I want to remind you of the gospel I preached to you, which you received and on which you have taken your stand. *By this gospel you are saved,* if you hold firmly to the word I preached to you. Otherwise, you have believed in vain. For what I received I passed on to you as of first importance: that *Christ died for our sins according to the Scriptures,* that he was buried [proof of his death], that *he was raised on the third day according to the Scriptures,* and that he *appeared to Peter* and then *to the twelve.* After that, he appeared to *more than five hundred* of the brothers at the same time, most of *whom are still living. . . .*" [proof of His resurrection]. Both Christ's death and His resurrection are indispensable for salvation—His death, the price of our sin (Rom. 6:23) and the Resurrection, which provides eternal life. "And this is the testimony; God has given us eternal life, and *this life is in his Son.* He who has the Son *has life:* he who does not have the Son of God *does not have life*" (1 John 5:11–12). It's as simple as that. Therefore, Jesus proclaimed, "I am *the way* and *the truth* and *the life. No one* comes to the Father *except through me*" (John 14:6).

Such blessings occurred in Jerusalem in the early days as the church grew that the Christians lost sight of the Great Commission (Matt. 28:18–20). God had to put them back on track.

"At Caesarea there was a man named Cornelius, a centurion in what was known as the Italian Regiment [therefore, he was a Gentile]. He and all his family were *devout* and *God-fearing;* he *gave generously to those in need* and *prayed to God regularly*" (Acts 10:1–2). Many people believe that with such a recommendation by God, Cornelius and his family were already saved.

An angel came to Cornelius and said, "Your prayers and gifts to the poor have come up as a memorial offering before God. Now send men to Joppa to bring back a man named Simon who is called Peter" (vv. 4–5).

Joppa was some distance from Caesarea, and there Peter waited for dinner but was praying when he fell into a trance and saw a large sheet being let down from heaven by its four corners. "It contained *all kinds* of four-footed animals, as well as reptiles of the earth and birds of the air. Then a voice told him, 'Get up, Peter. Kill and eat.' 'Surely not, Lord!' Peter replied. 'I have never eaten anything impure or unclean.' The voice spoke to him a second time, 'Do not call anything impure that God has made clean.' This happened three times and . . . [left Peter] wondering about the meaning of the vision" (Acts 10:12–27). A change of the law as found in Leviticus 11 had occurred. The Holy Spirit then told Peter to go with the men sent by the Gentile Cornelius.

Cornelius recounted to Peter what the angel had told him. Peter then explained the two essential facts of the gospel—that the Lord Jesus had been slain and that God had raised Him on the third day. Only one thing was lacking in order to receive eternal life: "All the prophets testify about him that *everyone who believes in him receives forgiveness of sins through his name*" (v. 43). This was what Cornelius and his house had been waiting to hear, and immediately the Holy Spirit confirmed their salvation, just as He had to the Jews on the Day of Pentecost.

But the story does not end there. Some time had elapsed since Pentecost, but the Jews still harbored a contentious attitude toward the Gentiles. "The *apostles* and the brothers throughout Judea heard that the *Gentiles* also had received the word of God" (11:1), and they were not happy. "So when Peter went up to Jerusalem, the *circumcised believers criticized* him and said, 'You went into the house of *uncircumcised men* and ate with them'" (v. 2).

Peter then explained how Cornelius told him "how he had seen an angel appear in his house and say, 'Send to Joppa for Simon who is called Peter. He will bring you a message through which you and all your household *will be saved*" (vv. 13–14). Cornelius—even with all of his godly characteristics and even though an angel appeared to him—was not already saved. No, he had to hear the gospel and, as the result, believe in the Lord Jesus.

Peter added, "As I began to speak, the *Holy Spirit came on them* as he had come on us *at the beginning*" (v. 15). This action of the Holy Spirit was not the norm when anyone was saved. In supporting his stand for accepting Gentiles into the church, Peter referred to *"the beginning,"* that is, Pentecost, arguing that if the Holy Spirit Himself accepted Cornelius, then so too should the Jews. The Pentecostal experience was used by the Holy Spirit to prove that in the church there was now no difference between Israel and the Gentiles: "For he [Christ] himself is our peace, who has made the two one and has destroyed the barrier, the dividing wall of hostility, by abolishing in his flesh the law with its commandments and regulations" (Eph. 2:14–15).

Salvific Knowledge Only Through Specific (Special) Revelation

That Cornelius could be a good and moral man yet still not be saved raises the matter of general and specific revelation. Paul writes in Romans 1:20, "For since the creation of the world God's invisible qualities—his eternal power and divine nature—have been clearly seen, being understood from what has been made, so that *men are without excuse.*" And the psalmist wrote, "The heavens declare the glory of God; the skies proclaim the work of his hands. Day after day they pour forth speech; night after night they display knowledge. *There is no speech nor language where their voice is not heard.* Their voice goes out into all the earth, their words to the ends of the world" (Ps. 19:1–4).

That every result has a cause is evidence of God's wisdom. His power is readily apparent by what He has made—the sun, the moon, the earth. When man went to the moon he had to take with him a special suit, food, and—because of the lack of oxygen—even his own atmosphere. The environment on the moon demonstrated that it was not made to be man's abode, and thereby we see God's wisdom in providing all that we need for life here on the earth. All that we can learn from general revelation, however, is that humankind is without excuse in not recognizing the existence of God; humans cannot learn the way of salvation from what we learn of God through what we see.

Don Richardson shares his experience with the cannibalistic Sawi people in Irian Jaya. The film and the book *Peace Child* depicted the difficulties that he and his wife experienced in presenting the gospel to those people. That is, until by "coincidence" they learned of the custom between two warring tribes of making peace by exchanging baby sons. That custom was the bridge that the Richardsons had been seeking. They could now make the gospel relevant to those pagan people—God gave peace by giving His Son (Eph. 2:14–18).

With this illustration as foundation, Richardson set about finding current customs and rites among peoples around the earth that could be applied for use with biblical doctrine and that were similar to practices and beliefs held for many centuries. He recorded many such instances in his second book, *Eternity in Their Hearts,* published by Regal Books.

It is unfortunate that Richardson used the term *redemptive analogies* to describe these traditions. Bruce A. Demarest, professor of Systematic Theology at Denver Seminary in Denver, Colorado, and Richard J. Harpel, associate pastor of the Bethany Evangelical Free Church, in Littleton, Colorado, wrote an article "to explore Don Richardson's concept of 'redemptive analogies' and assess the way he relates this concept to revelation broadly and general revelation specifically."[3] They also examined the implications of the "redemptive analogy" for the salvation of unevangelized people. According to Demarest and Harpel, "Saving faith, Richardson argues, need not involve knowledge about Christ and the plan of salvation."[4] They correctly observe, "It is important to realize that in its universal disclosure general revelation imparts no *redemptive* truths. Rather, general revelation performs the limited function of enabling all persons to know that God *is* and something of what He is like."[5]

Inexact knowledge is, in fact, reflected in *Eternity in Their Hearts.* It is difficult at times for the reader to understand what the author is claiming. Richardson writes, for instance, "For these reasons I propose that these particular facets of Mbaka lore be described as 'redemptive.'"[6] But he then explains, "(*Note:* 'redemptive,' not 'redeeming'! 'Redeeming' would mean that Mbaka people could find relationship with God through their own lore, apart from the gospel. 'Redemptive' in this context means 'contributing to the redemption of a people, but not culminating it). 'Redemptive lore' contributes to the redemption of a people solely by facilitating their understanding of what redemption means."[7]

At the same time, the author's ideas are indistinct. Early on the book says, "Both the Athenians and Cretans of Epimenides' time and the Incas of Pachacuti's day died without hearing the gospel of Jesus Christ. How about it? Are there no God-anticipating pagan peoples who *did* live to receive the blessing of the gospel?"[8] The question seems to suggest that although the exact gospel of Jesus Christ did not reach them, perhaps sufficient light was given so that some of them received the "blessing" of the gospel, which surely must refer to salvation.

Many Scripture verses (e.g., John 3:18, 36; 1 John 5:12) indicate that, today, saving faith is found only in the work of God's Son, which satisfies completely God's holiness in regard to sin (Rom. 6:23). Certainly the experience of Cornelius should be sufficient confirmation of this. Without question, Cornelius had advanced further in his spiritual knowledge than those persons referred to in Richardson's illustrations. Scripture does not tell us how Cornelius came to such knowledge, only that he was sincere and wanted to do what was right. But that was not enough. Only when Cornelius heard the good news about what Christ had done and placed his trust in Him as Savior did he cross over into salvation. In other words, with all of his knowledge, works, and sincerity, he was still totally lost and bound for a Christless eternity.

That God sent an angel to Cornelius in order to expedite a meeting between him and Peter indicates that God wanted Cornelius to hear the Good News. The angel might have at the same time shared the gospel. It would have been easier than sending men on foot to find Peter and then having them all return to Caesarea. Angels, after all, thoroughly know the gospel; they announced the Lord's birth, were no doubt present at His crucifixion, and they announced His resurrection to the women at the tomb. Surely angels would be more faithful than unpredictable humans. But God, in His sovereignty, has chosen redeemed sinners to be His witnesses when it comes to salvation. Paul tells us, "But God chose the foolish things of the world to shame the wise; God chose the weak things of the world to shame the strong. He chose the lowly things of this world and the despised things—and things that are not—to nullify the things that are, so that no one may boast before him. It is because of him that you are in Christ Jesus, who has become for us wisdom from God—that is, our righteousness, *holiness,* and redemption" (1 Cor. 1:27–30).

THINGS YET TO COME

God is not yet finished. And following His steps through prophecy will reveal His holiness and love in the future. At the conclusion of the Last Supper with His disciples, Jesus tells them, "I am going there [to my Father's house] to prepare a place for you. And if I go and prepare a place for you, I will come back and take you to be with me that you also may be where I am" (John 14:2–3).

Not only is a place prepared for His followers but another place is prepared for unbelievers. Jesus said, "Then he [the king] will say to those on his left, 'Depart from me, you who are cursed, into the eternal fire prepared for the devil and his angels'" (Matt. 25:41).

Scripture tells us of only two places that have been "prepared": the dwelling place for the saved in the Father's house, and the lake of fire prepared for the Devil and his angels. The only way to get to heaven is by the crucified Son of God, who not only died for us but also rose from the dead to give us eternal life. For the unsaved, there is no third place. Hell was not created for human beings but rather for the Devil and his angels. But if humans, even though not realizing it, have followed Satan in this life, they must follow him for all eternity.

The Rapture

Christians look forward to the Rapture, when Jesus will come for us: "For the Lord himself will come down from heaven, with a loud command, with the voice of the archangel and with the trumpet call of God, and the dead in Christ will rise first. After that, we who are still alive and are left will be caught up together with them in the clouds to meet the Lord in the air. And so we will be with the Lord forever" (1 Thess. 4:16–17). As far as we know, this is the next prophecy to be fulfilled.

The Rapture demonstrates God's love, because after that He will bring tribulation upon the earth in the judgment of those who have not yet received Him. Paul tells the Thessalonian believers, "They tell how you turned to God from idols to serve the living and true God, and to wait for His Son from heaven, whom he raised from the dead—Jesus, who rescues us from the coming wrath" (1 Thess. 1:9–10). He then adds, "For God did not appoint us to suffer wrath" (5:9). In his second letter to the Thessalonians, Paul writes concerning the time that will come upon the unbelieving world: "For the secret power of lawlessness is already at work; but the one who now holds it back [i.e., the Holy Spirit] will continue to do so till he is taken out of the way" (2 Thess. 2:7). The restraining ministry of the Holy Spirit will cease at the Rapture. He will take the believers to meet Christ, the Bridegroom, and Christ will take us to His (and our) home in heaven.

The Tribulation

To uphold His holiness, God will bring tribulation upon the earth in the judgment of those who have not accepted Christ as Savior. Unbelievers who are left on earth after the Rapture will experience horrible times: there will be earthquakes, famine, and death; trees and grass will be burned up; part of the sea will become blood; fish will die; ships will be destroyed; the sun will become black and at the same time the moon will turn blood red; demons will be loosed to torment the unsaved. But worse yet, sinners will have to face the wrath of God, and then they will be condemned to the lake of fire to live eternally with the demons and Satan. Revelation gives more details of how the unsaved will suffer.

Many people ask, "Will there be no hope for those who find themselves in this terrible time? Can anyone accept Christ during this awful period, or will it be too late? What about the destiny of those who have never heard of Christ? Will they have an opportunity to be saved, or will they have to go to a Christless eternity?"

God has told us in His Word how He will demonstrate His love and holiness. People in the first group—those who definitely rejected Christ, wanted no part of Him before the Rapture, and go into the Tribulation in that state—will not be saved. They chose to believe the lie about Christ before the Rapture, and they will continue to believe that lie in the Tribulation, and they will perish.

Satan has been waiting for the day when the Holy Spirit, who has been restraining the works of the Evil One, will be taken out of the way so that he can reveal his lawless one, the Antichrist: "And then the lawless one will be revealed, whom the Lord Jesus will overthrow with the breath of his mouth and destroy by the splendor of his coming. The coming of the lawless one will be in accordance with the work of Satan displayed in all kinds of counterfeit miracles, signs and wonders, and in every sort of evil that deceives those who are perishing. They perish because they refused to love the truth and so be saved. For this reason God sends them a powerful delusion so that they will believe the lie and so that all will be condemned who have not believed the truth but have delighted in wickedness" (2 Thess. 2:8–12).

The second group of people are those who might have heard the good news of salvation but did not understand it. Most people today do not accept the Lord the first time they hear the gospel. Many people hear the Good News several times before they comprehend what it's all about. But when the Tribulation takes place, it will be a fearsome, terrifying event for those who are left on earth. The part of their family who are Christians will have disappeared. Their Christian friends will have disappeared. If a pilot and a copilot are Christians, and the Rapture takes place, their plane will crash, killing all unbelievers who are aboard. If the driver of a car is a Christian, he or she will be taken and the car demolished. Runaway trains will crash because Christian engineers were taken. Millions of graves will be emptied because Christians will rise at the Rapture call of Christ.

The government will try to explain away all events, but the people who have heard the gospel will suddenly remember that their families or a friend had told them that this very thing would someday take place. With fearful hearts, they will grab a Bible and start reading it for themselves. The Holy Spirit, demonstrating God's love, will convict them of their sin and their need of Christ as their Savior. Possibly they will accept Christ, and they will become the first Christians in the Tribulation. They will also become the first people to witness to others, telling them of the salvation found only in Christ as Savior. Many of these new believers, though, will be martyred for their faith.

The third group of people are those who have never heard about Christ, those whom we Christians were unable to reach before the Rapture. God gives us hope that many of these will hear of salvation during the Tribulation: "After this I looked and there before me was a great multitude that no one could count, from every nation, tribe, people, and language, standing before the throne and in front of the Lamb. . . . These are they who have come out of the great tribulation; they have washed their robes and made them white in the blood of the Lamb" (Rev. 7:9, 14).

In Acts 2:14–41, the apostle Peter gets to his feet and begins to preach. On this great Day of Pentecost he explains to his hearers the work of the Holy Spirit. In his message, he quotes a prophecy of Joel 2:28–32, which also speaks about the work of the Holy Spirit from the Day of Pentecost to the Tribulation. The prophecy seems to merge these two events as if they were one, but they are, indeed, separate. Part of the prophecy was fulfilled on that great Day of Pentecost, and some of the things that occurred on Pentecost will also occur during the Tribulation. But in the Tribulation, other things will come to pass that did not take place at Pentecost.

On the Day of Pentecost, the Holy Spirit was given to the one hundred twenty believers who were assembled together praying. He entered into them and empowered them to go out and witness in unknown languages.

All of them were filled with the Holy Spirit and began to speak in other tongues [languages] as the Spirit enabled them. Now there were staying in Jerusalem God-fearing Jews from every nation under heaven. When they heard this sound [of the Holy Spirit coming down and indwelling the believers], a crowd came together in bewilderment, because each one heard them speaking in his own language [i.e., the language of the hearer]. Utterly amazed, they asked, "Are not all these men who are speaking Galileans? Then how is it that each of us hears in his own native language? Parthians, Medes and Elamites; residents of Mesopotamia, Judea and Cappadocia, Pontus and Asia, Phrygia and Pamphylia, Egypt and the parts of Libya near Cyrene; visitors from Rome (both Jews and converts to Judaism); Cretans and Arabs—we hear them declaring the wonders of God in our own tongues! Amazed and perplexed, they asked one another, "What does this mean?" Some, however, made fun of them and said, They have had too much wine." (Acts 2:4–13)

Some people will always reject the Word of God, but more than three thousand people were saved that day.

At the beginning of the Tribulation period, many people will, because of the Rapture, receive Christ as Savior and will in turn become witnesses for Him. After three and one-half years, however, something else happens. The Antichrist comes to Jerusalem to take charge and to present himself in the Jewish temple as God. Jews will then realize that they have been deceived and will search for the truth either in the Bible or through the testimony of those who have been saved.

Also, during this time 144,000 Israelites will be set apart and sealed (12,000 from each of the twelve tribes) as a special divine remnant to testify of God's mercy and saving power. Although the Antichrist, urged by Satan, will do everything in his power to destroy them, they will be sonvereignly protected by the seal of God. The fact that a description of the multitude who are saved out of the tribulation immediately follows the account of the 144,000 argues strongly that the special task that these Israelites will be fulfilling is the proclamation of the gospel of the kingdom to the world.

Those saved will be from "all nations and kindreds, and people and tongues" (Rev. 7:9). Thus, it appears that these "evangelist-missionaries" will be dispersed throughout the earth, probably as a result of persecution, to preach the gospel to all nations.

As well, during the Tribulation the Holy Spirit will empower believers to be witnesses of God's grace and His provision for their salvation. These witnesses will suffer much for their faith. Some of them will even be beheaded or die in other ways. The Tribulation will be so horrendous that John writes in Revelation 14:13, "Then I heard a voice from heaven say, 'Write: Blessed are the dead who die in the Lord from now on.' 'Yes,' says the Spirit, 'they will rest from their labor, for their deeds will follow them.'" John says in Revelation 20:4, "I saw thrones on which were seated those who had been given authority to judge. And I saw the souls of those who had been beheaded because of their testimony for Jesus and because of the word of God. They had not worshiped the beast or his image and had not received his mark on their foreheads or their hands. They came to life and reigned with Christ a thousand years." Revelation 12:11 tells us, "They overcame him by the blood of the Lamb and by the word of their testimony; they did not love their lives so much as to shrink from death."

But the result will be "a great multitude that no one could count from every nation, tribe, people and language, standing before the throne and in front of the Lamb. . . . These are they who have come out of the great tribulation; they have washed their robes and made them white in the blood of the Lamb" (Rev. 7:9, 14).

John tells us that those who were beheaded as martyrs "came to life and reigned with Christ a thousand years. (The rest of the dead did not come to life until the thousand years were ended.). This is the first resurrection. Blessed and holy are those who have part in the first resurrection. The second death has no power over them, but they will be priests of God and of Christ and will reign with him for a thousand years" (20:4–6).

As he sees the Bride—the church glorified—the apostle John falls down on his knees before the angel who had shown him this scene: "But [the angel] said to me, 'Do not do it! I am a fellow servant with you and with your brothers who hold to the testimony of Jesus. Worship God! For the testimony of Jesus is the spirit of prophecy'" (19:10).

The Return of Christ

The next scene revealed to John is the Lord Jesus as He leads the armies of heaven, wearing a robe with his name written on it, "KING OF KINGS AND LORD OF LORDS" (19:16).

John continues:

Then I saw the beast and the kings of the earth and their armies gathered together to make war against the rider on the horse and his army. But the beast was captured, and with him the false prophet who had performed the miraculous signs on his behalf. With these signs he had deluded those who had received the mark of the beast and worshiped his image. The two of them were thrown alive into the fiery lake of burning sulfur. The rest of them were killed with the sword that came out of the mouth of the rider on the horse, and all the birds gorged themselves on their flesh. (19:19-21)

The Final Judgment

In chapter 20 of Revelation, we find "an angel" binding Satan for a thousand years. Meanwhile, those who were martyred during the Tribulation are restored to life, and they reign with Christ a thousand years. These events are the final part of the "first resurrection," that is, of the saved, including the church, which had been raptured, thus ushering in the Tribulation (1 Cor. 15:51-53).

In Revelation 20:7, the Devil is released from his imprisonment. He again deceives the nations, gathering them to battle against the Lord. This battle is different from Armageddon or any other battle: "But fire came down from heaven and devoured them. And the devil who deceived them, was thrown into the lake of burning sulfur. . . . They will be tormented day and night for ever and ever" (v. 10).

Final judgment then takes place (vv. 11-14). The dead of all ages are brought together and will be judged "according to what they had done as recorded in the books" (v. 12). The book of life will testify against those who never received Christ as their Savior, and they will all be "thrown into the lake of fire" (v. 14). This judgement upholds the "holiness" of God, who endured the rejection of the lost since the Garden of Eden. Three times God initiated definite time periods (dispensations) peopled with only believers—Adam and Eve, Noah and his family, and the kingdom period after the Tribulation.

God's final victory is depicted in Revelation 7. The tribes of Israel are restored with their representative twelve thousand who were sealed from each tribe; the "great multitude that no one could count, from every nation, tribe people and languages"—saved mostly during the last half of the seven-year Tribulation—are redeemed and are reigning with Christ in the kingdom. How great is His love! Then all these, together with the redeemed of all ages, will live in the new creation (chaps. 21–22), where nothing will remain to remind God's people of sin. There will be only joy, and praise to the Lamb of God Who reigns with Him for ever and ever.

What a Savior we have. We wait only for the fulfillment of His final promise: "Yes, I am coming soon" (22:20). And we echo with the apostle John, "Amen. Come, Lord Jesus" (v. 20).

CHAPTER 7

THE CHALLENGE OF RELIGIOUS PLURALISM

CHUCK SUTTON

ACCORDING TO CONVENTIONAL WISDOM, one should avoid two topics at parties—religion and politics. Not any more. Religion is "in"! Not only is it fine to talk about religion, but people now create "designer religions." They can mix and match beliefs and practices according to what fits their lifestyle. Consider these few options:

> "I'm an Episcopalian, and I think of myself as a practicing non-Jew," says Katherine Powell Cohen, a 36–year old English teacher in San Francisco. . . . "I'm a Mennonite hyphen Unitarian Universalist who practices Zen meditation," says Ralph Imhoff, 57, a retired educator from Chandler, Ariz. . . . "I call myself a Christian Buddhist, but sort of tongue-in-cheek," says Maitreya Badami, 30, who works in the Contra Costa, Calif., public defender's office.[1]

So popular is designer religion that the Dalai Lama himself has called our country "the spiritual supermarket."[2] *The Wall Street Journal* observed, in fact, that

> Jews flirt with Hinduism, Catholics study Taoism, and Methodists discuss whether to make the Passover Seder an official part of worship. Rabbi Zalman Schachter-Shalomi, a prominent Jewish scholar, is also a Sufi sheik, and James Ishmael Ford, a Unitarian minister in Arizona, is a Zen *sensei*, or master. The melding of Judaism with Buddhism has become so commonplace that marketers who sell spiritual books, videotapes and lecture series have a name for it: "JewBu."[3]

Hey, why not! Each religion, after all, offers a viable path to God. And what if your religion is different from mine? All religious beliefs are relative, so don't worry about it. You have your truth, and I have mine.

Five minutes from my house, a group of Chinmaya Hindus meets weekly in a house that they have converted into a place of worship. Ten minutes away in the other direction, in northeast Philadelphia, stands a recently built two-million-dollar Buddhist temple, paid for by donations from Buddhists around the country and from Thailand.[4] A beautiful work of Thai architecture, this temple is sure to attract the attention of its neighbors, who can observe faithful Buddhists coming to worship together from different parts of the northeast United States. Five months after the inauguration of the Thai Buddhist temple, a local Vietnamese community of about eighteen thousand residents celebrated the opening of the first Vietnamese Buddhist temple in Philadelphia.[5]

Islam is growing even more rapidly. A Muslim leader in Philadelphia claimed that in the city's ten largely African-American mosques, five new people a week embrace Islam.[6] One report indicates that Philadelphia is home to the fifth-largest Muslim population in the United States, with approximately forty thousand followers of Islam.[7] American Muslims are finding a new political "voice" in what might be the fastest-growing religion in the United States. At events around the country, Muslims register their followers to vote. Some Muslims are entering politics, whereas others are learning how they can use their wealth to influence political interests that advance the growth of Islam.[8] In our nation's capital, in a park between the White House and the Washington monument, the crescent-and-star symbol of Islam was recently included as a part of the holiday display alongside the national Christmas tree and the Hanukkah menorah.[9]

The renewed interest in religion is evidenced by its coverage in the media. A full-page "Living Religion" section has been added to the Sunday edition of the *Philadelphia Inquirer*, one of the major daily newspapers on the East Coast. The new section offers something for everyone, from articles on praising Lord Krishna and honoring the Hindu deity Kali, to encouraging intercessory prayer among various Christian denominations, to a local Muslim college student seeking purification and holiness during the Islamic holy day of Ramadan. Other reports include the installation of a ritual bath for personal purification in a local Reform Jewish synagogue; reflections on the reality of reincarnation; lively notes from readers responding to an article about "pious agnosticism"; and the celebration of Le Vu Lan, or Mother's Day, by local Vietnamese Buddhists who are praying for the health and happiness of mothers as a means of rescuing souls. One account explored the interest in, dialogue about, and experimentation with Eastern religious traditions by Roman Catholics, Quakers, and other denominations. Readers were asked to respond if they supplement their "religious practice with elements of another religion," to tell how they do it, and whether they set boundaries.

Another article told about Sogyal Rinpoche, a Buddhist apostle-author who claimed to be the incarnation of a nineteenth-century Buddhist master. In a local Episcopal church, the Tibetan lama counseled his listeners on how to live a meaningful life and prepare for death. The Episcopalian rector commented, "My religion has a range to it, and I love having the Buddhists here because we have so much in common. There are many paths. The Buddhist path can be the path to Christianity, and Christianity can lead toward Buddhism."[10]

Even as I write, Muslim refugees from Albania, fleeing the crisis in Kosovo, Yugoslavia, have arrived at a military installation in New Jersey not far from where I live. The front page of *The Philadelphia Inquirer* displayed a large photo of a Muslim who is sitting on a prayer rug facing Mecca at the military base and carrying out his Friday prayers.[11] A few days later, page two of the same newspaper headlined a large photo of sixteen young men completing their ordination to enter the monastic life as Buddhist monks in Sri Lanka.[12]

The visibility of religious groups in Philadelphia is a microcosm of what is taking place across North America, not only in the large cities but also in smaller communities. So strong is the interest in religion and so fast the growth of new religions that a major textbook publisher is offering a book that introduces readers to the many recently emerging religious movements. The text, *Religion in the Twenty-First Century,* "probe[s] the role religion will play in the new millennium."[13] Some religious leaders argue that the existence of other religions and the emergence of new religions are evidence that Jesus is just one of many ways to God. Evangelicals struggle to make sense of and respond to the myriad and new challenges to the historic Christian faith.

ADRIFT IN A SEA OF CHANGE

Anthony Giddens, a leading sociologist, helps us understand why, relative to religion, our world is different from that of the past. Two phenomena apply particularly to the current topic: first is the rapid and bewildering *pace of change* (advancements in science and technology being but two examples).

Second is the broad *scope of change.* "As different areas of the globe are drawn into interconnection with one another, waves of social transformation crash across virtually the whole of the earth's surface."[14] The reasons for these changes are many.

The Global Community

In the past, most of the United States shared a common heritage grounded largely in the Judeo-Christian tradition. Such is not the case today. One reason is the increase of global communication and travel, which has helped to create a global community. Recent immigration has brought people from other cultures to our neighborhoods and classrooms. This diversity means that we as a society no longer share a cohesive bond or worldview. Instead, we are a composite of many different subsocieties, each with its own cultural traditions and religious beliefs.[15] Hindus, Muslims, and other religious groups frequent our communities. They are our neighbors, and their children are in the classrooms of our local schools, a situation that was seldom experienced just a generation ago. Rodger Kamenetz, the author of the *Jew in the Lotus,* claims, "We're no longer living in an Episcopal neighborhood or a Jewish neighborhood.[16] It's easy to look over the fence and see what the other folks are doing."[17]

The Influence of the Electronic Media

As earlier stated, global communication has permitted access to virtually any belief system—including paganism—via thousands of sites on the Internet.[18] *The Wall Street Journal* reports that an on-line search of *God* on the Internet will produce as many as six hundred thousand responses. One expert describes the presence of religion on the Web as "staggering" and says that it is "expanding exponentially."[19] "Yahoo! Inc. lists seventeen thousand sites devoted to religion and spirituality."[20]

The Growth of World Religions

The expansion of Christianity as a result of missionary efforts during the eighteenth and nineteenth centuries led some people to believe that the major world religions would decline in both size and influence. The opposite has been the case. Two missiological researchers, David Barrett and Todd Johnson, report that from 1900 to 1970, the number of Muslims grew from 200 million to 558 million, a growth of 180 percent.[21] And these researchers expect Islam to more than double its numbers again by the year 2000 (reaching 1.2 billion), and to grow still another 75 percent between 2000 and 2025, to almost 1.9 billion followers.

With regard to Hinduism, Barrett and Todd tracked a growth from about 200 million to almost 474 million from 1900 to 1970 with a projected 786 million by 2000 and more than one billion followers by 2025. If their projections hold, growth would be 502 percent from 1900 to 2025. Barrett and Johnson project that the number of Buddhists will have grown from 127 million to 423 million by 2025, a growth rate of 333 percent. While much of this growth is due to birth rates, it nonetheless indicates that the world's religions are not dying but rather are increasing in numbers and influence at a significant pace.

In addition to their population growth, Muslims, Hindus, Buddhists, and others are staking out new ground in the West. They are becoming evangelistic, reaching out to North Americans who, often disillusioned by the emptiness of materialism and suffering from lack of purpose, are drawn to attractive, alternative worldviews that offer a meaning for life.

Not only is growth occurring among the world's existing religions but *new* movements, too, are attracting followers. Barrett and Johnson report that the number of persons who embraced new religions amounted to a meager 5.9 million in 1900. By 1970 the number had risen to almost 78 million, and it is projected to reach 118 million by 2025.[22] One religion experiencing rapid growth is the Falun Gong movement in China. With an estimated 70 million followers, the Falun Gong is—according to the States Sports Administration of the Chinese government—larger than the Communist party.[23] The preceding figures and trends indicate that people are searching for something outside the existing religious systems, and they reflect the spirit of openness to new ideas and change that characterizes our age.

Religious Skepticism

Professor Harold Netland notes other factors that contribute to the acceptance of new religious ideas.[24] In the last two centuries, the writings of such men as David Hume, Immanuel Kant, and others have influenced the fields of philosophy and the larger arenas of academia, raising doubts about the possibility of knowing anything for certain when it comes to religious matters. Coupled with this view is the skepticism of the higher critical method in biblical studies, which has cast serious doubts on the historical accuracy and truthfulness of New Testament writers. Scholars argue that we cannot really know who Jesus was or what He said. They further claim that, in texts such as John 14:6, others put words in Jesus' mouth, and that it cannot be proved that Jesus Himself ever spoke them. Jesus' divinity, they argue, was a later invention of His followers—a result of their fervent commitment to Him. Such skepticism casts doubts on the truthfulness of Jesus' words not only in John 14:6 but in Acts 4:12 and elsewhere.[25]

Relativism

Relativism in the current context refers to the theory that no concept or conduct is normative or universally true for all people, at all times, and in all places. In other words, there is no absolute truth. Philosopher Roger Trigg notes, "Relativism has always proved tempting when people who had previously lived a settled and complacent life have suddenly been confronted with new and different ideas or practices."[26] Trigg's statement describes what has taken place in North America during the last several decades. Contact with the worldviews of other cultures has had the effect of making the truth of all worldviews relative.[27]

The influences of the social sciences and American higher education in general have also contributed to the assumption that all truth is relative. "Tolerance and openness—radical openness to anything and everything—are prized as the greatest of all virtues, and frequently the implication is that critically evaluating or rejecting as false the beliefs of others is incompatible with this spirit of tolerance."[28] Combined with religious skepticism, relativism attacks and undermines the historic beliefs of Christianity, challenging the Bible's claims to give us revealed, unchanging, universal truth from God. The truth-claims of Christianity are thought to be implausible and unbelievable, disqualifying them from serious consideration.[29]

A Distinction Between Public and Private Truth

Among others, Lesslie Newbigin, a missionary statesman and astute critic of Western culture, notes that a particularly troubling problem has developed in the West. Newbigin

> alerted us to the modern tendency to make a sharp dichotomy between the public world of "facts," exemplified especially in the physical sciences, and the private realm of personal values, opinions, and preferences, with religion being banished to the latter. Truth is said to belong to the public realm of "facts" and not that of

personal preference. And since religious statements are allegedly not empirically testable as are other "public truths," religious beliefs are eliminated from the public sphere and are reduced to matters of mere personal preference and opinion.[30]

As a consequence, religious belief has been marginalized to the private sphere, and this undermines it. People wonder if their beliefs are true, reliable, and dependable. If they cannot know for sure, they turn to the sphere of personal experience. People do, after all, still want to believe something, and they can at least verify if something works for them. If spiritual truth is no longer the primary issue, individuals are left to choose religion like they choose music, car color, or clothing: religious belief, like any other choice in our consumer society, now depends upon personal taste.[31] This means, however, that it is no longer permissible to try to persuade others that what we believe is the truth, because religion, although now acceptable, is based on individual preference. If no one religion is true for everyone, truth-claims become narrow-minded and intolerant. This way of thinking converges with the pragmatic view of religion and the rejection of Christian exclusivism that results.

A Pragmatic Approach to Religion

For many people, the primary purpose of religion is its ability to help them solve their everyday problems and find some measure of peace, contentment, or happiness. Such thinking underlies the quotations that opened this chapter. Setting aside concerns about the truthfulness of their beliefs, people only want to know what works—what helps them cope with their problems and provides them with an inner source of strength and stability in a world of increasing change, uncertainty, and instability. If Hinduism works for people in India, and Buddhism works for Southeast Asians, and Islam works for Muslims in the Middle East, it seems intolerant to criticize other beliefs and practices because they are different. Those other religions meet the needs of the people who follow them. If, however, Christianity meets our needs, they reason, that's what is important. If it doesn't work, we can find a religion that does. Or maybe a combination of, say, Zen Buddhism and Christianity will work best. "Since people and cultures differ widely and people's needs are so varied, it is only to be expected that a variety of religious traditions will be necessary."[32]

A Shift in Thinking About the Meaning of Religious Diversity

The United States may be described as a pluralistic society.[33] Religious plurality in the United States refers to the variety of religious beliefs that our society tolerates and permits to function without government interference. We take pride in our heritage of protecting the right of people to believe and practice as they desire, as long as their beliefs and practices do not infringe on the basic rights of others. Religious diversity recognizes that "there are many fundamentally different answers to the questions of human existence."[34]

But the trends and influences discussed earlier have contributed to a new way of understanding the many religious beliefs around us. In the past, our society tolerated different beliefs without necessarily accepting them. But a new system of thought or worldview—religious pluralism—goes beyond accepting religious diversity to make a judgment about the conflicting truth claims of groups such as Christians, Buddhists, Muslims, and others. Some theologians and church leaders conclude that "these fundamental differences do not *as truth claims* mutually exclude one another" (italics added).[35]

At this point it should be evident that the many factors involved in religious pluralism overlap. Together, they converge to produce a new, unsettling, and fragmented world. Peter Berger described it thus: "A world in which everything is in constant motion is a world in which certainties of any kind are hard to come by."[36] Such a world fosters doubt about which religion is true. And the attractive answer that some religious leaders offer to resolve the doubt and tension is religious pluralism.[37]

RELIGIOUS PLURALISM: AN ATTEMPT TO MAKE SENSE OF RELIGIOUS DIVERSITY

John Hick, a pluralist and a leading spokesperson for religious pluralism, describes it thus: ". . . God as known to Christians, Jews, Muslims, Hindus, Sikhs, and others represents different manifestations in relation to humanity, different 'faces' or 'masks' or *personae* of God, the Ultimate reality."[38] These different concepts about God, reflecting the differing human perceptions of God found in various cultures, lead Hick to conclude that "we can at once see how there is a plurality of religious traditions constituting different, but apparently more or less equally salvific, human responses to the Ultimate. These are the great world faiths."[39]

Paul Knitter, an influential Roman Catholic pluralist, states that pluralist theologians hold to "the possible independent validity and 'rough parity' of other religious paths . . . Christianity may be 'one among many'" paths to God, rather than being the superior or final revelation.[40]

Hick uses what is by now a well-known analogy to argue for a Copernican revolution in our understanding of religions. Just as the Ptolemaic—or geocentric (earth-centered)—model of the universe was demonstrated to be untenable and was replaced by the Copernican—or heliocentric (sun-centered)—model, so by analogy Hick argues that Christian exclusivism, with its belief that outside Christianity there is no salvation, must be replaced by a reality-centered focus. This theory claims that God (or ultimate reality) is working through other religious systems, which in their own ways point us toward ultimate reality.[41]

Religious pluralism, then, is the attempt by many church leaders to reconcile the diverse religious beliefs that surround us. To the questions of what God is like; what the origin, purpose, and destiny of humankind might be; how we might reconcile the different explanations for the presence of suffering and evil in our world—religious pluralism proposes that answers are found not in one religion but in many. That is, the different religious systems and their truth claims do not mutually exclude one another.[42] Note that pluralists, like exclusivists, are concerned about the eternal destiny of people. Strong disagreement exists, however, as to how each position addresses this concern.

Contemporary religious pluralists argue their beliefs on at least three basic grounds:

1. Historical consciousness: All knowledge and religious beliefs are relative to and limited by the cultural conditioning unique to a particular historical time frame, making it difficult to evaluate the "truth claims of another culture or religion on the basis of one's own."
2. The mystery of religious experiences: Because of their indescribable nature, religious experiences prohibit "any one religion from having the 'only' or 'final' word."
3. The need to promote justice: In the presence of the universal suffering of humanity, there is a need to promote justice, and this is an ethical basis for a new attitude of cooperation among the different religions.[43]

Hick argues that religions are the product of a complex interplay between the divine and human initiatives. The "Real"—God or ultimate reality—reveals itself to humankind; humankind, in turn, responds in historically and culturally conditioned ways to the "Real." Hick categorically denies the possibility that God has spoken to humans in propositional terms. That is, we cannot claim that God has communicated to us with factual, objective truth. He therefore asserts that the Bible is, at best, man's word about God; it is not God's inerrant and unique revelation to man. Rather, Hick believes, God has spoken to us through the holy writings of many religions, such as the Koran of Islam and the Bhagavad-Gita of Hinduism, as well as through the Bible. Jesus is not God, says Hick. Nor is He the perfect and final revelation of God to man in human form. Christians may regard him as *their* savior, but He is not the *only* Savior; He is only one of many. Other religions have their saviors and spokespersons (e.g., Buddha) who point them to God in the same way that Jesus Christ points Christians to God through His life and teachings.[44]

Hick further claims, "There is not merely one way but a plurality of ways of salvation or liberation . . . taking place in different ways within the contexts of all the great religious traditions."[45] Elsewhere, Hick states that the different religions are "equals, though they may each have different emphases." Christianity is only one partner in the quest for salvation.[46]

Pluralists argue that because salvation (or liberation or enlightenment) is more or less equally available in all of the major religions, no single tradition such as Christianity or Islam can claim to be the one true religion. Thus, tolerance of the differences among religions becomes very important. We should not, argue the pluralists, make judgments about the rightness or wrongness of the truth claims of other religious systems. To do so reflects the arrogance of exclusivism and is divisive. Because the major religions are on equal footing, harmony and unity are important goals of interreligious dialogue among the various parties.

By his own report, Hick reveals that the most powerful influence leading him to espouse religious pluralism was his extended contact with Hindus, Muslims, Jews, Sikhs, and Christians in Birmingham, England. His personal experience and observation led him to conclude that these groups were all doing the same thing: they were seeking God and attempting to live out their commitment to Him, although each did it in the framework of differing ancient and developed traditions.[47] The high standards of personal morality (kindness, compassion, love, honesty, and truthfulness) that are taught by and practiced among followers of the major world religions convinced Hick that they all reflected a right relationship with God. If Christianity is a religion that is superior to all others, asks Hick, why do we not find spirituality reflected more fully and perfectly in Christians? He argues that "it is not possible to establish the moral superiority of the adherents of any one of the great traditions over the rest."[48] Therefore, he concludes that Christianity is just one of many ways in which God is working to save people.

If, as Hick and others argue, Christianity is only one of many paths leading to God, then Christians should not claim that Jesus is the only way to God. Such talk would be arrogant and intolerant. Wilfred Cantwell Smith, a leading proponent of religious pluralism, states, "Exclusivism strikes more and more Christians as immoral. If the head proves it true, while the heart sees it as wicked, un-Christian, then should Christians not follow the heart? Maybe this is the crux of our dilemma."[49] Knitter believes that the "conservative Evangelical declaration that there can be authentic, reliable revelation only in Christ simply does not hold up in the light of the faith, dedication, love, and peace that Christians find in the teachings and especially in the followers of other religions."[50]

Pluralist writers argue that the narrow-mindedness of Christian exclusivism makes it impossible to dialogue with others in our communities and in the larger global community. How, they ask, can we possibly work together to solve the overwhelming problems that face the human race if we say that the religious beliefs of our dialogue partners are false?[51]

The corollary to rejecting Christian exclusivism is embracing some form of universalism, which claims that, in some way, God's universal love and sense of fairness will move Him to make provision ultimately to save all persons.[52] Hell, then, would at most be a temporary purgatory to prepare us for heaven. Or perhaps hell does not even exist but was merely an old, lingering myth from the first-century church that modern Christians no longer need to take seriously.[53]

AN INITIAL EVANGELICAL RESPONSE TO RELIGIOUS PLURALISM

Religious pluralism challenges the beliefs of evangelicalism in several areas, of which Netland identifies two:

First, the notion that one particular religious figure and one religious perspective can be universally valid, normative, and binding upon all peoples in all cultures—an assumption central to the Biblical understanding of Christ and salvation—is widely rejected today as arrogant and intellectually untenable in our pluralistic world. Even within the broadly Christian community it is increasingly accepted that there cannot be just one savior and one religion for all of the world's diverse peoples. And second, even if in principle it is granted that one religion might be superior to the rest, and that one religious figure might be universally normative, why should we assume that Christianity and Jesus Christ are in this privileged position?[54]

In responding to pluralists, evangelicals must realize that quoting Scripture is generally ineffective because pluralists do not view the Bible as authoritative. Although evangelicals should not abandon the appeal to Christian Scriptures, other approaches to countering pluralists are also effective. One approach is to point out the inconsistencies in the pluralist position, which is vulnerable at several points.

The Problem of Relativism

Most religious pluralists assume some form of relativism. Such an assumption is necessary in order to argue that the paths of all major religions lead ultimately to God, even though the beliefs of those various religions conflict with one another with regard to what God (or the "Real") is like and how one comes to know Him. Christians are sometimes intimidated by the threat of relativism. We understand that it neutralizes our belief in the existence of the objective, unchangeable truth revealed to us in the Bible, which we believe to be propositional (factual) truth given by God. A closer look at relativism, however, demonstrates that it is not a viable foundation upon which to build a belief system.[55]

First, a more precise term for *relativism* is *cognitive relativism*, which refers to "the view that truth, knowledge, and basic rationality norms are relative to particular contexts."[56] That is, there is no truth or knowledge that is universal or independent of a given context.

A significant weakness of cognitive relativism is that it is incoherent and self-refuting.[57] If, for example, I state, "*All* things are relative," I have just made a claim that is absolute. Thus, not every thing *is* relative, because I am stating that the *one* statement above is absolutely true. But if *all* things are relative, then nothing can be absolutely true. Both statements cannot be true at the same time.[58] The first statement, therefore, refutes itself and is inconsistent.

People embrace relativism, too, because when they observe the diversity of the culture that surround them, they realize that their way of life is just one of *many* ways of acting and thinking. When two people who follow different practices come together, they may each view the other's practice as unacceptable, but neither practice is wrong in its own context. I, for example, eat with my left hand. This practice is acceptable in the United States, but in many other cultures eating with the left hand is taboo and offensive. The left hand is used only for body functions; the right hand is used for eating. Each custom is acceptable in relation to its own cultural context.[59] Pluralists, however, carry context one step further. They state that—because each religion holds to different, even conflicting, beliefs—it can be concluded that there is no universal, objective truth about God and no one religion is binding upon all cultures. Hindu beliefs are true for Hindus even as Christian beliefs are true for Christians.

The fallacy in this thinking lies in the confusion of *diversity* with *truth*. These are two distinct (albeit related) concepts. All diverse beliefs are not equally true. Just because some people once believed that the earth was flat did not make it true. A lot of conflicting beliefs exist about God and the world. Are all beliefs, therefore, true? To answer "yes" to this question is to throw out all rational thinking. "Ultimately, truth is not dependent upon what people happen to accept; it is defined by what is in fact the case."[60] Relativism must face the problem of invalid conclusions.

Hick provides a statement that exemplifies an invalid conclusion. Having wrestled with the differences that exist among the world's religions, his contact and dialogue with the many different religious groups in Birmingham, England, influenced his thinking. He wrote that "in the great majority of cases—say, 98 or 99 percent—the religion in which a person believes and to which he adheres depends upon where he was born."[61] Thus, a person born in Saudi Arabia will probably be a Muslim; a child born in Dehli, India, will most likely be a Hindu; a youth raised in Thailand probably will become a Buddhist; and a person born in the United States will most likely be a Christian. Because one is born into a particular tradition, one's birthplace significantly influences the religion that one embraces.

Note again the confusion between diversity and truth. If geography (i.e., birthplace) determines one's religion—the beliefs of which are true—then "truth" would depend upon where one is born. If truth is merely a function of the circumstances into which one is born, then the beliefs of any home or culture into which children are born are true for those children, even if that "truth" includes an aberration such as child sacrifice.[62] In all fairness, we must note that Hick rejects stretching relativism to this point, but the weakness in his argument is still evident.

Another problem must be faced if a relativistic stance is adopted. If truth about God is relative to a particular context, how do we explain that such "truth" changes over time even within a given culture? The medieval church in Europe believed in the Virgin Birth, but many people in the West now reject this idea as unscientific and impossible. If truth is relative to a particular place or society, which time period of that place or society holds the truth? Is more recent truth (e.g., the twenty-first century) better than older truth (e.g., the twelfth century)? On what basis? Before claiming the superiority of modern knowledge over that of people who came before, thereby claiming "truth," we should pause and reflect. The next two centuries will surely demonstrate that much of what we believe in the twenty-first century is untrue. Given our tremendous gains in knowledge in all spheres of life, much of what we know will probably change in the next fifty years. "Once it is admitted that different people within a society believe different things, or that over a period of time they have believed different things, truth cannot be defined in terms of what is accepted in that society."[63] If we embrace relativism, we are again embarrassed by the problem of "changing truth."

Another unresolved matter exists relating to relativism. If truth is relative to a given culture, one can make no judgment about what is right or wrong, precisely because one's views are relative to one's culture. No universal norms exist for declaring what is right and wrong. All that exists is personal perspective and preferences. A sincere and consistent relativist dares not make any judgment whatsoever about another belief system. Even those who embrace religious pluralism shudder at the idea of throwing out all discernment. But this predicament leads us to see the ultimate price of relativism: forfeiture of the right to determine what is right or wrong.[64]

John Hick argues persuasively that his position is true. But how can he know this, given that his own view is culturally limited to the assumptions of modern historical consciousness? The fallacies inherent in cognitive relativism bring Hick's own position into serious question and render it doubtful.

In the end, we must agree with Sharpe's conclusion about relativism, spoken in the context of its implications for personal commitment: "[Relativism] is an intellectual position which, though it certainly has some ethical consequences, makes no personal demands on the individual, and of itself mediates little of the transcendent."[65] Thus a commitment to relativism ultimately leads to a commitment to nothing.

How, then, do we know what is true, apart from the dogmatic assertions we hear from all quarters? Evaluating truth claims is too broad a subject to address within the limitations of this chapter. Alister McGrath, however, suggests five guidelines that argue for the truth of Christianity's claims: discover the "reliability of its historical foundations, its internal consistency, its rationality, its power to convert, and its relevance to human existence."[66]

The Problem of Tolerance

A corollary of relativism is tolerance, or openness to the beliefs of others. If, as relativists claim, we do not have access to objective, religious truth, then we have no basis for judging the truth claims of other religious groups and thereby practicing intolerance toward them. Allan Bloom's landmark study on the impact of cognitive and moral relativism in American education recognized this corollary. With no little irony, Bloom observes,

> Relativism is necessary to openness; and this is the virtue, the only virtue, which all primary education for more than fifty years has dedicated itself to inculcating. Openness—and the relativism that makes it the only plausible stance in the face of various claims to truth and the various ways of life and kinds of human beings—is the great insight of our times . . . The point is not to correct the mistakes and really be right; rather it is not to think that you are right at all.[67]

Pluralism and relativism have contributed to a redefinition of *tolerance:* Any claim to truth is acceptable as long as it is tolerant of other positions, even when they contradict. Tolerance has historically been understood as "an issue of character and cultural awareness in a culturally and religiously diverse world."[68] That is, respect should characterize our relationship toward those who hold different beliefs and practices. This perspective is supported by the definition of *tolerance* provided by Maurice Cranston: "a policy of patient forbearance in the presence of something which is disliked and disapproved of."[69]

S. D. Gaede discusses tolerance as it relates to political correctness and multiculturalism in North America. Gaede's observations on societal trends reinforce and substantiate Bloom's concerns. Gaede charges, "Truth as a known commodity, attainable and worthy of pursuit, is not a pervasive influence in the modern world."[70]

Gaede provides a historical overview of the shift from a concern for truth and tolerance for those who disagree to the current understanding of tolerance as acceptance of conflicting truth claims. Traditional societies actually encouraged intolerance because of their homogeneity. Gaede points out that the definition of tolerance as the acceptance of conflicting truth claims came about when communal homogeneity broke down and cultural pluralism developed. The interdependence of economic relationships and other factors cited earlier indeed called for some form of tolerance. A lack of confidence in the concept of objective truth also clearly contributed to the shift in the meaning of tolerance. Cognitive and moral relativism now dominate our culture and are reflected in the current emphasis of style over content (that is, truth). The result is a multiplicity of worldviews that exists side by side in our society, and an insistence on the right of the individual to choose or mix and match any of the available options, a mind-set that contributes to the fragmentation of belief.

Consequently, tolerance regarding conflicting truth claims is now valued because it "conforms nicely to the world we live in. Having pretty much decided that truth is not attainable, we have made tolerance of a plurality of truths a virtue. Having no truths worth defending, we have made nondefensiveness a mark of distinction."[71]

The weaknesses of the pluralist view of tolerance are clear. The incoherence of relativism as a system of thought undermines its view of tolerance. Relativism cannot consistently promote the obligation for tolerance—whether it be over a moral issue or a truth claim—without contradicting itself. If relativists insist that tolerance means that we should not evaluate truth claims as right or wrong, they have set forth an objective rule about tolerance, one that they believe should apply equally to all people without exception. But in saying this, they have identified an absolute truth, which cannot exist if all truth is relative to a group or an individual or a particular time period. Furthermore, as Koukl points out, "Relativists violate their own principle of tolerance when they do not tolerate the views of those whose morality [or truth claim] is nonrelativistic. They only tolerate those who hold their ethical viewpoint. They are, therefore, just as intolerant as any objectivist appears to be."[72]

Perhaps better ways of dealing with religious differences exist. One illustration will suffice. Each year, I take my students who are enrolled in a World Religions class to visit Hindu, Sikh, and Buddhist temples and an Islamic mosque. The Muslims at the mosque that we visit typically receive us with gracious Middle Eastern hospitality and tell us about their beliefs and practices. They point out the superiority of Islam as a further revelation given by Allah to Mohammed superseding the revelation received by Christians at the hand of Jesus and the apostles. They evangelize because they are convinced that they know absolute truth, and it is found in Islam.

After their presentation, I am kindly offered an opportunity to respond. Discussing the differences between Islam and Christianity can be delicate. I explain, however, that if we are to take each other seriously and try to understand one another, we must take our differences seriously as well. And the differences are indeed significant, including our belief in who Jesus is, the nature of humankind, and how we receive salvation. To ignore the basic differences between Islam and evangelical Christianity is to trivialize both the Muslims' beliefs and mine. Precisely because I respect the Muslims, I not only tolerate and respect our differences but I also take their beliefs seriously by attempting to understand them. I do not gloss over the differences. I compare and contrast Muslim beliefs in light of the gospel message, which I believe to be true. Again, ignoring differences trivializes other people, their beliefs, and the very idea of truth itself. Of course, this approach is more effective when relationships of trust have been established, thus allowing each side to discuss these serious differences without animosity. At the same time, the offense generated by and inherent in the subject of the Cross cannot be avoided if I am faithful to all of the biblical themes that are interwoven into the gospel message.

The Pluralist View of Jesus

The pluralist attempt to trivialize the uniqueness of Jesus is necessary to allow for their agenda of promoting other saviors and religions as viable paths to God. To accept at face value the Bible's statements regarding the person and work of Christ would undermine the pluralist position, a fact that Hick recognizes.[73] He argues that the historical Jesus never taught that He was God. Rather, Hick claims, early church writers put words in the mouth of Jesus, making Him out to be God as a result of their developing theology. Hick relies upon the findings of liberal scholarship, which has embraced the higher critical method. Evangelicals have carefully critiqued this methodology and its findings and have ably defended the reliability of the Gospels and the Christology of the New Testament writers.[74] Such studies are, however, generally ignored by pluralists. Hick's view stands against twenty centuries of orthodox Christian belief in the full deity and humanity of Jesus Christ, and his position is unacceptable to evangelicals who desire to remain faithful to the historic creeds and to the biblical record as it stands.

Alister McGrath notes, "Pluralists have driven a wedge between God and Jesus Christ, as if Christians were obliged to choose between one or the other."[75] But for Christians, God is revealed in Christ. The Bible does not allow for the pursuit of "the new pluralistic theological strategy of moving away from Christ-centered faith toward God-centered faith." On the contrary, the New Testament affirms a both/and approach: "The only way in which we can be God-centered, then, is to be Christ-centered, for God is salvifically known nowhere else (Acts 2:36–38; 4:12; 13:26–41; 17:29–31). . . . The New Testament unequivocally sounds the note of Christ's uniqueness, the clarion call of historical particularity, which vitiates every other religious claim."[76]

We should take note of an additional result of the pluralist attempt to reduce Jesus to one of many saviors and thereby diminish His uniqueness as God. In trying to find an adequate understanding of ultimate reality—or the "Real"—that is broad enough to encompass the major religions of the world, pluralists such as Hick are driven to homogenize their concept of God. That is, they are forced to strip it of any significant content so that it is (presumably) uniform and acceptable to all major religious systems. But in doing so, pluralists trivialize the unique understandings of God (or the "Real") that are important to each religion. Such an approach is inadequate and unacceptable not only to evangelicals but also to many followers of other religions, for they also take seriously their own unique concepts of God. Furthermore, to describe ultimate reality, or the "Real," in such vague terms has no meaning. To claim that this understanding is a superior and adequate designation for the one whom we are to seek and worship is completely unsatisfactory to an intelligent, thinking person who wants to enter into a meaningful relationship with this being.[77]

Eric Sharpe's observation about a relativistic approach to understand other religions is appropriate here: "Commitment to relativity, in short, is not altogether what it seems, in that it does not affirm the equality of religious traditions as they are, but only the equality of what a certain type of mind has been able to distill out of them."[78]

The Pluralist Rejection of Eternal Punishment

As noted earlier, pluralists hold to some form of universalism. They argue that the idea of eternal punishment is unacceptable and repulsive, unworthy of a loving God. Such writers tend, however, to be selective in the choice of themes that bolster their position. Hell is obviously not an attractive idea; it is, in fact, offensive to most of us. But we cannot avoid the issue of hell if we admit to the problem of personal sin and guilt before a holy and righteous God as set forth in the Bible. The part of the gospel at which pluralists take offense comes to the foreground when discussing the necessity of the Cross and eternal punishment.

Even apart from the biblical data that pluralists reject, universalism has serious problems. The argument that God will ultimately save everyone overlooks the innate, moral outrage and desire for justice that most people experience when they think of the genocide of six million Jews during World War II, the murder of perhaps as many or more Russians under the reign of Stalin in the 1950s, and the more recent genocide in Rwanda, Kosovo, and elsewhere in the 1990s. Stetson indicts universalism on the "insignificance of the relationship between morality and salvation that inheres in it, and the affront this constitutes to the human moral sense."[79]

Stetson also criticizes universalism for its "divine usurpation of the human free will and autonomy" by assuming that God will ultimately save everyone even though some people have deliberately chosen to reject God. In addition, the claim by universalists that God will ultimately save everyone means that "this life on earth—how one lived and what one chose to do and believe—was in the final analysis irrelevant, since it apparently will have made no lasting impact on one's self-formation or destiny."[80]

The Morality of Christian Exclusivism

John Hick and other religious pluralists consider exclusivism to be immoral. Pluralists base their charge mainly upon two claims: (1) exclusivists judge as wrong the truth claims of others and thus wrongfully condemn them; (2) exclusivists have historically been intolerant of the beliefs of others. On the first count, as was stated earlier, it is important to distinguish between how people are treated and how their truth claims are viewed and evaluated. If we accept the position of pluralists that we should not critique the truth claims of others, we are committing intellectual suicide. Refusing to make such evaluations abdicates our responsibility to determine what is right and wrong. It also says that discerning right and wrong with regard to religious truth claims is not important and that truth and error are irrelevant.

Neither are pluralist charges correct in assuming that exclusivism equals animosity in its judgments on the truth claims of other religions. Disagreeing with other people about religious truth claims is not the same as treating them badly. Do we not all have the ability to be courteous while disagreeing with someone? Pluralists are naive in suggesting that Christian exclusivism is responsible for division among individuals and societies and that pluralists are exempt from such charges. As Stetson argues, *all* of us, without exception, have the capacity to treat people badly.[81]

Those who accept the existence of objective religious truth and the authority of the Christian Scriptures believe that truth does exist as distinct from error and that we are to accept revealed truth and reject error (see, for example, 1 John 4:1-6; cf. Paul's call to embrace "sound" or "healthy" doctrine as distinct from unsound, or false, doctrine in 1 Tim. 6:3-5; 2 Tim. 1:13-14; 2:14-4:6). The Bible assumes that we can recognize truth and error and, in fact, *insists* that we do so. Maturity requires such judgments; immaturity (and ultimately spiritual shipwreck) is the lot of those who refuse to submit to the truth and authority of God's Word (Heb. 5:11-14; Eph. 4:11-16; cf. 1 Tim. 1:19-20).

Also, regarding the second charge, at certain points in human history those who called themselves Christians did indeed demonstrate intolerance toward others (e.g., the Crusader attitudes against the Muslim "infidels" and the anti-Semitism that has reared its ugly head at various points in the history of the church). Most exclusivists, however, condemn such attitudes and actions. Scripture exhorts us to show respect toward *all* people (1 Peter 2:17), an exhortation given to Christians regarding how they should respond even when persecuted or treated unjustly. We are not to curse anyone, because everyone bears the divine image (James 3:9-10) and is therefore worthy of dignity and respect. Even when confronted by error, we are given clear directions about objecting to it in a manner that is consistent with Christian conduct (cf. 2 Tim. 2:20-26).

In sum, the charge that exclusivism is immoral simply does not stand. Pluralists might, in fact, examine their own claims of tolerance. They charge that the exclusivist position is wrong, yet they know that exclusivists believe exclusivism to be true. To be consistent with their own view of tolerance, then, should pluralists not withhold judgment? They are censuring exclusivists for dissenting, that is, for making judgments on the truth claims of other religions. But in doing so, pluralists are dissenting from our position; they, too, have made a judgment.[82]

HOW SHOULD WE RESPOND TO A PLURALISTIC WORLD?

Recovering a New Sense of Mission

These are indeed challenging times in which to live as a believer. No clear voice exists among evangelicals to point out the way we should go or how we should respond to challenges posed by religious pluralism. Confusion and fragmentation reign. With prayer and careful thought, consider the following suggestions.

The Need to Reaffirm Christian Exclusivism

Go to back to the basics. It must not be assumed that people know or understand the exclusivist position and what it entails. Christian exclusivism has been the dominant position, not only of evangelicals but also of Christendom in general. Although the exact formulation of exclusivism might vary among evangelicals, D. A. Carson notes that "until the modern period, this was virtually the unanimous view of Christians."[83] Dennis Okholm and Timothy Phillips agree: "Particularism [their preferred term in place of exclusivism] is a hallmark of the salvation-history scheme, the oldest enduring tradition in Christian theology."[84]

Millard Erickson's research identified the following belief principles of exclusivism.[85]

1. All humans are sinners who live apart from God. This combination of disbelief and disobedience means that we are under God's condemnation.
2. Even those who have never heard of Jesus Christ are responsible for their sin and guilt. A genuine general revelation of God exists both in nature and in the human personality from which all persons know God sufficiently to respond positively to Him but have in fact suppressed that knowledge.
3. Salvation cannot be achieved by works. It is available only through God's merciful, gracious provision in offering Jesus Christ as a sacrifice for the sins of all humankind.
4. To be forgiven and saved, one must understand the basis of this salvation, in other words, to have the special revelation that gives knowledge of the gospel.
5. No one is innocent. Because all have sinned, the question of the condition of the unevangelized is not a question of the innocent. All people deserve divine judgment. If God were to give each person what he or she deserves, none would be saved; all would be lost.
6. Adherents of other religions, no matter how sincere or committed, are spiritually lost unless they come to believe in Jesus Christ.

7. Death brings to an end the opportunity for accepting Jesus Christ and thus for eternal salvation. The decisions made in this life have eternal consequences.

8. Jesus Christ's return will be followed by a great judgment, at which point persons will be consigned to eternal fellowship with God if they have accepted Christ or to eternal separation from God and to eternal punishment if they have not.

9. In light of the foregoing facts, Christians have an obligation to take the Good News to unbelievers by telling them of Jesus Christ.

Christian exclusivists themselves differ with regard to the destiny of those who have never heard the message of the gospel. Some people argue that conscious faith in Christ is necessary to be saved; others suggest that in some way truths about salvation are transmitted by means of general revelation, that is, nature, for those who never hear. Still others say that we simply do not know and must trust the outcome of this matter to a wise and holy God.[86] (These issues are discussed in more detail elsewhere in this book.)

Address the Uneasy View of Hell in the Church

We may strongly disagree with pluralists regarding their universalism and their total disregard for the biblical revelation on eternal punishment. We might also affirm Erickson's principles of the orthodox position presented above. It is necessary, however, for all individuals to probe their attitudes on eternal judgement. Pluralism and relativism, as well as our desire to fit in with the world around us, have indeed influenced the church. Personal acquaintance with real people who share our concerns as parents, as neighbors, indeed as fellow humans makes it difficult to affirm that they face eternal punishment if they do not know Jesus Christ as their Savior. Most people we meet "are not so different from us—they are decent human beings who enjoy life, love family, work hard, and try to live morally respectable lives. What right do we have to tell them that our religion is correct and theirs is false?"[87]

Such a mindset, however, has contributed to a growing loss of consensus and a diversity of viewpoints among evangelicals on what the Bible reveals about hell and eternal punishment. These trends "signal a clear departure from Scripture, a lessening of biblical authority."[88] J. I. Packer expresses his concern, stating that the biblical teaching on hell and eternal punishment "is becoming more and more a problem area for belief. Uncertainty is growing, and growing in a way that has a very weakening effect on Christian witness." Packer identifies two areas of concern: first, "Christians in general are increasingly uncertain about the finality of God's condemnation on sinners at the judgment"; second, "Evangelicals in particular are increasingly uncertain about the ongoing existence of those who leave this world in unbelief."[89]

The unpopular teaching of eternal punishment has brought great pressure on the church to move toward a position that is less severe and more civil than the orthodox position, as perceived by many people in contemporary culture. The result is a shift on the part of some evangelicals toward annihilationism. Annihilationism generally acknowledges the reality of a final judgment; those who are condemned, however, will be punished and then destroyed, that is, they will cease to exist and will therefore not suffer eternal punishment.

Packer believes that between annihilationism and universalism, the former "is the more tempting by-path for Evangelicals at this moment."[90] A debate on annihilationism took place in May 1989 among evangelical leaders at the Consultation of Evangelical Affirmations at Trinity Evangelical Divinity School. Annihilationism was not addressed in the final document because of a lack of consensus, underscoring the current openness to this doctrine among evangelicals.[91] Packer's concern is also borne out by such influential evangelicals as John Stott, Clark Pinnock, Michael Green, Stephen Travis, Philip E. Hughes, Edward Fudge, and John Wenham, who have publicly acknowledged their acceptance of or sympathy with the annihilationist view.

The Scriptures, though, are replete with teaching regarding hell and eternal punishment (e.g., Matt. 5:22, 29–30; 8:12; 10:28; 18:9; 25:46; Mark 9:47–48; Luke 16:19–31; Rom. 2:5–16; 2 Thess. 1:7–9; Jude 7; Rev. 14:6–20; 20:10–15). Several recent orthodox writers treat the topic in careful detail.[92] Eternal punishment must be studied afresh, along with its sobering implications both for those who do not have a living relationship with God through Jesus Christ and for those of us who bear the burden of this truth.

Help Believers to Understand the Ambiguity of Our Times and to Live as Pilgrims

Major paradigm shifts have taken place in our postmodern culture, with the accompanying loss of traditional norms and values. Merely lamenting the loss of these things is not helpful. Praying for revival is important but still not enough. Neither is it effective to confront relativism and blatant sin with an angry and pugnacious attitude.

How, then, from a position lacking in both power and influence, can the church respond prophetically? The church has been marginalized. We no longer have an influential voice in our culture; we are simply one voice among many. And the church's commitment to exclusivism further separates her from a "culture of disbelief."[93]

So do we give up? Or do we revisit old truths but with fresh applications? What does it mean, for example, for the church to live as a minority in a hostile environment? What does it mean for the church to die to self (cf. Mark 8:34–38) in the postmodern era? As we walk in the spiritual heritage of Abraham (Heb. 11:8–19), what does it mean to be a pilgrim or sojourner in this world? Do we have the courage to look critically at our lifestyles and to then ask God for help in making changes in the way we use our time and resources in order to promote the gospel in our neighborhoods and around the world?

These questions show the challenges facing the pilgrim and the serious disciple. No one can do it alone. Therefore, we must encourage one another to live out biblical truths before God and the world. It is never easy. And it will cost us.

Evaluate Candidly the Church's Response to the Pressures of a Pluralistic World

As a result of the influences wrought by pluralism and relativism, the church is experiencing the erosion of belief among its members.[94] Peter Berger identifies four ways in which the church may respond to the cultural trends around us and which may serve as a starting point for self-evaluation.[95]

Some Christians adopt the approach of "cognitive bargaining," in which some truths that might be offensive are surrendered and others are maintained. Such an approach leads to the "slippery slope" of compromise. A second approach is that of "cognitive surrender," which concedes that religious pluralism is correct and tempts the church to adapt its message accordingly, thus allowing contemporary ideas to subvert Christianity. A third approach is "cognitive retrenchment," a *defensive* mode in which a church community adopts a fortress mentality to avoid cognitive contamination. This response leads to isolation from the culture that surrounds us. The fourth approach is "cognitive entrenchment," an *offensive* mode by which evangelists attempt to "reconquer society in the name of traditional religion."

We might not be happy with any of these responses, but they can serve as a basis for evaluating how our particular Christian community has responded to the pressures of modern culture. Berger issues a warning regarding the impact of culture and pluralization on religious belief. Although contact with conflicting belief systems affects all the parties involved, the traditionalists generally are the ones who experience the greatest pressures to compromise their worldview.[96] Such pressure occurs because traditionalists fit in least with the culture that surrounds them. Assuming that one fits under the rubric of "traditionalist," one should heed Berger's words; experience corroborates his view.

Os Guinness seems convinced that much of evangelicalism has compromised its witness before the world. He describes the subtle, even unconscious, process by which we have bought into the nonbiblical values of our culture. The first step on the road to compromise is "assumption." Without any intention to compromise, the believer uncritically accepts some feature of modern life or thought "as superior to what Christians now know or do, and therefore worth assuming as true." The second step is "abandonment," when religious values that do not fit with the new assumption of what is true are ignored or removed from the believer's world view. The third step is "adaptation"—"what remains of traditional beliefs and practices is altered to fit in with the new" and now controlling assumption. The final step of compromise takes place through "assimilation," which is the "logical culmination of the first three [steps] . . . Christian assumptions are absorbed by the modern ones," resulting in a modified or different way of thinking that now reflects the culture around it.[97]

Evidence suggests that all of this bargaining and compromise leads us to a diluted theology. Theologian and historian David Wells surveyed evangelical seminary students regarding the influence of theology on their lives. More than one-third of the respondents reported a small influence. These seminary students, the future leaders of the church, expressed doubt about the value of historic church doctrine for knowing religious truth. Wells's conclusion: "They have little confidence that the church's 'long-standing' doctrines are the 'surest guide for knowing ultimate religious truth.'"[98]

Wells, himself a seminary professor, also observed, "Students now enter seminary with less biblical literacy than they used to have, often with less moral literacy, and with a considerable indebtedness to modernity for their self-understanding and for the values by which they live."[99]

Wells's observations reflect a national attitude toward religion. George Barna's 1991 survey of 1,005 American adults led him to conclude that Christianity is becoming viewed "just as one of many competing alternatives in life."[100] Barna's research of the adult population also demonstrated a shift in thinking away from a belief in absolute truth. In 1993, Barna reported that 62 percent of the general population agreed that "it does not matter what religious faith you follow because all faiths teach similar lessons." Forty percent of those who claimed to be born again also agreed with that view, leading Barna to suggest that most people were naive about the differing religious faiths that are around them.[101]

A survey of evangelical youth commissioned by Josh McDowell in 1994 reported that 21 percent of 3,795 young people from thirteen denominations said "it does not matter what religious faith you follow because all faiths teach similar lessons." The survey results of McDowell and Hostetler link a belief in relativism to an openness to other religions and low views concerning the uniqueness of Christianity.[102] A description of the current youth scene, *Generation Next,* published by Barna in 1995, also noted the growing trend in universalism among young people.[103]

Why is there such an openness to other religious groups whose truths contradict the basic tenets of Christianity? Barna proposes that people are exposed to many different religious faiths but only on a superficial level. As a result, they conclude that religions are similar. Such thinking

> embodies a series of philosophies or truths geared to enable a person to lead a happier, more successful life without undermining the ability of others to do the same. In our life-on-the-run culture, who has time to dig deeper to flesh out the idiosyncrasies of each faith, or to determine which is and is not valid as a life foundation? More importantly, from the view of adults, why bother since they all appear to offer the same basic assistance anyway?[104]

In sum, the evidence points to a weakening of integrity in doctrine and practice in the church. Evangelicals have, through the influences of culture and pluralization, been pressured to conform to modernity's own form of orthodoxy. The result is a softening of the conviction with which beliefs are held and practiced.[105] How do individual Christian communities stand in light of these trends?

Practice Honest Reflection and Repentance

When God's people found themselves surrounded by overwhelming circumstances, finding a way out began with a response of humility and repentance along with a renewed confession of dependence on Him.

- When the sons of Israel cried out in the midst of their idolatry and bondage in Egypt, God graciously responded (Exod. 2:24–25; cf. Josh. 24:14–15; cf. also Ezek. 20:5–10, 22).
- During the period of lawlessness recorded in the Judges (2:11–23; cf. 3:7, 9, 12, 15; 4:1, 3; 6:1, 7; etc.), God consistently responded with grace and mercy to the pleas of his disobedient people.
- When Hezekiah found his city surrounded by the Assyrians he, wearing sackcloth and sprinkled with ashes, earnestly sought the Lord, and God again answered and saved his people (Isa. 36–37).
- When with brokenness and repentance over the sins of his people in captivity Daniel appealed to God's great compassion, God again responded with hope and the promise of future restoration.
- God showed Himself able to deliver his people when Nehemiah wept and prayed before Him about the condition of the remnant and the walls of Jerusalem (Nehemiah 1; cf. Ezra's prayer, 9:1–15).
- When the apostles were threatened by the religious leaders, they beseeched their Sovereign God to defend them (Acts 4:1–31).
- The apostle Paul recounts the desperate circumstances that he and others faced, when they despaired even of life, and a sentence of death hung over them. Yet God delivered them. Paul relates the lesson of that experience: ". . . that we should not trust in ourselves, but in God who raises the dead," using the prayers of others on their behalf (2 Cor. 1:3–11).

One might well ask how this discussion relates to the challenges of religious pluralism. If the church is weak spiritually, she will not withstand the pressures of pluralism. The worldliness of the church in the United States is self-evident. In many places, the church has bought into the values of materialism, pragmatism, and the health-and-wealth gospel.[106] Evangelicals are quick to condemn abortion and homosexuality—and justifiably so; but many succumb to self-righteousness, gluttony, and infatuation with the toys of our culture, all of which dull their sensibility to God's concern for personal and corporate holiness. It is right to pray with devotion for those around us who are lost and facing eternal punishment (Col. 4:2–6). Charity is said to start at home but so does repentance of sin. Our appeals to God's grace and mercy must be accompanied by a corresponding admission of our bankruptcy before God. With all of our possessions, technology, and methodological knowledge, do we sincerely believe that without Christ we can do nothing? Those who speak of the coming judgment of the world must also remember that judgment first begins with the family of God (1 Peter 4:17).

Reaffirm Biblical Teachings with Careful Instruction from the Scriptures

The church is the "pillar and foundation of the truth" (1 Tim. 3:15 NIV). As such, one of her primary tasks is to proclaim and defend biblical truth, as well as to display this truth in its corporate conduct. Strong Christian spirituality is tied to a solid understanding and personal application of the Christian Scriptures.[107] But the hard evidence presented by Hunter, Barna, Carson,[108] Wells,[109] and others regarding biblical illiteracy in the church and the new openness to other religious faiths should be of great concern to church leaders. Part of the new reality with which church leaders must contend is that to a greater extent than they realize, church members have been influenced by the religious currents that surround us. The result has often been syncretism, which is the mixing of different forms of religious beliefs and/or practices, even when they contradict one another. If left unchecked, this tendency will alter the Christian faith such that it no longer remains true to its theological foundations. (The statements of various persons at the beginning of this chapter are examples of syncretism.)

As those who are responsible for biblical instruction (or who are preparing for that task), readers—before condemning the erosion of what were once firmly held beliefs on such basic doctrinal truths—must ask themselves some hard, personal questions. Have we mistakenly assumed that believers in our churches firmly hold to the uniqueness of Christ as the only Savior of the world? Do those we teach truly believe that people who do not hear about Christ are without hope and face eternal punishment? We cannot assume that people know what they believe—or that they believe what they know.

Bruce Camp, a missions consultant for the Evangelical Free Church, was skeptical of reports that evangelical Christians indicated a growing interest in universalism. He conducted his own survey among 816 Christian adults across the United States. He found that 55 percent of the respondents did not fully support or agree with the statement "Men and women who don't hear the gospel will go to hell."[110]

Have we been naive about the influence that a religiously pluralistic world has on church members? How recently have we provided instruction on the person and work of Jesus Christ, clearly relating these teachings to the crosscurrents of religious pluralism at work in our culture? Are we keeping ourselves fully informed about the vast cultural changes taking place around us, and are we able to address them from a biblical perspective? If church leaders have isolated themselves from these realities, how much more may this be the case with church members who are trying to balance their daily responsibilities of work and family and, at the same time, are trying to understand the bewildering changes taking place around them?

Biblical illiteracy should be an embarrassment to evangelicals. And the problem must be laid at the feet of the shepherds who lead the flock. The teaching function is one of the pastor's primary tasks (e.g., Eph. 4:7–16; 1 Tim. 4:6–16; 2 Tim. 2:2; 4:1–4; Titus 1:9), and pastor-teachers are responsible for teaching the whole counsel of God (Acts 20:27; cf. Col. 1:9). The least this task involves is grounding believers in consistent Bible exposition and theology, carefully showing the Bible's relevance to daily life (cf. Titus 2:1). The New Testament letters are still a remarkable model for communicating truth.

This process of teaching and learning the Bible will not be easy for many pastors or for their congregations. Some preachers and teachers will have to change from merely preaching stories or homilies that entertain to doing the harder work of digging into the Scriptures. In some cases, pastors might need to relearn how to wrestle with the meaning of a text in order to explain its significance to believers. For some leaders, digging deeper into Scripture will mean rethinking priorities and readjusting schedules in order to find time for renewing the discipline of study. This does not mean that pastors should hide behind their desks and ignore other pastoral responsibilities. But other church members might be trained so that pastors can delegate the administration of programs and other aspects of ministry so that, like the early church leaders, the shepherds can dedicate themselves to prayer and the ministry of the Word (cf. Acts 6:1–6).

A second reason the process might be difficult is that pastors often feel constrained to fulfill the expectations of people who don't want to be challenged to think. Some congregations have been socialized into expecting an entertaining message that is long on stories but short on substance. Replacing substance for style might be threatening to pastors because congregants might decide to "walk." But the long-term consequences for perpetuating our biblical ignorance will be reflected in the church's spiritual well-being. If biblical illiteracy is a problem, pastors and congregations must work together to rectify it. Refocusing on serious Bible study will not be easy, but it will be a step forward.

Consider one more word regarding the content of preaching: Pastors cannot afford to teach and preach piecemeal. Communication by sound bytes might be fashionable and popular, but it does not produce mature, discerning Christians. Teachers of the Word must think and communicate in terms of the larger story line of the Bible so that people see how the various parts of the Bible relate to the whole. Teaching a part of the Bible as it relates to the whole, illustrated by D. A. Carson in the *Gagging of God*, is essential in communicating the meaning of Scriptures to listeners.[111] A long-range plan of teaching can be developed that addresses pluralism in the context of the Bible's story line. The pulpit themes addressed in ministry can easily be supplemented with teaching in small groups and in Sunday school classes as part of a missions curriculum.[112]

The authority of Scripture as the basis for examining the truth claims of other religions must be reaffirmed in the minds of Christians. Wells reminds us that the biblical writers believed that God's revelation was true "in an absolute sense. It was not merely true *to them;* it was not merely true *in their time;* it was not true *approximately.* What God had given was true universally, absolutely, and enduringly."[113]

Recover the Meaning of Verbal "Witness"

The influence of pluralism has also affected our witness. Hunter suggests that those who hold to absolute truth claims may still yield to the pressures of contact with people from other religious traditions by refusing to evangelize because of a "a softening of the dogmatic insistence on conversion (i.e., 'God is a just God. Who am I to pass judgment? Let Him be the Judge')." The result is that believers trivialize the public implications of their religious beliefs and compensate by overemphasizing implications in the private sphere.[114] Pluralism's pressure threatens evangelicalism's ability to remain orthodox and defend its public claim to universal truth against the claims of other religious systems.

Although exclusivism normally incites strong hostility, evangelicalism, as Hunter notes, has been widely accepted. The reason, he suggests, is found in evangelicalism's "cultural demeanor," which softens and polishes the more rigid elements of the Christian worldview in an attempt to make it more sociable and acceptable.[115] In contrast to earlier, more repugnant forms of evangelicalism, contemporary evangelicalism has attempted to be more civil in its relationship to those outside the Christian faith. Hunter suggests, however, that this "civilizing process" has involved less frequent mention of orthodox teachings that are deemed offensive to outsiders. These "offensive" doctrines include the sinfulness of man, sinful conduct and lifestyles, the consequent wrath of God experienced in future judgment, eternal death, and torment in hell.

The trivialization—or softening—of certain biblical teachings is often accompanied by an emphasis on the benefits of the gospel (inner peace, true joy and happiness, dependable fellowship, and a source of strength in times of need, all in addition to an eternal life in heaven) and a redefining of love in terms of civility rather than a "self-effacing and sacrificial giving." This approach, Hunter observes, creates a social posture that says, in effect, "Don't take offense, but here is the truth." The result is a perception that evangelicalism reflects "good taste" and is superior to other religions, not because of its truth claims but because it offers superior benefits.[116]

With regard to how faith is reduced to private and internal belief, Wells assesses the influence of modernity on the witness of the evangelical church:

> Many Evangelicals quietly assume, perhaps even without much thought, that it would be uncouth and uncivil to push this private dimension too noticeably or noisily on others or into the public sphere. The right of each individual to his or her own private thoughts and beliefs is held to be both axiomatic and inviolable. So it is that the particularities of Evangelical faith—the things that make it *different*— are dissolved. Modern culture grants me absolute freedom to believe whatever I want to believe—so long as I keep those beliefs from infringing on the consciousness or behavior of anyone else, especially on points of controversy.[117]

Wells reminds us that the New Testament witness was grounded in the objective facts of Christ and His death on the cross, not in a personal experience with God. He argues that

> . . . it is anything but clear that this [witness in the early church] should be understood as the use of personal autobiography to persuade others that they should commit themselves to Christ. New Testament witness was witness to the objective truth of Christian faith, truth that had been experienced; our witness today is witness to our own faith, and in affirming its validity we may become less interested in its truthfulness than in the fact that it seems to work.[118]

When sharing our faith, then, we often embrace a subjective approach. The emphasis is placed on *our* experience and the benefits *we* have received as a result of trusting in Christ. The danger in this approach is that people will simply acknowledge our experience and perhaps even be happy for us because we have found something that "helps" us. Listeners, however, may ignore what our truth means for them. It is *our* experience, after all, not theirs. Everyone's experience is different. So why should they consider it, *unless* it is true not only for us but for everyone and is necessary and urgent for *everyone* to hear?

The witness of the early church bears out the Christian message as true and urgent. Although it is certainly valid to bear witness to a changed life, David Wells also observed that

> The early Christians did not preach their *experience* of Christ; that would have been to promote a form of religion like any other form of religion. Rather, they preached the Christ of that experience. They preached not what was internally interesting but what was externally true. God had raised him from the dead, and this was a matter of history, not simply of internal perception. . . . The fact that God's truth was transmitted through events external to the individual meant that it was objective, and the fact that it was objective meant, further, that his truth was *public*.[119]

Take a fresh look at the book of Acts to see how early Christians bore witness to the risen Lord.[120] It is necessary to teach and train Christians to share their faith from a more biblical perspective, and at the same time listen carefully to learn where new believers stand in their respective spiritual journeys. The "quick-fix" approach to evangelism is to be avoided. The biblical illiteracy apparent in our culture means that people do not understand basic terms such as *sin* and *salvation*. Committing to long-term relationships allows us time to sow the seed and give people time to absorb and understand what they have heard.

Defend the Morality of Evangelism

Evangelism is morally offensive to pluralists because Christians ask non-Christians to recognize the error of their beliefs and change their minds about them. Truly, we call people to receive God's free offer of salvation in Christ through faith in Him and repentance from their sin (cf. Acts 2:38). Many people equate such efforts with proselytism (or "sheep stealing"). But evangelism and proselytism are different. Proselytism involves the use of morally unacceptable coercion and manipulation to persuade people to accept a certain point of view. Exclusivists reject such motives and methods (cf. 2 Cor. 4:1–2; 1 Thess. 2:2–13).[121]

Evangelism, however, means simply proclaiming the gospel, the good news that "Christ died for our sins according to the Scriptures, and that He was buried, and that he was raised on the third day according to the Scriptures" (1 Cor. 15:3–4 NASB). Evangelism is the logical result of our belief that Jesus is the only Savior of the world. It is this belief that gives believers an urgent, moral obligation to share the Good News. The apostle Paul recognized this: "Woe is me if I do not preach the gospel!" (1 Cor. 9:16 NASB).

John Hick's statement, that what people believe is usually determined by their birthplace, should give us pause. If people are indeed born into spiritual darkness, what is our responsibility if we have tasted forgiveness and have been entrusted with the Good News? Do we share God's concern for those who are "dead in their trespasses and sins," earnestly desiring that they should not perish but come to repentance (2 Peter 3:9)? Are we genuinely concerned about those who have never heard, and are we driven to ask the Lord of the harvest to send forth laborers around the world? Do we give sacrificially to support those whom God raises up to take the Good News to the unreached? Can we say with Paul, "I have great sorrow and unceasing grief in my heart. For I could wish that I myself were accursed, *separated* from Christ for the sake of my brethren, my kinsmen according to the flesh . . ." (Rom. 9:2–3)?

Would we not attempt to rescue people trapped in a burning home? How much more should be our compassion and concern for those who face the consequences for their sin—eternal punishment and separation from their Creator. God is concerned for them (cf. Ezek. 18:23–32; 2 Peter 3:9), and as imitators of God we should be concerned, too.

Learn How to Engage with Integrity People from Other Faiths

True tolerance means treating people with respect even while disagreeing with them. Our witness involves communicating the truth not only with words but also with our lives. Never underestimate the impact of modeling truth with loving actions toward others. All that believers do should be done with a loving spirit, avoiding a condescending or belittling attitude, even when we speak truth that will offend. No place exists for the pugnacious, mean-spirited attitudes that sometimes characterize Christians. Hick's observation that the morality observed in Christians is not much different from that observed in followers of other religions serves as a reminder. God expects believers to display ethical standards that are grounded in His character and that grow out of our relationship to Him through Jesus Christ (cf. 1 Peter 2:9ff.; Eph. 4-6; Rom. 12-16; Col. 3:1-4:6).

Christ calls us to engage all people, not just those who are "like us." Reaching out to those of other faiths means stepping out of our comfort zones. And, when building relationships with others, it is necessary to be sensitive to cultural differences. Visiting missionaries can offer tips on how to reach out to Muslims, Hindus, and others.

If you live near a college or university, international students would love to be invited to your home. Just being friendly is important. Those who stand out as different in our culture usually feel as we would if we lived in their country—strange! We all share the human condition and have the same need to be loved and accepted. Focus, then, on what all humans have in common. People from other countries are often lonely and are usually open to a person who befriends them and accepts them without being condescending or patronizing. Ask them to tell you about their culture, then listen. We are often more interested in talking about our own lives than in listening to others tell us about their countries, their interests, and their concerns. As your friendship grows, ask gently about their religious beliefs. In response, be respectful, and do not attack what they believe; criticism usually causes people to withdraw. Explain what you believe without being pushy, and if they are open to discussing religious beliefs, you might suggest having a Bible study. If you invite them to your church, expect that they might invite you to their place of worship.

Be confident that God has placed people with other religious beliefs in your life for a reason, but don't expect them to respond to the gospel the first time you share it. Be committed to a long-term relationship. Cultural and religious differences are not quickly overcome. One person has said that a Muslim must hear the Good News a hundred times before being saved. Just love people. If you make a mistake, and it appears you have offended them, apologize and keep working at just being a loving and caring friend. Be involved in their lives, and welcome them into yours. Remember that ultimately God is the evangelist; He is the one who saves. Our responsibility is to be witnesses with our lives and words. Sow the seed, and trust God for the harvest in His time. God does not give up on such people; He did not give up on us. Let us not give up on those whom God brings into our lives.[122]

PROCLAIMING THE NAME

The "religious supermarket of modern pluralism" has complicated religious discussion. As Eastern and Western religious thought interact, the question of *why* one should believe in God is usurped by *which* God one should believe.[123] The current challenges are to rethink our approach to defending the Christian faith and answer the new questions that confront us.

The current formulations and claims of religious pluralism are sophisticated and intimidating. Christians often find themselves on unfamiliar ground and uncertain about how to respond. Some of the weaknesses (and there are many) of the pluralist position have already been outlined. But evangelicals would do well to be self-critical as well, acknowledging areas—such as Christian exclusivism—where we have succumbed to the pressures of the world.

The challenge of living in a religiously pluralistic world, although new to North Americans, is not a new phenomenon. The early church was founded in an environment where people were faced with many religious alternatives. But, as we see in the New Testament and especially in the book of Acts, the early church fathers were convinced of the truthfulness of the gospel and proclaimed it with boldness. The church in Asia and elsewhere has, for centuries, confronted and wrestled with the problem of bringing the gospel into places where followers of other religions abound. Those believers have much to teach us in the West about living faithfully for Jesus Christ in a pluralistic world.

Religious pluralism is related to postmodernism (discussed in chapter 8), a movement that is currently popular in many segments of North American and European society.[124] Understanding how religious pluralism reflects the larger cultural ideas and values that surround and influence the church and society will help us offer a broader-based response. This is more helpful than merely addressing isolated, personal concerns while overlooking the larger issues.

Prominent evangelical scholars such as Ronald Nash and D. A. Carson view religious pluralism as one of the most serious contemporary threats to the Christian faith.[125] If current trends continue, the church will find itself increasingly marginalized. Charges of arrogant intolerance might so threaten us that we will allow our voice to be silenced.

Rather than display a superficial triumphalism, let us ask God for the courage, grace, and sober discernment to respond with the integrity that marked so many first-century followers of Jesus. In the midst of a pluralistic world, they willingly paid the price of following Christ and boldly proclaimed that name that is above all names—Jesus Christ, God's only Son, the only Savior and hope of the world.[126]

CHAPTER 8

THE CHALLENGE OF POSTMODERNISM

STEVEN MCAVOY

CAN TRUTH BE KNOWN?

The concept of truth, absolute unchanging truth, is primary to Christian orthodoxy and thus to Christian missions.[1] As Jesus stood before Pilate, He claimed to bear witness to the truth and said, "Every one who is of the truth hears My voice." Pilate asked, "What is truth?" (John 18:37–38).[2] His question addressed, not *the* truth that stood before him, but the *concept* or *nature* of truth. Pilate was either convinced that there was no answer or did not want to hear it, for he did not wait for an answer.

A Centuries-Old Search

Down through the centuries, other "Pilates" have questioned the nature and knowability of truth. But until the time of the Enlightenment, humankind, and especially Immanuel Kant (1724–1804),[3] traditionally held truth to be absolute, objective, and having a propositional correspondence to reality. It was knowable.[4] Such is no longer the case. Since the Enlightenment, relativism (the belief that truth is relative, not absolute) has made inroads into the intellectual and philosophical landscape. Relativism has so eroded the thinking of today's world that contemporary thought and culture are awash, without intellectual and moral roots. Relativism is now the underlying assumption of Western culture.

In the early battle between modernism and fundamentalism, modernists evidenced a tendency to abandon absolutes. Still, the battle did not so much concern the *concept* of truth as it did the *content* of truth and how truth was to be ascertained. Among other things, modernism held (1) that truth is determined strictly by reason; (2) that belief in the supernatural is irrational and anti-intellectual; and (3) that all knowledge is determined by empiricism, that is, what people can experience by their own senses. Christians opposed these ideas.

Modern Developments in the Search

The question now is no longer "What is true?" but "What is truth?" The very *nature* of truth is in question. Postmodernism holds that truth—hence, morality—is relative. Contrary to modernists, postmodernists teach that there "is no such thing as objective rationality (that is reason unaffected by bias) in the sense that modernists use the term. Objective reason is a myth."[5] For the postmodernist, "reality is in the mind of the beholder. Reality is what's real to me, and I construct my own reality in my mind. . . . We cannot judge things in another culture or in another person's life, because our reality may be different than theirs. . . . Intuition and feelings might tell us more about reality than does reason."[6] Rationalism having failed, postmodernism is giving way to irrationalism. Modernists did not believe that the Bible was true; postmodernists have thrown out the category of truth altogether.

> Before, in both the modern and the premodern eras, religion involved beliefs about what was real. There either is a God, or there is not. Jesus was either the incarnate Son of God, or He was just a man. Miracles happened, or they did not. Some Christians vehemently disagreed with each other: Is there such a place as Purgatory? Does Mary intercede for us in Heaven? Are some predestined to damnation? But these were disagreements over questions of fact. Today religion is not seen as a set of beliefs about what is real and what is not. Rather, religion is seen as a preference, a choice. . . . We believe in what we like. We believe what we want to believe.[7]

Signs of this intellectual revolution appear everywhere—on university campuses and television screens, in the citadels of higher learning, and in the lifestyle of the average American. Relativism, widely accepted by postmodernist society, has gained a foothold even within evangelical churches.[8] More than a decade ago, Professor Allan Bloom of the University of Chicago said, "There is one thing a professor can be absolutely certain of: almost every student entering the university believes, or says he believes, that truth is relative."[9]

The Effect on America and Beyond

In 1991, the Barna Research Group reported that 28 percent of Americans agree strongly, and an additional 39 percent agree somewhat (for a total of 67 percent), that "there is no such thing as absolute truth; different people can define truth in conflicting ways and still be correct."[10] What is more alarming, 53 percent of "born again" Christians and 53 percent of adults associated with evangelical churches held a relativistic view of truth. When polled again in 1994, "a staggering 72 percent of American adults— almost three out of four—affirmed some kind of relativism."[11]

Moreover, relativism is not just an American phenomenon. As Veith recently stated,

> Now the assumptions of modernism have fallen apart, from Moscow to San Francisco. The enlightenment is discredited. Reason is dethroned, even on university campuses. The Industrial Revolution is giving way to the Information Age. Society, technology, values, and basic categories of thought are shifting. A new way of looking at the world is emerging.
>
> . . . These views respond to the failure of the Enlightenment by jettisoning truth altogether. The intellect is replaced by the will. Reason is replaced by emotion. Morality is replaced by relativism.[12]

And one philosopher of ethics puts it,

> Ours is an age where ethics has become obsolete. It is superseded by science, deleted by psychology, dismissed as emotive by philosophy. It is drowned in compassion, evaporates into aesthetics, and retreats before relativism. The usual moral distinctions between good and bad are simply drowned in a maudlin emotion in which we feel more sympathy for the murderer than the murdered, for the adulterer than the betrayed, and in which we have actually begun to believe that the real guilty party, the one who somehow caused it all, is the victim and not the perpetrator of the crime.[13]

Carl F. H. Henry said, "Never has the question been more important whether our beliefs are simply scientific tentatives, speculative conjecture, private psychic certitudes, or universally valid truth."[14]

The New Tolerance

One of the watchwords of postmodernism is *tolerance*. But this tolerance no longer means that "all people have a right to their opinions" and that everyone should recognize and respect that right. Today's definition of *tolerance* considers every person's beliefs, values, lifestyle, and truth claims to be *equally true* or *equally valid*. So now not only do all people have an equal right to their opinions and beliefs but all opinions, beliefs, values, and truth claims are equal. Never mind that this position defies the laws of reason and logic; reason and logic are also *passé*.

Thus, the Christian who speaks against such things as homosexuality, pornography, abortion, and so on, is labeled "intolerant." To the postmodernist, "what is true for you is not necessarily true for me; what is right for you might not be right for me." For the postmodernist, there is no transcendent, fixed polestar by which to judge morality. On the surface, this new "tolerance" appears to be a very charitable worldview. It treats all opinions, human ideologies, and moral viewpoints as equal. Herein lies the problem. The issue is no longer the *truth* of the message but whether one is *right* to proclaim it. Exclusivistic truth claims such as "there is no salvation apart from Jesus Christ" (John 14:6) are dismissed as intolerant, closed-minded, arrogant, or bigoted. Truth has been abandoned for the new tolerance.

Reason has also been abandoned. As Professor Harvey Cox of Harvard Divinity School noted in 1984, "Both reason and science, which arrived in the modern world as its darlings, have fallen from their previous positions of esteem."[15] With the failure of modernism's empirical rationalism, postmodernism views skeptically such objective notions of reality and questions whether pure objective reason even exists. The heirs of modernism, which deified reason, have recognized its fraudulence and have responded by jettisoning truth and reason altogether. The result is intellectual confusion and moral anarchy.

A World Adrift

As postmodern civilization enters the twenty-first century and the new millennium, it does so without a fixed reference point outside of itself by which to determine what is true and what is false, what is right and what is wrong, what is important and what is trivial. Relevance is determined by feelings, intuition, and emotion. Right and wrong are determined by individual preference. Postmodernism has "sanctified the rights of the self and charged malice to any obstructer of those rights."[16] Charles W. Colson did not overstate the case when he said that "the greatest controversy of our age is the crisis of truth."[17] *Perhaps the greatest challenge that the church faces as it enters the twenty-first century is the issue of relativism and its denial of absolutes.* Leith Anderson is correct:

> Some mistakenly think the crisis centers on pluralism. Actually the issue is that of relativism. . . .
>
> Cultural pluralism is already a reality in North America, just as it was a reality in the first-century Roman Empire. While this is uncomfortable for many people, it is not necessarily a negative for the gospel of Jesus Christ. Christianity has often flourished when openly competing with contrary ideas.
>
> The greater crisis is in the growing acceptance of relativism, which denies the existence of absolutes. There is a popular belief that "the only absolute is that there are no absolutes." Individualism and tolerance are elevated as the highest virtues. Where relativism prevails, there is no call to choose between competing claims for absolute truth. Instead the call is for isolation and acceptance that "you have your truth and I have my truth and let's just leave each other alone."[18]

What Is at Stake?

The Christian faith is founded on the God of truth and His true Word (2 Sam. 7:28; Pss. 119:160; 146:6; Isa. 65:16; Jer. 10:10; John 17:17).[19] If people are to be saved from sin and death, made heirs of the "spirit of wisdom and of revelation in the knowledge" of God (Eph. 1:17), and made "alive . . . together with Christ" (2:5), then what we believe and understand about the nature of truth matters a great deal. If we hope to evangelize, preach, teach, and proclaim the gospel of Jesus Christ as the truth of Scripture, then we must understand not only the nature of truth but also the culture to whom we speak and its viewpoint of truth. Pilate's question is relevant in light of today's relativism. The church must have an answer to the question, "What is truth?"

Focusing, then, on the nature and knowledge of truth, particularly as it relates to the issue of relativism versus absolutism, the following questions will be addressed:

1. What is the nature of truth?
2. Can truth be known? If so, how?
3. What must we then do about it?

THE NATURE OF TRUTH

Although many conflicting theories on the nature of truth exist, it is fair to say that all views other than the correspondence view can legitimately be categorized as *non*correspondence views.[20] It is not the purpose here to engage with representatives of the different schools of thought but to explore the biblical and philosophical evidence, which weighs decisively in favor of the correspondence view of truth.

Biblical and Philosophical Evidence

Evidences for discovering the nature of truth are both biblical and philosophical. Objections have been raised to both categories. Of philosophy, some say that it has no place in theology. In this view, Colossians 2:8 is a warning to avoid philosophy. But philosophy is the "handmaid" to theology. Philosophical thinking "is an integral part of the way that we understand and disseminate revealed truth."[21] Logic is a necessary presupposition of all thought, including thought about God. God has revealed Himself and created man with the ability to use reason and logic that we might know God.[22] It is inconceivable, therefore, that humankind's reason and logic would be different *in nature* than God's own. *A* cannot be non-*A* either for God or our world. Reason and logic are essential to knowing truth and the true God. Moreover, certain truths are undeniably self-evident. Philosophical arguments, therefore, do have validity.

Regarding the biblical evidence, some people conclude that the Bible does not teach a concept or theory of the *nature* of truth. A. F. Holmes says, "Scripture does not directly address the question of the nature and tests of truth which has received so much philosophical attention."[23] According to John S. Feinberg, the biblical writers do "seem to incorporate some form of the correspondence theory . . . but they do not teach (assert as correct) any *theory* of truth."[24] He concludes his discussion with a question-answer: "Does Scripture, then, teach a theory of truth . . . ?" His answer is *no*.[25]

Although the Bible might not provide a *systematic account* of the nature of truth in either its theological or philosophical dimensions, we cannot conclude that the Bible teaches us nothing about the nature of truth.[26] It might be true that the *writers* did not teach or "assert as correct" any theory of truth, but that doesn't necessarily mean that *Scripture* does not teach a theory of truth. Should not the focus be on the completed body of Scriptures (i.e., the *writings*) rather than on the writers? It is Scripture, after all, that is inspired (2 Tim. 3:16), not the writers. The writers were "moved by the Holy Spirit" (2 Peter 1:21), but it is the writing, the body of Scripture, that is said to be inspired. Therefore, it is not invalid to draw doctrinal conclusions from Scripture, conclusions that an individual writer might not have intended but that, taken as a whole, the Scriptures do teach.

It may be said, for example, that nowhere did the biblical writers *teach* or *assert* the doctrine of the Trinity, yet every evangelical Christian would affirm that *the Bible teaches it*. It might also be said that no writer of Scripture "bothers to give proof of God's existence, of which they were all only too aware."[27] Yet we do not conclude that the Bible teaches nothing about the existence of God. Nor do we stop short of systematic "theology proper" (doctrine of God) based upon what the Bible says.

It is possible, therefore, to arrive at a biblical concept of truth much the same as we arrive at a biblical concept of God and the Trinity. By induction, we gather the evidence from which certain principles can be formulated. From these principles, logical deductions can be made that should prove to be true as long as our premises are true and our logic is sound. In short, because God is rational and has communicated to us rationally, we may in like manner (by the use of reason) determine not only *what* He has said but also *how* He has said it. If God is the God of truth (and the Bible says that He is, Deut. 32:4; Isa. 65:16), and He has communicated to us truthfully (and the Bible says that He has, Ps. 119:160; John 17:17), and if the Bible is God's inspired Word to us (and it claims to be just that, 2 Tim. 3:16), then we should be able to determine with confidence something about the nature of truth, and this regardless of whether it was any given writer's intention to teach anything concerning the *nature* of truth. John V. Dahms states "that what we consider to be the view of truth implicit in the Scriptures need not have been the conscious understanding of any biblical writer."[28]

According to Norman Geisler, one of the implications of the correspondence view of truth is "that whatever the writer of a scriptural book actually *affirmed* is to be taken as true, even if he did not intend to affirm it. That is to say, the Bible could say *more* than its human authors intended it to, since God could have intended more by it than the authors did."[29] God is, after all, the ultimate Author of Scripture. The human writers of Scripture, superintended as they were by the Holy Spirit, composed and recorded without error God's revelation to humankind as He wanted it recorded (Isa. 59:21; Matt. 22:43; Acts 4:24-25; 1 Cor. 2:13; Heb. 1:1-2; 2 Peter 1:20-21).[30]

The Sum of Biblical Evidence

The Bible, then, should teach us something about the nature of truth, as indeed it does. Scripture affirms a number of basic propositions or principles concerning the nature of truth that may be reduced to the following two over-arching propositions:

1. Truth is theocentric and absolute (to affirm the one is to affirm the other).
2. Truth is correspondence to reality.

From these two propositions, a number of logical deductions—termed philosophical implications—can be made.

Biblical Perspectives

Although a biblical theory of truth cannot be built on word studies alone, the words for *truth* studied in context direct us toward a biblical concept of truth. The word *truth* occurs 201 times in the *New American Standard Bible* (92 times in the OT, 109 times in the NT); *truthful* 4 times (2 in the OT, 2 in the NT), *truthfully* once (Luke 9:27), *true* 87 times (28 in the OT, 59 in the NT), and *truly* 141 times (31 in the OT, 110 in the NT).

The Old Testament. The most common Old Testament word for *truth* is *emet* and its cognate, or kindred term, *emunah*. Both words are derived from the verb *aman* (cf. English "Amen"), which in its basic stem means "to confirm, support or uphold" and, in its derived stems, "to be established, be faithful, be certain," and "firmness, fidelity, and steadiness." The basic root idea is firmness or certainty.

The word *truth* in the English versions of the Old Testament almost always corresponds to the Hebrew *emet*, although it is not always translated that way. Sometimes it is rendered "faithfulness." That meaning, however, more properly and frequently belongs to *emunah*. The noun *emet* (the most common form of the root *aman*) is frequently used of speaking the truth as opposed to falsity or falsehood (Josh. 9:15–16, 19; 1 Kings 17:24; Isa. 48:1; 59:13–14; Jer. 5:1, 3; 9:3, 5–6); hence, *emet* is "what is true" or "that which corresponds to the facts."

This term is used in several categories of context, "all of which relate to God directly or indirectly."[31] It is sometimes used of God's Word (e.g., Ps. 119:142, 151, 160; Dan. 10:21). At other times, it is used to denote the "ways" of God toward humankind (e.g., Josh. 10:21; 24:14; 1 Kings 2:4;

Pss. 26:3; 86:11; 91:4; Isa. 38:3), who in turn are obliged to reflect this same characteristic toward God and one another (e.g., Exod. 18:21; Neh. 7:2; Ps. 15:2; Zech. 8:16). Because God is true, He expects His people to be true. As Moberly says,

> A fundamental principle of OT (indeed biblical) ethics is the imita-
> tion of God: as Yahweh is, likewise Israel is to be. This is most fa-
> mously expressed in Lev. 19:2, "Be holy because I, the LORD your
> God, am holy" (for NT formulations of this principle, see, e.g., Matt
> 5:43-48; 1 Cor. 11:1). It is no surprise, therefore, that if Yahweh is
> faithful, it is expected of Israel that they should be faithful too.[32]

More important, *emet* is also used to depict the *character* of God (e.g., Exod. 34:6, *by God's own testimony;* Pss. 31:5; 40:10-11; 57:10; 86:15; 89:14; Isa. 65:16; Zech. 7:8). Often it occurs in couplets or in combination with other words that ascribe attributes to God such as *lovingkindness* (Gen. 24:27; Exod. 34:6), *righteousness* (Ps. 85:10-11), *living* (1 Thess. 1:9; 1 Tim. 3:15), and *justice* (Ps. 111:7).

Similar in meaning to the noun *emet* is *emunah*, usually translated "faith-fulness." *Emunah* also occurs frequently as an attribute of Yahweh (e.g., Pss. 33:4; 36:5; 40:10) and, like *emet*, is often used in close association with other words depicting the nature or character of God (e.g., Deut. 32:4; Pss. 92:2; 143:1).

Again, the principle of imitation applies. Just as God is a God of faithful-ness, so must His people be. The Bible does not lack examples of God's people failing to be faithful, but never do we read this of God. He is the God of truth; a faithful God who cannot lie (Titus 1:2; Heb. 6:18).

The major theological significance of the Old Testament word for *truth (emet)* is its frequent use in depicting the character of God. The same may be said for its kindred word *emunah* and, more indirectly, its root word *aman* and its cognates. Jack B. Scott concludes his study of *emet:* "As we study its various contexts, it becomes manifestly clear that there is no truth in the biblical sense, i.e., valid truth, outside God. All truth comes from God and is truth because it is related to God."[33] Truth in the Old Testament, then, is (1) a characteristic of God, also to be reflected by His people, and (2) facticity, or correspondence to reality. Truth is theocentric and corresponds to things as they really are.

The Septuagint. In the Septuagint (LXX)—the Greek translation of the

Old Testament—*aletheia* almost always is used to translate the Hebrew *emet,* which, as we have seen, denotes "what is true." It was necessary for the translators of the Hebrew Old Testament to use some word to translate *emet,* and the word they chose was *aletheia.* According to Spicq, "In the LXX, *aletheia* never expresses a metaphysical concept."[34] Thus, regardless of the way the word *aletheia* was used by some Greek philosophers (see next section below), to say that in using *aletheia* the translators imported a metaphysical concept into the Old Testament or that they understood the Old Testament word *emet* to carry such a metaphysical meaning would be incorrect.

The New Testament. In the New Testament, too, the primary word for "truth" is *aletheia,* occurring 109 times in the Greek New Testament. With few exceptions, it is always translated "truth." Kindred words are *alethes,* "true, truthful"; *alethinos,* "authentic, genuine"; and *alethos,* "truly, really."

Sometimes, too much is made of the etymology of *aletheia* and the fact that in secular Greek (e.g., Parmenides and especially Plato) *aletheia* is sometimes used metaphysically to refer to "the notion of truth as against mere appearances and as that which belongs only to the realm of timelessness and immateriality."[35] But as Thiselton demonstrates, first, little evidence exists that the etymology of the word played any part in determining its meaning in the later Greek of the Classical and Hellenistic periods. Second, even within Greek philosophy itself, abundant evidence exists that *aletheia* is used to denote "truth" that "has a more positive relation to the material world."[36] In short, secular Greek also commonly used the word *aletheia* for (1) that which stands in opposition to falsehood, (2) that which corresponds to the facts, and (3) that which is real, authentic, or genuine. These secular uses are in conformity with the New Testament, in which *truth* is used in contrast to falsehood or falsity and to denote that which corresponds to reality, or the facts of the matter (John 8:44–47; Rom. 1:25; 3:4–8; 9:1; Acts 26:24–25; 2 Cor. 13:8).

The New Testament, therefore, does not present a different concept of truth than that of the Old Testament, a fact particularly apparent in the New Testament writers' importation of the Hebrew *aman* to the Greek *amen* (cf. English "amen"). *Amen* occurs 129 times in the New Testament, most of which are found in Jesus' words, "*Amen,* I say to you," usually translated "truly." In Revelation 3:14, Christ is called "the Amen, the faithful and true Witness." This verse clearly recalls Isaiah 65:16, where Yahweh is *twice* called "the God of *amen,*" that is, the God of truth. "The maintenance of the Semitic 'amen' in the midst of a text written in Greek (Rev. 3:14) manifests the impact of Hebraic concepts and language on the thought world and worship of the early church."[37]

The Synoptic Gospels. In the Synoptic Gospels, *aletheia* occurs infrequently and is used most often to point to speech that is true, exactly correct, or trustworthy as opposed to false or deceitful. Jesus' sayings often attack hypocrisy or any discrepancy between word and deed or between word and reality (Matt. 23:2-3, 23-24; Luke 11:46; cf. Matt. 23:4). Contradiction between word and deed is considered untruthful or deceitful and *aletheia*, used to describe this contradiction, reflects the moral nature of truth that is seen in the Old Testament.

The Pauline Usages. The Pauline usages of the word are (1) as truth in general as revealed in the Law or creation (e.g., Rom. 1:18, 25; 2:8, 20); (2) as a reference to the gospel, hence, his use of the phrase, "the truth" (e.g., Col. 1:5; 2 Thess. 2:10, 12-13); (3) of truth as opposed to lying or deception (2 Cor. 4:2; Gal. 4:16; 1 Tim. 2:7); (4) as an attribute of God (Rom. 1:25; Eph. 4:21; Titus 1:1-2); (5) in keeping with the Old Testament principle of the imitation of God, truth characterizing our relationship with God and one another (1 Cor. 5:8; 13:6; 2 Cor. 6:7; Gal. 5:7).

The New Testament (especially John) also uses *true* and *truth* in a comparative sense to convey the idea of reality in contrast to appearances or to what was hitherto only a type or shadow of the "real thing." John, for example, speaks of "the true light which, coming into the world, enlightens every man" (John 1:9 NASB). Jesus identifies Himself as "the true bread out of heaven" (6:32) and "the true vine" (15:1). Commenting on John 6:55, where Jesus says that His flesh is "true food" and His blood "is true drink," Thiselton explains, "It is more genuinely food and drink than other things that go under these names. Real food gives more lasting satisfaction and nourishment than other things which men call 'food.'"[38] True worshipers are those who "worship in spirit and truth" (4:23-24). "Spirit and truth" do not refer to worship in sincerity and inwardness. "The Samaritans are not criticized for lacking sincerity [but for idolatry]. True worship is that which accords with reality, which men grasp on the basis of revelation."[39] The only *true* worship, then, is that which is in accord with the God of truth, the true God, the only God.

Apart from John, *aletheia* in the rest of the New Testament denotes (1) a synonym for the gospel (1 Peter 1:22; 2 Peter 2:2); (2) correspondence to the facts, or facticity (1 Peter 5:12; 2 Peter 2:22); and (3) a characteristic of God (James 1:18).

John's Writings. In John's writings, the word for "truth" *(aletheia)* occurs some forty-five times and its related terms about forty-eight times. John does not use *aletheia* in the book of Revelation, but he uses *alethinos* (true) ten times in that book. Other related words are *alethes* (truthful, valid, true, genuine, real) and *alethos* (truly, really, actually). Also important in understanding John's concept of truth is his frequent reference to lies and falsehood. In keeping with the rest of the New Testament writers (and the Old Testament ones), John often sees truth as the opposite to lies and falsehood (John 5:33; 8:44; 16:7; 1 John 1:6-10; 2:21-24; 4:6; 2 John 1:2; cf. v. 7; 3 John 1:12).

Like the Old Testament writers who incorporated the concept of "doing" the truth, John also conceives of truth as the divine rule or standard by which people should live and by which obedience is measured. The disciple of Christ is one who "practices the truth" (John 3:21). In John 3:21, then, moral absolutes are not merely assumed; they are categorically affirmed. *Truth* here is not only the opposite of falsehood but also a way of life that is aligned with the nature and Word of God. "When John speaks of doing the truth in 3:21, it is evident that the thought is in sympathy with the Hebrew connotations of the term."[40]

John also sees truth as revealed, as the revelation of God. In the prologue to John's gospel, Jesus, the incarnate Logos, is described as "full of grace and truth" (1:14). Here, John harkens back to the Old Testament, Exodus 34:6 being widely acknowledged as the background for John 1:14 and 17.[41] In Exodus 34, God renews His covenant with Israel. In so doing, He reveals His glory to Moses on Mount Sinai: "Then the Lord passed by in front of him and proclaimed, 'The Lord, the Lord God, compassionate and gracious, slow to anger, and abounding in lovingkindness and truth'" (Exod. 34:6). In His own words, Yahweh declares Himself to be abounding in "lovingkindness" *(hesed)* and "truth" *(emet)*, a phrase that occurs frequently in the Old Testament and expresses Yahweh's covenant loyalty and unchanging truth. "What then is the point of John's connection with Exodus 34? *Revelation.* The incarnation of God in the Logos is presented as the supreme disclosure of the Lord who revealed himself to Moses in the giving of the Law at Sinai (1:17). Jesus shows us God as he really is."[42] Jesus, the incarnate Logos, then, is the truth of God revealed. His person, work, and word are a revelation of truth. Jesus is both the Messenger and the Message of truth (John 14:6).

As has been stated, the New Testament writers (including John) did not

derive their concept of truth from the Greek philosophers, nor did the etymology of the word derive, as some people have suggested, from its use in
the New Testament.[43] John's concept of truth is not so different from that of
Old Testament writers, nor does it need explaining in terms of preconcep-
tions about Hebrew versus Greek concepts of truth. "J. Barr and A. Thiselton
have shown that the common distinction made between Greek and Hebrew
meanings for truth simply does not work linguistically. John's usage is not
'Greek,' it is 'Johannine,' and . . . it is not incompatible with an OT/Hebrew
background."[44]

Perhaps John's greatest contribution to the biblical concept of truth is
his perception that all truth is rooted in God. Truth is thus absolute and
theocentric. It has been shown that John presents truth as an attribute of
God revealed in the incarnate Logos or Word of God. God's ontological
reality is ultimate reality. No standards exist outside of God by which to evaluate His reality. As ultimate reality, God is the only absolute standard by which
all truth or falsehood, light or darkness, and right or wrong are measured in
this world (John 5:33; 8:31–32, 42–47). Moreover, both Jesus and the Holy
Spirit are said to be "the truth" (14:6, 16–17; 15:26; 1 John 5:7). So the
Father is truth, the Son is truth, and the Holy Spirit is truth. The locus of
truth is the Triune God. God *is* truth.

The Word of God *Is* Truth

Finally, with regard to evidences for the nature of truth, the Word of God
is truth. This is the unequivocal claim of Jesus Christ: "Thy Word is truth"
(John 8:31–59). And John declares the apostolic word to be "the spirit of
truth" as opposed to "the spirit of error" (1 John 4:6). *Error* here does not
mean simply "mistake," but "deceit" or "leading astray."[45] When God speaks,
His words are true because He is true. It is impossible for God to speak falsehoods (Titus 1:2; Heb. 6:18; 2 Sam. 7:28). Whether He speaks directly (Exod.
34:6) through Jesus (Matt. 22:16; Luke 9:27; John 8:45; Rom. 15:8), or by
the prophets and apostles (1 Kings 17:24; Deut. 18:18; Isa. 66:1; Jer. 1:1–4;
Acts 26:25; 2 Tim. 3:16; 1 Peter 1:11–12; 2 Peter 1:21), His Word is reliable
because it is rooted in and ruled by the divine absolute. His Word corresponds
to reality because reality is measured by God, the ultimate reality.

Thus, the New Testament concept of truth conforms to that of the Old
Testament and is predicated upon it. Truth originates in God, who is the
source of all truth. All truth is God's truth. Truth is opposite to falsehood
and lies. Truth is that which corresponds to things as they really are. Truth

can be witnessed to, stated propositionally, and tested. Truth is reliable and right because it is valid; it is from God, measured by God, rooted in God, and required by God. Truth finds its absoluteness in God, that is, because God is absolute, truth is absolute. Because God is authentic, real, genuine, and perfect reality, all truth corresponds to reality.[46] The same concept of truth is reflected in the lives and in the writings of the apostolic fathers.[47]

The Truth According to Scripture

We may conclude the following concerning the biblical concept of truth:

1. God is truth. Truth is ontologically rooted in God. Truth is an unchanging, fixed, absolute attribute of God. *Truth* is thus unchanging, fixed, and absolute.
2. Truth is correspondence to reality. Truth is what is true as opposed to falsehood and lies.
3. Truth is propositional and verifiable.
4. Truth is revealed and therefore objective, knowable, and subject to systemization. Because God's Word was spoken and written, it may be taught and learned.
5. Truth may be personally practiced inasmuch as truth determines what is right and wrong, moral and immoral, righteous and unrighteous, real and unreal. The person who is faithful to God is so because he or she is "true to God," that is, ideologically and morally aligned to the true God, the God of truth.

The biblical concept of truth may thus be summarized by two overarching propositions: (1) truth is theocentric and therefore absolute; (2) truth is correspondence to reality. Given these two premises, the following implications or propositions may be logically deduced.[48]

Philosophical Implications

If truth is *absolute* and *correspondence to reality*, then the following implications must be true.

Truth is universal. Whatever is true at one time and in one place is true at all times and in all places. Relativists object, saying that a proposition such as "it is raining" might be true in Portland but not in Pittsburgh. But this fact does not vitiate absolutism; it merely demonstrates that meaning—rather than truth—is relative to context. Once context is considered, meaning is understood and truth is clearly absolute. Granted, it might be raining in Portland but not in Pittsburgh, but the proposition "it is raining in Portland" is true in Pittsburgh as well as in Portland as long as it is really raining in Portland. The laws of gravity, mathematics, physics, and so on are true in the East as well as in the West. So too, are the reality of God and the claims of Christ.

Truth is, by definition, exclusive. Christianity is an exclusivistic religion. Christianity and any other religion cannot both be true. Both could be false, but both cannot be true. If Christianity is objectively true, it is true everywhere for everyone. Cultures may differ, but truth is transcultural. In any age, in any place, at any time, and for anyone the truth of God's Word is enough to answer the questions raised by reality. "When people refuse God's answer, they are living against the revelation of the universe and against the revelation of themselves."[49]

What is true for one person is true for all persons. All people are entitled to their own opinion but not to their own truth. People do not create truth; they can only discover it. Religion and moral behavior are not a matter of consensus or personal preference. If they were, and if truth were relative, then Hitler's views, policies, and deeds would have just as much validity as do Mother Teresa's. Whatever is true and right, is true and right for all people, in all places, and under all conditions. Absolute truth does not change from person to person or from place to place. Absolute truth does not, in fact, change.

An epistemological infinite regress is impossible. Self-evident truths exist, and the fact that truth is absolute is based on first principles. Every truth claim cannot rest upon another. If every truth claim rested upon another, you would have an infinite regress, which is logically impossible. There must be an absolute first principle upon which all other truths rest. This first principle is, of course, God.

The universe cannot contain contradictory conditions or truths. If truth were relative, then the universe would have contradictory properties *(A is non-A)*. To deny this fact is to employ the law of noncontradiction *(A is not non-A),* which is self-defeating. The fact that truth is absolute forbids contradictory conditions or truths. Relativism would require that the universe be full of contradictions.

Truth claims may be made and believed. If truth were relative, it would be impossible to rationally believe or claim that anything is true or false. Nothing would be true; nothing would be false. To say that "truth is relative" is itself an absolute truth claim. To deny absolutes is an appeal to absolutes. McDowell and Geisler demonstrate the dilemma of the relativist with an illustration from one of the *Winnie the Pooh* stories:

> Winnie the lovable bear has a notorious appetite, which brings him to the door of Rabbit for something to eat. When Winnie the Pooh knocks, Rabbit, who has no intention of feeding the bear, calls out, "Nobody home." Wise Winnie responds, "There must be somebody home or else he could not say, 'Nobody home.'"
>
> Winnie is right, of course. Rabbit cannot deny his own presence unless he is present to deny it. Similarly, those who deny the existence of absolutes cannot hold that all things are relative unless there is some unchangeable ground on which their affirmation can stand. It's senseless to pronounce everything relative while not allowing that very position to be relative as well. In reality, the relativist stands on the pinnacle of his or her own absolute in order to pronounce everything else relative.[50]

Truth can be stated in terms of propositions. Truth must be absolute to be propositional. If truth were relative, then no statements could be made about truth that were not relative in themselves. "Any attempt to deny that truth is expressible in propositions is self-defeating because it is a truth claim expressed in a proposition."[51] A recent television talk show hosted a forum that consisted of a group of teenagers on one side and their parents on the other. When each side was asked what it considered "acceptable" behavior, each side disagreed with the other. Much of what the teenagers considered "acceptable" the parents rejected as *un*acceptable. When asked, "Why?" the parents' best answer was, "Well, we just feel it is." They made no appeal to absolutes and, of course, no solution was achieved. In fact, no solution to this dilemma *can* be achieved apart from absolutes. Parents who embrace relativism as their own criterion of ethics have no basis on which to deny their children the same criterion.

One can be mistaken, wrong, or deceived. If truth were relative, no one could be mistaken or utter a false statement. With regard to theology, this prospect would mean that no such thing as heresy exists. Lies would be impossible. As a child, I remember hearing my uncle call upstairs to my little cousin, who was supposed to be asleep, "Karen, are you asleep?" Much to our amusement, she answered, "Yes." Her truth claim, of course, did not correspond to reality (unless she was talking in her sleep). If truth were not absolute, this incident would have been unremarkable, without humor, and meaningless. It was humorous because we saw the implication of her truth claim. We were in much the same position that Winnie the Pooh was in when he knocked on Rabbit's door and received the answer, "Nobody's home."

Learning is possible. One can learn only if one moves from what is really false to what is really (i.e., absolutely) true. If truth were relative, one could never learn. There would be no point in trying.

Truth is static. That is, truth is unchanging and constant as opposed to "dynamic." Truth remains the same throughout all ages, as opposed to the idea of "process" or temporal truth. "Truth," says Carl F. H. Henry, "is not subject to revision as are the airline schedules . . . the good and the true cannot be reduced to whatever Hollywood and Madison Avenue momentarily approve, or to whatever culture-ridden sociologists and secular humanists command."[52] It will always be true that $2 + 2 = 4$. Error will never become true, and truth will never become error. "Perspective, geography, or the time on the clock may change the way we view reality, but reality remains unchanged. When reality is described accurately, we encounter truth. Absolute truth."[53]

Truth is knowable. One can become cognizant of truth. Truth is not just "livable"; one can conceptualize, or *know,* truth. Indeed, in order to "live" truth or "do" truth, one must know truth. Knowledge of truth is cognitive and intellectual. That some truth is self-evident, even relativists must admit, for the denial that truth can be known is itself an assertion of truth. Because truth is revelation from God, it comes to us in a form that we can understand and *test* or *verify.* Jesus said, "You shall know the truth and the truth shall make you free" (John 8:32). Whatever else this statement affirms, it affirms that truth can be known.

Truth lies within the realm of the rational as opposed to the existential. Truth is not something "wholly other" but is attainable by the rational powers of the human mind.

Truth doesn't come in degrees. Something can't be partly true and partly false.

Something can be true only if it affirms or denies something.

Truth is theocentric. If truth is absolute, it must have a basis for its "absoluteness." This basis can only be God, implying that all truth is God's truth and that all truth is theocentric. Augustine wrote, "Every good and true Christian should understand that wherever he may find truth, it is his

Lord's."[54] Gordon R. Lewis says, "Every story has three sides—your side, my side and God's. Our assertions are true insofar as they conform to God's mind. . . . all truth is God's truth, whether on your side or my side, or wherever it may be found."[55] Recall the thesis of Frank E. Gaebelein's notable book *The Pattern of God's Truth:* All truth is God's truth.[56] Christian education (ideally all education) should present all subjects of study as parts of an integrated whole with the Scripture at the center. Every truth, wherever found, is part of the whole, behind which is the divine absolute.

God can be known. God is truth. Truth is absolute and objective and can thus be known. God, therefore, can be known. That God can be known does not mean that we can have absolute knowledge of God or of truth in general, but it does mean that the *basis* of our knowledge, or the *object* of our knowledge (i.e., God), is itself absolute.

All systems of systematic theology, although relative in themselves, are based upon what is unchanging. The job of systematic theology may be done and improved upon, and it follows that systematic theology is worth doing. If truth were not absolute, we would have no "goal" toward which to shoot in doing systematic theology. Categories would be unrelatable and systematizing impossible.

Everything that is not true is false. This statement implies that we must be diligent in searching for the truth and that no one can say (truthfully) that it doesn't matter what you believe. No middle ground exists between what is true and what is not true. Aristotle's definition of truth demonstrates the polarity of truth and falsehood: "To say of what is, that it is not, or of what is not, that it is, is false; while to say of what is, that it is, and of what is not, that it is not, is true."[57] By the facts of the matter being so or not being so, a statement is found to be true or false.

It matters what you believe. The implications of this statement are enormous. My eternal salvation depends upon what I believe. My immediate safety or well-being depends upon what I believe—and upon what those around me believe. Many people today seek to justify their lawlessness by saying, "It's my moral right." But meaninglessness is the result of humankind's pursuit of autonomy. Meaning is contingent upon reality—that which is true. When truth is diminished, knowledge disappears. If it doesn't matter what we think, then what we *feel* will be our guide. No stable society can be built apart from absolute truth. Everyone has a moral responsibility to know truth (Titus 1:1; Pss. 51:6; 119:51; Prov. 3:3; 23:23), and relativism's rejection of this stand robs human existence of meaning and worth.

When our pastor came to our church, he said, "We cannot be just a crowd; we must be a church where people care, and truth matters."[58] No genuine caring exists in the absence of truth. Where there is no truth, there is no love. To be a church that really cares, we must embrace the truth. Truth matters. And if truth matters, it matters what we believe. Dorothy L. Sayers said, "It is worse than useless for Christians to talk about the importance of Christian morality, unless they are prepared to take their stand upon the fundamentals of Christian theology. It is a lie to say that dogma does not matter; it matters enormously."[59]

Truth is objective rather than subjective. It is objective because God exists outside ourselves. And it is universal because God is above all.

> It is impossible to arrive at an objective, universal, and constant standard of truth and morality without bringing God onto the stage. If an objective standard of truth and morality exists, it cannot be the product of the human mind (or it will not be objective); it must be the product of another Mind. If a constant and unchanging truth exists, it must reach beyond the human timelines (or it would not be constant); it must be eternal. If a universal rule of right and wrong exists, it must be above us all. Yet, absolute truth must be something—or Someone—that is common to all humanity, to all creation. . . . it is God's nature and character that defines truth. He defines what is right for all people, for all times, for all places. But truth is not something He decides; it is something He is.[60]

Christianity is predicated upon this "claim to absolute, objective *truth,* . . . To surrender this ground is to surrender the faith itself."[61]

Truth can be systematized because there are grounds for relatability. Without correspondence to facticity or reality, you have no grounds for systematizing.

Truth can be tested. If truth did not correspond to reality, neither truth nor falsity could exist. In order to know whether a thing is true or false, a real difference must exist between the thing and the statements about the thing. But this difference is precisely what is entailed in a correspondence view of truth.

An error must be defined not as "intentional misleading" but as "that which is false." If truth did not correspond to reality, one could redefine error as an intent to mislead, and maintain that whatever a writer intends to affirm is true regardless of whether it corresponds to the facts. In the inerrancy debate of the '70s and '80s, noninerrantists (i.e., *errantists*) proposed what might be called an intentionality view of truth, according to which a statement is true if it accomplishes what the author intended it to accomplish, regardless of whether it corresponds to the facts.[62] This position is contrary to the biblical view of truth.

The law of noncontradiction applies. If truth did not correspond to reality, then contradictory properties (an impossibility) could both be true. As J. Oliver Buswell Jr. says,

> If we accept the sovereign Triune God as revealed in the Bible, it follows that we accept propositional truth, and the laws which are inherent in the nature of propositional truth. These laws are not imposed upon our basic presupposition but are implicit in it and derived from it. The Bible is a book in human language. If we are not talking nonsense we must then believe in the rules of linguistic expression. The Bible as a book written in human language claims to speak the truth. If the word truth is not meaningless, it implies the laws of truth, that is, the laws of logic.[63]

Truth cannot be defined as "that which works." The pragmatic view of truth is false.

Truth is an expression *of reality, not an existential experience.* Geisler and Brooks illustrate the propositional nature of truth when they say,

> Meaning is a disclosure of the author's intentions, but it can only be discovered by looking at what he actually said. Since we cannot read the author's mind when we want to know the meaning of a statement, we look at the statement itself. Only when we see the proper relation of all the words in the sentence, and the sentence to the paragraph, etc., do we understand the big meaning of the affirmation. Then we check it against reality to see if it is true or false.[64]

The Bible is true. The ninth commandment is predicated on a correspondence view of truth. "You shall not bear false witness against your neighbor [Exod. 20:16] depends for its very meaning and effectiveness on the correspondence view of truth. This command implies that a statement is false if it does not correspond to reality."[65]

Lies, falsehood, and heresies are possible. If truth did not correspond to reality, lies could not exist. If one's statement need not correspond to the facts to be true, then any factually incorrect statement could be true. And if this is the case, then lies could not exist because any statement is compatible with any given state of affairs. That situation would rob the Bible of its authority and make systematic theology impossible.

Factual communication would break down without a correspondence view of truth. Factual communication depends on informative statements. But informative statements must be factually true to inform correctly.

Missionary activity, gospel witnessing, biblical preaching, and Christian educating are therefore worthy and necessary enterprises.

Systematic theology is essential. Systematic, disciplined reflection on biblical truth is essential for Christian living and ministry. If truth resides in God, every person must be a theologian.

THE KNOWLEDGE OF TRUTH

As we have indicated, truth can be known. But more may be said. In addition to the two premises already stated, namely (1) that truth is absolute, and (2) truth corresponds to reality, three more premises may be postulated that are both biblically and philosophically justified and that help explain how we can come to a knowledge of truth: (3) logic applies to reality; (4) creation resembles the Creator; (5) religious language is analogous.

Premise Three: Logic Applies to Reality

If logic applies to reality, the following can be concluded:

1. *Two contradictory statements cannot be true.* The law of noncontradiction applies. *A* is not non-*A*. Otherwise, theological paradox is inevitable.
2. *Naturalistic arguments—the cosmological, ontological, teleological, and anthropological arguments—for God are valid.* If logic did not apply to reality, one could not argue from the observable to God or from the known to the unknown.
3. *Humanity can know God.* Epistemologically, logic is the basis for all knowledge of God. Ontologically, God is the basis of all logic. Epistemologically, reason and logic are the starting point to the knowledge of truth. Ontologically, revelation is the starting point.
4. *We have a methodology for testing truth.* We can test the accuracy of systematic theology.

5. *Logical deductions can be made.* Argumentation can take place and be profitable. The law of rational inference applies; otherwise, theological argumentation is implausible. By logical deduction, we arrive at doctrines we would otherwise not know, such as the Trinity, inerrancy, and so on.

6. *Systematic theology is possible.* Systematic theology is dependent upon the premise that logic applies to reality. If logic does not apply to reality, there is no connection between systematic theology and reality.

7. *We can study apologetics and offer proofs.*

8. *The law of identity applies. A is A.* Otherwise, theological unity is unachievable.

9. *Doctrinal heresy is possible.* If logic did not apply to reality, then doctrinal heresy would be impossible. Here, the law of the excluded middle applies. Either something is *A* or non-*A*. If relativism were true, then *A* could be non-*A*, right could be wrong, and evil could be good (cf. Isa. 5:20, "Woe to those who call evil good, and good evil"). Orthodoxy is impossible unless logic applies to reality.

10. *Religious language, or "God-talk," is meaningful.* We can make meaningful and affirmable statements about truth.

Premise 4: Creation Resembles the Creator

If creation resembles the Creator, the following can be concluded:

1. *Man is made in the image of God, and we can assume the* via eminentiae *(the way of eminence).* Fallenness does not destroy this similarity. The *via eminentiae* is "the method for the positive derivation of divine attributes . . . by raising attributes of things in the finite order, particularly spiritual attributes of human beings, to the order of the infinite. E.g., power becomes omnipotence; wisdom becomes omniscience."[66]

2. *We can know God.* If creation did not resemble the Creator, we could not know anything about God through nature, or the Bible, which is a creaturely manifestation, or even the incarnation of Christ.

3. *The logical arguments for God are valid.* It is legitimate and justifiable to reason toward God from that which He has created.

4. *There is a correspondence between reality and what is proposed about reality.*
5. *We have a basis for analogical language—the only possible way to talk of God.*
6. *We can study systematic theology, using the Bible and all of nature.*
7. *Logic and reason apply.* If creation did not resemble the Creator, then we could not assume that being produces being, and only so.

Premise 5: Religious Language Is Analogous

If religious language is analogous, the following can be concluded:

1. *God can be talked about in a meaningful way.* Only three alternatives exist for descriptive God-talk: (1) equivocal language (totally different), (2) univocal language (totally the same), or (3) analogical language (both the same and different). Equivocal language either reduces God to the mortal or elevates man to deity. Univocal language leads to skepticism.
2. *At least two beings exist in the universe.* Thus, ontological pluralism is a necessity, and monism and pantheism are false.
3. *Only because religious language is analogous can we use the* via negativa *(the negative way) arguments or deny any imperfections in God.* The *via negativa* is "a method of defining or identifying the divine attributes . . . by negating the attributes of the finite order. Thus, creatures are measurable, mutable, and finite; God is immeasurable or immense . . . , immutable . . . , and infinite. . . . In addition, creatures are complex and temporal; God is simple and eternal."[67]
4. *The transcendence of God is preserved.* If language were not analogous, we could not speak of God as transcendent. Or, to put it another way, because God *is* transcendent, only analogous language applies. If God is both immanent and transcendent, analogous language is the only God-talk that is possible.

An interrelationship exists between each of the preceding five premises. If one of these premises were not true, none would be true, and systematic theology would be impossible. A Creator-creature relationship exists that sets up a basis for analogy. If this were not true, then there could be no correspondence between reality and what is proposed about reality. The fact that creation resembles the Creator necessitates language that is analogical. That religious language is analogous depends upon the fact that logic applies to reality. The application of logic to reality depends upon truth, which is unchanging and absolute. The fact that logic applies to reality is a necessary presupposition to religious language, or God-talk. Ultimately, all of these premises are necessary to, and make possible and meaningful, the study of systematic theology. In his inimitable way, Ravi Zacharias says,

> as a sloganeering culture, we have unblushingly trivialized the serious and exalted the trivial because we have bypassed the rudimentary and necessary steps of logical argument. Reality can be lost when reason and language have been violated. . . . It is understandable why textbooks in logic do not hit the bestseller list, but the laws of logic must apply to reality else we may as well be living in a madhouse.[68]

REASON AND TRUTH

Given the preceding premises, the conclusion that reason plays a fundamental role in ascertaining truth and in studying theology is inescapable. Indeed, the Bible not only is predicated on the human capacity for reason but directly instructs and commands us to reason. Speaking to Judah, God said, "Come, let us reason together" (Isa. 1:18). This statement is hardly a fair and plausible invitation if people are incapable of reason.

Peter told us to be ready to give a reason for the hope that is in us (1 Peter 3:15). In what Jesus declared as "the great commandment," He said, "You shall love the Lord your God with all . . . your *mind*" (Matt. 22:37, italics added). The apostle Paul urges, "Whatever is true . . . let your mind dwell [i.e., *think*] on these things" (Phil. 4:8). God Himself asks, "To whom will you compare me or count me equal? To whom will you liken me that we may be compared?" (Isa. 46:5 NIV). Comparison necessitates intellectual reasoning. "Thinking is not an option for the Christian; it is an imperative."[69]

But how much can we count on reason? What can reason do, and what can it *not* do? What role does reason play in knowing God and in studying theology? What is the relationship between reason and faith? In Christian apologetics, differences of opinion exist regarding the relationship of faith and reason. Some people have argued for the priority of reason; others insist on the priority of faith. The best answer seems to be, *There must be a proper balance of both.*[70] In whatever way the Fall affected humankind's ability or capacity to reason, it is the certain testimony of Scripture that we both *can* reason and *must* reason. Without getting sidetracked onto the topics of *imago Dei,* the *noetic* effects of sin, and the doctrine of revelation,[71] the following statements are what reason *can* do and what it *cannot* do in theology.[72]

What Reason *Can* Do

1. *Reason can prove the existence of God.* Aquinas insisted on as much. This does not mean that by reason alone people can know God personally or that by reason alone they can come to faith in God. It does mean, however, that unregenerate humanity can clearly see, through nature (general revelation), "the eternal power and divine nature" (Rom. 1:20). As Thiessen says, "The revelation of God in nature reveals that there is a God and that he has such attributes as power, glory, divinity, and goodness."[73] According to Aquinas, "To know that God exists in a general way is implanted in us by nature."[74] Thomas C. Oden affirms, "A limited reasoning toward and about God . . . can proceed, without direct reference to Scripture or the history of revelation, on the basis of natural human intuition, moral insight, and reasoning."[75]

2. *Reason is a means of understanding revelation.* Revelation must be grasped by the only faculty with which we are endowed for that purpose—reason. Revelation presupposes reason.

> Truths, to be received as objects of faith must be intellectually apprehended . . . knowledge is essential to faith. In believing we affirm the truth of the proposition believed. But we can affirm nothing of that which we know nothing. The first and indispensable office of reason, therefore, in matters of faith, is the cognition or intelligent apprehension of the truths proposed for our reception.[76]

3. *Reason tells us what is reasonable to believe.* Reason, having grasped the message of revelation, then determines whether it is coherent or believable—that is, noncontradictory.

4. *Reason verifies the credulity of revelation.* "It is not enough to understand the revelation and declare it free of contradiction; reason must determine its credibility."[77]

5. *Reason argues for the dependability of revelation.* By reason, we know that divine revelation is to be depended on.

6. *Reason interprets the content of revelation.* When we claim to recognize, acknowledge, or know God through His revelation, reason is by no means suspended. Without reason, we could not identify or interpret revelation. Faith needs reason, else we could not recognize in what and in whom we believe. This is not to say that reason takes priority over revelation. Once reason tells us "this" is revelation, it is reasonable to accept that revelation as worthy to be believed, and our reason now subjects itself to revelation. Once one has determined, by reason, that the Bible is the Word of God, it is absurd to sit in judgment on Scripture.

7. *Reason helps confirm faith.* Faith is not an unreasoned leap. Faith does not mean believing in God despite a lack of evidence. On the contrary, faith rests on the certitude of objective truth, or facticity. Faith is the willingness to accept the evidence for what it really is (John 7:17). As Shedd says, "Faith . . . is yet an intelligent act."[78]

What Reason *Cannot* Do

1. *Reason cannot form the basis for faith.* The basis for faith is revelation, what God has told us. Reason considers revelation; faith receives it. Revelation has to do with content and message; reason has to do with method. Reason learns; it never teaches.

2. *Nor can reason attain to faith.* If reason were the only way open to us for the knowledge of God, we would remain in the most miserable ignorance. People must reason, but reason must be assisted by the Spirit of God as reason considers the Word of God.

3. *Reason cannot yield a supernatural, salvific revelation or even ascertain it on reason's own initiative.* Apart from the work of God in the human heart, reason cannot reach salvific knowledge of God.

4. *Reason alone and apart from the illuminating work of the Holy Spirit cannot effect adequate knowledge, understanding, or comprehension of revelation.*

5. *Reason cannot supersede revelation or replace faith. It is the servant of both.*

All finite reason must resemble the infinite reason in kind. We cannot conceive of God's creating two diverse kinds of rational mind. When God creates a rational mind, He must, from the nature of the original case, make it after His own likeness. "When finite mind and reason are created, they are made after the divine image, and therefore can be of only one species and quality."[79] Ronald H. Nash states,

> A blank mind . . . cannot know anything; human knowledge of any-thing depends upon *a priori* possession of innate categories of thought. These categories are ours by virtue of having been created in God's image, a fact that guarantees that the human structure of reasoning matches the divine reasoning. Reason subsists in the mind of God eternally. Reason also characterizes the human mind. And reason is objectified in the world because of its relation to the divine Logos. Language is a divinely-given gift to facilitate a communion between God and humans that is both personal and cognitive. . . . Any flight from reason and logic is a flight from reality. All who re-pudiate logic automatically cut themselves off from any possible knowledge of God and His creation. The Word of God (that in-cludes revealed information from God and of God) is not alien to the human mind. Neither the nature of God nor the nature of hu-man knowledge and language preclude the possibility of the human mind attaining cognitive knowledge of the Word of God.[80]

LET US THEREFORE SEEK THE TRUTH

Without absolute truth, we are not equipped to evaluate moral issues. Without a sound spiritual and moral standard, we cannot hold the truth of the Christian faith "which was once for all delivered to the saints" (Jude 1:4). Strong, reliable convictions concerning right and wrong cannot long remain afloat in a sea of relativism. If we do not hold to truth as absolute, knowledge will disappear; tyranny will follow in the wake of moral anarchy; all that is good, right, and just will be engulfed in a tide of intellectual and moral nihilism. Under such conditions missions will fade away like a wisp of smoke, and the world will be without a witness of *the truth*.

As Christians, we must *pursue* truth. We must renew our conviction and enlarge our understanding that truth is rooted in God and recorded in His Word. Jesus said, "If you abide in My Word, then you are truly disciples of Mine; and you shall know the truth, and the truth shall make you free" (John 8:31–32). The pursuit of truth requires that we love the truth (2 Thess. 2:10) and embrace it (John 7:17; 8:47; 18:37; 1 John 4:6; 2 Chron. 15:2). Blaise Pascal (1623–1662) said, "Truth is so obscure in these times and falsehood so established, that unless we love the truth, we cannot know it."[81] Truth must be allowed to reign. Justice, fairness, kindness, love, righteousness, goodness, comfort—all that is true and right—are to be found in our proper alignment to the God of truth. [82] To seek justice, love, comfort, and so on while ignoring the fixed nature of truth—the ultimate, absolute, ground of all truth—is pointless. C. S. Lewis said, "Comfort is the one thing you cannot get by looking for it. If you look for truth, you may find comfort in the end. If you look for comfort, you will not get either comfort or truth."[83] Christians, then, have a responsibility to pursue truth. "If God's truth is what we call people to live by, it needs to be pursued afresh and restated anew in every generation."[84]

The Christian church must *proclaim* the truth. Truth must be taught in the home (Deut. 11:18-19). It must be proclaimed in the world. B. B. Warfield said, "Christianity is in its very nature an aggressive religion; it is in the world just in order to convince men; when it ceases to *reason*, it ceases to exist."[85] More than 120 years ago, J. C. Ryle said, "If ever there was a time in the world when churches were put upon their trial, whether they would hold fast the truth or not, that time is the present time."[86] One can only wonder what Ryle would think of today's church and its flirtation with relativism. The cost of relativism is relevance. There is no meaning if truth is relative. Truth is what "gives relevance to 'relevance,' just as relevance becomes irrelevance if it is not related to truth. Without truth, relevance is meaningless and dangerous."[87] Alister McGrath says,

> To allow relevance to be given greater weight than truth is a mark of intellectual shallowness and moral irresponsibility. The first and most fundamental of all questions must be this: Is it true? . . . no one can build his personal life around a lie. Christian doctrine is concerned to declare that Christian morality rests upon a secure foundation.[88]

As Christians we must also *practice* the truth. We know so much yet do so little of what we know. Again, McGrath is on target:

> An obedient response to truth is a mark of intellectual integrity. It marks a willingness to hear what purports to be the truth, to judge it, and—if it is found to be true—to accept it willingly. Truth demands to be accepted because it inherently deserves to be accepted and acted upon. Christianity recognizes a close link between faith and obedience—witness Paul's profound phrase "the obedience of

faith" (Rom. 1:5)—making it imperative that the ideas underlying and giving rise to attitudes and actions should be judged and found to be right.[89]

Let us therefore seek truth while it may be found. Pilate asked the question, "What is truth?" But he didn't wait for an answer. He might now wish that he had. Rollin T. Chafer once told of hearing a well-known preacher declare

> that he had never forgotten having once read in a work entitled "Letters from Hell," of one who was discovered in the world of lost spirits to be occupied in the ceaseless routine of washing his hands, and every now and then looking up to ask, "What is truth?" When questioned why he so acted, he appeared to have no answer save to go on washing his hands and putting the same question. *"What is truth."* [90]

It is an apocryphal story to be sure, but it does urge us to pursue truth while it may be found and to bring others with us.

In the end, we must accept one of two alternatives: Truth is either relative, or it is absolute. Either we live in a universe where truth and morality are relative and all is meaningless and irrelevant, or truth is absolute, moral rules exist, and we are accountable to a holy and righteous God. No other choices exist.

This chapter is based on *The Fundamentals for the Twenty-First Century,* ed. Mal Couch (Grand Rapids: Kregel, 2000), 29–55.

CHAPTER 9

THE NECESSITY OF THEOLOGICAL TRAINING FOR THE MISSIONARY

J. RONALD BLUE

THEOLOGY![1] WHY IN THE WORLD DOES a missionary need theology? All missionaries need is a good blade and the Good Book—just chop the grass and chatter the gospel. If a missionary has enough stamina to chop through the jungle with a machete and enough sense to share the gospel with poor lost pagans, then that person will be a great success!

It would be a terrible waste to send out a missionary who has been well trained in theology. In fact, theology would only cause confusion. How can a missionary benefit from knowing the ontological arguments for the existence of God or the eschatological significance of the pretribulation rapture?

Many people share this view of the missionary task. To those individuals, *missionary* is synonymous with *mediocrity* in relation to theological training. They think that a little biblical knowledge and a lot of brawn are all that a missionary needs. But nothing could be further from the truth. Of all of the people who are engaged in the Lord's work, the missionary is probably in greatest need of sound, thorough, theological training.

THE BIBLICAL PATTERN

The Sending of Paul and His Missionary Journeys

Although the church began on the Day of Pentecost when the Holy Spirit came to baptize believers into Christ's body (Acts 1:5; 11:15–16; 1 Cor. 12:12–13; Eph. 1:22–23; Col. 1:18), it did not begin sending missionaries until Acts 13:1–3. By this time, the church in Antioch—which began as the result of persecution that scattered believers from Jerusalem after Stephen's death (7:54–60; 11:19)—had benefited from a year of Paul's and Barnabas's instruction (11:26).

In this mature congregation were "prophets and teachers" (Acts 13:1), in response to the fasting and ministering of whom God spoke: "The Holy Spirit said, 'Set apart for Me Barnabas and Saul for the work to which I have called them'" (v. 2). As the first missionaries sent to "the field," Paul and Barnabas—not the least equipped theologically or having the minimum thirty-two credit hours of theological training—were gifted teachers, trained in God's Word. Thus, God's Spirit chose Paul and Barnabas from the *most* equipped of those in the church at Antioch.

The wisdom of this choice becomes apparent in what Scripture records about Paul's missionary thrusts. On Paul's first missionary journey, for example, he needed theological astuteness to deal with the lies of a magician (13:8, animism), with legalistic Judaism (vv. 15–47; 14:1–5), and with Greek paganism (14:8–18, polytheism).

During his second missionary journey, he again confronted many false systems, including demonism (16:16), the philosophies of Epicurianism and Stoicism (17:16–34), and Judaism (18:4–17). In Corinth, he taught the Bible for a year and a half (18:11).

Paul's third journey was no different from his first two. He confronted Judaism (19:8) and taught for two to three years in the school of Tyrannus (v. 9; 20:31). Paul's theological instruction not only equipped the existing disciples but spawned missionary activities by his disciples. The cumulative result was that "all who lived in Asia heard the word of the Lord, both Jews and Greeks" (19:10 NASB).

Thus, a cursory look at Paul's missionary endeavors proves that the pattern of the early church was to send theologically trained individuals to the field (13:1–3), and it proves the wisdom of that choice as well. Paul's missionary activities demonstrated the instruction and theological understanding necessary to continue the process of equipping his converts and to correct error and heresy that arose in the congregations.

Other Missionaries in the New Testament

Although Paul had many colleagues and fellow missionaries (e.g., Erastus, Sopater, Aristarchus, Secundus, Gaius of Derbe, Gaius of Macedonia, Tychicus, and Trophimus [Acts 19:22, 29; 20:4]), of only Timothy and Titus does enough information exist to evaluate their theological training. Because

Paul "sent out" Timothy and Titus to teach, instruct, and correct doctrinal error (1 Tim. 1:4; 2 Tim. 4:1–2; Titus 1:5; 2:15) it is clear that both men had adequate training in those areas to fulfill the task. Timothy was even left to continue this work in a well-established church, and both men remained under Paul's tutelage.

Similarly, Apollos was sent from the house church of Aquila and Priscilla in Ephesus to Corinth (Acts 18:24–28; 1 Cor. 16:19). He was said to be "mighty in the Scriptures" (Acts 18:24) and able to "powerfully refute the Jews" (v. 28).

New Testament Missionary Qualifications

One can infer from the activities of Paul and Barnabas and their position in the church at Antioch that both were elders in that church (Acts 11:26; 13:1). From what Scripture reveals about Titus and Timothy, it can be assumed that all of the people whom Paul and others sent out for missionary activities were qualified elder "material." That all of the men sent out could and did meet the qualifications set forth by Paul in his first letter to Timothy (1 Tim. 3:1–7) makes sense.

They had to be "able to teach" (1 Tim. 3:2). Paul's list of qualifications is preceded by the statement, "An overseer, then, must be. . . ." The Greek particle *dei*, translated "must be," could also be accurately translated "it is necessary." Rienecker states, "The word speaks of the logical necessity according to the binding needs of the circumstances."[2]

In the list of qualifications for elders sent to Titus, Paul further exhorts that an elder must "hold fast the faithful word which is in accordance with the teaching, that he may be able both to exhort in sound doctrine and to refute those who contradict" (Titus 1:9). Each elder, then, would have to know sound doctrine and be able to identify the theological error of an errant position.

Even in the first century, the need to evangelize, train, and equip believers to establish churches and to counter false religions and worldviews made the theological training of missionaries imperative. Thus, the chop-and-chatter-the-gospel view is shown by Scripture to illustrate two fallacies.

Fallacy One: The Perception of Missionary Territory

Although much remains to be done in primitive areas of the world, the vast majority of missions work today is accomplished in the arena of sophisticated societies and progressive peoples. Of the more than two billion "unreached" people (i.e., those who have not yet heard a clear presentation of the gospel), most are not primitive pagans. They are more likely enlightened individuals who are quite religious but wrapped up in complex counterfeit religious systems. The God-given vacuum in their souls has been stuffed with a virtual smorgasbord of religions that supposedly give meaning to life. Islam, for instance, claims more than one billion adherents, Hinduism boasts more than 700 million followers, and Buddhism is embraced by about 300 million people.[3]

The modern missionary is called upon to penetrate these complicated religious systems, which seem to grow like weeds from strange theological substructures. The roots might be hopelessly entangled, but they all claim to draw from mysterious revelation, issued by a divinity or god.

Non-Christian religions are only a part of the challenge. Divergent theologies are also found in the spectrum of denominations included in the world's largest religion—Christianity. Almost 30 percent of the world's population, or 1.7 billion, profess to be Christian.[4] Included among that number are those who claim allegiance to the Roman Catholic Church, with a total membership in the early 1990s of 958.4 million or about 17 percent of the world's population.[5] The number also includes the Orthodox Church, which has communities in Europe, Africa, and Asia and numbers more than 174 million adherents throughout the world.[6] Much missionary endeavor is directed to areas of the world where "Christianity" has become as garbled and confused as non-Christian religions.

In addition to those who claim some kind of religious affiliation, the missionary challenge encompasses the estimated one-fourth of the world's population who are enmeshed in "secularism." More than one billion secularists—men and women who have fallen prey to the gods of humanism, Marxism, existentialism, hedonism, and materialism—too, are mission territory.

The mission field is hardly some uncultivated plot of enriched soil waiting to receive the good seed. Rather, it is a jungle infested with weeds and parasitic plants that have matted the soil of people's souls, repelling the true gospel. The modern missionary is called upon to wade into that jungle of diverse ideologies and divergent theologies.

Fallacy Two: The Perception of the Missionary Task

The missionary endeavor involves more than gospel proclamation. And although missionary evangelism is perceived as glamorous, it has often been reduced to sharing a standardized presentation of the gospel or spouting a few key verses to the unfortunate and unsuspecting pagans of the world. Colorful tracts in strange languages are dropped over jungle villages; sound trucks race through dusty streets, blaring recordings of John 3:16; powerful transmitters hum on remote islands, sending the Good News to isolated souls who huddle around their radios. The outreach is alluring, but the task is exceedingly more complex.

The missionary must acquire a new language, adapt to a new culture, analyze a new religious system, appreciate new values, avoid new dangers, adopt new habits, account for new emotions, attain new expectations, ascribe to new regulations, abstain from new taboos, address new problems, anticipate new opposition, answer new conflicts, apply new criteria, advocate new solutions, advance new goals, effect new changes, admit new defeats, acknowledge new limitations, and proclaim the old gospel message.

And this is but the beginning. Once the missionary has penetrated the target culture and effectively proclaimed the good news of life in Jesus Christ, they must then work with those who have responded, bringing them to productive spiritual maturity.

The territory in which missionaries work is as big as the world, and the task that they must perform is as wide as God's diverse work in that world. Neither the arena nor the assignment is for theological neophytes. Thus, the purpose here is to substantiate the need for missionary theologians in today's world and offer suggestions for meeting that need.

THE NEED FOR MISSIONARY THEOLOGIANS

Never in the history of the church has there existed a greater demand for missionaries who are well trained in the Bible and theology. The day when a simplistic approach to missions was acceptable—if, indeed, this ever was the case—no longer exists. It is all too easy, however, for Christians in the United States to view missions as a "foreign endeavor," unrelated to life in America.

The United States is, in fact, an ecclesiastical compound that has fenced out the rest of the world. It is difficult to sense the needs of the world while living in a self-sufficient state. A nation that has but 6 percent of the world's population and yet consumes 50 percent of the world's goods tends to be provincial and complacent.[7] And the churches, with their freshly painted spires punctuating the landscape of "Compound USA," tend to be rather provincial as well. They boast a staff of well-trained leaders even when membership or attendance may not warrant it.

When we step outside the borders of the United States, however, we are engulfed in a crowded, convulsing, and chaotic world—a world that is in desperate need of sensitive and culturally aware theologians who want to serve others and obey God. The need is acute for at least three reasons: demographic explosion, ecclesiastical expansion, and theological erosion.

Demographic Explosion

According to the U.S. Census Bureau Web site, 5.9 billion people were living on the earth in 1989, and the numbers have kept rising. Every day, an additional 216 thousand mouths must be fed. "According to Census Bureau projections, world population will increase to a level of nearly 8 billion persons by the end of the next quarter century and will reach 9.3 billion persons—a number more than half again as large as today's total—by 2050."[8]

The vast majority of the world's people live in Asia. China alone now has more than 1.2 billion inhabitants, India claims 967 million, Indonesia more than 209 million, and Japan 126 million. Indo-Asia, however, does not have the greatest population growth rate. While world population is increasing at a sizable 1.27 percent per year, "ninety-six percent of world population increase now occurs in the developing regions of Africa, Asia, and Latin America, and this percentage will rise over the course of the next quarter century. In 1998, 90 percent of the world's births and 77 percent of its deaths took place in less-developed countries (LDCs). Ninety-nine percent of global natural increase—the difference between numbers of births and deaths—occurs in the developing world."[9]

The astounding growth of the global village can best be seen by tracing population increases throughout history. Scientists estimate that humankind did not reach the 1 billion mark in population until the early nineteenth century. Then it took only 120 years to add a second billion. In a mere thirty-two years, a third billion was added. In but fifteen years, the fourth billion joined the world crowd. If the population explosion continues at the current rate, the next billion people will push their way into the teeming masses of humanity in less than a decade.[10]

Because God's work is "people work," this astounding population growth carries implications for missions and theology. Missions involves *reaching people* and theology involves *teaching people*. More people means more work, and that is the plight facing the church today. Every day, 216,000 more people are born who must be evangelized and edified.

With the fast-paced population increase, the world scene has changed. In an age of acceleration in every area of life, the world is on a racetrack, or perhaps a better analogy is a drag strip. Starting from a virtual standstill, change for centuries seemed to spin its wheels. Then changes began to take place at a reasonable speed. Now they scream down the track at a frightening pace. As the world explodes numerically, the missionary's task takes on a new sense of urgency. Today is not a time for a relaxing journey to the field on a slow-moving steamship. It is time to board jetliners and try to keep pace with the endeavor called world missions. That does not mean, however, that men and women should depart without being prepared theologically. On the contrary, the missions enterprise will produce nothing of lasting value if preparation is defective. To board that jetliner without the benefit of adequate training is nothing short of missions suicide. The increased complexity and urgency of missions today demands more, not less, preparation. If theological proficiency ever was an option, such is no longer the case; it is a prerequisite.

Ecclesiastical Expansion

Not only is the world population growing at an astounding rate but so, too, is the church expanding. The church in America is often unaware of that worldwide growth. Throughout the Third World, particularly in Africa, Christianity is experiencing the largest growth in followers in church history. David Barrett—a Nairobi-based researcher who is completing a major multivolume work on world religious trends—has estimated that in the last decade more than six million Africans were being converted to Christianity every year—at an astonishing rate of 16,600 believers a day.[11]

Similar spectacular church growth has occurred in some areas of Asia. In South Korea, for example, the Protestant church is growing five times faster than the population. One third of all government leaders are Christian, and at least one fourth to one half of the six hundred thousand men in the armed forces of South Korea are Christians.[12] In 1980, an estimated six new churches were being established every day, and every forty-five seconds a new Christian was added to the church.[13]

Advances for the Christian church have been seen in Indonesia, the world's fifth largest nation. Of the 20 million Christians in Indonesia today, 10 million had turned to the Christian faith during the '70s, the largest increase in Christians ever recorded in a Muslim country.[14] In India, one pastor baptized seven hundred new believers during the first two months of 1980. His group of churches grew from two thousand members in 1972 to twenty thousand in 1980.[15]

Latin America is also experiencing unbelievable growth among evangelicals. Johnstone reports that in 1900 there were only two to three hundred thousand Protestants in all of Latin America, but by 1980 that number had increased to 21 million, and by 1990 it was 46 million.[16] Some recent breakthroughs among ethnic subgroups in Latin America demonstrate remarkable growth spurts. Read, Monterroso, and Johnson reported in 1969 in their *Latin American Church Growth*, "The thin end of the wedge of Christianity has barely entered among the Quechua Indians. Perhaps five per cent of this population has been won to Christ."[17] Today, the vast majority of the Quechuas have come to Christ.

In Central America, where the population growth is soaring, church growth is skyrocketing. One mission reported that, whereas the annual rate of population growth in Honduras stood at a record-breaking 3.5 percent per annum, the churches associated with CAM International reported an astronomical 16.5 percent rate of growth for the same year. Costa Rica's rate of population growth is a more modest 2.5 percent, yet the churches there reported a 20.4 percent increase in baptized believers during the year.[18]

It should be noted that the growth of the church in the Third World is not like church growth in the United States. Most American churches that grow usually do so at the expense of neighboring churches. The growth is mainly through transfer. In contrast, almost all who join the church overseas are new Christians. They are not veterans of the faith who have decided to sip sermons from a more scintillating fountain. These are babes in Christ who, in many cases, have never peeked inside a Bible before.

The pressing need for theologically trained teachers, then, is obvious. With so great an influx of new believers, the Third World church is at the point of crisis. If adequate teaching is not soon forthcoming in the exploding churches of Africa, Asia, and Latin America, a warped, ill-conceived, self-wrought theology will likely develop that will hardly be recognized as Christian.

When new Christians are not adequately taught the Word of God, they naturally devise their own standards, their own regulations, and their own systems of religious experience. Rampant legalism and complex religiosity are but symptoms of a more severe disease called Bible anemia. Crippled saints will manufacture crooked canes on which to lean while they hobble through life. God-starved believers will sacrifice their prized possessions to forge some golden calf that they can see and worship. Blinded Christian neophytes will grope for a leader and will embrace anyone who comes along.

If better care is not taken to store the grain from one of the greatest harvests in the history of the church, there may be nothing left but piles of rotting seed so stricken with blight and mildew that future plantings will be impossible. One bumper crop is not enough. The Lord of the harvest *demands* reproduction. A key to that process is proper care of the seed and prudent cultivation of each tender shoot in God's garden.

The marvelous growth of the church overseas brings to every true believer great joy and thanksgiving. At the same time, the growth should bring deep concern to thinking Christians. Too few seem to sense the world crisis. *While the theologically trained stand behind church pulpits in the United States and deliver sermon masterpieces to sleepy audiences, masses of new Christians in the rest of the world are crying to receive biblical answers to the difficult questions hurled at them from a hostile environment.* They plead for training from God's Word, and they look for guidance in their new-found faith. Thus, the need for well-trained theologians is acute.

Theological Erosion

The world is exploding, the church is expanding, and in the midst of all the growth, theology is dissipating in confusing and contradictory directions. Where the Bible is not faithfully taught, insipid substitutes for the true gospel are concocted by brilliant but spiritually destitute pseudo Christians. Self-made designers have conceived several popular—if alarming—theological fashions. Even more alarming is the eager reception given them by unsuspecting seekers. Two examples should suffice to demonstrate the need for biblically trained theologians both to correct the damage done and to prevent further erosion.

Liberation Theology

Claimed by Latin Americans as their own unique contribution to the church today, the "theology of liberation" is one of the most talked-about innovations on the theological spectrum. In truth, this system should not be labeled "theology" because its dominant themes are economic, social, and political. One of the best-known spokesmen and designers of the popular movement, Gutierrez, states,

> Indeed, *liberation* is a term which expresses a new posture of Latin Americans. They believe that there can be authentic development for Latin America only if there is liberation from the domination exercised by the great capitalist countries, and especially by the most

powerful, the United States of America. This liberation also implies
a confrontation . . . a social revolution.[19]

The thrust of liberation theology is clearly toward the social, political, and
economic liberation of people who are oppressed by sins that are seen as
collective rather than individual. Yet liberation theology is, in reality, an old
tune—or rather a symphony comprising old melodies rearranged and passed
off as a new composition. The theology proper of liberationists is pantheism, their soteriology smacks of universalism, their ecclesiology is ecumenical, and their eschatology is an echo of More's utopianism.[20] Perhaps the
most devastating aspect of liberation theology is its admitted Marxism.[21] Not
only are millions of people being deceived, they may soon be devoured.

Latin America, as elsewhere, is desperate for biblical theologians who can
answer effectively this counterfeit theology of "praxis," who can demonstrate
what God has already done for those who "do" orthodox theology, who
can teach that the central issue of individual sin and Christ's personal redemption will transform corrupt societies through changed lives, who can
represent the true revolutionary forces of moral righteousness and biblical
justice.

African Theology

Someone said that the continent of Africa is a large question mark that
sprawls out below Europe. Africa today is no question mark. It is a gigantic
exclamation point poised at the center of the globe—a continent so recently
controlled by foreign masters that has suddenly issued eviction orders to them
and has seized its own destiny. Many of the title holders have been thrown
out with violence, and colonialism has essentially ended. A new breeze is
blowing across the continent, and borne on that breeze are the seeds of in-
credible church growth, especially in the sub-Sahara regions.

With this increased political independence and rapid church growth has
come a rather volatile theological movement. Whereas Latin Americans are
crying for a liberated society, the Africans are suggesting a sentimental return to traditional practices.

African theology is a label that defies precise definition. The label has been
indiscriminately attached to far too many concepts. Mbiti, probably the greatest exponent of the so-called African theology, admits this dilemma. "It is
all too easy to use the phrase 'African theology,' but to state what that means
or even to show its real nature, is an entirely different issue."[22]

Although the specific forms might vary, African theology is primarily a reactionary theology that resulted from the battles for independence. The leaders in the movement equate Christianity with colonialism.

> It is the imposition of western culture in the garb of the Gospel that people react against. It is the interpretation of the Bible by the standard of the western social and cultural yardstick, without reference to the indigenous African spiritual heritage and social norms, that stings some African politicians, Christians and theologians.[23]

The "African spiritual heritage and social norms" are apparently key ingredients within the African theological movement. Turner suggests that African theology attempts to amalgamate elements of Christianity and elements of traditional African belief.[24] That being so, Kato has surmised that African theology poses a threat to biblical Christianity through the influence of syncretism and universalism.[25]

Africa needs biblical scholars who can present God's truth to the searching believers of today. It needs theologians who can provide a refreshing but intellectually alert flow of spiritual nourishment to the thousands of new babes in Christ across the African continent. Africa needs missionaries who can expound the Word to a scripturally starved African leadership.

Many other variations of Third World theologies could be cited. In every case, though, it is apparent that the leaders of the most dynamic churches of the world—Latin America, Africa, and Asia—are not sitting in their studies waiting for the latest shipment of theological treatises from Europe or the most recent packages of well-bound commentaries printed in the United States. They are writing their own versions of theology, which all too often bear little relationship to the Bible.

The Need for Biblically Trained Missionary Architects

Well-trained biblical scholars and adept, sensitive theologians are desperately needed to establish a solid foundation—not *for* but *with* the Third World church—grounded in the bedrock of God's unchanging Word. The missionary theologian may then assist in the structure that rises from that foundation—a structure that will reflect the beauty and unique tastes of the culture in which it is built but that, at the same time, will be true to God's plumb line. National architects will lend the edifice an aesthetic appearance, but a divine building code will ensure that every beam is level and every corner square. The missionary theologian is needed not as a building inspector but as an invited consultant, a colaborer in the gigantic, history-making project.

The influence of aberrant theologies is limited primarily to the distant countries in which they are developed. But few conservative evangelicals are aware that the ecumenical movement finds its roots in a missionary conference held in Edinburgh in 1910, from which time Hoekstra has traced what he calls the "demise of evangelism."[26] Johnston sounds a warning lest the same trend away from evangelistic outreach occurs in the world congresses and missions consultations arranged with greater frequency among evangelicals. He contends, "Evangelicalism by its very nature is ecumenical."[27] And Bassham contends that the ecumenical, evangelical, and Roman Catholic traditions "have developed a significant convergence on the main issues in mission theology."[28] If he is correct, then good cause exists to heed the alarm that Johnston sounded. Could Pinnock be right when he suggests, "Today's evangelicals may be tomorrow's liberals"?[29]

A missionary today needs to know more than just simplistic slogans. The tendrils of hybrid theology penetrate the mission field, and in no way may they be confined to one locality. More well-trained, biblically sound theologians are needed to husband and guide these tendrils before they choke the sprouts of the true gospel.

THE PROVISION OF MISSIONARY THEOLOGIANS

Throughout most of the world, the church is reeling under the tension of an exploding world population, a rapidly growing church membership, and an increasingly diverse array of theologies. At the same time, the Western church has become increasingly provincial and complacent. It is time for the materially rich and spiritually blessed Western church to review her responsibilities and renew her commitment to her sisters abroad. To help alleviate the severe shortage of trained theologians, the Western church would do well to consider three suggestions. First, individual Christians must resolve to make theological education in the non-Western church a priority in their own prayers and financial commitment. Second, churches must reassess their missionary outreach and develop a new emphasis in the area of theological training. Third, mission boards must actively recruit candidates with biblical and theological proficiency and encourage the current missionary force to upgrade its training in those areas.

Individual Resolution

Christians are like yeast, acting as a catalyst to change the group. If individual Christians resolved to make theological training in missions a priority, their commitment would affect others in their churches. Soon, the entire body would dedicate more attention to this need.

Individuals and families in the church can, for example, "adopt" Third World countries and start praying daily for God's work in that area. Country profiles prepared by the conveners of the International Congress on World Evangelism in Lausanne,[30] Johnstone's *Operation World,* or the information-packed cards on fifty-two spiritually needy nations compiled by Operation Mobilization can serve as a starting point in assembling information about the adopted country. [31] A small card with a silhouette of the country and a few ongoing prayer requests can be placed in some strategic location in the home as a constant reminder for daily prayer. A strategically located and appropriately labeled clock may be set to the time of the adopted nation so that families can relate more readily to the country's schedule. Concern for a nation and its people, concern especially for the theological welfare of that country, will grow with increased information. Perhaps the family, or several families together, could ensure that a well-deserving student from the adopted country receives three or four years of theological training in his or her own country, a nearby country, or a reputable institution in the United States. Thus, information would yield more involvement, and that involvement could spell new hope for a theologically needy nation.

Outreach Reassessment

Church leaders must assign new importance to their congregations' responsibility for world outreach. The myths about missions already outlined in this chapter must be exploded. World missions is a vibrant activity, offering adventure and opportunity, as well as challenges that have never existed before in the history of humankind.

Because of the need for theological training in the growing church abroad, every church in the West should reevaluate its current emphasis. In many churches, missions has been relegated to an annual pep rally; but missions is more than an occasional conference. In other churches, missions is calculated only in dollars and cents; but missions is more than a budget. In still other churches, missions has been dressed entirely in skirts; but missions is more than a women's guild. And in still other churches, missions has been confined to a bulletin board in the church foyer; but missions is more than a map.

Missions can come alive as a part of the regular church services through occasional long distance telephone calls to missionary members overseas. With new computer technology, it is possible to talk to the missionary on the field during the service as the congregation watches him or her on an overhead screen! Or missions can come alive through relevant, engaging interviews with visiting missionaries followed by a special emphasis in prayer for current activities and challenges overseas. Continuing education and missions exposure is necessary at all levels of the Sunday school curriculum, with a special emphasis on career opportunities at the junior high and high school levels.

Above all, a new commitment should be evidenced toward training theological leaders and supporting those leaders in overseas assignments. A truly missionary church is one that provides personnel for the needs of the world. To the extent that a church is financially able, it should fully support the people from that church who are emerging for missionary service. In addition to sending missionary personnel, the church can "adopt" international students during their years of theological training. A scholarship accompanied by loving, personal concern is an investment with both immediate rewards for the church and long-term benefits for God's work. If a church could provide just one well-trained theologian who is totally committed to investing his or her life for the benefit of a Third World country, that church would do more toward justifying its existence than all of its self-perpetuating services and self-centered promotional programs combined. In most churches, much attention is given to increased attendance and budgets and not enough to what God could be doing through increased numbers to reach the world for His glory.

Missions Recruitment

Missions leaders must give priority to recruitment at the seminary level, challenging capable students with specific opportunities for service. Soliciting from chapel pulpits is counterproductive. Consider, when a church looks for a pastor, it doesn't send an elder or deacon to a seminary to tell about the church in a chapel service there and then ask people who want to serve as pastor to sign up at a literature table. Rather, a church searches out individuals who are best equipped to meet that church's specific needs. Similarly, field surveys conducted by mission leaders will yield specific challenges. Then talented and well-trained individuals who are equipped to meet those challenges can be individually recruited.

Opportunities for theologians on the mission field need not be confined to classroom teaching. Pastoral retreats, leadership seminars, theological education by extension, camp and conference ministries, and untold other areas of service also demand the best in theological training.

Missionary organizations must take a new interest in recruiting key national leaders for advanced theological training. In some cases, adequate institutions are available overseas. In all too many instances, however, such is not the case. The United States, for example, has more than eight hundred Christian colleges and a number of excellent theological seminaries. Africa, however, with more than three times the land area and more than one and a half times the population of the United States, has only a handful of Christian schools.[32]

Not only does the need exist to establish top-level theological institutions in most Third World countries but scholarships are needed to provide proven leaders of those countries the opportunity for study abroad. No investment could yield greater dividends. Sudan Interior Mission's Byang Kato, who received his doctorate from Dallas Theological Seminary, provided leadership to the Association of Evangelicals of Africa and Madagascar at a time when such high-caliber leadership was desperately needed. Wakatama pleads, "Africa urgently needs fifty Byang Katos."[33] Since Kato's untimely death, another doctoral graduate, Tokunboh Adeyemo, has provided leadership while acquiring an additional doctorate—one in philosophy—from the University of Aberdeen.

Another recent example of the dividends reaped from investing in the education of key nationals can be seen in Dr. Chris Marantika, said to be the first Indonesian evangelical to hold a doctoral degree in theology. During his years in the United States, he gathered a team of several Western couples to assist in founding the Evangelical Theological School of Indonesia. The well-trained faculty team hoped for an initial enrollment of thirty; they launched the seminary in late 1979 with more than seventy students! As part of their training, the seminary students must plant a new church. In the first six months of 1979, twenty-seven new congregations were formed. In one location, seventy converts—primarily from Islam—were baptized after the required preparation, which included three months of study and an oral examination.[34] Mission leaders and church leaders alike would be wise to become involved in activities that respond to the need for theological leaders overseas.

A HEALTHY BODY

The missionary's territory and his task are as immense and as complex as the twenty-first-century world. The modern missionary endeavor is centered in sophisticated societies of highly religious peoples, and it includes both evangelism and edification. Thus, theological training for today's missionary is a necessity.

Because of demographic explosion, ecclesiastical expansion, and theological erosion, trained biblical expositors and theologians are needed. World population is increasing at astronomical rates, and much of the Third World church is growing at an even greater rate. In the midst of this growth, diverse nonbiblical theologies proliferate.

It is often easier to identify needs than to provide solutions. Providing biblical theologians to missions demands the attention and sacrifice of every Christian, every church leader, and every mission leader. Church members can "adopt" a country or group of people, working and praying toward the theological welfare of that area or group. In their mission outreach, church leaders can give priority to theological training and to the development of competent workers. Mission leaders can more actively recruit theologically equipped candidates and can provide opportunities for their current missionaries to upgrade their training in theology.

Mediocrity in missions theology must cease. God's growing church demands biblical strength and theological precision. Without a solid foundation in the Word, the structure of Third World churches will be laid low by "every wind of doctrine." Without a theological anchor, the church will be split open on the shoals of false teaching.

"Speaking the truth in love, we are to grow up in all aspects into Him, who is the head, even Christ" (Eph. 4:15). Every member of the body is responsible for the biblical health and theological well-being of the whole body—the church around the world.

This chapter is reprinted with additions and adaptations from J. Ronald Blue, "The Missionary as a Theologian" in *Walvoord: A Tribute* (Chicago: Moody, 1982), 315–31.

CHAPTER 10

WOMEN ON THE MISSION FIELD

RUSSELL L. PENNEY

THE SAINTLY WOMEN MISSIONARIES OF THE PAST

Since the inception of the modern missions movement, women have played a key role in the spread of the gospel to the ends of the earth. Their earliest form of participation was financial support. Dana L. Robert writes,

> In 1800 a Baptist "invalid" named Mary Webb founded the Boston female Society for Missionary purposes, a group of Congregational and Baptist women whose purpose was to encourage current efforts to spread the gospel throughout the world.[1]

From this beginning, the many women's missionary fellowships and auxiliaries in local churches across our nation were established. "As the only public institution that encouraged the participation of women, the church became the focus of women's extra-domestic activity."[2]

But women's participation in missions has not only been through financial means. Women such as Narcissa Whitman, Eliza Spaulding, Charlotte Carey, and Ann (Nancy) Hasseltine Judson served faithfully with their husbands during the difficult early years of the missions movement. The motivation of these women was much the same as that of their husbands. Robert writes,

> Missionary wives shared with their husbands the view that without the God found through Jesus Christ, the souls of humanity would not obtain eternal life. Seeking the salvation of the heathen through the spreading of the gospel motivated much of the female missionary sensibility.[3]

Because of their deep reverence for Scripture, these godly missionary wives "assumed that their primary mission work would be directed toward women and children."[4] Robert writes of Ann Judson,

> Just as she had led children to Christ in her career as a school teacher, Ann Judson assumed that the great object of her mission work was to lead women and children to Christ.[5]

"Although public opinion throughout much of the nineteenth century was opposed to the idea [of single women missionaries] . . . beginning in the 1820s single women began to trickle overseas."[6] Later in history came single missionary women of note such as Lottie Moon (evangelism and church-planting), Amy Carmichael (Christian orphanage work), Gladys Aylward (Christian orphanage work), and Helen Roseveare (medical missions). These women were convinced that the Bible was inspired and inerrant and that it should be literally interpreted. They believed that faith in Jesus Christ alone was the only way the pagan or anyone else could be saved. Thus, the driving force for most of these women was a desire to evangelize the heathen, a goal in direct contrast to that of the liberal denominational missions of the early 1900s, which emphasized "social reform, pacifism, and friendship among the world's Christian women."[7]

Because of their belief in Scripture, the majority of these early women missionaries held that the prohibitions for women outlined in the Bible were as applicable on the mission field as they were in their local assemblies. Married women saw their primary task as supporting their missionary husbands through the nurturing and training of their own children and the evangelization and discipling of women and children of their host culture. Single women believed that their primary ministry was evangelization and discipling of women and children. Whether through their work in orphanages, medical missions, home Bible studies, or the planting and establishing of local churches in conjunction with male missionaries, evangelical women missionaries lived out their biblical convictions.

WHY THIS CHAPTER?

Because of the social environment in the United States and in much of Western society, anyone who points out the biblically mandated roles of the sexes causes a stirring of emotions. Any controversy over the place of women that arises in local churches, within mission agencies, and on mission fields is the product of cultural influences ("do not be conformed to this world," Rom. 12:1 NASB). The result has been an overall deterioration in the modern church's purity and holiness, and this deterioration has reduced the church's effectiveness in carrying out the Great Commission.

THE HEART OF THE PROBLEM

Scriptural Inspiration, Inerrancy, and Sufficiency

Some churches, mission organizations, and mission agencies no longer believe in an inspired and inerrant Bible. They have begun to doubt the reliability of Scripture and its sufficiency to deal with modern problems. Culture is allowed too much influence, with the result that, as Schaeffer states, "the Bible is made to say only that which echoes the surrounding culture at our moment of history. The Bible is bent to the culture instead of the Bible judging our society and culture." This has a practical effect on daily life and on missions practice. Schaeffer again writes, "Compromising the full authority of Scripture eventually affects what it means to be a Christian theologically and how we live in the full spectrum of human life."[9] Such compromise also affects the missionary zeal and effectiveness of the local church. So, in coming to a biblically guided view of the role of women on the mission field, we must hold up Scripture as the ultimate authority for objective truth. We must recognize not only its supreme authority but also its sufficiency in dealing with all doctrinal issues.

Scriptural Interpretation and Application

Among those who hold strongly to inspiration and inerrancy are two major groups. The first consists of those who take their view of women's roles predominately from contemporary culture. This first group approaches Scripture with a cultural and contextual interpretation that nullifies the prohibitions on women in ministry. Included in this approach is the practice of redefining terms. Seeing the scriptural prohibition on women in ministry as a matter of sexual superiority or inferiority clouds the issue. The Bible is clear that mandated roles are a matter of function and not superiority and inferiority.

The second group historically has held to a more biblical view of manhood and womanhood. This group, however, struggles with how the doctrinal truths that guide the conduct and function of women in the local church play themselves out on the mission field. This important topic will be discussed in the concluding pages of this chapter.

Many of the larger mission agencies—most of them interdenominational—fit into the latter group. As a result of their failure to clarify their position on women's role in missions, they have given in to the liberal denominations and opened up areas of service to women that Scripture forbids. Other agencies tell missionaries that they should abide by the policies of their sending churches, which, in essence, is no stance at all. In researching this chapter, the general editor contacted fifteen of the major independent mission agencies about their views on women's roles in missions. Most of them did not respond. Of those that did, their positions were found to be disappointing. One major mission agency, for instance, wrote,

> I would say that over the years [name of the agency] has grown in its understanding of the role of women and in practice as well. Our roots were more from the Brethren Church, which traditionally had more of a male leadership model. Over the years we have had more women assuming leadership roles and have provided more freedom for women to develop the kind of ministry that they feel God is leading them into.[10]

Note that not once is an appeal made to Scripture to defend the move away from a biblical male-leadership model to one that places women in spiritual authority over men. Another mission agency summarized their thoughts on the matter by quoting from a December 1992 *Pulse* article by Jim Reapsome, in which he wrote,

> Perhaps the strongest signal we send women is the role we give, or do not give, to them in mission leadership. Some of our institutions would be better served if the wives of the men in charge were given their job. In these cases, the wife is gifted in management and administration, while her husband's gifts are in teaching, preaching and counseling. The point is to use people in their strengths, regardless of sex. The work of God could be considerably expedited if we got serious. Men, it's long past the time to change.[11]

Notice the pragmatism in the author's view. This mission agency has, apparently, bought in to such thinking.

That major mission agencies have taken such a stance is not only damaging to the women involved but also potentially harmful for the churches with whom they will be working or helping to establish. In the case of church planting, the unbiblical pattern and doctrinal compromise will be modeled to the converts from the very first day.

God's Design for the Family

To understand the doctrinal truths of the woman's role on the mission field, it is important first to understand the woman's role in the family and in the local church. The roles of men and women in the church and in missions are tied to God's creation of man and woman and the function of each in the family. This connection is most strongly stated by the apostle Paul in 1 Timothy 2:11–15. The following diagram shows how the institutions of the family, society, and the church are connected ("God's Design of Male Leadership"). Understanding the functional distinctions inherent in God's original design of man and woman clarifies the logical connection between male leadership in the home and in the church, of which missions is simply an extension.

GOD'S DESIGN OF MALE LEADERSHIP

Church	The Mission Agency	Society
Elders	Elder Leadership	Elder Leadership
(1 Tim. 3:1–7; 2:12)		

Family
God (Gal. 4:6)
Christ (1 Cor. 11:3)
Man (Eph. 5:22–23; Col. 3:18; 1 Peter 3:7)
Woman (1 Tim. 2:11–15)
Children (Eph. 6:1)

The Bible mandates that the leadership of the family is to be male. Considering that the church is referred to as "the household of God," it naturally follows that the leadership of the church is to be male. Because the mission agency is an extension of the church, the same doctrinal prohibitions apply. And since the society in which we live is made up primarily of families, it is logical that God meant there to be male leadership of society. Thus, women are not to be in positions wherein they teach doctrinal truths to or exercise authority over men.

The Bible on Sexual Equality

Before discussing biblically mandated roles for the sexes, we must first begin by defining some terms. Ortlund defines biblical *male-female equality* thus: "Man and woman are equal in the sense that they bear God's image equally."[12] The second important term is *male-headship,* about which Ortlund states, "In the partnership of two spiritually equal human beings, man and woman, the man bears the primary responsibility to lead the partnership in a God-glorifying direction."[13] Ortlund also clarifies the distinction between *male-headship* and *male-domination.* He writes, "The model of headship is our Lord, the Head of the church, who gave Himself for us. The antithesis to male headship is male domination. By male domination I mean the assertion of the man's will over the woman's will, heedless of her spiritual equality, her rights, and her value."[14]

According to Genesis 1:26–28, which gives us an overview of the creation of mankind, Adam and Eve were both made in the image of God. Mankind exists as male and female, two distinct sexes. Earlier, Genesis states "let *them* rule," indicating that both sexes are to be involved in the ruling process. In verse 28, mankind's responsibilities are recorded, which is a directive to both sexes. Thus, from this passage we see (1) that man and woman are both equal image-bearers of God; (2) that both are called to be fruitful and multiply, to fill the earth, and to subdue it; (3) that both are called to rule over the rest of God's creation.

THE BIBLE ON MALE HEADSHIP

Genesis 1:26–28 depicts full equality between men and women with regard to their bearing the image of God, carrying out the command to rule over the rest of God's creation, and being fruitful and increasing the population of the world with godly progeny. The passage also suggests male headship. From the beginning, for instance, God's creation was called "man." Ortlund writes,

> God did *not* name the human race "woman." If "woman" had been the more appropriate and illuminating designation, no doubt God would have used it. He does not even devise a neutral term like "persons." He called us "man," which anticipates the male headship brought out clearly in chapter two, just as "male and female" in verse 27 foreshadows marriage in chapter two.[15]

Thus, male and female bear equally the image of God, but Genesis 2 denotes a clear difference in function; God made man to be the head and woman to be the helper.

In Genesis 2:18, God stated, "I will make him a helper suitable for him." The Hebrew term translated "helper" (Heb. *ēzer*) means "a helper," "a help," or "a support."[16] Woman would be "suitable for him" in the sense that only she, of all of the creatures, shared a common nature with Adam. "And the Lord God fashioned into a woman the rib which He had taken from the man, and brought her to the man. And the man said, 'This is now bone of my bones, and flesh of my flesh; She shall be called Woman [Heb. *Ishshah*], Because she was taken out of Man [Heb. *Ish*]'" (Gen. 2:23).

This new creation could meet Adam's inner longings, and this is the reason, as Moses explains in Genesis, that throughout history man and woman have paired off and created homes: "For this cause [that woman was taken out of man] a man shall leave his father and mother, and shall cleave to his wife; and they shall become one flesh" (v. 24). The institution of marriage is not a result of tradition; it is a part of God's sovereign plan. The attraction between a man and a woman, eventually leading to marriage, is the result of woman being taken from man in the original creation. Thus, the reunion of what was originally one flesh is God's natural design. That man and woman were naked and were not ashamed demonstrates the perfection of the original creation. They perfectly complemented each other.

God said that she was "a helper suitable for him" (vv. 18, 20). The fact that she alone was suitable for him demonstrates her equality with him. She was the only creature that shared his nature. Only she could provide him with companionship on an equal level. At the same time, she is called his "helper." Ortlund writes,

> The man was not created to help the woman, but the reverse. Doesn't this striking fact suggest that mankind and womankind are distinct and non-reversible? Doesn't this make sense if we allow that, while the man and the woman are to love each other as equals, they are not to love each other *in the same way?* The man is to love his wife by accepting the primary responsibility for making their partnership a platform displaying God's glory, and the woman is to love her husband by supporting him in the godly undertaking. (italics his)[17]

Kassain writes,

> Adam recognized the unity between himself and the female. However, he also recognized his God-given responsibility and authority by naming her. (Adam's act of naming the woman occurs again in Genesis 3:20 when he gives her the name "Eve"—mother of all living.) If the woman and man were meant to have identical roles, God would have named the woman, just as He had named the man. In giving Adam the responsibility to name the woman, a hierarchical relationship between Adam and the woman is established from the very outset. This in no way belittles the woman or assigns her a lesser role. It simply reflects the differences between the roles that God had assigned for each. Adam was to be the leader in the relationship and the woman was to be the helpmate. These assigned roles blended together and coexisted alongside perfect oneness and unity.[18]

In summary, from the creation account we see that (1) man and woman are both equal image-bearers of God, (2) man's headship in the relationship is clear, (3) woman is created as man's equal in nature but is functionally different, and (4) their roles blend together and coexist in perfect oneness and unity—an ideal and complementary relationship.

GOD'S PERFECT DESIGN CORRUPTED

Although God's design for the family was perfect, something occurred that altered it, and this has resulted in turmoil in our families down to the present day. Humankind's fall in the garden, the eating of the forbidden fruit as recorded in Genesis 3, drastically affected family relationships.

The penalty for man and woman's violation of God's prohibition is given in Genesis 3:16–20, in which the woman was given three primary punishments: she would have increased pain in childbirth, she would have a strong desire for her husband, and he would "rule over" her.

The Hebrew word, here translated "rule," carries the meaning of "to have dominion, to reign, rule."[19] As we have seen, the pre-Fall condition consisted of a beautiful complementary relationship with full spiritual equality under a loving male headship. Man and woman worked together to fulfill God's design for them. But, because the woman usurped the headship of the man by taking the forbidden fruit, she would now have to deal with the sinful male tendency to dominate her. The woman's sinful reaction to sinful male domination is to rebel, a reaction that has resulted in various feminist movements throughout history.

God's punishment for man perfectly fitted his sin. First, because he had submitted to his wife (Gen. 3:17), whom he should have lovingly led, he would now have to deal with the insubordination of the soil. No longer would the tillage of the earth be easy; now it would involve "misery." Only through toil could enough food be produced to sustain him and his family. Work would now be more grievous (Heb. *'itstsebhōn,* "misery," "toil," or "sorrow"). Second, the man's actions resulted in the human race itself being infected by sin (Rom. 5:12).

Note the distinction between the roles of the sexes did not come as the result of the Fall but were a part of God's original design. From the beginning, God created the two sexes to fulfill different roles in society. The Fall, however, created enmity between the sexes, plunging us all into a state of separation from our Creator and creating a need for a Savior and world evangelization.

MAN'S ROLE IN SOCIETY

Because society comprises a community of families and God created man as the spiritual head of the family, it follows that God intended that man should lead in society. Throughout the Old and New Testaments, leadership was always male, both in the nation of Israel and in the church. Only in cases of spiritual apostasy were women put in a position of authority (see especially Isaiah 3:12, where God condemns Israel for allowing the women to lead).

MAN'S ROLE IN THE CHURCH

The Church: God's Family

Much misunderstanding about the roles of men and women in the church results from ignoring that the body of believers—the church—is viewed as a family. Poythress writes,

> The Bible teaches us to call God "our Father" (Matt. 6:9). We who are redeemed by Jesus Christ are children of God (Gal. 4:1-7). These two Biblical affirmations are among many in which the Bible employs an analogy between a human family and the church. By means of this family analogy God makes some of His most precious promises

to us concerning His present love, our future inheritance, and our intimate fellowship with Him (for example, Rom. 8:12–17; Heb. 12:5–11; Rev. 21:7).

The practical implications of these "family teachings" are so deep and so many-sided that we can never fully fathom them. Let us here concentrate only on one strand of implications, those for our conduct toward one another within the Christian community. The Bible invites us to use these family teachings to draw some particular inferences about the respective roles of men and women within the church. In brief, the argument runs as follows: just as husbands and fathers ought to exercise godly leadership in their human families, so wise, mature men ought to be appointed as fatherly leaders in the church (1 Tim. 3:1–7). A particularly important role also belongs to more mature women (1 Tim. 5:9–16; Titus 2:3–5). Likewise mothers of the church, they are to train their spiritual daughters by example and word. But just as in the case of marriage (Eph. 5:22–33), the respective functions of men and women are not reversible in all respects. Men—and not women—are called on to exercise the decisive fatherly leadership as elders.[20]

"According to Paul, the fundamental principles regarding the structures of the human family are to be applied to the church as God's household (1 Tim. 3:15)."[21] As Poythress points out, Paul refers to Timothy as his "son." In addition, Timothy should view older men as fathers, younger men as brothers, older women as mothers, and younger women as sisters (5:1–2). Widows, if they lack immediate family, should be cared for because they are in the Christian family (vv. 5, 16).[22] Paul writes in 1 Timothy 3:14–15 (NASB),

> I am writing these things to you, hoping to come to you before long; but in case I am delayed, I write so that you may know how one ought to conduct himself in *the household of God*, which is the church of the living God, the pillar and support of truth. (italics added)

The Elder/Overseer/Pastor-Teacher

Under the preceding relationship, one can understand why Paul required that an elder of the church "manage his own household well" (1 Tim. 3:5). The same management skills required in the home were those required in the church, "the household of faith." It is not surprising, then, that headship/

leadership roles in the church are restricted to men, just as they are in the home. Therefore, when looking at the qualifications for the pastor-teacher/elder of the church, Paul speaks only of *men* aspiring to that position (v. 1). Paul has, in fact, just addressed the prohibition of women "to teach or exercise authority over a man" in the church assembly (2:12). A woman's attitude and actions should reflect her submission to her husband (1 Cor. 11:2–16).

But, as in the family, the male leadership of the church should be reminded that the women of the church are equal image-bearers of God. In addition, women, like men, have been given spiritual gifts (12:7–11) and are called to use them to minister to the body (1 Peter 4:10).

The biblical pattern for leadership in the local church, then, is a group of men referred to as elders, who meet the criteria established in 1 Timothy 3:1–7 and the corresponding list in Titus 1.

The Deacon

In addition, the biblical pattern includes a group of men called "deacons." The term *deacon* (Gk. *diakonos*) literally means "servant," or "helper."[23] This office probably developed from the benevolent ministries in the early church, as described in Acts 6. The lists of qualifications for elders and deacons are similar, with one exception: absent in the list for deacons is the ability to teach. Thus, it is likely that deacons performed any task in the church that would have taken the elders away from their tasks of praying, teaching, and preaching.

Although some people have argued for female deacons (deaconesses) from 1 Timothy 3:11, this passage probably refers to the wives of deacons. Even if this passage is referring to female deacons, the position would still not give them license to violate Paul's directive in 1 Timothy 2:12 and 1 Corinthians 14:33–35.

THE ROLE OF WOMEN IN THE CHURCH

The Biblical Prohibitions

Several passages in the New Testament address the role of women in the church. The key New Testament text is 1 Timothy 2:10–15, which succinctly states the prohibitions against women presented in the broader text of 1 Timothy 2–3 (cf. 3:15). Women are prohibited from *teaching or exercising authority over men* in public worship, that is, in the church (2:11–12, italics added). Note, Paul has just mentioned the proper adornment of a Christian woman who makes a claim to godliness. Here he further notes that her inner attitude should manifest itself through "quietly receiv[ing] instruction with entire submissiveness" (v. 12; cf. 1 Cor. 14:33b–35). But what does Paul mean here by the term *teach?* Moo writes,

> The word teach and its cognate nouns teaching *(didaskalia)* and teacher *(didaskalos)* are used in the New Testament mainly to denote the careful transmission of the tradition concerning Jesus Christ and the authoritative proclamation of God's will to believers in light of the tradition (see especially 1 Tim. 4:11 "Command and teach these things," 2 Tim. 2:2; Acts 2:42; Rom. 12:7). While the word can be used more broadly to describe the general ministry of edification that takes place in various ways (e. g., through teaching, singing, praying, reading of Scripture [Colossians]), the activity usually designated by teach is plainly restricted to certain individuals who have the gift of teaching (see 1 Cor. 12:28–30; Eph. 4:11). This makes it clear that not all Christians are engaged in doctrinal instruction. As Paul's own life draws to a close, and in response to the false teaching, Paul is deeply concerned to insure that sound, healthful teaching be maintained in the churches. One of Timothy's main tasks is to teach (1 Tim. 4:11–16; 2 Tim. 4:2) and to prepare others to carry on this vital ministry (2 Tim. 2:2). While perhaps not restricted to the elder-overseer, "teaching" in this sense was an important activity of these people (see 1 Tim. 3:2; 5:17; Titus 1:9).[24]

Paul, in this instance, was prohibiting women from any position or situation where they would be giving out doctrinal instruction or exercising authority over any group in which men were present.

Paul gives two reasons for this. *Note that Paul's theology has nothing to do with culture.* First is the creation order. The Greek text reads, "For Adam first was created, then Eve" (1 Tim. 2:13). God's creation order indicates a distinction in function. Adam was created first and placed in the headship position. Thus, men are to lead in the church. Second, a literal rendering of the following verse reads, "And Adam was not deceived [misled], but the woman having been completely deceived, has come to be in transgression" (v. 14). Although many commentators avoid making a judgment on Paul's intention, the only conclusion possible is that the woman, because of the way she was created to fulfill her role, is more easily deceived. Her emotional sensitivity and nurturing capabilities are a strength for her role as mother and wife but are a weakness in doctrinal discernment. As can be seen from this passage, the reasoning behind forbidding women to teach or exercise authority over men has nothing to do with culture. It is tied to the creation design, thus making the principle transcultural and fully applicable for today.

Some people have raised the question as to whether Paul was here referring to one activity or to two different activities; that is, was Paul prohibiting women from the authoritative teaching of men, or was he prohibiting them from teaching *and* directly exercising authority over men? This question is best answered by resorting to grammar. Moo, referring to the Greek conjunction that joins the two infinitives "to teach" and "to exercise authority," writes,

> While the word in question, *oude* ("and not," "neither," "nor"), certainly usually joins "two *closely related* items," it does not usually join together words that restate the same thing or that are mutually interpreting, and sometimes it joins opposites (e.g., Gentile and Jew, slave and free; Galatians 3:28). Although teaching in Paul's sense here is authoritative in and of itself, not all exercising of authority in the church is through teaching, and Paul treats the two tasks as distinct elsewhere in 1 Timothy when discussing the work of elders in the church (3:2, 4–5; 5:17). That teaching and having authority are "closely related" is, of course, true, but here and elsewhere they are nonetheless distinct, and in 1 Timothy 2:12, Paul prohibits women from conducting either activity, whether jointly or in isolation, in relation to men.[25]

Another passage that addresses the issue of the role of women in the church is 1 Corinthians 11:2–16. There, Paul states the theological principle (v. 2) for headship in the church as Christ–man–woman, and again the context is public worship (v. 2; 16). Paul indicates that, if a woman prays or prophesies (*prophesy* here is probably referring to foretelling; i.e., 12:10; Luke 2:36; Act 21:9, which later ceased with the completion of the canon of Scripture; 13:8–13), she is to have her head covered, the culturally accepted way of showing submission to her husband. Although space does not allow for a full explanation of the passage, it is important to note that Paul gives several reasons—including the divine order (1 Cor. 11:3–6) and creation (vv. 7–9)—

for this sign of subordination in the assembly. The same reasoning is found in Paul's first letter to Timothy. Thus, women who show the proper subordination to male leadership in the assembly should be allowed to offer oral prayer in public worship.

In 1 Corinthians 14:33–35, Paul points out that his theology of woman's submission is drawn, as is the theology on other prohibitions, from the creation account. In that passage, he states,

> . . . as in all the churches of the saints. Let the women keep silent in the churches; for they are not permitted to speak, but let them subject themselves, just as the Law also says. And if they desire to learn anything, let them ask their own husbands at home; for it is improper for a woman to speak in church.

Paul notes here that the prohibition against women speaking in the church assembly is based on the Law. The "Law" here is not the Mosaic Law but the first five books of the Hebrew Bible—the Torah (Genesis–Deuteronomy; specifically Gen. 2:20b–24). From the creation account of Genesis, Paul draws the theology on male headship that he applies in the 1 Corinthians passage. The prohibition is against women being involved in discussing the meaning and application of prophecies received in the worship service. Paul makes clear that a woman is certainly allowed to learn, but if she has a question about what is being discussed she should ask her husband. He, being the spiritual head, is responsible for gaining an understanding of the Scripture and ensuring that his wife (and his children) are spiritually nourished (Eph. 5:26). This passage (and others that we have discussed) does not prevent women from giving testimony, offering the Scripture reading, making announcements, leading songs, or even offering a public prayer, because none of these activities violates Paul's prohibition.

Galatians 3:28 has sometimes been used to counter the argument for biblically mandated functions in the church based on sex. The context of Galatians 3:28, however, does not support such a stand. There, Paul is responding to the Judaizers who were teaching that the Galatian believers would have to continue observing the Mosaic Law as a means of sanctification. These teachers of false doctrine appealed to their descendancy from Abraham, thinking their legacy gave them authority in the eyes of the Galatians (Gal. 3:7). Paul reminded the Galatians that, just as Abraham was justified by faith, only those who demonstrated the same kind of faith were children of Abraham

(vv. 6–7, 9), and that God would justify the nations through the Abrahamic covenant: "All the nations shall be blessed in you [Abraham]" (v. 9).

In verses 10–25, Paul responded to the question that would naturally arise: "Why, then, the Law?" He asserted that the Law was never meant to justify and could not do so (vv. 10–12). Christ now had redeemed all from the curse of the Law so that all might receive the blessing of Abraham by faith and that all might receive the promise of the Holy Spirit (v. 14). Paul then demonstrated the superiority of the covenant given to Abraham over the Law and emphasized that the Law was given for a brief time for specific reasons and did not replace the covenant given to Abraham (vv. 15–18). The Law was given alongside the existing Abrahamic covenant to restrain sin (v. 19, "because of transgressions") and to lead the Jews to the knowledge that they could not keep the Law and that they needed a Savior (v. 23–24). Paul's point was that everyone has equal access to God's blessing through Christ and to receiving God's promise of the Spirit (v. 14). All who accept God's blessing in Christ and thereby receive the Spirit are Abraham's seed (vv. 7, 9). And, in that sense, no one has an advantage. Piper and Grudem comment,

> Most evangelicals still agree that this text is not a warrant for homo-sexuality. In other words, most of us do not force Paul's "neither male nor female" beyond what we know from other passages he would approve. For example, we know from Romans 1:24–32 that Paul does not mean for the created order of different male and female sex roles to be overthrown by Galatians 3:28.
>
> The context of Galatians 3:28 makes abundantly clear the sense in which men and women are equal in Christ: They are equally justified by faith (v. 24), equally free from the bondage of legalism (v. 25), equally children of God (v. 26), equally clothed with Christ (v. 27), equally possessed by Christ (v. 29), and equally heirs of the promises of Abraham (v. 29).
>
> This last blessing is especially significant, namely that equality of being a fellow-heir with men of the promises. In 1 Peter 3:1–7, the blessing of being joint heirs "of the gracious gift of life" is connected with the exhortation for women to submit to their husbands (v. 1) and for their husbands to treat their wives "with respect as the weaker partner." In other words, Peter saw no conflict between the "neither-male-nor-female" principle regarding our inheritance and the headship-submission principle regarding our roles. Galatians 3:28

does not abolish gender-based roles established by God and redeemed by Christ.[26]

When all the above points are examined and considered, it becomes clear that there are biblically mandated roles for men and women, based on God's creation order. It follows, therefore, that in some areas of ministry the Bible places prohibitions on women.

MODERN PRAGMATISM

The church today has, by and large, tended to move from a position of relying on the sufficiency of Scripture to that of being pragmatic, saying in essence, "If it works (or seems to work), do it that way." True, God often "blesses" ministries, regardless of whether they are conducted in His way; people still receive Christ even under the ministry of those who are not holy. When Moses was told to speak to the rock, he struck it. He disobeyed God (and later paid a high price for that disobedience), but he got the desired *results*—the water gushed from the rock. God did not deprive His people of the water they needed just because it was procured in the wrong way. Results do not, however, validate the method. Disobedience, no matter what the results, does not honor God.

The Biblical Latitude

In the local church and on the mission field, tremendous latitude exists for women's ministry, including areas of teaching. I agree with the author who writes, "Women who teach, whether in conformation to the Scriptures or otherwise, are under the same divine scrutiny and ultimate accountability as are men" (see James 3:1).[27] The qualifications for a woman in a position such as director of children's ministries, women's ministries, Sunday school teacher, or missionary should be as stringent as those required for positions held by men; in such positions both men and women need to exhibit responsibility and teach through both word and deed. Those who fill these positions must exemplify Christian maturity to those whom they teach. Thus, most of the same qualifications that are placed on elders and deacons should also be placed on women teachers (1 Tim. 3:1–13; 2 Tim. 2:21–26).

Clearly, based on 1 Timothy 2:11–12, women are not to teach or exercise authority over men. Neither the educational level of the culture engaged nor their view of women's roles changes this prohibition. Nonetheless, numerous areas exist in which women *can* serve in the local church. The following is a nonexhaustive list of areas in which women can exercise their spiritual gifts:

1. Teaching women (small groups, large groups, or conferences)
2. Teaching children (boys until puberty)
3. Writing (all manner of publication presenting a Christian perspective)
4. Authoring Bible study materials (especially for women and children)
5. Personal evangelism and discipleship (especially among women)
6. Visiting the sick
7. Counseling
8. Children's church director
9. Children's ministry director
10. Church secretary
11. Church treasurer
12. Assisting deacons in benevolence ministry
13. All of the preceding ministry opportunities in the area of missions

In each church or missions situation the elders, or the board of the mission agency, should examine the job profile in light of biblical injunction and be convinced that the principle of women not "teaching or exercising authority over a man" is not being violated.

THE ROLE OF WOMEN IN MISSIONS

Studying God's design for men and women, their roles in the family, and their roles in the church has helped us to understand the role of women on the mission field. As the chart on page 193 shows, God's original design mandates that leadership—in family, church, or missions—is to be male.

The overarching principle for women in mission work is given by Paul in 1 Timothy 2:12: "I do not allow a woman to teach or exercise authority over a man." Some examples of how this principle applies in missions will further clarify the functions that are appropriate for women.

Frontier missions work (i.e., reaching unreached peoples and planting churches) does not necessarily exclude women. Women could be part of church-planting teams and involved in the initial evangelization of both men (depending on the culture) and women. As the church is being organized, a woman could help to teach children and to teach and prepare other women of the church to carry on the ministry and to continue teaching the children. She could also teach and help with the application of God's Word in the marriage relationship and the home (Titus 2:3–5). Many other ministry activities are also open to her (see the list above).

In situations where missionaries help disciple nationals in the faith and in the truth of God's Word in established churches, women have a vital role in the discipleship of women and children. In missions organizations, women can certainly be a part of the structure, but any position that puts women in authority over men violates God's Word.

Medical missions, too, is an area where women can be effective. Consider the work and testimony of Helen Roseveare and the scores of women like her who have given much of their lives to ministering to the medical needs of those in foreign cultures while sharing the gospel.

Many saints will populate the corridors of heaven as a result of godly women like Gladys Aylward and Amy Carmichael, who have reached out to rescue and evangelize the unwanted children of foreign cultures. Missionary women have, in conjunction with their primary ministry, written journals of their experiences and struggles that have inspired millions to serve Christ abroad. Women missionaries have also written Christian literature of every sort to encourage and strengthen Christians in their walk with the Lord.

TO HONOR GOD'S WORD

Endless examples could be given of the ways in which gifted women can use their talents on the mission field. But the guiding principle by which to evaluate all of these areas is the same (1 Tim. 2:12). God established an authority structure from the beginning. Male and female were created spiritually equal yet functionally suited to different purposes. As Paul clearly teaches, the authority structure in the local church, and thus in missions (see chap. 14, "The Role of the Mission Agency"), is based not on the culture but on the creation order (1 Tim. 2:13–15). Because of this distinction in function, women are prohibited from any ministry that places them in positions of teaching or exercising authority over men. These prohibitions are minor in limitation, however, when one considers the spectrum of ministry that God provides on the mission field. Women can exercise their spiritual gifts in many arenas for the glory of God.

May God continue to raise up godly women who honor God's Word and who desire to commit their lives to evangelizing the world until Christ's return. Amen.

Adapted in part from *A Biblical Theology of the Church,* ed. Mal Couch (Grand Rapids: Kregel, 1999), 213–23.

CHAPTER 11

DEMONOLOGY AND THE MISSION FIELD

JOHN F. HART

IN RECENT YEARS, MISSIONARIES AND mission agencies have demonstrated sharply increased interest in the demonic.[1] Several factors account for this intensified interest. The rise of the Third Wave in the 1980s and its emphasis on deliverance and exorcisms[2] have caught the attention of charismatics in regard to deliverance ministries, and many noncharismatics have expressed support.[3] One might also attribute the fascination with spiritual warfare to Frank Perretti's popular fictional stories, *This Present Darkness* and *Piercing the Darkness*, in which the Christian church is under attack from New Age occult activities. Yet some of the books' portrayals of the spirit world are the result of the current Western worldview rather than the direct testimony of Scripture.

THE FOUNDATION FOR ERROR

In Western culture, the pendulum has swung from a humanistic, rationalistic worldview to a New Age, antirational outlook in which inner feelings and existential experience dominate. Add to the mix the postmodern rejection of knowable truth, and the stage is set for propositional truth grounded in the Scriptures giving way to anecdotal illustrations verified only by experience. Unfortunately, evangelical missionaries have not always been alert to the subtle influence that the non-Christian and experiential may exert on their theology of the spirit world.[4] In its approach to demonology, modern missions has often bought into the secular culture's mind set. A paradigm shift has taken place with the result that many missionaries are now unknowingly interpreting the spirit world in light of existential rather than exegetical principles.

Suppose, for example, that a counselor interviewed several demons in a counselee, asking each one its name, the kind of pernicious activity in which it is involved, and the name of the ranking demon to which it is under authority. For many missionaries, nothing sounds more biblical. But there is nothing specifically Christian or evangelical about the elements of this technique. Rather, they form the essential features of Jewish and Greek practices found in texts of the second-century A.D.[5]

With the recent missionary attraction for doing battle with demonic forces comes the danger of relying upon empirical data against the final authority of the Scriptures. Doing so, even in ignorance, allows experience to take precedence over exegetical methods. Ice and Dean write,

> The empiricist will gather all the information he can from those who claim to have some experience with an angel or demon, or those who have helped deliver people from demonic influence. He will find out what they learned from these encounters and which methods, in their opinion, proved successful in delivering a person from the demonic oppression. He will collect these case studies and then draw conclusions about what we are to do when we encounter a demon. Even when the Bible is consulted with this process, no matter how high the empiricist's view of Scripture, in practice the Bible is treated as just another voice or witness to demonic activity. This always results in adjusting the biblical teaching on demons until it fits with the conclusions of various experiences.[6]

Evidence to demonstrate the validity of Ice and Dean's criticism can be produced *ad nauseam,* but a few examples suffice. After a demon has been expelled, one counselor crawls on the floor next to the collapsed body of the counselee. His experience has shown that the only proven method of determining if a demon has left upon command is to look into the eyes of the counselee and demand, "If there is a spirit in there, I command you to manifest."[7] Another evangelical counselor has discovered a female demon in a "demonized" person, a "reality" he accepts despite his study of the Bible, which confirms that demons always appear as males.[8] Through conversations with demons, another counselor has learned that directly under Satan are six worldwide spirit-leaders whose names are Damian, Asmodeo, Menguelesh, Arios, Beelzebub, and Nosferasteous.[9] Still another counselor commands a patient to wake up immediately from an unconsciousness that has been caused by demons.[10]

These examples are cited not to prove that the counselors are wrong but to emphasize that, apart from biblical input on spiritual reality, humankind (and, of course, Christians) cannot know any spiritual data with certainty—in either the demonic or the angelic realms. There might indeed be six leader-demons under Satan's leadership. But because such information goes beyond biblical revelation, its veracity can be neither affirmed nor denied.

God has not seen fit to make known to human beings—including believers of the Old Testament or New Testament era—countless facts about the angelic and demonic world. Gathering information about the spirit world that goes beyond revelation is strictly forbidden to human beings and is labeled in the Bible as spiritism (Deut. 18:9-14).[11] Isaiah challenged Israel (8:19a NIV), "When men tell you to consult mediums and spiritists, who whisper and mutter, should not a people inquire of their God?" Missionaries, too, need to consult with God both in the Scriptures and by prayer, despite temptations to inquire of demons, shamans, and former occult leaders for insights into the demonic world.

Moses warned the Israelites against an unsettled curiosity about the unknown spiritual dimension: "The secret things belong to the LORD our God, but the things revealed belong to us and to our sons forever, that we may observe all the words of this law" (Deut. 29:29 NASB). Evangelical missions must come to a settled conviction that numerous details about the spirit world *cannot* be known without transgressing into the private knowledge of God. As Moses admonished, "the things revealed" are what the missionary must accept as legitimate knowledge and grounds for obedience. Consider the case of Saul. The disobedient king was dissatisfied with God's refusal to answer his question about the battle with the Philistines. So Saul sought out illegitimate information from a spiritist, and God brought judgment for his rebellion (1 Sam. 28:6-7).

> Epistemology—how we come to know truth—is at the heart of the issues of modern missions, and among many evangelicals empiricism is equally reliable to Scripture in developing a theology of the spirit world.[12]

SPIRITUAL MAPPING AND TERRITORIAL SPIRITS

Brief History of the New Movement

Although spiritual realities cannot be established through scientific method as can earthly, material realities, demonology is nevertheless becoming similar to a Western social science, involving case studies, inventive experimentation, and the gathering of an information base from all sources.[13] Some world missions experts are employing the technique called "spiritual mapping" as a systematic attempt to uncover Satan's strategies.[14] The first International Consultation on Spiritual Mapping met in November 1997 in Tacoma, Washington.[15] George Otis Jr., president of the Sentinel Group (a Christian research agency) and co-coordinator of the United Prayer Track of the A.D. 2000 and Beyond Movement, organized the meeting. Otis also leads the Spiritual Mapping Division, the most prominent division of the United Prayer Track.[16] The phrase "spiritual mapping" was coined by Otis in 1991 to describe the creation of a "spiritual profile of a community based on careful research."[17] The 10/40 Window (the area of the globe between ten degrees and forty degrees north from North Africa to China) is the primary target of spiritual mapping since 95 percent of unreached peoples live in the window. But for Otis, Satan never left the Garden of Eden (in ancient Mesopotamia in the center of the 10/40 Window) at the human fall described in Genesis 3. Instead, he established a global command center in the air above the Garden. This information helps explain the "strongholds" of the 10/40 Window and how we should pray.[18]

With the assistance of specialists who have "gifts of prophetic espionage" or a spiritual "hunting instinct to track down the enemy's manipulations," Peter Wagner—a leading expert in church growth and coordinator for the United Prayer Track[19]—hopes to "map out" the geographical activity of demons so that Christians can pray more effectively against Satan's schemes.[20] "We in the A.D. 2000 Movement are no longer discussing whether we *should* do spiritual mapping. We are now concentrating our energies on *how to do it well*" (italics original).[21] Collecting the names of "territorial spirits" is essential to the project because these spirits are controlling demons who manipulate political powers and prevent the reception of the gospel.

The Faulty Theology of Territorial Spirits

A theology of "territorial spirits" is not only relatively new but also has little biblical support on which to stand.[22] Foster, although an ardent supporter of binding demons and Satan, has surveyed the biblical passages that might support an idea of territorial demons and concludes, "Far and away, the first major obstacle to the concept of territorial spirits is the scarcity of biblical texts."[23] This admission in itself should warn us against making much ado about any teaching on territorial demons.

The most prominent passage suggesting territorial spirits is Daniel 10:10–21. The "prince of the Persian kingdom" (vv. 13, 20)—that is, a demon—opposed the movement of an angel (or of the angel of the Lord, the preincarnate Christ) in bringing an answer to Daniel's prayers. Michael, the archangel, assisted in the heavenly battle (vv. 13, 21). When the angel left Daniel, he would again do battle, this time with the "prince of Greece" (v. 20).

Several important factors must be considered when discussing the relevance of this passage to any teaching on territorial spirits. First, Daniel's prayers for three weeks had nothing to do with the outcome of the heavenly battle. He was not praying against territorial demons or any demon for that matter. Daniel certainly did not seek the names of the princes (demons) or any information about their sinister intentions (their functions, plans, and so on). Information about the princes was *revealed* to Daniel by the supernatural knowledge of God. It was part of divine revelation—not knowledge gained by experimentation, specialized gifts, or exorcism. Daniel's prayers might have affected the results of the spiritual battle, but if information about the battle had not been given to him by revelation, Daniel would have seen only the human results. Nor was Daniel given any instructions about prayer against territorial spirits regarding the future battle between the angel and the prince of Greece. This passage from Daniel is in full harmony with the rest of the Bible, which never directs God's people to pray in regard to territorial demons. "Therefore, in Daniel 10, the *locus classicus* for territorial spirits advocates . . . Daniel does not 'discern,' 'map,' 'bind,' or 'pray against' a territorial spirit."[24]

Second, despite popular presentations of heavenly battles in which myriad demons battle with myriad angels, we have in Daniel 10 only two demons and two angels.[25] A large-scale heavenly battle between the unclean spirits and the holy angels will take place in the Tribulation (Rev. 12:7).

Third, if territorial demons indeed exist, it is logical, as well as biblically supported, that territorial guardian angels also exist. Consider, for example, the angels who are addressed in regard to the seven churches of Revelation (2:1, 8, 12, 18; 3:1, 7, 14). But even if we grant this perspective on territorial angels, the Bible gives absolutely no teaching on how this knowledge should affect prayers or any other aspect of Christian living. If no practical procedures exist in a Christian's relationship to guardian territorial angels, neither do applications exist regarding territorial demons.

Fourth, that the demons maintain their powers through geographical localities rather than political entities is not clearly demonstrated in Scripture.

Because Satan's primary design is to deceive the nations (Rev. 20:3, 8; cf. also 16:13–14), however, it is reasonable to think that the princes of Persia and Greece are concerned with the governmental program of these nations more than their geographical boundaries. Consider, though, that Michael the archangel (Jude 9) is specifically assigned to the Jewish people (Dan. 10:21; 12:1), not to the geographical boundaries of Israel. If anything, then, the book of Daniel stresses the sovereignty of God, not the role of human agents, in breaking the powers of evil. Very little emphasis is placed on how the Old or New Testament believer can defeat the spirit powers behind world governments. Political powers such as the great Babylon are controlled by the will of God, who sets up and disposes them according to His own purposes (Dan. 2:21, 27; 4:25, 32; 5:21). In the years of the Babylonian captivity, for an Old Testament saint to pray against the "prince of Babylon" (if such a demon existed or still exists) would have been futile. Such a prayer would have been in contradiction to the will of God, who set Israel's captivity in Babylon to be nothing short of seventy years.

A danger of the radical spiritual warfare movement is its tendency to ignore the sovereign will of God. For a believer to exercise some imagined authority over the demonic world might be foisting humankind's will on God. To bind the demons behind Job's illness and to rebuke the spirits behind the tragedies to his family and their possessions (Job 1:13–19) would be to oppose God's permissive will (v. 12). To confront the demons that tormented Saul (1 Sam. 16:14–16, 23; 18:10; 19:9) would be to fight against the discipline of the Lord.[26] For Paul to have rebuked the "messenger (lit., *angel*) of Satan" that caused his thorn in the flesh would have been a rebellion against God's purpose of preventing pride (2 Cor. 12:7). To exorcise an evil spirit who had supposedly "demonized" an incestuous Corinthian man (1 Cor. 5:1) would be to take the very opposite course of the apostle Paul. He decided to judge the man rather than "free" him and to deliver him *to* Satan, rather than to deliver him *from* Satan (1 Cor. 5:3–5, italics added).[27]

Finally, advocates of the territorial spirits idea imply that the angel of Daniel 10 was attempting to reach Daniel, and in the process the angel had to pass through the geographical region of Persia but was delayed by a powerful demon for twenty-one days. But that the angel was delayed by weakness (i.e., the demon overpowered the angel until Michael arrived) is unlikely. Instead, he was delayed by choice (in his superior strength) to prevent the prince of Persia from carrying out some harmful scheme against the Jews through the political powers of Persia. Daniel's prayer, recall, was for the Jewish people to fare well under the new Persian government, but Satan had other plans. Michael, being the angel especially assigned to the Jews, came most appropriately to assist in the battle and replace the first angel.

DISPENSATIONALISM AND DEMON POSSESSION

A controversy concerning a biblical approach to demonology revolves around whether a Christian can be possessed by demons. Those involved in deliverance ministries and charismatic spirituality believe that Christians can be inhabited by demons. But more recently, noncharismatic Christians have expressed concern that believers might become inhabited, despite the fact that there is no evidence of a believer being demon possessed in the Scriptures. [28]

Several dispensational teachers have now come to believe that Christians can be possessed. Merrill Unger, for years a professor at Dallas Theological Seminary, moved theologically from an earlier belief that Christians were protected from demon possession. In 1952 Unger wrote his first book, *Biblical Demonology,* in which he held that Christians could not be inhabited by demons. But, he explains, in the intervening years before his second book, *Demons in the World Today* (1971), he had received many letters from missionaries all over the world who questioned the theory that true believers could not be demon possessed. Unger gradually reconsidered his position *based on these experiences and some of his own.*[29] He reasoned, "If consistent experience clashes with an interpretation, the only inference possible is that there is something wrong with the experience itself or the interpretation of the Scriptures that runs counter to it. . . . The sincere truth seeker must be prepared to revamp his interpretation to bring it into conformity with facts as they are."[30] Note, however, that Unger admits that when "consistent experience clashes with an interpretation," it is possible that there is "something wrong with the experience itself." Should we not be willing then to reinterpret experience? Consider that the "facts as they are" argue against the doctrine of the Virgin Birth.[31] Should we, then, adjust our doctrine?

C. Fred Dickason, a friend, former colleague, and retired chairman of the Theology Department at Moody Bible Institute, maintains a dispensational perspective on speaking in tongues and on miracles.[32] On the one hand, he wants, to some degree, to model his deliverance counseling after Jesus and the apostles. On the other hand, he wishes to distinguish the miraculous nature of the exorcisms performed by Jesus and the apostles from modern-day deliverance attempts. In his view, "The Bible does not suggest that demons can be removed only by miraculous gifts. It does teach that it can be accomplished only by the supernatural working of God."[33] He contends that exercising authority over demons does not require miraculous powers.[34]

But the New Testament always presents the casting out of a demon as both a healing and a miracle. Demon expulsion is explicitly described as a miraculous ability "to heal" (Gk. *therapeu*, Matt. 4:24; Luke 6:18; 7:21; 8:2; Acts 5:16) or "to cure" (Gk. *iaomai*, Matt. 15:28; Luke 9:42; Acts 10:38). Demon expulsion is also implied to be a healing by its repeated associations in Scripture with the healing of other diseases (Mark 1:32, 34; 3:10–11; 6:13; Luke 13:32). In Matthew 12:22, Jesus casts out a demon that caused a man to be blind. Apart from a known medical cure, can making a blind person see, as did Christ by casting out the demon, not be called a healing and a miracle?

Even a dispensational understanding of Jesus' offer of the kingdom should lead one to reject the casting out of demons as a valid ministry for today. When Jesus commissioned the Twelve, He told them to go and proclaim, "The kingdom of heaven is at hand" (Matt. 10:7). Then He instructed them, "Heal the sick, raise the dead, cleanse the lepers, cast out demons" (v. 8). He made no distinction between the first three miraculous events—healing the sick, raising the dead, cleansing the lepers—and the fourth—casting out demons. All four events were directly related to the message of the nearness of the kingdom. Jesus further clarified the issue in Matthew 12:28: "But if I cast out demons by the Spirit of God, then the kingdom of God has come upon you."[35]

In Scripture, demon expulsion is not only referred to as a healing but also is described as a "sign" (Gk. *semeion*, Acts 8:6–7; Mark 16:17–18), a "wonder" (Gk. *teras* [always plural in the New Testament], Acts 5:12, 16), and a "miracle" (lit., "a power"; Gk. *dunamis*, Acts 19:11–12; cf. Luke 6:18–19). John reported that the Twelve had tried to hinder an unknown disciple from casting out demons in the name of Jesus. Jesus replied, "There is no one who shall perform a *miracle* [Gk. *dunamis*] in My name, and be able soon afterward to speak evil of Me" (Mark 9:39, italics added). In Matthew 7:22, Jesus also listed the casting out of demons with other supernatural phenomena. In the book of Acts "extraordinary miracles" (NASB, Gk. *dunamis*) are associated with Paul. When handkerchiefs and aprons, carried from Paul's body, touched the demon possessed, the demons were expelled (Acts 19:11–12).

Today casting out demons would be to participate in a dramatic sign and wonder. Thus, people of a charismatic or signs-and-wonders persuasion are—

although perhaps misguided—at least more consistent theologically with regard to the miraculous nature of exorcism than are some dispensationalists who participate in deliverance ministries.

"DEMON POSSESSED" OR "DEMONIZED"?

Confusion over Word Meaning

Those who advocate that Christians can be demon inhabited redefine the Greek word *daimonizomai,* which in English is translated as "demon possession." In the minds of most Christians, "demon possession" means ownership. But every Christian knows that Satan cannot own a person who is saved. That person belongs to God. Thus, because Christians cannot be "demon possessed," theologians and lay people do not believe that Christians can have demons. Teachers of demon inhabitation, however, attempt to demonstrate that the Greek word translated "demon possession" does not, in actuality, mean ownership and is therefore an inadequate translation.[36] Instead of the translation "demon possession" they suggest that *daimonizomai* be translated as "demonized" or "demonization." This translation, they argue, rids the word of connotations of "ownership" or "possession" by Satan.

But Webster's primary definition of *possessed* is "influenced or controlled by something (as an evil spirit or a passion)."[37] This definition is recognized in modern Bible versions, which have continued to use the term *demon possessed* rather than the term *demonized.* To interpret *daimonizomai,* the *New American Standard Bible* uses *demon possessed* not only when *daimonizomai* is used but also when another Greek construction occurs (Mark 3:22; 9:17; Luke 4:33).[38] The *New International Version* also uses *demon possession* or *demon possessed* seventeen times, six times when *daimonizomai* is not used (Luke 8:27; John 7:20; 8:48, 52; 10:20; Acts 19:13).

In determining the basis for the retranslation of *daimonizomai* as "demonized" one writer states, "When we look at the word for demonization, improperly translated 'demon possession,' it is highly instructive to notice its root and structure."[39] Advocates of inhabitation use primarily morphology and etymology to define the Greek word. But, as Silva argues, etymology and morphology are weak contributors to word meaning. *Usage and context are the final determinants.*[40]

Wimber, however, goes so far as to state that the Greek words for demon possession are unclear:

The Greek terms used to describe people having demons are impre-
cise. In fact, many English translations are misleading when they
describe people who "have a demon" as "demon-possessed." The
original Greek terms may not be translated this precisely.[41]

In response, several important observations must be raised. First, no known
lexicon—including Thayer, Cremer, Liddell and Scott, and Bauer, Arndt,
Gingrich, and Danker—translates *daimonizomai* (or the participle
daimonizomenos) as "demonized." Defining the Greek word contrary to all
available Greek lexical works would certainly require substantial evidence to
justify the change. *In all of these lexicons, the translation "demonization" or
"demonized" is never recognized even as one of the variant ways to translate
the Greek term.*

The translation of *daimonizomai* as "demonized" is not, in fact, a translation at all but a transliteration. Because no understanding is commonly
attached to the word *demonized* by the majority of English Bible readers,
this transliteration is no improvement over the common term *demon possessed*. The value of this transliteration, then, is similar to that of transliterat-
ing the Greek word *skandolizomai* (cause one to stumble) as "to scandalize."
In both cases, additional clarification is needed to define the terminology.

The transliteration "demonize" neutralizes the biblical concept of demon
possession by removing some of the stigma and repulsiveness inherent in it.[42]
The result is that a harsh biblical reality becomes a euphemism. By using the
word *demonized*, certain teachers/counselors have tried to convince Christians
of the unbiblical concept that a believer can be inhabited by demons. Christians are familiar with the Bible stories about demon-possessed people. *Demon possession* rightly brings to mind certain extremes that are portrayed vividly
in the Bible. So it might be more difficult to convince them that they can be
inhabited by demons when the term *demon possession* is used.

Demon Habitation: Spatial or Spiritual?

Many recent authors have attempted to speak in terms of various degrees
of "demonization."[43] Wimber, for instance, states, "The term 'demonized'
refers to people who are in varying degrees or levels of demonic bondage."
He believes that mild "demonization" includes being tormented by troubling thoughts.[44] Unger cites a case in which a godly woman was invaded by
a demon, causing her to have a disturbing confusion in the work of God.[45]
Demon deliverance advocates claim that suicidal thoughts are a common

indicator of demon invasion.[46] Many also teach that evil spirits can hide in their victims,[47] and some teach that degrees of deliverance are also possible.[48]

Varying degrees of demon possession do exist in the Scriptures. Jesus spoke of a demon returning to its victim to possess him, taking along seven additional demons that were even more wicked. Jesus concluded that the man's latter condition was now worse than his former state. In other words, this latter state was more severe because of the greater number of demons dwelling in the man and the deeper depravity of the last seven demons (Matt. 12:44-45). But by speaking of various degrees of demonization, focus is drawn away from fundamental issue, which is whether possession is indeed the condition. Consider the following viewpoint:

> So the issue is not whether a demon is in my body causing some undesirable activity, but whether it has access to my mind through my failure to use my defenses against it. . . . This is not a spatial matter. It is a spiritual one and *the location of the demon— inside or outside—is not the real issue.* The issue is, to whom do I yield control? (italics added)[49]

This conclusion is simply not true. The concept of demon possession must not be based on one Greek word, *daimonizomai,* and its definition. A study of semantically related and contextually related terms demonstrates that the issue in demon possession is indeed one of location—inside versus outside!

The Greek word *ekballein* is used thirty-three times in the New Testament—exclusively in the Synoptic Gospels (in Matthew twelve times, in Mark twelve times, and in Luke nine times)—to mean "to cast *out*" a demon, unclean spirit, or Satan. Such use comprises the majority of the total fifty-seven uses of *ekballein* in the Synoptics. If location was not the issue, no need would exist for a demon to be "cast *out*" of a person, and Jesus' ministry of expelling demons would become meaningless.

The New Testament also speaks of demons "going *out*" (*exerchomai;* italics added) of a person, either by compulsion or by choice. The Greek word *exerchomai* is used twenty-five times and two additional times *ekporeuomai* ("to go *out*"; italics added) is used.[50] One's concept of demon possession must also be influenced when Scripture mentions a demon "entering *into*" (italics added) a person or animal. The Greek word for entering into, *eiserchomai,* is found ten times in relation to Satan or demons.[51] Once again, *eiserchomai* becomes meaningless apart from demonstrating a sense of location that indicates demon possession.

Further, the most often used expression is a construction of *echein* (to have) followed by one of the terms for a demon (i.e., in English, "to have a demon [or unclean spirit]"). This construction appears seventeen times in the New Testament. Hanse comments, "*[Echein]* expresses a *spatial relationship* and means 'to bear in oneself'" (italics added).[52] A careful study of this *echein* construction shows that it is used in connection with each of the three words "to cast out" (*ekballein,* Mark 7:25–26), "to go out" (*exerchomai,* Mark 7:25, 29–30), and "to enter in" (*eiserchomai,* Luke 8:27, 30, 32–33). The conclusion is unavoidable: the construction of *echein* (to have) with the object being an evil spirit speaks of a demon residing *within* a person.[53]

The biblical concept "to have a demon" or "to be demon possessed"—together with the terms for a demon entering, leaving, and being cast out of an individual—is clearly an indwelling. The translation "demon possessed" is still an adequate translation for the Greek *daimonizomai.* The translation "demonize" is incommunicable and most often contains a hidden agenda. If one seeks an alternate to the English translation "demon possessed," the term *to be under the power of an indwelling demon* might suffice.

Regardless of the preceding analysis, the term *demonization* has gained significant popularity and is probably here to stay. The best response for Bible teachers and missionaries is to fill the word *demonization* with the biblical meaning as far as is possible, making it understood that the concept clearly indicates a demon *within* a person.

CAN CHRISTIANS BE DEMON POSSESSED?

The Crippled Woman Bound by Satan (Luke 13:10–17)

When advocates of inhabitation seek proof from the Bible that Christians can be possessed by demons, one passage in particular is given attention: the crippled woman who was healed in Luke 13.[54] After discussing the interpretation of the passage, Dickason concludes, "Here we have a fairly clear case of a believer who has been demonized."[55] This statement, however, is qualified in the next paragraph. "Though we cannot come to a settled conclusion that she was a genuine believer who was inhabited by a demon, the weight seems to balance in that direction."[56]

Two issues must be identified in this passage: (1) Was the woman a believer? (2) Was she in fact demon possessed? The latter question, although it is often treated as a foregone conclusion, deserves serious consideration.

Before it can be assumed that Christ diagnosed the woman as being "plagued by demonic illness," it must first be established that this was indeed the woman's condition. The majority of English translations tend toward the perspective that the woman was demon possessed. The *New International Version* says that she was a woman "who had been crippled by a spirit for eighteen years" (v. 11). The *New American Standard Bible* states that for eighteen years she "had had a sickness caused by a spirit."[57] Dickason comments, "The expression in Greek is *pneuma echous astheneias,* which actually should be translated as 'having a spirit of illness.' It may refer to a sickness or a weakness, but the expression, 'having a spirit' is equivalent to demonization. There is no doubt that the woman was demonized."[58] In addition, the text states that the woman was "bound" by Satan (v. 16) and that Jesus had "freed" her (v. 12).

But she might not have been inhabited by a demon at all. First, the normal vocabulary for demon possession or demon expulsion is not found in the narrative. As was discussed earlier, normal language for demon possession/expulsion includes such phrases as "(to) have a demon," "(to be) demon possessed," "casting out (a demon)," "(a demon) entered in," an "evil spirit" or an "unclean spirit," and "(a demon) came out."[59] Even Jesus' methods in this incident do not parallel how He cast out demons elsewhere. Jesus, rather than speaking to a demon, spoke to the crippled women directly. Elsewhere, Jesus did not lay hands on a person to cast out a demon as He did to heal this woman (13:13).[60]

The literal term in the Greek for the phrase "a sickness caused by a spirit" (NASB) is "having a spirit of weakness" or "having a spirit of infirmity" (cf. KJV, NKJV, ASV, or RSV of Luke 13:10). But this unmodified use of the word *spirit* (Gk. *pneuma*) might not refer to a demon at all.[61] When the word *spirit(s)* is used without a modifier and a demon is referenced, Luke and other authors offer clues in the context that identify a demon.[62] Otherwise an angel or a facet of the human spirit might be referenced.[63] If we consider the whole phrase "a spirit of . . . ," the same point is true. Luke and others always identify demons and demon possession using clear modifiers with the phrase.[64] Luke's writings contain no parallels to 13:10, where the phrase "a spirit of . . ." without a modifier identifies a demon.[65]

That the Greek phrase "a spirit of . . ." in Luke 13:10 does not in itself refer to a demon is confirmed by similar phrases elsewhere in the New Testament. Other modifiers must be present to demand an interpretation involving demons and demon possession. Note, for example, Paul's statement that "God has not given us a spirit of timidity" (2 Tim. 1:7 NASB). No one would suggest that "a spirit of timidity" refers to an indwelling demon who causes fear. In Romans 8:15, Paul writes, "You have not received a spirit of slavery." The verse contains no impression that Paul desires us to think of a demon that causes slavery. If one considers the verbal form "(having a) spirit of . . . ," 2 Corinthians 4:13 is analogous: "having the same spirit of faith."

Nolland's evaluation of Luke 13:10 is to the point: "It remains uncertain whether we should consider a 'spirit of weakness' as descriptive of a demon (see 'spirit of festering' in the Genesis Apocryphon of Qumran Cave 1 [1QapGen] 20:26; cf. v. 16, 'spirit of divination' in Acts 16:16) or whether it is simply an idiom for having a debilitating ailment."[66]

When all of the facts of the passage are put together, the phrase "having a spirit of infirmity" seems best understood as a Greek construction that simply describes the woman's disabling and discouraging physical condition.

Neither is the phrase "Satan has bound" (Luke 13:16) determinative of demon possession. The phrase might simply express a physical illness that was caused by the Devil. The concept of Satan's oppression and affliction of people (including Christians) encompasses his use of physical illness.[67]

Acts 10:38 (NASB) declares that Jesus "went about doing good, and healing all who were oppressed by the devil" (NIV, "under the power of the devil"). This verse seems to describe the overall healing ministry of Jesus. As such, it suggests that Satan is at work behind many diseases although we cannot see or know this fact. Job's boils were a physical disease allowed under God's sovereignty, but they were caused by Satan and demons. A "messenger of Satan" produced Paul's thorn in the flesh. The apostle saw his affliction as being figuratively beaten by the Devil or tormented by him (2 Cor. 12:7). Nolland's conclusion on Luke 13:16 is the most sound: "'Satan bound' in v. 16 is not a decisive indicator [of demon possession], since 'healing all who were oppressed by the devil' in Acts 10:38 is best taken as referring to healing in general. In all other respects the language of the account [in Luke 13] suits a healing better than an exorcism."[68]

Concerning the evidence that addresses the second issue—Was the woman a believer?—Dickason explains,

> First, she was well known in the synagogue as a person plagued by demonic illness (no objection is lodged against Christ's diagnosis) and was probably a regular attender at the services (13:10–11). Second, she knew immediately that God had healed her; and she gave Him the glory (13:13), a seeming natural response in her heart. Third,

Jesus labeled her "a daughter of Abraham as she is." This expression
"daughter of Abraham" could be ethnic in that she was Jewish.
However, Luke's record shows Jesus applying this term to the newly
converted and remade Zaccheus: "Today salvation has come to this
house because he, too, is a son of Abraham" (Luke 19:9).[69]

In response, note that the scriptural text yields no clues that the woman
"was well known in the synagogue as a person plagued by demonic illness."
If this were the case, it is unlikely that she would have been permitted to
attend the synagogue services. Wilkinson agrees: "If this woman's defor-
mity was generally believed to indicate that she was demon-possessed, it is
unlikely that she would be allowed to worship in the local synagogue. The
fact that she was allowed to worship there suggests that she was not regarded
as demon-possessed by the people of the community in which she lived."[70]
But even if she was a regular member of the synagogue—known or unknown
as having demonic illness—her attendance there is no proof that she had faith.
What good Pharisee, with his heart of unbelief, failed to attend the synagogue service?
   What, then, is the meaning of the phrase "daughter of Abraham" (Luke
13:16)? Does this phrase imply salvation? Contrary to those who teach that a
Christian can be demon possessed, the parallel phrase "son of Abraham" implies Jewish ethnic background, not salvation. The phrase is used only three
times (Matt. 1:1; Luke 3:34; 19:9), twice of the Jewish genealogy of Christ.
Granted, Paul uses the phrase "sons of Abraham" in a spiritual sense in Galatians
3:7 of all who place their faith in Christ for salvation. But this post-Pentecost
meaning must not be carried backward to interpret its use in the Gospels. The
LXX has only one use of a related phrase: "the daughter of God-fearing
Abraham" (4 Macc. 15:28). Jewish descent is the obvious meaning. In Luke
19:9, Jesus remarks, "Today salvation has come to this house" of Zacchaeus
(or spelled Zaccheus, NASB) because he is "a son of Abraham." Although the
term *son of Abraham* might point to the faith of Zacchaeus, more probably
the meaning is Jewishness.[71] This announcement was for the benefit of those
who had labeled Zacchaeus a "sinner" and unworthy of salvation (19:7). Jesus,
on the other hand, pointed out that although Zacchaeus had been sinful, he
was still a part of Israel to whom Christ had come to bring salvation (John
4:22; Rom. 1:16).[72] Viewing all three citations of the term *son of Abraham* as
designating Jewish physical descent has the advantage of consistency. Therefore, to understand the phrase "daughter of Abraham" in Luke 13 in the very

same manner is natural.[73] "In keeping with Luke's purpose, this designation highlights the priority of the Jews in the program of the Gospel. It shows that the woman deserved immediate healing."[74]

It may be concluded that if the story of the crippled woman in Luke 13 is the most noteworthy text to demonstrate that Christians can be inhabited by demons, the exegetical case for this theology is extremely weak if not nonexistent. It is highly questionable that she was demon possessed. Nor do any indicators show that she had faith before Jesus healed her. The fact that she gave God the glory for her healing (13:13) might speak of a newfound faith. Consider the Gadarene demoniac, who, immediately responding in faith after the demons were expelled, desired to follow Christ wholeheartedly (Mark 5:18). His desire, however, is not evidence of prior faith.

The Contributions of Matthew 12

Contrary to those who argue that demon possession does not mean to be "owned" by anyone, possession is in fact central to the parable of the strong man in Matthew 12.[75] The Lord taught that two opposing kingdoms exist— God's kingdom and Satan's kingdom (Matt 12:26; Luke 11:18). When He cast out demons by God's power, that action presupposed that Satan's kingdom was being destroyed and that God's kingdom had arrived. Christ explained in Matthew 12:28 (NASB; par. Luke 11:20), "But if I cast out demons by the Spirit of God, then the kingdom of God has come upon you." Demon possession and the kingdom of God are, therefore, mutually exclusive.[76] Thus, it seems logical to assume that one's participation in the kingdom of God prohibits demon possession of the participant.

By using the word *or* to begin the next verse, Jesus now describes another way to think about His ability to cast out demons: "Or how can anyone enter the strong man's house and carry off *his property*, unless he first binds the strong man? And then he will plunder his house" (Matt. 12:29, italics added). For Jesus to bind the strong man and carry off the property he owned meant to confiscate Satan's servants from him by delivering them from demon possession (v. 29).[77] To be demon possessed is to be the property of Satan and to be part of his kingdom. One cannot stress too strongly that, in the context of Matthew 12, the property of Satan refers most specifically to those who are demon possessed. In fact, the healing of a demon-possessed man (vv. 22–23) stimulated the whole discussion with Christ (vv. 24–37). If Christians can be demon possessed, then they must be the property of Satan.

But Satan's house cannot be described as plundered in the fullest sense unless redemption is implied in the parable. For Christ to "carry off" Satan's property involves the transfer of Satan's property to Christ. A Christian is transferred from Satan's house-kingdom to God's house-kingdom. When the Lord at salvation transfers the new believer into the kingdom of the Savior, he or she has been released from the kingdom of darkness (Col. 1:13). The implication follows that the Christian can no longer be inhabited by a demon. If "it is therefore inappropriate to speak of a Christian's coming under the ownership of Satan," it is just as inappropriate to speak of a Christian's being indwelled by a demon.[78]

In Matthew 12:43–45, Jesus used an analogy to explain the evil nature of that generation of Jews. A demon leaves a man only to return later. When it arrives, it is able to reenter the man because it finds the human "house unoccupied" (Gk. *scholazonta* "to stand empty," v. 44). Seven other demons join it inside the man, thereby making his last condition much worse than when only one demon was living there. Logically, if the house had not been empty, the demon could not have returned. What, then, could have occupied the house so that it was not empty? The prominence of the ministry of the Holy Spirit in the context (Matt. 12:28, 31–32) suggests that salvation and the reception of the Holy Spirit prevent demon possession because the "house" becomes "occupied." In the context of the Lukan parallel, Jesus taught how "your Heavenly Father [will] give the Holy Spirit [some mss. read 'a good spirit'] to those who ask Him" (11:13). *"This is God's only alternative to the unclean spirits* (11:24–26) which threaten all (even entire generations) who reject the work of God" (italics added).[79] Jesus was teaching that to receive the Holy Spirit is to become an "occupied house" and to gain God's protection from demon possession.

With the comment "while He was still speaking to the crowds" (Matt. 12:46 NRSV), Matthew also closely ties the story of the returning demon to the teaching about Jesus' true family (12:46–50). Jesus' explanation that those who had faith in Him were His true brothers and sisters, His true family—coming upon the heels of the parable of the strong man—gives the firm suggestion that being a member of the Lord's spiritual family is to become a house with a resident, unavailable for additional occupancy.

This understanding can be taken one step further. Christ unmistakably applied the story of the eight demons inhabiting a house to the Jewish nation: "That is the way it will also be with this evil generation" (Matt. 12:45). In other words, by His ministry Jesus had cast out a demon from the nation and had swept and put their house in order. But by rejecting Him as Messiah and committing the blasphemy against the Holy Spirit, they were susceptible to a more severe demon possession.[80]

In a metaphorical but spiritual sense, a national demon possession was under way. The nation could not have received Jesus as Messiah and still have committed the blasphemy of the Holy Spirit. So, also, the nation could not have been "demon possessed" at the same time that it received Him as Messiah. If Israel had welcomed her Messiah, then she would have been an "occupied house," incapable of being repossessed by demons. The nation could not have been redeemed and at the same time been inhabited by evil spirits. The exact same reasoning must also apply to Christians. To be redeemed means that one cannot at the same time be demon possessed.

Other Passages Considered

According to Arnold, "The one passage in the Epistles that comes closest to the language of demonization is Ephesians 4:26–27."[81] In the *New International Version* this passage reads, "In your anger do not sin: Do not let the sun go down while you are still angry, and do not give the devil a *foothold* [Gk. *topos,* italics added]." Although in some contexts *topos* ("place") carries a spatial idea, this concept must not be illegitimately transferred to the meaning of the word itself.[82] Paul gives no indication that he is developing a theology of "grounds" given to Satan that must be reclaimed through specific steps to freedom.[83] Nor is the apostle indicating that believers "should not allow any portion of their dwelling to be occupied by a demonic spirit."[84] Of the ninety-four uses of *topos* in the New Testament, only one implies even a metaphorical "place." In the *New American Standard Bible, topos* is used several times in the sense of "possibility, opportunity, chance" (Acts 25:16; Rom. 12:19; 15:23; Heb. 8:7; 12:17), and that version translates 4:27, "Do not give the devil an opportunity." [85] In Greek, the phrase may be translated, "Don't give the devil a chance to exert his influence."[86] The "opportunity" that the Devil can gain is likely that of promoting disunity among believers (Eph. 4:25).[87] But no impression is given in Ephesians 4:27 that a Christian who permits his anger to seethe overnight is in danger of demon invasion. If such were the case, what is to be said of non-Christians who never have control of their anger? Are most non-Christians demon possessed? Or do only Christians have a vulnerability to this form of demon possession? If the latter is the case, then salvation offers *less* protection from demons than remaining unredeemed.

The Loud Silence of Scripture

The Gospels appear to mention demon possession quite frequently. Remember, however, that many of these references are snapshots taken from the broad vista of Jesus' healing ministry (e.g., Mark 1:32–34, 39; 3:7–12). Only six separate incidents of demon possession are treated in detail by the Gospels (without paragraph references, Matt. 9:32–34; 12:22–23; Mark 1:23–28; 5:1–20; 7:24–30; 9:14–29). Although Acts covers more than thirty years of history, it mentions demon possession only four times: two references are summary statements about the ministries of the apostles (Acts 5:16; 8:7), and two other references are treated more descriptively (16:16–18; 19:11–16). The Epistles never mention demon possession, demon expulsion, or any equivalent terminology that is used in the Gospels and Acts.

A biblical response to demonology and missions must consider that the Epistles rather than the Gospels or Acts contain the central guidelines for Christian conduct today. The apostle Peter claims that God has given us in Scripture everything that we need for godliness and successful Christian living (2 Peter 1:3).[88] Yet the absolute silence of the New Testament letters on the subject of demon possession or demon expulsion is inexplicable if unclean spirits can possess a Christian. It is unthinkable that the Epistles would have failed to address such an extreme crisis in the life of a redeemed person as the struggle with a resident demon. Even more surprising, Paul's great treatise on justification by faith and Christian living—the book of Romans—references demons and Satan only twice (8:38; 16:20).[89]

Consider, then, the epistle to the Ephesians. Ephesus was perhaps the center for occult activity in the first-century Roman world.[90] It would not be surprising, then, to find people in the Asian city who were possessed by demons (Acts 19:12). Jewish exorcists also practiced in the region, attempting to help the demon possessed (vv. 13–14). Yet in all of the New Testament materials written to believers in Ephesus—Ephesians, 1 and 2 Timothy, and the book of Revelation (Rev. 2:1–7),[91] and probably 1 John—no instructions are given regarding Christians being inhabited by demons.[92] In the same way, demon-possessed non-Christians lived at Philippi (Acts 16:16), but in the book of Philippians Paul is silent on the topic. Satan and demons are not even mentioned. Such silence is inexplicable if Christians face the danger of demonic invasion.

Teachers of radical spiritual warfare object that argument from silence provides weak support. They offer an analogy between a Christian being demon possessed and a Christian getting cancer. The Bible is silent on the matter of Christians developing cancer, but clinical evidence (i.e., experience) has shown that believers do indeed develop the disease. In the same way, the Bible is silent about the matter of Christians being inhabited by demons, but experience has shown that they sometimes are.[93]

Although this argument sounds logical, it is flawed. Many subjects that are not addressed specifically in Scripture are included in *biblical principle*. Take the subject of abortion, for example. Although the Bible never directly addresses abortion, by biblical principle evangelicals affirm that abortion is murder.[94] Abortion is wrong because it is one type of murder, and murder is wrong. The same biblical principle teaches that Christians can develop cancer. Although cancer is not mentioned specifically in Scripture, it is a life-threatening disease, and the Bible makes it evident that Christians can contract life-threatening diseases (e.g., Phil. 2:27). Because Christians contract life-threatening diseases, and cancer is one type of life-threatening disease, the Bible teaches by principle that Christians can develop cancer.

On the basis of silence alone, the cancer analogy used by spiritual warfare advocates is inadequate, but consider that the demon possession of a believer is not an argument *from* silence as much as it is an argument *about* silence.[95] A true argument from silence must follow this syllogism: "Since the Bible says nearly nothing about whether a person can be demon possessed, it is highly unlikely that Christians can be demon possessed." If the Bible did not speak about demon possession, then this line of reasoning would be a worthless argument from silence. But on the contrary, the Bible says an enormous amount about demon possession. But *all* of the Scriptures— especially the Epistles—are silent about believers being demon possessed. The Bible is able to make us "thoroughly equipped for every good work" (2 Tim. 3:16–17 NIV), but the New Testament epistles give no instructions on how a believer handles demon possession. The real question, then, is, Why does the Bible speak so often about demon possession but is silent about Christians having this problem?

Finally, the greatest weakness in the cancer analogy is that cancer is an amoral issue, but demon possession is not. Those who opine that believers can be inhabited by demons are themselves offering an argument from silence—the entire Bible is silent on this spiritual and moral issue of stupendous magnitude. Konya states,

The Bible never claims to be a book of diagnosing disease, but it *does* claim to be a book of diagnosing moral and spiritual problems.

In fact, it claims that equipping the believers for every good work is its *exclusive* domain, and that it is fully sufficient for instruction in these areas. The silence of Scripture in such matters as diagnosing and treating demon possession speaks forcefully to the fact that those practices *must not be an essential issue.* (italics added)[96]

People who claim that Christians can have demons list numerous reasons why a demon can enter the believer: prolonged unconfessed sin,[97] persistent rebellion,[98] involvement in false teaching,[99] child abuse,[100] dysfunctional home life, demonic transference through sexual relations, sexual sins,[101] or ancestral involvement in the occult. The list is so comprehensive that one wonders how any Christian is protected. And the list can be greatly enlarged. Some people even believe that God might allow demons to infest godly believers as a discipline either to cleanse certain sins from their lives or to prepare them for future deliverance ministries.[102] Those of us who believe that Christians cannot be demon possessed might be even more susceptible to demon invasion because of the "deception" that we are insusceptible.[103]

Not one of the above reasons, however, can be produced from Scripture. The Bible gives, in fact, no reason whatsoever for demon possession.[104] It is interesting to note, too, that Jesus never rebuked anyone who was demon possessed. Never did He say to a demoniac after He delivered that person, "Go and sin no more," as He sometimes did to other people whom He healed (cf. John 5:14; 8:11). If persistent unconfessed sin is a cause for demonic invasion, it is strange indeed that Paul never mentions that any of the fleshly Corinthians (1 Cor. 3:1–3) were possessed. And it would be likely that non-Christians who never genuinely confess their sins are demon possessed.

Even though Christians cannot be inhabited by demons, it doesn't mean they are not influenced by Satan and demons. Advocates who hold that believers can be indwelt by demons sometimes imply that those who reject their teaching also believe that Christians are not susceptible to demonic attacks.[105] Ice and Dean express my own sentiments when they deny the possibility of *internal* control by demons but affirm that *external* influence on believers can be substantial.[106]

In essence, then, where the Bible is silent, modern missiologists and spiritual warfare counselors focus their attention. Although Jesus' ministry of delivering the demon possessed was exclusively among unbelievers, many modern deliverance ministries, claiming that Jesus' ministry is the model for what they do, specialize in freeing believers. Other deliverance ministries suppose that, after non-Christians are delivered from demon infestation, the demons might—if the demonized person does not respond to the gospel—return. No biblical record exists, however, in which demons returned to reinhabit a demon-possessed person once Jesus had cast out the unclean spirits. Jesus often commanded the demons to come out and never return to their victim (Mark 9:25), and it is unlikely that it was necessary on all occasions for Jesus to verbalize this command. If believers have the same authority as the apostles and Jesus, their exorcisms should produce permanent results just as the Lord's did. Because Jesus delivered many nonbelievers in His earthly ministry, and no evidence exists that He delivered believers in a like manner, it is difficult to understand why modern deliverance ministries give so little attention to demon-possessed non-Christians.

DO BELIEVERS HAVE AUTHORITY OVER SATAN AND DEMONS?

The Great Commission

Spiritual warfare adherents often claim that believers are both able and obligated to challenge the domain of darkness. The obligation includes asserting authority over Satan and his hosts and is said to be the inherent right of every New Testament Christian.[107] The first and primary argument for their theology is the belief that Christ delegated this authority in the Great Commission.[108] One author writes,

> The Great Commission indicates that Christ delegated to His disciples and to those who follow in their train that same authority over demons. . . . The authority to successfully oppose and cast out demons still remains throughout the age until Jesus comes (Matt. 28:18–20).[109]

The same author concludes elsewhere that the Christian "should assume his position in Christ as far above all demonic forces and exercise his God-given right to directly charge the enemy to obedience."[110] Another author writes, "We are delegated by this commission to enforce the victory won at the Cross."[111] Note that the alleged authority given concerns aggressive, offensive warfare and not simply defensive resistance of Satan.

A closer examination of the Great Commission, however, does not substantiate the above claim. The text of the commission (Matt 28:18–20) contains no mention of a transfer of authority of any kind to the believer. The

Great Commission refers solely to the authority of Christ by which He commands us to go into the entire world. Jesus simply states, "All authority has been given to Me in heaven and on earth. Go, therefore . . ." (v. 18). This authority is unlimited ("*all* authority"), personal to Christ ("has been given *to me*"), and universal ("in heaven *and on earth*"). It includes authority over the angelic realm, not just the demonic realm; it involves authority over all human supremacy as well as all heavenly powers. Such an extensive authority cannot, and is not, given to any believer today. As is the case of any other command, the command in the Great Commission has no need for authority for it to be obeyed: "The church has no—and needs no—delegated authority to carry out its obligation to evangelize and disciple the world (28:19–20). What it has is the Holy Spirit, and what it needs is obedience."[112]

The Book of Ephesians

Teachers of radical spiritual warfare also claim that, because the Bible says that believers have been raised up with and are seated with Christ in the heavenly places (Eph. 2:6), Christ has granted believers the authority over Satan and the demonic army.[113] This claim can be illustrated in the following syllogism based on their interpretation of Ephesians 1 and 2:

1.   Christ was raised up above all dominion and power, including Satan and demons. He has authority over them in His exalted position (Eph. 1:21).
2.   All believers have been raised up with Christ and seated with Him in heaven (Eph. 2:6).
3.   Therefore, all believers, by virtue of their position in Christ, also have authority over Satan and demons.

A closer examination of the relevant Ephesians passages, however, uncovers the fallacy of the above syllogism. In Ephesians 1:21a, Paul does tell us that Christ has been raised up far above "all rule and authority and power and dominion." The same verse emphasizes the unique, all-inclusive nature of this position when it says, "and [far above] every name that is named" (v. 21b). This authority of Christ is comprehensive because it is over every person named, "not only in this age, but also in the one to come" (v. 21c). Christ's position at the right hand of God also means that "God placed all things under his feet and appointed him to be head over everything for the church" (v. 22 NIV).

The statement "God placed all things under his feet" is a quotation from Psalm 8 and is also found in 1 Corinthians 15:25-28. The latter passage tells us that Christ's authority over all things means that He will abolish death forever at the end of the age. Hebrews 2:5-9 also quotes the Psalm 8 text. The writer of Hebrews suggests that all things will be put under the authority of Jesus but not until the end of the age. The Cross has, of course, firmly secured the subjection of all things under Christ's rule, but complete subjection does not occur until the future reign of Christ. Revelation 12:10 looks prophetically to the Second Coming: "Now the salvation, and the power, and the kingdom of our God and the authority [Gk. *exousia*] of His Christ have come." This authority is the eschatological sovereignty of Christ over all creation. So even Christ is not now reigning supremely over the demonic realm in all aspects. When He sets up His millennial kingdom, He will bind Satan and put down all demonic opposition (Rev. 20:1-6).

Christ is not assigning Satan or demons to the Abyss now but is waiting at the right hand of God until all of His enemies are made a footstool under His feet (Heb. 1:13). Despite this fact, some deliverance ministers attempt to bind Satan, cast out demons, and send them to the pit. Doing so takes on more authority than even Christ is exercising in the present age. Thus, if Christ is not now "binding" Satan, it is hardly likely that the believer has authority to do so.

Consider, too, that according to Ephesians 1, Christ's authority is over not only the demonic dominions but also the elect angels and all earthly rulers. If believers have the authority Jesus does, we should have not only authority to direct the good angels for the benefit of the church but authority to command and rebuke earthly rulers and all political powers. Such authority is, of course, without biblical support. Even though, in our future position in Christ, we will be exalted above all angels, good and evil (cf. 1 Cor. 6:3; Heb. 2:6-7, 10), and above all existing earthly powers, we do not have this privileged authority now.

In Ephesians 2:6, when the believer is said to be now raised up with Christ, the phrase "far above all rule and authority and power and dominion" found in 1:21 is noticeably absent. Our new position seated with Christ in the heavenly places is not identical in every respect to that of Christ. His position most certainly pertains to matters that we will never share with Him. No major passage on the believer's position in Christ applies this truth of Christ's authority to the Christian's warfare with the spirit world (cf. Rom. 6:1-14; Col. 2:12; 3:1-11). On the classic passage of Ephesians 6:10-18, Paul does raise the subject of the believer's warfare with Satan and his dark forces. But if our position in Christ grants us authority over Satan, the Ephesians 6 passage is an anomaly because it mentions neither our position in Christ as being raised up with Him nor any authority over these "world forces of this darkness" (v. 12). This silence is peculiar if the perspective of much of modern spiritual warfare theology is correct. Instead, the weapons mentioned are defensive weapons rather than offensive weapons for an aggressive, direct confrontation with the demons.

The Book of Romans

Every mention of our position in Christ refers to our need to conquer the flesh, not to our need to command demonic forces. Romans 6:4, for example, tells us that "we have been buried with Him through baptism into death, in order that as Christ was raised from the dead through the glory of the Father, so we too might walk in newness of life." This verse indirectly implies that, in some sense, we have been raised up with Christ, but the purpose of this identification with Christ is that we may have a newness of life—a resurrection kind of life. Paul adds, "For if we have become united with Him in the likeness of His death, certainly we shall be also in the likeness of His resurrection" (v. 5). This newness of life is silent, however, on the subject of commanding Satan and the demonic. Paul's challenge is not to focus on demonic warfare but to focus on God: "Therefore . . . *present yourselves to God* as those alive from the dead, and your members as instruments of righteousness *to God*" (vv. 12–13, italics added).

Parallel passages that refer to the exalted position and authority of Christ never include thoughts of the believer's authority over all rule and dominion (Eph. 4:10; Phil. 2:9–11; 1 Cor. 15:24–28; Heb. 1:3–13; 4:14–16; 8:1; 9:24). But they do tell us to avail ourselves of our merciful and faithful high priest, so that "we may receive mercy and may find grace to help in time of need" (Heb. 4:16).

Rebuking Satan?

Perhaps the clearest example of falsely claimed authority over the demonic is found in the current emphasis on "rebuking" Satan. An examination of both Old and New Testament uses of "rebuking" demonstrates how demonic warfare advocates have misapplied the term. In the Old Testament, the word *rebuke (gā'ar)* is consistently used (twenty-one of twenty-eight times) of God's triumph over His enemies (Isa. 17:13; 50:3; Nah. 1:4; 2 Sam.

22:16; Ps. 104:7). The defeat of the "waters of chaos," or the sea, is an Old Testament motif figuratively describing the defeat of all God's enemies in preparation for the establishment of His kingdom. In rabbinical literature, only God rebukes Satan, demonstrating His sovereign control over him. In the New Testament, the Greek word for "rebuke" *(epitimaō)* is unmistakably related to the Hebrew word for "rebuke" *(gā'ar)* by the allusion in Jude 9 to Zechariah 3:2, which uses *gā'ar*.[114] Evidently, the Jews in both the Old Testament and extrabiblical literature recognized that only God could rebuke Satan. Therefore, when Jesus "rebuked" *(epitimaō)* demons, He was making an unmistakable messianic claim to deity.

The gospel writers also make a parallel between rebuking demons and rebuking the realm of nature and disease when they use the Greek word *epitimaō*. In Mark, Jesus rebukes the demons (1:25; 3:12), but later He rebukes the wind and the sea (4:39). In Luke 4, Jesus rebukes a demon (v. 35), then He rebukes the fever in Simon's mother-in-law (v. 39), and still later He rebukes more demons (v. 41). The close proximity in which these instances are placed in Scripture suggests an intended association—that is, rebuking Satan and demons is no different from rebuking diseases. Thus, to be consistent, those who claim that the Christian has authority to rebuke Satan should also claim the same authority to rebuke diseases or the elements of nature (and have the same miraculous and instantaneous success that Jesus had). But to do so seriously impugns the uniqueness of Christ and His deity.[115]

Finally, Jude 9 substantiates the conclusion that rebuking Satan is the sole prerogative of God. The *New International Version* reads, "But even the archangel Michael, when he was disputing with the devil about the body of Moses, did not dare to bring a slanderous accusation against him, but said, 'The Lord rebuke you.'" Ice and Dean comment, "This passage is telling us that even Michael, the highest-ranking elect angel, would not rebuke the devil; yet many Christians do it on a regular basis."[116] Second Peter 2:11 adds that all of the other elect angels also refuse to accuse evil spirits slanderously in the presence of the Lord.[117] These texts imply that the Lord alone has the right to stand in judgment of Satan and to use harsh criticism against him.

One author explains that in Jude 9, Michael's refusal was to bring a *blasphemous* (sinful) accusation against the Devil.[118] "We should not suppose that the apostles did anything like that when they commanded demons to leave men. They were following the example of the Lord Jesus."[119] Christians can therefore rebuke the Devil by their authority in Christ. If this is the meaning of the text, then Michael did not need to refuse to rebuke the Devil. He could have rebuked the Devil while still avoiding a blasphemous accusation. The verse could then read, "Michael did not dare to bring a slanderous accusation against him, but said, 'I rebuke you.'" But Jude sets the "slanderous accusation" in direct connection to what is involved in rebuking. For Michael to rebuke the Devil would have been an accusing "judgment" (Gk. *krisis,* Jude 9).[120] The "slanderous accusation" is not a sinful action in itself. One could hardly speak evil against Satan and have the statement deemed untrue. The error that Michael avoided was in pronouncing a judgment or rebuke that was not his prerogative—and is not our prerogative—to do.

It is interesting to note that although the apostles might have truly "rebuked" demons when they cast out evil spirits, the Greek word for "rebuke" *(epitimaō)* is never used in these settings. When evil spirits (and not other humans) are the objects of a rebuke in the New Testament, the word *epitimaō* is reserved strictly for Christ's use. Jude 9 is in keeping with this. The rebuke of the Devil is reserved for the Lord. As Green suggests, "The point of the story lies just here. If an angel was so careful in what he said, how much more should mortal men watch their words."[121] The righteous angels have no authority to judge the fallen angels. Believers will *one day* judge angels (1 Cor. 6:3) but not in the current age. Believers have not received delegated authority in the Great Commission, nor does their position in Christ at the right hand of God constitute a delegated right to command the demons to obey or the right to pronounce judgment upon them.

WHAT'S A MISSIONARY TO DO?

Missions will continue to debate the role of spiritual mapping, territorial spirits, "strategic-level spiritual warfare," and other issues. Those missionaries who seek to honor the all-sufficient Scriptures will confront the temptation of compromising truth in the face of repeated experiences that contradict biblical principles. What, then, should be their response with regard to spiritual warfare?

Concentrate on Evangelism and Discipleship (Church Planting)

Remember that the gospel and salvation, not a "power encounter," are the greatest displays of God's might. Expelling a demon can never compare with the change brought about in a person's heart by faith in Christ and growth in His truth. As Konya remarks, "At no time in the New Testament era did an individual have the ministry of casting out demons, with the gospel taking a position in the background."[122] If deliverance is sought, it should be remembered that the word *salvation* really means deliverance. Romans 1:16 describes more than justification when it states that the gospel is the power of God for salvation (deliverance) to everyone who has faith.[123] Prayer and evangelism are God's methods today for dealing with demonic oppression and possession. As James 5:16 promises, "The effective prayer of a righteous man can accomplish much." Never underestimate the power of prayer.

Prayer, language acquisition, evangelism, personal discipleship, and church planting will all demand tremendous commitments in time and energy, both physically and spiritually. Radical spiritual warfare offers quick but unbiblical solutions to winning the lost and solving their struggle with sin. "What missionary candidate would not love to find some key or shortcut obviating the need for laboriously acquiring linguistic and cultural competence—something missions is dangerously in short supply of?"[124] Mature Christians must follow God's methodology.

Fight Defensively, Not Offensively

The constant emphasis in the New Testament is to keep up our guard, not to seek out the enemy. We are exhorted in three different places to "resist" the Devil (Eph. 6:13; 1 Peter 5:9; James 4:7), a command all the more emphatic when we consider that three different authors taught it to believers with regard to spiritual warfare.

1. Peter teaches that we do not resist the Devil by using commanding words or direct address but by "standing firm in the faith" (1 Peter 5:9 NIV).
2. Three times in Ephesians 6, Paul clarifies that to resist also means to "stand firm" (vv. 11, 13–14). The armor with which we are to clothe ourselves is completely defensive. Even the "sword of the Spirit," which is the word of God (6:17), is used to defend rather than to attack.[125] No offensive terminology such as "challenge the power of Satan" or "aggressively confront demonic spirits" is used in the Bible.
3. Christ's use of Scripture in His temptation in the desert (Matt. 4:1–11) is our example. Jesus did not seek out the Devil, but when Satan arrived, Scripture forced him to leave (cf. James 4:7).

The New Tribes Mission video, "Delivered from the Powers of Darkness," documents how a team of four missionaries reached the Taliabo people on a remote island of Indonesia. After spending four years learning the language and witnessing the tribe's spiritistic and animistic habits, these missionaries decided to avoid using direct power encounters to deal with the demon possession and satanic control in the tribe. Instead, they taught the Bible, using the chronological method, building a base of truth about the character and work of God from the Old Testament. After four more years of Bible teaching and waiting for the right time to introduce the New Testament and the death of Christ, they presented the gospel. When the Taliabo people dramatically turned to Christ, demons were forced to leave the new believers. As the missionaries discipled these new Christians in biblical truth, demonic phenomena disappeared and unusual attacks diminished. The power of the Word of God, not "command words," won the victory over the demonic forces.[126]

Talk to God, Not to Satan

Even Paul, when he learned that his thorn in the flesh was caused by a demonic agent, did not cast it out or demand that Satan back off. Instead, he took his request to God three times and then accepted the Lord's answer (2 Cor. 12:7–9). Believers, then, should refuse to address Satan and refuse to command the evil spirits. Conversing with demons is labeled spiritism in the Bible (Deut. 18:10–12). Believers are to speak only with the Lord of the universe. He will never belittle us for not using our so-called authority in Christ. Christ has authority to talk to demons; Michael and the angels have this privilege, too (cf. Jude 9). But until Christ returns to set up His kingdom, believers have neither the authority nor the privilege. As believers have no authority to command even good angels for "good causes" (the end does not justify the means), neither can we speak to the demonic realm without doing what God has forbidden. Conversing with angels, commanding them by our position in Christ to carry out our directives, is nothing less than spiritism. But unlike Christ, who could command demons to leave with a word or cast them out without the demon-possessed person's even being in His presence (Mark 7:29–30), those practicing modern exorcisms usually hold extended conversations with demons as a necessary element in their "success."

Reject the Unbiblical

Occult sins do not require a different set of techniques in order for the sinner to experience freedom and deliverance.[127] Occult sins are always listed with the sins of the flesh (Gal. 5:19–20; Rev. 9:21; Lev. 19:31; Exod. 22:18), which demand confession, repentance, and living by the power of the Spirit. Although verbally sharing with others our resolute intent to follow Christ and to turn from past sins is healthful, a theology of "renouncing" past involvement with the occult and other such sins is not found in Scripture. Neither is it necessary to pray special "warfare prayers" that must include certain words or concepts so that "those in bondage" might find victory. Such practices might involve meaningless rituals (Matt. 6:7) or a superstitious talisman.

Reject Syncretizing Biblical Faith with Superstition

Such ideas as the transmission of generational demons,[128] the Christian's susceptibility to being placed under a curse by those in the occult, or the teaching that demons attach themselves to objects have no support in the Bible.[129] Paul taught that meats sacrificed to idols were sacrificed to demons (1 Cor. 10:19–20). But if he had believed that demons could attach themselves to objects, he wouldn't have told the Corinthians to feel free to bring those meats into their homes and eat them (v. 25).

On one occasion, I was teaching on spiritual warfare in one of my college classes. The windows normally brought in enough sunshine that the lights were not needed, but on this particular day it was dark and cloudy so all of the lights were on in the classroom. Suddenly, all the lights in the entire building went out. I knew what the students were thinking, and I used the occasion as an opportunity to teach them the truth. My response was something like this: "You're probably thinking that Satan and demons have made the lights go out because we were discussing spiritual warfare," I said. "Satan doesn't like it when we talk about that. But suppose we were discussing salvation by faith alone through the death of Christ or the need for sexual purity and the lights went out. What would you be thinking? You'd probably think that there was a power failure in the building.

"In both cases," I continued, "your thinking might be incomplete because Satan hates talk about salvation or sexual purity just as much as he hates talk about spiritual warfare. Satan might be involved at both times in turning out the lights in the building. But the more important question is, Why did God in His sovereign control allow Satan (assuming that he was involved) to cut the power in this building?" I explained further that the Bible never suggests that Satan dislikes talk about spiritual warfare or himself more than he dislikes talk about Christ or other biblical truths. Rather, it is likely that Satan's real intention was to tempt us into this kind of super-stitious belief.

If I had not instigated this discussion in the class, I'm convinced that many students would have fallen into a pattern of fear. If the lights flickered that evening in their dorm room, they would have thought demons were the cause. If they woke up with a horrible dream two days later, they would have con-cluded that Satan was attacking them. Before long, they would be more fo-cused on Satan than on Christ, and an obsession with the demonic would result.

"What God is really trying to accomplish in the event," I said, "is to test us in the matter of superstitious beliefs. He wants us to be wise enough to reject superstitions and to resist being drawn away from Christ. Satan, on the other hand, wants to enslave us with false and deceptive ideas."

Colossians 2:8 in the *New Revised Standard Version* reads, "See to it that no one takes you captive through philosophy and empty deceit, according to human tradition, according to *the elemental spirits of the universe,* and not according to Christ" (italics added). Missionaries will inevitably experience many mysterious phenomena—in animistic cultures, in Native American cul-tures, in American culture, and others. Our interpretation of these experi-ences—not the experiences themselves—will be crucial in demonstrating that we will not be taken captive by them.

A DIVINE PREROGATIVE

Sins such as bitterness, lust, anger, and greed are attributed to the flesh (Gal. 5:19-20). Although demons might entice us to sin, our yielding to sin is never ultimately attributed to demons. James declares that when we are tempted, we are being enticed by our own desires (James 1:14). No evi-dence exists in Scripture that demons have names associated with particular sins (demon of lust, demon of smoking) or with ailments (e.g., the demon of allergies). Only once did Jesus ever seek the name of a demon ("Legion," Mark 5:9), and the name does not appear to be a sin or a disease. The only other names of demons recorded in Scripture are names for Satan himself, and only two names of angels are ever revealed to us (Michael and Gabriel). Unlike modern warfare advocates, God apparently does not consider that we need to know the names of angels or demons to live a godly life in this evil world.

In responding to demonology and missions, evangelical missionaries must call each other to account for speculation and existential thinking. Although we have been promised divine protection from the demonic realm, we must await the revelation of Christ for the exercise of our God-given rights over the spirit world. Paul left the Romans with this benediction: "And the God of peace *will soon* crush Satan under your feet" (Rom. 16:20, italics added). From Paul's perspective, the subjugation of Satan under the believer's feet was a future privilege, not a current obligation; it was a divine prerogative, not an exercise of positional authority. May Paul's perspective be ours as we attempt to win the lost to Christ.

PART 3

PRACTICAL MATTERS
IN MISSIONS

CHAPTER 12

FINANCIAL SUPPORT OF THE MISSIONARY

RUSSELL L. PENNEY

IF YOU'VE SERVED AS A MISSIONARY—whether long- or short-term—you've probably had to do some deputation work. You've probably had a variety of feelings about it. You might have thought, "I hate to beg people for money," or "Why can't we just take it out of the general account?" Every missionary has struggled at one time or another with raising support to serve Christ abroad. Have you ever thought, "I wonder how Christ or the apostles or Paul were supported?" "Did they ever feel as though they were begging?" And as a church member, have you ever thought, "Why can't that missionary get a real job?"

Considering that the church is commissioned to "go and make disciples," it's important to understand what the Bible teaches about the church's responsibility materially to support the missionaries they send out. It's also important for the missionary to understand how God meant to support His full-time servants, for when God calls people to special service, He always meets their needs as they carry it out.

THE BIBLICAL PATTERN OF MISSIONARY SUPPORT

In examining what Scripture says about missions support, it can be seen that throughout the course of redemptive history God has provided for His servants in similar ways: provision both for those in full-time ministry and for the first missionaries has always been through the generous giving of God's people.

Supported by Spiritual Beneficiaries

A principle seen throughout Holy Scripture is that those who benefit directly from spiritual instruction from an individual are materially to support that individual.

The Old Testament

Support by spiritual beneficiaries is seen in the Old Testament as early as Numbers 18:21–24:

> And to the sons of Levi, behold, *I have given all the tithe in Israel for an inheritance, in return for their service which they perform, the service of the tent of meeting.* . . . Only the Levites shall perform the service of the tent of meeting, and they shall bear their iniquity; it shall be a perpetual statute throughout your generations, and among the sons of Israel they shall have no inheritance. *For the tithe of the sons of Israel, which they offer as an offering to the Lord, I have given to the Levites for an inheritance; therefore I have said concerning them, "They shall have no inheritance among the sons of Israel."* (NASB, italics added)

Thus, God established early that those who rendered full-time service for Him on behalf of others were to be supported by those who received the benefit. Among the nation of Israel, the Levites were given no inheritance in the land; they were to receive the tithe because they were designated to perform the spiritual "service of the tent of meeting." The Levites performed the spiritual service for the Israelites, and the Israelites, through the tithe, provided materially for the Levites. The tithe was to sustain them ". . . in return for their service which they perform" (Num. 18:21; see also Deut. 14:27–29a).

The New Testament

This same principle continued into the New Testament. Even Jesus' ministry was characterized by it.

> And it came about soon afterwards, that He [Christ] began going about from one city and village to another, proclaiming and preaching the kingdom of God; and the twelve were with Him, and also some women who had been healed of evil spirits and sicknesses: Mary who was called Magdalene, from whom seven demons had gone out, and Joanna the wife of Chuza, Herod's steward, and Susanna, *and many others who were contributing to their support out of their private means.* (Luke 8:1–3, italics added)

During Christ's ministry, He allowed others to provide *physically* and *materially* for His needs. He was not embarrassed to receive support from others, whether in the form of goods, possessions, or property. Scripture also says, ". . . and the twelve were with Him." So as Jesus and the twelve apostles were involving themselves in full-time ministry, those to whom they ministered were providing for them. Matthew wrote the following about Jesus' sending out of the Twelve:

> These twelve Jesus sent out after instructing them, saying, "Do not go in the way of the Gentiles, and do not enter any city of the Samaritans; but rather go to the lost sheep of the house of Israel. And as you go, preach, saying, 'The kingdom of heaven is at hand.' Heal the sick, raise the dead, cleanse the lepers, cast out demons; freely you received, freely give. Do not acquire gold, or silver, or copper for your money belts, or a bag for your journey, or even two tunics, or sandals, or a staff; for the worker is worthy of his support." (Matthew 10:5–10)

Jesus specifically told the Twelve not to take anything with them but to depend on the support of those to whom they ministered, because, He states "The worker is worthy of his support." The same principle is seen in passages such as Galatians 6:6–10: "Let the one who is taught the word share all good things with him who teaches." Paul tells Timothy,

> Let the elders who rule well be considered worthy of double honor, especially those who work hard at preaching and teaching. For the Scripture says, "You shall not muzzle the ox while he is threshing," and "The laborer is worthy of his wages." (1 Timothy 5:17–18)

The Greek term *timē* translated "double honor," can be used in the sense of "respect" and also in the sense of "financial remuneration." Although, as Aalen states, "It is unclear whether it should be rendered honour or honorarium, i.e., remuneration," in this case—because Paul quotes from Deuteronomy 25:4 and Luke 10:7, where the idea is remuneration—it is likely that Paul has *remuneration* in mind.[1] Paul's instruction to Timothy clearly supports the principle that *God's full-time servants are to be supported by those who benefit directly from their ministry.*

Colaborers

It could be argued that all this does not speak directly to the subject of missionary support because the support of most missionaries today does not come from those who directly receive ministering. In the case of the Levites, as well as the New Testament examples, those who were being supported were ministering directly to those who gave the support. This observation is accurate. Today, missionaries in a foreign field are supported by Christians back home who believe in their work and want to colaborer with them. Scripture offers precedent for this pattern as well.

Philippians 4:15–20 says,

> And you yourselves also know, Philippians, that at the first preaching of the gospel, after I departed from Macedonia, no church shared with me in the matter of giving and receiving but you alone; for even in Thessalonica you sent a gift more than once for my needs. Not that I seek the gift itself, but I seek for the profit which increases to your account. But I have received everything in full, and have an abundance; I am amply supplied, having received from Epaphroditus what you have sent, a fragrant aroma, an acceptable sacrifice, well-pleasing to God. And my God shall supply all your needs according to His riches in glory in Christ Jesus. Now to our God and Father be the glory forever and ever. Amen.

This passage makes clear that the Philippians "colabored" with Paul (and his companions) through financial gifts as he ministered to others (i.e., the church in Thessalonica). Here is a pattern closer to what is seen today in the support of foreign missions: *God's full-time servants are supported by the financial giving of those who believe in their work and desire to be colaborers with them.*

MAKING NEEDS KNOWN

Many missionaries struggle over the idea of making their needs known and then asking for a response. Some mission agencies, in fact, teach that making needs known is unscriptural and that missionaries simply need to pray and trust God. The agency's desire in this teaching is to honor God, but Scripture teaches the pattern established by Paul. Second Corinthians 1:15–16, says,

And in this confidence I intended at first to come to you, that you
might twice receive a blessing; that is, to pass your way into
Macedonia, and again from Macedonia to come to you, and *by you
to be helped on my journey to Judea.* (italics added)

Here, Paul mentions to the Corinthians that one reason for his passing
through Corinth on the way to Judea was to "by you be helped on my journey." The Greek infinitive *propemfthenai,* here translated "helped on my journey," means "to outfit for a trip."[2] Paul lets the Corinthians know that he
would like their material help in his ministry. He informs them that he has a
financial need and that he wants their help to meet that need.

In Paul's letter to the Roman church he lets them know, too, that he has
a need:

. . . whenever I go to Spain—for I hope to see you in passing, and *to
be helped on my way* there by you, when I have first enjoyed your
company for awhile. . . . (Romans 15:24, italics added)

Paul uses the same Greek infinitive (the infinitive expresses purpose in
this case), *propemfthenai,* from the verb *propempō,* which means, according
to Bauer, "[to] *help on one's journey* with food, money, by arranging for
companions, [and] means of travel, etc."[3] Paul is writing to a church that he
had never even visited, although he did know many people in it (Rom. 16:3–
16). Again, Paul makes clear that he has a need and that he wants these believers to help him meet that need.

THOUGHTS ON THE BIBLICAL PATTERN

If we look at the record of the first missions, we do not see any clear statement that the church in Antioch provided for the material needs of Paul,
Barnabas, and John Mark; we can only speculate on how they were provided
for. At the same time, it would not be surprising if the church in Antioch did,
indeed, provide some help. It would seem highly unlikely that the church would
send the missionaries off without gathering an offering to assist them, especially since Paul, in at least two other instances, felt comfortable asking churches
to help in the support of his missionary activities. Paul apparently considered
requesting support a normal practice for those involved in missions work.

One may well wonder, however, if Paul communicated to his sending church and other supporting churches *specific, "essential" needs for his trip.* Again, nothing in the text of Scripture indicates that he did. But it is not unlikely that, when he arrived at Corinth and Rome, the believers asked about his needs for the trip. Recall, the term Paul used in Romans 15:24 , meaning, according to Bauer, "[to] *help on one's journey* with food, money, by arranging for companions, [and] means of travel, etc."[4] It would not then be unnatural for the believers, in response to Paul's request, to ask him about specific needs. Such conclusions can be inferred from the use of the term *propemfthenai* and from a general understanding of human nature.

SUPPORT SUMMARY

From Scripture, the following principles have been established:

1. God's full-time servants are supported by those who benefit directly from their ministry.
2. God's full-time servants are supported by those who believe in their work and desire to be colaborers with them through financial giving.
3. God's full-time servants let believers know about their needs generally (and probably specifically) and directly ask them to help with those needs.

MODERN APPROACHES TO MISSIONARY SUPPORT

Since modern approaches to missionary support vary based upon the type of mission board, an examination of types will provide an overview of their approaches to addressing missionary finances.

The Modern Mission Boards

Upon examining modern mission boards, it is observed that they can be categorized into two general types: the associational or denominational mission boards and the independent mission boards, which are usually nondenominational or sometimes interdenominational. There follows a broad description of how these different types of mission boards handle their financing.

Denominational Mission Boards

The denominational mission boards are, as their name implies, subject to the authority of the denomination under which they work. Usually, a missions committee reports to the leadership of the denomination.

For funding, denominational mission boards depend on the churches that are members of their denomination or association. Rarely, if ever, are candidates sent to the field from outside the denomination.

In some instances, a percentage of missions giving is suggested to local churches. This percentage is, however, only a suggestion, and giving obviously varies from church to church. Throughout each year, the missions committee might plan and advertise specific events in the local churches (e.g., Missions Sunday) to promote missions and encourage giving. The plans that the board for missions activity might make each year would be based on an estimated budget.

When missionaries are elected by the committee, they are put on a regular salary or living allowance. In most instances, the amount is based not on the responsibilities the missionary bears on the field or the value of the work but on the cost of living in the host country. The number of children a missionary has is taken into account as well in assigning a salary.

Strength of the Approach

Missionaries do not have to raise support themselves because they are given a regular salary. This arrangement takes a heavy burden off missionaries and allows them to concentrate on the task at hand.

Weaknesses of the Approach

Many, if not most, people who donate to missions prefer giving to an individual missionary or a special project rather than to a denominational board.

Missionaries who receive a regular salary tend to feel less obligated to maintain close contact with their sending and supporting churches, which stifles missions giving and enthusiasm.

With the salaried system, missionaries who work hard at putting together a good presentation to raise support, benefit no more than those who visit only a handful of churches while on deputation. (In light of this fact, some boards now allow gifts to be designated toward a specific missionary's ministry.)

Independent Mission Boards

Independent mission boards are, as their name implies, independent of any denominational structure or control. They tend to be nondenominational or interdenominational and are usually run by a board chosen from among independent and denominational churches around the country that share a similar vision and doctrinal position with the founders of the mission. These boards have generally been conservative in their theology at the time of their founding.

Most of these independent mission boards are called "faith" missions, a title that comes from their financial policies. They choose not to solicit funds directly but simply make their needs known and trust that God wants certain people to give toward those needs and that He will move hearts. Independent mission boards depend on a multitude of independent churches and some denominational churches for both the financial support of the mission's endeavors and for missionary candidates. While these boards tend to be nondenominational in their doctrinal stance, and many are quite conservative, they accept missionaries from both independent and denominational churches. Missionaries are usually required to raise a certain amount of support, but the mission often does the research for estimating the approximate amount needed on their field.

Missionaries usually raise support by traveling to churches they have contacted and giving presentations of the work in which they will be involved. At this time, the missionaries will explain their financial needs. The process of raising support is most often referred to, in missions circles, as "deputation." Churches and individuals may offer either a lump-sum amount to the missionary work or establish a monthly amount. Some churches might include the missionary in their missions budget at an annual or monthly level. When the missionary has enough money for initial set-up costs, and enough in monthly pledges to cover the estimated salary (living allowance) needed, the mission board then allows the missionary to travel to the field. If at any time in the future the salary consistently falls below the amount needed, the missionary may be recalled.

Some of these independent mission boards use a plan similar to the denominational boards—they pool contributions and establish allowances for the missionaries. Again, these allowances are based on marital status, cost of living in the host country, and the number of dependents.

Strength of the Typical Faith Mission Approach

The individual support plan tends to promote missions giving because supporters can identify with specific missionaries and the work they are doing.

Missionaries feel a greater responsibility for keeping their supporters current with the work because their salaries are being paid directly by them.

The pooling plan among independent missions has the advantages of leveling out inequalities among missionaries. Some missionaries, for instance, are more dynamic speakers and are better support raisers although their work might not be any more valuable than that of less successful fund raisers.

Weaknesses of the Approach

If financial support falls below the minimum needed, missionaries might have to leave the work on the field at an unfortunate time and return home to do deputation.

As with the salaried system, in the pooling system the missionary who works hard at putting together a good presentation and raising support benefits no more than the missionary who visits only a handful of churches while on deputation.

The Independent Missionary

The independent missionary chooses to go to the field without being a member of any mission board. Missionaries make this choice for various reasons. Some, for example, feel called to a particular and sometimes unique work in a country where no mission boards are involved. Some independents find it difficult to work with others and do not want to become accountable to a mission board. Others might have been rejected by several mission agencies and have chosen to go to the field anyway. Some independents end up ministering with an established ministry and fit in very well. Others seek to start their own work and have varying degrees of success.

Most independent missionaries address their financial needs in one of two ways—through churches or through nonprofit organizations. Those sent to the field by their local churches depend on the sending churches to manage their finances. These missionaries raise support, however, in the same way that missionaries who work through independent mission boards do—by gaining support from individuals and churches and having it sent directly to their sponsoring churches. The missionaries are considered employees of the sending churches, which send a monthly or bimonthly check to them on the field. Other independent missionaries establish their own nonprofit organizations/missions that handle their funds exclusively. The finances are then usually managed by a trusted supporter back in the homeland.

Obviously, the independent missionary's approach has weaknesses similar to those of the independent mission board. It has, however, one additional disadvantage: Unless the missionary is associated with a group of counselors or a board of advisors, the missionary alone controls the expenditures and also suffers from the limitation of self-counsel.

FIGURING THE FINANCING

Calculating the financial needs of the missionary involves estimating costs that include (1) training, (2) field setup, (3) field expenses, (4) supporting services, (5) airfare, and (6) personal living allowance. A Financial Worksheet (see reproduction below) tells missionaries and potential supporters the amount of funds needed to be effective on the field.

Training

Some mission agencies require prefield orientation and training in addition to the theological education necessary to apply for candidacy. The length of training varies from a few months to a year and typically covers (1) Bible training, (2) cross-cultural adjustment and communication, (3) language acquisition skills, and (4) evangelism. Classes that address support raising, interpersonal relationships, Teaching English as a Second Language (TESL), church planting, and so on might also be required.

Field Setup

Learning the language of the host country is a necessity if one is to be effective on the field. One year of finances for language training is a minimum—two years is preferable.

Household furnishings might be too expensive if purchased on the field; shipping furnishings to the field might be more cost effective. Other ministry supplies include Bible study materials, pens, paper, computer equipment, and so on. The type of supplies needed depends upon the specific type of ministry.

In some countries, a vehicle, if needed, can be purchased inexpensively on the field, whereas in other countries shipping a vehicle is a better option. In most cases, the least expensive approach to shipping either a vehicle or other belongings is to purchase an ocean-worthy container and ship well in

FINANCIAL WORKSHEET

Training _____

Field setup
    Language school _____
    Household furnishings _____
    Ministry supplies and equipment _____
    Vehicle _____
    Shipping costs _____
    Visas _____

Airfare _____

TOTAL SETUP SUPPORT NEEDED $_____

Field expenses
    Rent, utilities, and food _____
    Medical insurance _____
    Social Security _____
    Retirement _____
    Vehicle insurance, gas, and repairs _____
    Work fund _____
    Prayer/support letters and postage _____
    Conferences _____

Supporting services _____

Personal living allowance _____

TOTAL MONTHLY SUPPORT NEEDED $_____

advance of arrival on the field. Remember that the cost will include transportation both to and from ports. Some countries charge significant customs fees, and other extraneous expenses should be well researched to avoid significant "hidden" costs. The missionary should always raise more than needed, however, because unexpected costs will invariably arise.

Last, but certainly not least, in setup expenses is the visa. Resident visas can be very expensive and, in many countries, difficult to obtain. Various types of visas are available, and the laws of the host country may either be favorable or unfavorable toward missionaries, a circumstance that will affect the status under which the missionary enters and resides in the country. Information about the costs for visas and most of the other expenses mentioned in this section can be obtained from the U. S. State Department and/or from missionaries who already reside and work in the host culture.

Field Expenses

The items in the category of field expenses are much the same as they would be if one were living and ministering in the United States. In most cases medical insurance, Social Security, retirement, and so on will be administered by the mission, but amounts for these things should be included in the amount to be raised for support. Other field expenses include the "work fund," which allows the missionary to travel to different ministry sites throughout the host country. It also allows for the purchase of tracts, Bibles, printed materials, computer upgrades, and other helpful ministry equipment. Work funds must sometimes be approximated until one arrives on the field and gets a feel for the nature and extent of the ministry.

It is important that missionaries keep their supporters well informed. One effective and practical way of doing this is the prayer/support letter. Envelopes, duplication costs, and postage are expenses to be considered when missionaries are raising support.

Conferences—although looked upon by some supporters as luxuries—are necessary for maintaining missionaries' mental health and perspective, especially for those who have difficult field ministries. At conferences, missionaries receive encouragement, instruction, and fellowship. A typical conference consists of a week-long retreat where the missionaries of a given agency gather to share what God is doing in and through them on their given fields. Friendships are renewed and nurtured, common problems are shared, and solutions are considered. For some missionaries, this is a time during which they can be ministered to after months, if not years, of ministering to others.

Supporting Services

The small amount that is needed for an agency's support services reaps a tremendous return. In chapter 14, "The Role of the Mission Agency," Dr. Albert T. Platt gives the following examples of the supporting services that mission agencies provide for their missionaries.

> For example, services to mission members include purchasing, shipping, letter service, banking, receipting, bill payment, insurance, emergency services, travel arrangements, doctor appointments and just about anything else one might imagine. Services rendered to entities in the homeland include information regarding the field, consultation regarding missions, conferences, field activities, visits to the field, receipting, emergency reports, literature, films, videos, speakers, etc.[5]

Airfare

Airfares are a significant expense today. Round-trip tickets to most European, Asian, and South American countries are around $1,000 per passenger. That's a lot of money for a family of five. Again, missionaries should raise more than they think is necessary because prices always fluctuate.

Personal Living Allowance

Personal living allowance is a category that has developed in recent years as a result of missionaries thinking ahead. It includes planning for a salary that is above their immediate needs, taking into consideration such things as future college costs, home purchase, retirement, and so on. Many, if not most, mission agencies strongly suggest that support be raised to cover these areas.

A Final Note

Most of the information discussed in this chapter is gathered by mission agencies for their missionaries or can be obtained from the U.S. Department of State. Also, organizations such as Overseas Research Consultants (ORC) are dedicated to providing financial cost-of-living numbers for each country. Many missions subscribe to the ORC service instead of setting their own rates. Remember, it is always easier to raise support at home than it is on the field. No matter how anxious people are to get to the field, they should not depart undersupported and risk having to return home before the term is complete.

RAISING THE SUPPORT

Scripture shows that missionaries received financial support from those who shared their desire to carry out the Great Commission. It was the pattern of Jesus and Paul; it is not "begging." Kane writes,

> The missionary is not a beggar. He is a laborer in the Lord's vineyard, and the laborer is worthy of his hire. Jesus said so. He is also a servant of the church; the church *owes* him a living wage. Every true church is a church for others. The church, like Paul, is a debtor to both Greeks and to the barbarians. It is under moral obligation to share the gospel with the world, especially that part where Christ has not been named. The church can fulfill this obligation only through the missionary. When the missionary, therefore, comes seeking support he is not a beggar in disgrace; he is a benefactor in disguise.[6]

The missionary "is a laborer in the Lord's vineyard." When missionaries communicate their need for support on the foreign field, they are providing information. They are explaining the ministry to which God has called them, what God is doing there now, and how the churches that they visit can colabor with them.

Note, too, that Paul wrote to the Philippians, "Not that I seek the gift itself, but I seek for the profit which increases to your account" (Phil. 4:17). The spiritual benefits are immeasurable for churches and individuals who give to missionary work.

Where to Start

The starting point for raising financial support is the same as for any true need—prayer. God is the One who will move the hearts of people to give. It can be seen repeatedly in Holy Writ that God meets the needs of those whom He calls to a ministry.

But prayer is not the end-all in raising support. Kane writes,

> Missionaries do look to God for the supply of their needs, but everyone knows that these supplies are not sent direct from heaven. They are channeled through the church. In the case of the American church we have money in abundance. There is no need to "pray it down." All we need to do is "pry it out." God is not likely to work miracles for His servants on the mission field when the church

at home has the resources to underwrite the entire operation ten times over.[7]

Whom to Approach

In presenting their work, missionaries make two types of contacts: *individual* contacts and *group* contacts.

Individuals whom the missionary might contact include

1. family members
2. friends
3. former church members
4. former classmates
5. neighbors
6. former coworkers
7. banker, doctor, dentist, and so on

This list gives some idea of the many sources that God might use to meet the financial and prayer needs of missionaries while they are on the field. Missionaries should contact prospective supporters by telephone and set up face-to-face meetings. Whether they meet with them personally or send an information packet, missionaries should supply prospective supporters with literature that includes (1) a support-raising letter (see appendix 2 for a sample), (2) a financial needs worksheet (see appendix 3 for a sample), and (3) information on the missions agency with which the missionary is associated, including its doctrinal statement and financial policy. Conscientious supporters will want to know this kind of information. Missionaries who have visited the field on which they will serve have an advantage in this regard because they will be more informed and have extra resources such as video shots and pictures of the work and the people there.

The second type of contact is with a *group* of potential supporters, a meeting that will often involve a presentation of the work before a local church but could also be to men's groups, women's groups, Sunday school classes, and so on. Again, missionaries who have taken a short-term missions trip to the field will have an advantage. Quality video shots are an excellent way to present one's work, and because all video cameras now include editing capabilities, poor shots can be eliminated and music and comments added. Music from the area in which the missionary will work enhances the presentation. Information packets that include the items mentioned above should be available for those who want them. Also helpful is an informative handout describing ways that people or groups can help missionaries (see sample in appendix 4).

Speaking engagements at local churches should be arranged well in advance because most churches have full schedules. Contact the pastor or the chairman of the missions committee to ask for an opportunity to speak to the church or a group in the church.

When a date has been scheduled for a presentation, the missionary should be on time, be organized, be informative, and allow God to work. Whatever method of presentation is chosen, it should be high quality and presented with passion. Zeal and enthusiasm go a long way toward exciting people about the work.

Finally, missionaries must trust that, if God has called them, He will supply all needs. Kane's comments are fitting:

> Raising funds may be hard on the flesh but it is good for the spirit. When the young candidate first starts out he is filled with fear and trepidation. How will he ever be able to raise that huge amount of money? It seems like an impossible task. In his dilemma he is cast on the Lord in a new way, and early in his experience, before he ever gets to the field, he learns not to depend on his own understanding or trust in his own ability, but to look to the Lord for the supply of every need.
>
> When the meetings are over he settles down to wait and watch. As the funds come in, sometimes from the most unexpected sources he rejoices in the goodness of God. Each additional gift not only brings him closer to his desired goal, but it further confirms his call to missionary service. By the time the last dollar is in he is ready to sing the doxology. He is the happiest person in the world. God has provided abundantly above all that he ever dared expect. He will never be the same again. Looking back on the ordeal he decides that he would not be without the experience for the world.[8]

GO TO ALL NATIONS

The church of Jesus Christ has been called to make disciples by going to all nations, and baptizing and teaching all those who come to Him. With this in mind, it is proper that resources in the local church be prioritized to support missions (both home and foreign). As we see in the New Testament, Paul and his companions were supported by those who had directly benefited from their ministry. But their support also came from those who wanted to be colaborers with them in their missionary work. Like Christ, Paul was not embarrassed to let his needs be known and ask that certain saints share in meeting them. Missionaries have successfully followed this pattern in the past, and it is still just as effective today.

Adapted in part from *A Biblical Theology of the Church,* ed. Mal Couch (Grand Rapids: Kregel, 1999), 249–63.

CHAPTER 13

THE RESPONSIBILITY OF THE LOCAL CHURCH

RUSSELL L. PENNEY

MODERN MISSION AGENCIES PROVIDE inestimable blessing in carrying out the Great Commission. Through these organizations—which facilitate and support missionaries who are commissioned and sent out by local churches—the work of thousands of missionaries has been multiplied.

At the same time—and probably not because of any faults in the mission agencies—their development has made many local churches in the United States delegate their own responsibilities for carrying out the Great Commission to these professional agencies. "John Bennett of ACMC (Advancing Churches in Missions Commitment) says that there are 300,000 churches in America and yet only 10 percent have a missions program."[1] Yet, the Bible states that the local church—not the mission agency—is "the pillar and support of the truth" (1 Tim. 3:14). Even as they facilitate and enhance missions, mission agencies should consider themselves an extension of the local church, since it is the church itself that has been commissioned to take the gospel to the ends of the earth.

Dr. Robert Lightner states that the threefold mission of the church includes

> (1) the exaltation of God (John 4:23-24; Phil. 3:3); (2) the education, edification, and equipping of the saints in and through the Word of God (Eph. 4:11-16; 1 Thess. 5:11); and (3) the evangelization of the lost (Matt. 28:19-20; Acts 1:8; 2 Cor. 5:20; 1 Tim. 3:15).[2]

Any local churches whose hearts do not beat for missions (both home and foreign) are in need of a pacemaker. They have strayed from the goals of their Head, and they must rethink and readjust their ministry focus.

For those churches that do have the right focus and for those that are willing to readjust their goals, this chapter will be helpful. It will explain both biblically and practically the responsibility of the local church in missionary endeavor, and how the church can best carry out that responsibility.

The Responsibility to Promote Missions

Churches should keep foreign missions and the need for foreign missionaries ever before the people. Doing so helps remind members that believers are commanded to make disciples among *all* the nations (Matt. 28:19–20; Acts 1:8; 2 Cor. 5:20; 1 Tim. 3:15). The church that focuses on missions is constantly reminded of God's bigger program and is less likely to become ingrown, working solely toward "building a bigger local church." The leadership of the church must be the driving force in the promotion of missions. The bottom line is that *the local church will not be missions-minded unless the leadership of the church is missions-minded.* Harold Cook notes,

> The life of any missionary program in a local church depends largely on the leadership. Someone has to have the interest, the vision, the initiative to inaugurate a program, plus the persistence to carry it through. Normally, the pastor should be that leader. People usually look up to the leadership, and in this matter they expect him to be much better informed than the members. Besides, he must cooperate if missions is to be a church concern and not just a fringe activity of a small group within the church.[3]

Thus, the elders and pastor-teachers of the church must, through their actions, demonstrate that foreign missions is a priority. Church leaders don't have to do all the work in promoting awareness of the world's need for the gospel and the activities of the missionaries they support. Church leaders do, however, need to ensure that everything done in the church to promote missions is carried out with quality and consistency. Elders and pastor-teachers can and should, of course, delegate some of the work to others.

When the leadership is committed to missions, certain objectives can be established that will enhance and maintain the church's focus. Cook lists the following seven objectives for establishing an effective missions program:

1. Create interest in and enthusiasm for missions on the part of as many members as possible;

2. Support that interest and enthusiasm with accurate and current information;
3. Secure as much prayer support for missions as possible;
4. Contribute as much material support for missions as possible;
5. Provide personnel for the missionary enterprise;
6. Train prospective missionaries as far as is possible for a local church;
7. Assist missions in other ways as circumstances permit (e.g., the promotion of joint missionary conferences).[4]

Cook's objectives are worthy, but reorganizing them might be helpful. Objectives 1, 3, and 7 can be organized under the broader category of "Create interest in and enthusiasm for missions and the missionary"; objective 2 as "Encourage prayer support for missions and the missionary"; objective 4 as "Encourage material support for missions and the missionary"; and objectives 5 and 6 as " Train, commission, and send missionaries."

We will look at the biblical pattern in these areas and suggest practical ways that the local church can achieve its objectives.

CREATE INTEREST AND ENTHUSIASM

The key to the creation of interest and enthusiasm is providing information, a pattern that can be seen in the ministry of the early church. We live in the information age, but information about what God is doing around the world through His church generally and what God is doing through the missionaries your church supports particularly must meet certain criteria. First, the information must be current. Second, it must be visually appealing. And third, it must create enthusiasm in the church member.

Current Information

The missionary prayer/newsletter has, for decades, been a valuable tool for informing, encouraging, and exciting supporters back home about work on the field—which is sometimes thousands of miles away. The letter is also a way for missionaries to let their supporters know about the progress of the ministry, particular prayer concerns, and sometimes particular material needs.

But, in the past, by the time the supporter (including the supporting church) got the information, it was often old news. With the "snail mail" available in most countries, the letters took from two to four weeks to get to their destinations. If the events described in the letter had taken place over a one- to two-month period, then the information was several months old by the time supporters received it. Although a need for prayer letters still exists, modern communication through electronic mail eliminates delays in field updates.

Local church leadership, by using modern technology, can keep their congregations current about the work in which they are taking part.

Speeding up the Prayer Letter

The missionary can send written communications directly to church leadership shortly after the ministry events occur from any place where a phone line is available. This information can be announced either at the services that week or in an attractive mini news/prayer letter formatted, duplicated, and placed in the bulletin for the services. Communiqués help to keep the church's hand "on the pulse" of what is occurring on the field. The adage "Out of sight, out of mind" is, unfortunately, true. But the reverse is true as well. If the work of missionaries is kept constantly in the sight of the congregation, it stays very much in their minds and prayers.

The Audio/Visual Connection

To keep current with their missionaries, churches in the past several years have employed conference calls during a church service. By connecting the telephone to the public address system, questions can be posed to missionaries, and the missionaries can give a brief report and share prayer concerns. This system works well and helps the congregation to feel more connected to work on the field.

New technology now allows churches not only to hear their missionaries on the field in "real time" but to see them. Imagine going to church on Sunday morning and hearing that a report from your missionary will be presented live from Irian Jaya, halfway around the world. After the typical announcements, the lights dim and the overhead screen descends. Suddenly, Joe Missionary is projected onto the screen. The pastor asks him a few questions, and he gives you a report on all that God is doing there. Joe is also able to express his appreciation for your prayer and financial support.

With this new technology, both the church and the missionary only need a personal computer with Internet access and Web Cam. Both computers must have a USB port, which now is standard, and the church must have a digital projector. Currently, the quality of the video image as well as the audio can vary from near perfect to very poor, depending on the quality of the telephone line. But the technology is sure to advance. Never in history have churches had such opportunities to keep congregations excited about the work of the missionaries they support.

Appeal to the Eye

We live in a visual age. Our society is used to information that is visually appealing. In marketing, how an advertisement looks is at least as important as what it says. Because our culture is "spoiled" by graphic excellence, any presentation about mission work placed before a congregation must be done with quality and excellence. With the advent of personal computers, the church, working with the missionary on the field, should put together presentations with plenty of graphics.

If, for instance, the church is receiving information from a missionary on the field via electronic mail, in addition to the text, a picture can be scanned in as an attachment and then printed out on a color printer. Then an attractive mini news/prayer letter with pictures could be formatted, duplicated, and placed in the bulletin for the services. The equipment needed to produce presentable material (e.g., a computer, color printer, scanner, and, of course, an Internet connection) is within the budget of even small churches.

Prices for video cameras continue to drop, so a VHS or VHS-C video camera for missionaries is a worthwhile investment. The missionaries should, of course, be given some training and guidelines on how to produce quality video shots. If they are savvy in this area, they can add background music from the area where they serve. If not, someone in the church might be able to do it, the aim being a quality production.

Creating Enthusiasm

Current, visually appealing information helps church members realize the value of the missions ministry they help support. Members can read about, see, and hear from the actual people they are helping bring to Christ. Members see the life transforming power of the gospel firsthand in the lives of the people to whom the missionary is ministering.

Information should include specific and personal ways, too, that a church member can be a part of the ministry. The missionary could, for instance, give specific prayer requests (i.e., Pastor Julio's health or the evangelism campaign in Valle Grande, and so on). If a need exists for material items, such as in the construction of a church building, the missionary should let church members know and explain the overall benefit that the items will bring to the Christian nationals. If a work team would be beneficial, the missionary should let the church know specifically what kind of skilled workers are needed and what unskilled "helpers" can do.

The more missionaries engage congregations, the more enthusiasm they will maintain and the more they will be supported. Church leadership, too, can stimulate interest in their churches' missions endeavors by disseminating information. And that information can take several forms.

The Bulletin Board

The information provided and the overall attractiveness of the missionary bulletin board depends on the creativity of those who coordinate and care for it. As with all forms of information, the bulletin board should be eye-catching. The inclusion of maps is especially important. A map could show the location of the featured country in relation to the rest of the world, and another map of the featured country could highlight the city or region in which the missionary is working. The board should also include photos of the missionary, letters from the field, photos showing the nationals with whom the missionary is working, and pictures that give a sense of the cultural differences (animals, different customs, traditional clothing, and so on). A specific area of the board could feature current prayer concerns of the missionary.

A bulletin board that is current, attractive, and informative will benefit both the missionary and the congregation, and will be the result of good cooperation between the missionary and the caretaker of the board.

The Missions Conference

A well-planned two- to three-day missions conference will stimulate interest in the work of the missionaries that your church supports. A conference of this kind challenges people, young and old, to enter missionary service and can do much to increase the missions budget of the church. [5]

Churches that are part of a denomination or association that supports and sends missionaries would benefit from contacting that denomination or association for help with the planning. These central offices will have considerable experience and can advise about which ideas do and do not work at conferences. They can also help in arranging speakers. A church would be well advised to schedule a conference at a time of year when other conferences have been well attended. Since the regular Sunday morning service has the largest attendance, the conference could be "kicked off" at that time. Other local churches should be notified in advance, and if they are theologically compatible they might be included in organizing the meeting.

The missionaries who speak should have eye-catching displays that show the work in which they are involved. Artifacts, pictures, and national regalia stimulate the imagination and get people interested.

Although one speaker is sufficient, two or three would be even better. It is preferable that each missionary giving a presentation work in a different culture and practice a different type of ministry—variety gives listeners a broader view of what foreign missions is like.

Time should be allowed for questions after the missionaries' presentations. The audience should be encouraged to interact with the missionaries and ask for specific information regarding areas in which they might have an interest. A small-group or a round-table discussion led by a moderator for asking pertinent questions and stimulating discussion might be of value if several missionary speakers are present.

Well-organized missions conferences can challenge congregations, inform them about what God is doing around the world, and prevent churches from becoming ingrown.

The Missions Message/Sermon

World evangelization is part of the threefold mission of the church. It follows, therefore, that sermons and teachings on world missions should be a regular occurrence. A church that is interested in seeing souls come to Christ will be interested in missions. The Sunday message should help the congregation feel compelled to evangelize. Even messages that are keyed toward everyday Christian living can include illustrations from great missionaries of the past.

PRAYER SUPPORT

The Biblical Pattern

From the very outset, the missionary endeavor was bathed in prayer. Luke writes in the New Testament, "And while they were ministering to the Lord and fasting, the Holy Spirit said, 'Set apart for Me Barnabas and Saul for the work to which I have called them.' Then, when they had fasted and *prayed* and laid their hands on them, they sent them away" (Acts 13:2–3 NASB, italics added). Paul, too, in his letters to the churches he planted, requested prayer for his missionary efforts and for those of his colleagues.

While sitting in a Roman jail, for instance, Paul entreated the believers in Ephesus to "pray on my behalf, that utterance may be given to me in the opening of my mouth, to make known with boldness the mystery of the gospel, for which I am an ambassador in chains; that in proclaiming it I may speak boldly, as I ought to speak" (Eph. 6:19–20). During that same imprisonment, he wrote to the Colossians, "Devote yourselves to prayer, keeping alert in it with an attitude of thanksgiving; praying at the same time for us as well, that God will open up to us a door for the word, so that we may speak forth the mystery of Christ, for which I have been imprisoned; in order that I may make it clear in the way I ought to speak" (Col. 4:2–4).

Paul not only told the Thessalonians to "pray without ceasing" (1 Thess. 5:17) but also asked them, "Brethren, pray for us" (v. 25). On a later occasion, he wrote, "Finally, brethren, pray for us that the word of the Lord may spread rapidly and be glorified, just as it did also with you" (2 Thess. 3:1). Paul realized that prayer was needed for success in reaching the nations.

Prayer and God's Sovereignty in Missions

Prayer support is necessary because, no matter how gifted, talented, educated, and adaptable to another culture a missionary might be, God is ultimately the One who accomplishes the work of missions.

The Great Commission given in Matthew 28:19–20 is preceded and followed by statements that affect the outcome of how the commission is carried out. As a prelude to the commission statement, Christ said, "All authority has been given to Me in heaven and on earth," and He followed the commission with "and lo, I am with you always, even to the end of the age" (vv. 18, 20). Thus, the Messiah, who is sovereign in all things, was with them and is still with us today, carrying out His will in calling out a people for His name through His disciples. God through Christ produces the fruit by proclamation of the gospel, and He does so to glorify Himself. Christ stated, "By this is my Father glorified, that you bear much fruit" (John 15:8). John Piper writes,

> So how is God glorified by prayer? Prayer is the open admission that without Christ we can do nothing. And prayer is the turning away from ourselves to God in the confidence that He will provide that help we need. Prayer humbles *us* as needy and exalts *God* as all-sufficient.[6]

He continues,

> This is why the missionary enterprise advances by prayer. The chief
> end of God is to glorify God. He will do this in the sovereign tri-
> umph of his missionary purpose that the nations worship him. He
> will secure this triumph by entering into the warfare and becoming
> the main combatant. And he will take the engagement plan to all
> the participants through prayer. Because prayer shows that the power
> is from the Lord.[7]

Thus, the local church should be urged to pray for their missionaries,
understanding that it is "God who gives the increase" (1 Cor. 3:7 NKJV).

Missionary Service Is Warfare

Whether or not we are aware of it, a battle rages constantly for the hearts and
minds of people. Biblical evidence shows that Satan, like God, has organized his
angelic host (demons in Satan's case) into ranks. Paul writes, "For our struggle
is not against flesh and blood, but against the *rulers,* against the *powers,* against
the *world-forces of this darkness,* against the *spiritual forces of wickedness* in the
heavenly places" (Eph. 6:12, italics added). Many scholars believe that Paul is
listing the different ranks of fallen angels. The battle for the souls of those whom
the missionary is attempting to reach with the gospel is a spiritual battle.

Missionaries often go into areas over which Satan has held sway since the
descendants of Noah began to depart from God, and it is certain that Satan
will not be pleased with their presence. Knowing that the gospel "is the power
of God unto salvation" (Rom. 1:16), Satan responds by attacking the bearer
of the gospel. Although Satan can do nothing that God does not allow, the
missionary can become discouraged by difficulties such as the moral failures
of the converts, extreme weather conditions, the different culture, physical
illness, and countless setbacks. John Piper, in *Let the Nations Be Glad,* comments on the connection between "the sword of the Spirit" and "prayer" in
Ephesians 6:17–18:

> In the original Greek, verse 18 does not begin a new sentence. It
> connects with verse 17 like this: "Take the sword of the Spirit, which
> is the word of God, praying through prayer and supplication on every
> occasion . . ." Take the sword . . . praying! This is how we are to
> wield the word—by prayer.

Prayer is the communication with headquarters by which the weapons of warfare are deployed according to the will of God. That's the connection between weapons and prayer in Ephesians 6. Prayer is war.[8]

The Bible never exhorts prayer against demonic forces, but it does encourage prayer for missionaries (1 Thess. 5:25) and for boldness and opportunity for them as they proclaim the gospel to the ends of the earth (Eph. 6:19-20; Col. 4:2-4; 2 Thess. 3:1). Prayer is the indispensable ingredient for successfully reaching the nations.

MATERIAL SUPPORT

The Biblical Pattern

As mentioned earlier, when we look at the record of the first missions thrust, we do not see any clear statement that the church in Antioch provided for the material needs of Paul, Barnabas, and John Mark. We can only speculate about whether the church supported them materially. At the same time, it would not be surprising if the Antioch church did provide material help. That the church would send the missionaries off without gathering an offering to assist them in their endeavors seems highly unlikely, considering that Paul, in at least two other instances, felt comfortable in specifically asking churches to help with the support of his missionary activities. That Paul requested support indicates that the practice should be normal for those who are involved in missions work.

In writing to the church in Corinth, for instance, Paul stated, "And in this confidence I intended at first to come to you, that you might twice receive a blessing; that is, to pass your way into Macedonia, and again from Macedonia to come to you, and *by you to be helped on my journey to Judea* (2 Cor. 1:15-16, italics added). Here, Paul mentions to the Corinthians that one reason for his passing through Corinth on the way to Judea was "by you [to] be helped on my journey." The Greek infinitive *propemfthenai*, here translated "helped on my journey," means "to outfit for a trip."[9] So Paul is expressing his desire that the Corinthian church help him materially in his ministry.

Similarly, Paul let the Roman church know that he had a need and that he wanted them to help meet that need. He wrote, "whenever I go to Spain— for I hope to see you in passing, and *to be helped on my way* there by you, when I have first enjoyed your company for awhile" (Rom. 15:24). Here again, Paul expresses his purpose, using the same Greek infinitive *propemfthenai* from the verb *propempō*, which means (according to Bauer) "[to] *help on one's journey* with food, money, by arranging for companions, [and] means of travel, etc."[10] Paul makes known to local churches specific needs and asks them to support him in his missionary efforts.

Look closely at his exhortation to the church in Philippi, which was generous in supporting his missions work:

> And you yourselves know, Philippians, that at the first preaching of the gospel, after I departed from Macedonia, no church shared with me in the matter of giving and receiving but you alone; for even in Thessalonica you sent a gift more than once for my needs. Not that I seek the gift itself, but I seek for the profit which increases to your account. But I have received everything in full, and have an abundance; I am amply supplied, having received from Epaphroditus what you have sent, a fragrant aroma, an acceptable sacrifice, well-pleasing to God. And my God shall supply all your needs according to His riches in glory in Christ Jesus. (Philippians 4:15–19)

Although verse 19 is well worn, it is often quoted without considering its context. The church in Philippi had their priorities straight; they consistently gave toward world missions. Paul points out two things to the Philippian Christians. First, he points out the impact that their gifts had on God. The analogy he uses in verse 18 is probably a reference to the grain or meal offering of the Old Testament (Lev. 2:1–6; 6:14–23), which was given as an expression of gratitude to God and an offer of their lives to Him for service. The offering was an acceptable sacrifice to God and well pleasing to Him. The same can be said of our gifts toward world evangelization—they are well pleasing to God.

Second, Paul states that in light of God's pleasure at their offering, He will supply all of their needs according to the riches in glory in Christ Jesus. The Philippians needn't worry that, having committed so much to world missions, they might now have to do without. God would meet all of their needs.

The percentage of a local church's budget that should be committed to missions must be determined by the leadership. The amount, however, should be significant. Tom Telford has worked with hundreds, if not thousands, of churches, and he states that if a church desires a top-notch missions program, it should commit at least 30 percent of its annual budget to it. He notes that some churches give as much as 75 percent to cross-cultural ministry.[11]

It is important not to finance one ministry in a way that will make other ministries suffer. After prayerful consideration of the Scriptures and existing needs, church leadership must decide on the percentage of the budget to be dedicated for missions. But I've never heard of a church that had to close its doors because it committed too much of its budget to missionary work.

RECOGNIZE, EVALUATE, TRAIN, COMMISSION, AND SEND

The Biblical Pattern

As mentioned in chapter 2, not long after the stoning of Stephen (Acts 7:54–60), some of the scattered believers made their way to Antioch (11:19). There, a large church was established and its leaders spent time grounding followers in the faith (vv. 20–26). This growing church in Asia Minor became an early center of missionary activity, and from there the first missionaries—Paul and Barnabas—were sent.

Paul's missionary activity began when God chose him and Barnabas, and the leadership of the Antioch church set them apart (13:2). Acts 13:1–3 says,

> Now there were at Antioch, in the church that was there, prophets and teachers: Barnabas, and Simeon who was called Niger, and Lucius of Cyrene, and Manaen who had been brought up with Herod the tetrarch, and Saul. And while they were ministering to the Lord and fasting, the Holy Spirit said, "Set apart for Me Barnabas and Saul for the work to which I have called them." Then, when they had fasted and prayed and laid their hands on them, they sent them away.

From the preceding passage, four principles delineate the responsibility of the local church in sending out missionaries:

1. Leadership is to recognize those whom God has chosen to be sent out.
2. The missionaries sent are to be theologically equipped.
3. The missionaries sent out are to be commissioned by the local church.
4. The missionaries are to be evaluated. Those chosen must have the personality traits and ability to carry out the missionary task.

The following suggestions will be helpful to local churches in implementing the above principles.

Recognizing and Evaluating Those Who Are Called

The Spirit of God communicated to the church at Antioch that Paul and Barnabas had been "called" to a certain work (Acts 13:3). The Greek *proskeklēmai* (from *proskaleō*) means "to call to a special task or office" (see also 16:10).[12] Usually, the prospective missionaries will themselves feel the spirit urging them to go to the mission field. Individuals who feel such a call should communicate this to church leaders, allowing them to pray and to direct the candidates to opportunities for service, education, and training.

Because Paul and Barnabas were active in the teaching ministry of the local church in Antioch, both the congregation and the leadership had had the opportunity to see them exhibit spiritual maturity and effective service (Acts 11:25–26). Prospective missionaries today, then, should be involved in ministry in their local assemblies, allowing leadership and the congregation to evaluate their spiritual maturity (1 Tim. 3:1-7; 2 Tim. 2:24-25a), Scripture knowledge, and wisdom in applying that knowledge. If candidates exhibit the requisite qualities in their lives and in their service to their local bodies, it is likely they will do the same on the field. Telford writes,

> I believe one of the reasons we see a high rate of failure among missionaries is because people have made decisions to go into missions without the counsel and blessing of church leaders. It is a dangerous thing to make major ministry decisions apart from the body of Christ. My pastor often says, "Don't let people lay hands on themselves." An individual must certainly feel called of God and have a willing heart. But when God calls people, he usually calls loud enough that their church and friends who know them can hear it too. . . . the church community must help confirm that person's call and his or her readiness for service.[13]

Cook provides a list of questions for leaders to consider as they evaluate a candidate:

1. Does the candidate have real strength of character, or does he/she usually go with the crowd and let others make the decisions?

2. Is the candidate self-centered, or does he/she take a real interest in the affairs of others?
3. Is the candidate easily discouraged by difficulties? Does he/she usually finish what he/she begins?
4. Does the candidate work well when not under supervision? Can he/she be depended upon to fulfill obligations?
5. Is the candidate usually tactful and reasonable, even under moderate stress? Or does he/she easily lose his/her head?
6. Does the candidate have common sense?
7. Does the candidate show initiative and willingness to assume leadership responsibility?
8. Is it difficult for the candidate to cooperate with others or to obey those in authority?
9. Does the candidate readily adapt him/herself to new situations?
10. Does the candidate endure difficulties *without complaint?*
11. Does the candidate exhibit emotional stability? Is he/she given to despondency? Does he/she have a sense of humor?
12. Can the candidate stand criticism and even ridicule?
13. Is the candidate willing to serve in any capacity if needed, no matter how humble?
14. Does the candidate have a teachable spirit?[14]

During the evaluation process, it is an excellent idea for candidates to be sent on several short-term missions trips (see chap. 16) to witness the ups and downs and the ins and outs of missionary life. Firsthand experience will help them determine if missions work is really God's leading for their lives.

Training for the Missionary

As noted earlier, those who were sent out from the church at Antioch were not among the *least* qualified from the church but two of the *most* qualified. One can infer from their activities and their position in the Antioch church that both Paul and Barnabas were elders there before they were sent as missionaries (Acts 11:26; 13:1). The biblical evidence indicates that those whom Paul and others sent out for missionary activities were also qualified elder "material." Thus, it is highly probable that those sent out for missions work met the qualifications for elders set forth in 1 Timothy 3:1–7: "able to teach" (v. 2) and "holding fast the faithful word which is in accordance with the teaching, that he may be able both to exhort in sound doctrine and to refute those who contradict" (Titus 1:9). Elders, then, were to know sound doctrine and have the ability to point out theological errors. No less can be expected of missionaries today (see chap. 9).

Because the main task of missionaries is to baptize, teach, and establish leadership while planting new churches, it is only sensible to send those who are both knowledgeable in the Word and fully capable of teaching it. As Hesselgrave states, "Actually, the central missionary undertaking is to win men to Christ and establish churches in new areas."[15] With this goal in mind, the local church should ensure that those whom they send have the theological training needed to meet the demands that will be placed upon them.

Because in the early church God used the *most* qualified people to perform missions work, the missionary today should have the evangelism and disciple-ship skills needed to proclaim the gospel and establish others in the faith. Since "church planting" is the main task of frontline missionaries, they must have a good understanding of biblical missions strategy. An excellent book on this topic is David Hesselgrave's *Planting Churches Cross-Culturally: A Guide to Home and Foreign Missions.*[16]

The training required to develop candidates' spiritual gifts and prepare them for the task ahead should come from two sources. The first is the local church. The local church is "the pillar and support of the truth" (1 Tim. 3:15). Hesselgrave says,

> How then might we proceed with this process of missionary educa-tion? It seems that the very best way is to start with the local church itself—to see what God says about it in His Word and to conform the local church as much as possible to that model. The local church, then, becomes a microcosm of what needs to be duplicated and re-duplicated around the world. Evangelism is not something different "out there." Mission isn't something totally incomprehensible which is "somewhere else in the world." Essentially, both are what every local church should be doing in the here and now.[17]

Thus, the missionaries' education both in evangelism and in the nature of the local church should take place in their own churches. Good local churches produce the best missionaries because candidates have been taught, have seen, and have lived out the New Testament pattern for local churches there.

Second, the candidate should receive a sound theological education at a Bible institute or, even better, at a seminary (see chap. 9 for more on this).

In modern missions, places exist, of course, for theologically untrained helpers. Today, anyone who has a heart for missions—from a mechanic to a computer programmer—may benefit the frontline missionary as a support worker. We are concentrating, however, on the frontline missionary whose main task is to reach unreached peoples and plant churches, just as Paul did.

Commissioning and Sending the Missionary

Commissioning

In Acts 13:3, Luke writes, "Then, when they had fasted and prayed and *laid their hands on them,* they sent them away" (italics added). The ceremony in which the local church publicly recognizes and "lays hands" on their missionaries before sending them to the chosen mission field has come to be known as the "commissioning" service. Steven McAvoy, writing about the Old Testament rite of laying on of hands, comments about what the commissioning of a missionary represents:

> A . . . ceremonial use of the laying on of hands was in the ordination or consecration of someone to office. Beginning with the laying of hands on the animal sacrifice for the ordination of the Aaronic priesthood (29:10, 15, 19; Lev. 8:14, 18, 22), and the laying on of hands on the heads of the Levites to consecrate them (Num. 8:10, 12, 22), the laying on of hands set apart persons for spiritual office. Moses officially commissioned Joshua to be leader of Israel, transferring his role and authority to Joshua by laying his hand upon him (Num. 27:18; Deut. 34:9). . . . Moses . . . invested Joshua with his office and authority. Here the basic ideas seem to be ordination, separation, and perhaps transfer.[18]

The laying on of hands—for ordination and the transferring of authority— were carried over into the New Testament church. Thus, when the leadership of the church at Antioch laid their hands on Paul and Barnabas, they communicated the following messages:

1. We recognize that you have been called of God for this purpose (i.e., missionary service).
2. We separate you from among this congregation to proclaim the gospel to the people God has called you to serve.

3.   We invest in you the authority of this local church to baptize, teach, and establish new congregations in keeping with the doctrine and practice of the church of Jesus Christ.

Peters comments,

By the laying on of hands, the church and the individual missionary become bound in a bond of common purpose and mutual responsibility. It is thus not only a privilege and service; it is also the exercise of an authority and the acceptance of a tremendous responsibility. The identification of the church with the sent-forth representative is inclusive doctrinally, spiritually, physically and materially. It is the constituting of a rightful representative who will be able and who is responsible to function as a representative of the church. The church, therefore, by the laying on of hands, declares herself ready to stand by and make such representation possible. . . . Laying on of hands is not a favor we extend, but a divine authority we exercise and a responsibility we assume. A church should think soberly before it performs the act.[19]

It is hoped that understanding what "commissioning" communicates will prevent churches from commissioning and sending to the field—or commending to a mission agency—missionaries who do not measure up to New Testament standards.

Sending

Acts 13:3 states that, after they had prayed and laid hands on their missionaries, the leaders at Antioch sent them out. The Greek term translated "sent" is *apoluō*, which means "to release, to let go, or to send off," carrying the idea of a release from previous responsibility or obligation.[20] *Apoluō* is used in the New Testament for the release or pardon of prisoners (Matt. 27:15; Mark 15:6; Acts 3:13) and of divorce (Matt. 1:19; Mark 10:2, 4, 11; Luke 16:18). Acts 13, then, conveys the sense that the missionaries were released from their responsibilities as teachers in the church and were sent away to fulfill the work God had called them to.

In light of what has been discussed thus far, it is reasonable to suggest that, in the present day, churches should assist their missionaries with obtaining visas, scheduling travel plans, and securing any documents needed to enter the host country—unless, of course, the mission agency takes care of these details.

Once the missionary is on the field, the responsibility of the local church does not end. Ways in which the church creates enthusiasm for missions and the missionary have already been discussed, but local churches also need to minister to their missionaries personally.

CARE ON THE FIELD AND ON FURLOUGH

To many missionaries, the adage "out of sight, out of mind" is all too true. Churches that do well in recognizing, training, equipping, and sending out their missionaries often fail at field and furlough care. Below are suggestions for the proper care of missionaries while they are on the field and home on furlough.

Field Care

1. Keep abreast of the ministry in which the missionary is involved.

The how-to of keeping abreast has already been discussed. Suffice it to say that, from the missionary's perspective, it is discouraging to return home and be introduced to the congregation as their missionary from Romania when the missionary has been serving in Bulgaria. Church leaders should be in touch enough with the work that they can give the missionary a call and share in the missionary's spiritual victories as well as offer encouragement when the work is going slowly and things are tough.

2. Write letters and send care packages.

Missionaries who are sent off with a bang often receive cards and letters for a month or two, and then the correspondence trickles to nothing. It is not prudent to depend upon well-meaning family and congregational members to be faithful in writing. Rather, it would be well to designate specific members of the congregation, or perhaps specific groups—the men's group, the women's missionary auxiliary, the missions committee—to take on the task of writing, each pledging to take part of a calendar year.

Letter writing can also be a project from which children and teenage Sunday school classes can benefit. God could use this as an avenue for challenging children and young adults to support and participate in the Great Commission around the globe.

Furlough Care

1. Make arrangements for a missionary's furlough.

Missionaries returning from the field may need housing. Inviting a missionary to stay in your home during the furlough benefits both the missionary and the host. The host receives encouragement and challenge from the missionary, and the opportunity can be life-transforming for children. If the furlough is to last for an extended period of time, someone in the congregation might have a rental house or a place where the missionary can live free or at a reduced rate. The spiritual dividends from such generosity will far outweigh any loss in revenue.

A vehicle is another expense for the missionary on furlough. On one furlough, a couple allowed my wife and me to use their extra car for several weeks. Renting a car for that same period would have been a significant expense. It was a blessing to us and would be to any missionary.

Help in replacing clothing, getting dental work done, purchasing new eyeglasses or contacts, and getting a general health checkup are other ways that generous people who believe in and support the ministry can care for the missionary.

2. Meet with missionaries when they return from the field.

The leadership of sending churches should make a point of meeting with missionaries and talking to them about the work. Missionaries should be allowed to discuss their ministries and goals. This allows the leaders to get a firsthand understanding of the ministry, and it communicates to missionaries that the sending churches are genuinely interested and that they see mission work as an important part of their overall ministry. A meeting will also allow leadership to detect any personal problems that their missionaries might have and that may need to be addressed in further counseling.

3. Help missionaries continue their education.

Missionaries are often feeding others spiritually but may not have the opportunity to be spiritually fed themselves. This pattern of constant giving with little receiving is a leading cause of missionary "burnout." While the church must certainly ask the missionary to address many groups, including perhaps other supporting churches, the sending church must also realize that missionaries need to relax and receive teaching and encouragement from others. Instead of asking missionaries to teach a Sunday school class or fill in for the pastor while he is away on vacation, just allow them to sit and learn for a while.

Another good idea is inviting missionaries to further their education while they are at home. Pay for them to attend a few classes at a local Bible institute, seminary, or community college. Or maybe they could attend seminars in areas of interest to them.

4. Give missionaries a vacation.

Some missionaries have a personal conviction that it is not right for them to take a vacation while they are serving on the field. One of the ways to minister to missionaries is to provide some kind of vacation when they return home for furlough. The vacation doesn't have to be expensive. A member in your congregation might loan a cabin or a house on an area lake. Providing money for transportation and groceries might be the only expenses involved. Be creative. Your missionary will be extremely grateful.

REENTRY

Reverse Culture Shock

Reentry is the process of readjusting to life in the home culture after missionaries have spent time in a foreign culture. Jordan writes,

> Surprising as it may seem, some of the difficulty experienced by re-turning missionaries during re-entry is a result of their *success* on the mission field. Unfortunately, that success must be reversed when they return home. And what is their success? Cross-cultural adaptation. They have adapted so well to the culture in which they have been serving that they must undergo a reverse cultural adaptation back to their home culture.[21]

As with any culture shock, missionaries may feel frustrated and experience swings in emotion. Missionaries will have scrutinized the ways of their host cultures. Then they will have accepted many of the local customs and mores, becoming integrated into a new manner of life. The same process must occur in reverse when the missionary returns home.

Also, while missionaries were away, advances in technology may have affected everything from going to the grocery store to paying bills. People who have never lived abroad cannot imagine the frustration a returning missionary feels.

Concerning the signs of reverse culture shock, Jordan writes,

> One is *feeling "out of place,"* as though you are a spectator watching from afar. . . . Another sign is *feeling lonely.* You feel isolated from your closest friends and family members. . . . [In addition] you may also find yourself *reacting in odd ways;* weeping at a children's television program or being completely overwhelmed by the number of television movies from which to choose on a typical Saturday night. . . . However, one of the biggest aspects of reverse culture shock is the *reaction to western materialism.* (italics added)[22]

Often, returning missionaries react to materialism by becoming critical and cynical, an attitude that further alienates them from friends, family, and fellow church members.

How Can the Church Help?

The leadership of local churches should be aware of the effects of reentry on their missionaries. Steps can be taken to help them deal with those effects and slowly reorient to their own culture. The following are some suggestions for helping the missionary readjust:

1. Send missionaries books on cultural readjustment before their return from the field.[23] It would be a good idea for the elders or missions committee of the church to read these books as well.
2. The pastor and elders and/or missions committee should meet as a group, or one-on-one if possible, with missionaries and just listen. The time should also be used for asking informed questions about their experiences and future plans.
3. Give missionaries opportunities in informal settings to discuss both their experiences on the field and their struggles in transition.
4. Friends and families should regularly call their missionaries, inviting them over to their homes to listen and to encourage them through the transition.
5. Missionaries need gracious and loving people to help them at this time. A person's speech, behavior, and demeanor will let missionaries know that person is willing to help. Pray for missionaries regularly. Like most things that God allows, readjustment is another sanctifying activity He uses in our lives.

BRINGING GOD GLORY

The mission of the church is threefold: (1) the exaltation of God (John 4:23-24; Phil. 3:3); (2) the education, edification, and equipping of the saints in and through the Word of God (Eph. 4:11-16; 1 Thess. 5:11); (3) the evangelization of the lost (Matt. 28:19-20; Acts 1:8; 2 Cor. 5:20; 1 Tim. 3:15).[24] This being the case, every local church should feel a responsibility to take part in reaching the ends of the earth for Christ.

The Bible has much to say about the responsibility of local churches in missions. In light of this responsibility, practical ways exist to enhance and support the work of missionaries on the field. Active support and encouragement for missionaries also promote general enthusiasm for, awareness of, and participation in missions as a whole.

The church that implements the suggestions in this chapter will find a vision to reach the world for Christ—a vision supported by informed and enthusiastic members, realized by training and challenging the next generation of missionaries, and maintained by supporting and caring for those missionaries on and off the field. That church will not only be an exciting place to attend but it will bring glory to God. And that is the best result of all!

CHAPTER 14

THE ROLE OF THE MISSION AGENCY

ALBERT T. PLATT

FOR MANY YEARS AND TO most of Christendom (with the possible exception of Generation X believers) the terms *missions* and *mission boards* have been virtually synonymous. Either term would evoke images of Africa, China, someplace "south of the border," or, more recently, Eastern Europe. The terms might also conjure up noble spiritual warriors, wearing pith-helmets, and paddling canoes along equatorial waterways. Or perhaps "color slides"—some overly graphic, some underexposed, some very enlightening—ending, of course, with the sunset. More recently, video cameras have added the element of motion, some of which was intentional.

For older believers, the terms would be associated with historic mission societies—the China Inland Mission (now Overseas Missionary Fellowship) or the Sudan Interior Mission. Many people would think of missionary martyrs—John and Betty Stam in China, Jim Elliot, Roger Youderian, Nate Saint, and Ed McCulley on the river Curaray in Ecuador, and Chet Bitterman in Colombia.

The informed reader, however, understands that *missions* and *mission agencies*, though related, are not really one and the same. The former term represents the cross-cultural, evangelistic outreach ministry, which is the responsibility of the body of Christ. The latter term refers to a group of special entities committed to implementing said cross-cultural, evangelistic outreach. Warren Webster refers to them as an organizational structure . . .

> . . . composed of dedicated Christians who have banded together in
> a commitment to the Lord and to one another, to make special efforts
> to cross-cultural frontiers, in order to evangelize and disciple those

people who have not been reached with the gospel through the normal movements of history and commerce.[1]

THE LEGITIMACY OF MISSION AGENCIES

Before we address the role of mission agencies, we first need to examine their biblical and historical legitimacy. Some people suggest that mission agencies came into being only because local churches have failed to evangelize cross-culturally. Even if true, that alone would not automatically disenfranchise agencies. A biblical pattern for mission agencies, in fact, exists that might not have received sufficient attention. The second part of this chapter validates the legitimacy of mission agencies by examining the role that agencies play.

Legitimacy in the Light of the New Testament

Although no chapter and verse in Scripture mandates a specific, organizational structure for mission agencies, that absence is not sufficient reason to invalidate them. Consider the existence of the church itself. Its nature (including the purpose, function, and destiny) is certainly a subject of New Testament revelation, yet a number of modern church elements—both organizational and functional—are *not* covered in the New Testament, yet all are considered legitimate, important, and even indispensable. Perhaps the most significant example of such an element is Sunday school, although one could add specialized young people's ministries, the use of media, baptisteries, sound amplification, and so forth.[2]

In establishing a pattern for "missions," few people would quarrel with the pivotal nature of Acts 13. But that portion of Scripture and what follows in Paul's ministry constitute a *de facto* mission structure, that is, an embryonic agency. Bible scholars have always noted that the Holy Spirit—not the church—initiated (*set apart* is an aorist imperative) the missions movement (v. 2). The Spirit, too, mandated the method by which the ministry would be implemented. Barnabas and Saul—numbers one and five in the list of noted prophets and teachers (v. 1)—were set apart. Although in all probability, the list proceeded in order from the eldest statesman to the newest, still, not even number five was a neophyte; Paul, already well schooled in the Old Testament, was at least fourteen years in the faith and the ministry. Thus, the Spirit chose spiritually mature, theologically knowledgeable "missionaries" to establish an independent ministry movement.

Also, these men, although very much a part of what God was doing at Antioch, were *not* the product of the church at Antioch; they came there as teachers. In essence, then, the Antioch church itself was the beneficiary of ministry. Furthermore, the Antioch church did not decide to send two of their teachers elsewhere to minister, although the church is certainly to be commended for their response to the Spirit's message. Nothing indicates, however, that the Antiochan assembly accepted any financial responsibility for the new "missionaries." In fact, the Holy Spirit directed Luke to choose the interesting verb *apoluō*, "to cut loose," in describing the new relationship between the church and these two teachers. At the very least, the men were freed from the responsibility *for* the local ministry in Antioch. Obviously, all ties were not severed. Consider the later periodic fellowship the missionaries enjoyed with that church (Acts 14:26; 15:35; 18:22).

Still, in the light of the absence of any evidence that the church supported the two teachers financially, the verb *apoluō* has more in view.[3] Paul and Barnabas had come from elsewhere, had contributed to the edification and the grounding of the church in faith, and now were to move on, as it were, an independent entity. From this time forward in Paul's missionary ministry, no recorded directives issue from the church in Antioch to the missionary in the field. Periodically, Paul shared with them what God was doing through his ministry, but such could hardly be construed as consultation.

Without question, by total compliance with the Spirit's directive, Antioch became the nest of missions, the launch site of a world movement. As such, the Antiochan church and its response became the example, the role model, the epitome of what should be a local church's response to God's revealed will—they obeyed. The two prophets/teachers were not only "set apart" but also "let go," that is, released to follow the spirit's direction in their ministry.

That entity constituted the embryonic structure of an organization. As noted earlier, the sending of the first missionaries is attributed to the Holy Spirit; He gave the directive. Furthermore, that same Spirit guided Luke in selecting the word he employed for that sending—*ekpempō* (in this case, an aorist passive participle, masculine, nominative, plural), a somewhat more ordinary word than *apostelō*.

> *Pempo* is a more general term than *apostello; apostello* usually "suggests official or authoritative sending" (Thayer). A comparison of the usages mentioned above shows how nearly (in some cases practically quite) interchangeably they are used, and yet on close consideration the distinction just mentioned is discernible . . . ; the two are not used simply for the sake of variety of expression.[4]

The drama of the situation, complete with a direct message from the Holy Spirit, is without question. The word used for the sending, however, is very ordinary. It could be argued that the Spirit wanted to emphasize the ordinary—that is, that training, selecting, and sending missionaries was to be and should continue to be routine.

The activities that ensue in and proceed from the book of the Acts constitute the developing ministry of the apostle Paul in the work to which the Spirit called him and, along with those who worked under his direction, provide "a 'model' or 'prototype' for the modern missionary movement."[5] Paul led a missionary band that totaled as many as two dozen individuals, the majority of whom had no official association with the church at Antioch. Paul, recognizing the divine imperative of his calling as an apostle and under the guidance of the Holy Spirit, acted as administrator, overseeing the activities of these coworkers in evangelism, the establishment of local churches, and the edification of believers. Whereas Paul was admirably careful about the vertical dimension of his source of guidance, his leadership methodology apparently did not include horizontal consultation with Antioch in assigning his band of workers to countries, cities, assemblies, and ministries.[6]

Although in much that Paul did he was highly individualistic and autonomous, no serious early church-mission (i.e., Antioch) tension in regard to outreach ministry seems to have existed. Paul obviously recognized the importance of local churches and was committed to their establishment wherever he ministered. In addition, he was plainly concerned about relating well with Antioch.

Thus, Scripture provides evidence for establishing not only missions and missionaries, but under the direction of the Spirit, who selected and guided His administrators, Scripture provides the rudimentary framework of a mission organization.

Peters's offers an apt summary:

> The Bible presents broad organizational patterns. These broad principles certainly provide authority for the organization of missionary societies and justify their continued function.[7]

History and the Legitimacy of Agencies

Simply because something works doesn't mean that it is good, right, or worthy of emulation. It must be admitted, however, that mission agencies have a generally impressive track record. That record is intact despite criticism:

sometimes agencies have been considered unnecessary, have been belittled for their personnel who "couldn't-make-it-at-home," have been accused of having political agendas, judged for grandstanding, maligned as having to "beg" for funds, accused of usurping authority rightly belonging to the local church, censured for a competitive spirit . . .

Despite the rare apple of questionable freshness, however, the agency bushel has yielded "select fruit." In a worldwide kaleidoscope of culture, witness the number of believers; the number of local churches, Bible schools, Bible colleges, seminaries, and hospitals; the number of local dialects into which the Bible has been translated; the quantity of Christian literature; radio and television stations that have produced a long list of gospel-preaching and Bible-teaching programs—all have been the result of mission agency involvement. In great part, all this fruit is due to the ministry of mission agencies since the time of William Carey, results that would have been virtually impossible without the agency structure. Since the beginning of the eighteenth century the thrust of Spirit-generated, God-honoring missions emphasis has had tremendous impact. Wagner writes,

> Once missionary societies gained strength, wonderful things began to happen. More men and women have been led to Christ and more Christian churches have been planted in the world in the 190 years since William Carey than in the eighteen hundred previous years all put together.[8]

Although "the home and the church are the only two God-ordained institutions for carrying out His work," Charles Ryrie adds, "this is not to say that God does not use other organizations in His program, but it is to emphasize that the church is of primary importance in His purpose. When we abandon the church we abandon God's organization (1 Tim. 3:15)."[9] Neither the apostle Paul nor his group of missionaries abandoned the church. Instead, they provided a New Testament basis for mission agencies, which history has vindicated by revealing God's blessing upon them. And mission agencies still have a role to play today.

THE CONTRIBUTION OF THE MISSIONARY AGENCY

Missionary agencies serve God and the body of Christ in virtually all parts of the world. Through their experience, expertise, and organizational structure, agencies provide the church with a biblically based and efficient way to fulfill cross-cultural outreach ministries. No one claims that agencies are perfect, as indeed local churches are not. The failings of human beings undoubtedly have plagued every agency and should serve as a disclaimer when considering the functions of mission agencies. The section that follows considers some of those functions.

A variety of agency organizations and attitudes exist. Some are progressive, others are paternalistic. Some are autocratic, others democratic. In all of them, as is true of all organizations in general, both written and unwritten policies exist.

Biblical Base

First and paramount, most mission agencies provide what most local churches require—a biblical framework for cross-cultural ministry. *If the agency does not adhere to biblical principles of operation, then churches should avoid that agency.* The Bible and proper theology should be the driving force—organizational and operational—of every agency. When considering "mission," the agency and the church must recognize the priority of the New Testament commission.[10] Much "missionary" energy has been dissipated in endeavors that, although hardly ignoble in either intent or function, do not qualify biblically as outreach or as fulfilling the Great Commission cross-culturally.

Organization

The organization of a mission agency is designed to provide help at every stage, from the expression of general interest to participation in cross-cultural ministry. Although an agency might have been the vision of one man—who was driven by holy ardor and who, perhaps, considered the agency "his" to run during his lifetime—in reality the board of directors (at times called the home council) provides overall direction and stability to the organization. The board is responsible for keeping the organization on track as a mission agency while fulfilling legal requirements that Paul's missionary band did not face. Fulfilling these responsibilities facilitates the work of both the local church and the individual missionary.

When the board's responsibility is properly undertaken, everyone concerned is assured of the agency's ongoing soundness in the faith as well as the stability of its goals, regardless of changes in personnel or the personal agenda of some charismatic new leader at any level.[11] A mission agency's consistency provides both security and confidence, assuring the church and the missionary of a continuum. Just as the fidelity of a local church to the Word of God depends on the leadership, so it is with a mission agency. A doctrinal statement is only as strong as those who hold it. Thus, only when care is exercised in the choice of board members for a mission agency can hope exist for ongoing theological soundness. (The same truth applies to membership at the missionary level.) Board leadership for any part of God's work should be entrusted only to godly leaders who are well taught in the Word and who keep themselves unsullied by the world. No one should be vested with board membership simply because of personality, professional title, training, ability, or wealth.

Shared goals also contribute to the sense of "belonging" for everyone involved with the agency. In fact, one great advantage of service with such a group is the deep, abiding relationships that one makes with colleagues of like faith and function. That sense of "belonging"—although not something into which the missionary retreats—is of particular significance in the early stages of a missionary's cross-cultural experience. While the importance of an authentic appreciation for and intimate association with the host culture can hardly be overemphasized, the early ventures into cross-cultural circumstances can, nevertheless, be lonely for the expatriate. Association with a mission agency helps missionaries remember, "The arena in which one plays is not as important as the team on which one plays."

But the reputation of the team is also important. Respect for the name and stance of the sponsoring missionary agency translates into trust for the person and work of the missionary who belongs to it as well as for governmental and ecclesiastical authorities connected to the board. Confidence is earned, of course, but association with a recognized and approved agency opens the door for that to occur.

Another benefit of continuity in ministry is the ability to "pick up the slack" when a missionary must be absent from the work. When a missionary works independently, absences can create significant difficulties, but association with a missionary agency ensures the survival of long-term ministry. The agency is equipped to initiate short-term personnel adjustments to cover certain ministry posts.

Agency structure, then, contributes significantly both to the work and the worker on the field. Nomenclature might differ from agency to agency, but field councils, committees, and field directors are the on-the-spot representatives of agency principles, policies, and plans, and are as well real-life missionaries who understand their colleagues' points of view. Thus, the function of leadership at the level of field director—whether that person is appointed or elected—assures the missionary, the board, and the local church that decisions are made by knowledgeable people who are on-the-scene, rather than made arbitrarily by some distant, uninformed body. At some point, either the field director or an interfields council meets with the agency's board of directors, thus increasing the board's knowledge of the field and improving their decision-making ability as they incorporate suggestions and recommendations into mission strategy. Multiple input in the decision-making process helps avoid major errors.

Knowledgeable and compassionate on-the-field leadership can also be especially helpful to the new missionary, making available the accumulated wisdom of many years. Field leaders are acquainted with the language, the customs, the geography, the personality of and the personalities in the national church. They are familiar, as well, with the specific area of ministry with which the new missionary will be involved and that ministry's relationship to the entire field.[17]

Furthermore, in conjunction with missionaries and their immediate supervisors (i.e., the directors of an area or an institution), field leaders help establish the game plan and the individual job description. New missionaries are then able to check their individual performance against a job description. Field directors can also determine how a missionary's performance measures up and this can, in turn, be an encouragement to that missionary.

An abundance of difficult situations, pressure, and stress can result from adjusting to the new culture and from implementing the ministry, to say nothing of tensions arising in the missionary's personal and family life. There is much that can discourage a new missionary, but the wise field director and/or supervisor will be alert to problems and can take steps to correct or alleviate them.

The missionary body is comprised of not only self-starters and overachievers but also of the "laid-back" and "they-do-well-when-they-are-told-to-do-something" types who often don't see what needs to be done unless they are told. The latter type person might excel in personal witnessing and be fearless in it but never get around to making financial reports or writing thank-you letters to those who pray for and give to the work. Even in this technological age, without the presence of field leaders, agency leadership (i.e., the board of directors or a local church in the homeland) would have great difficulty in providing the supervision and direction necessary for the average missionary, let alone for those at either end of the personality spectrum.

Field directors, too, address the occasional serious and all-too-real problems that require immediate personal confrontation with the missionary. Such a need can arise in even the most godly of families. All sin is of the same hue and displeasing to the heavenly Father, and certainly the sin of His people must be particularly grievous. The mission organization can quickly be made aware of problems, can quickly confront them, and quickly provide counsel while relating *properly* to the receiving (i.e., national) church. The emphasis is on *properly* because, in many instances, missionaries in serious offense against both the Lord and the receiving church have been spirited away to the homeland and the action taken is never made clear to the receiving church. It is true that a mission board would be reluctant to allow someone in grievous sin to remain on the field as a representative of that mission, and that having a missionary "under discipline" by a receiving church would be embarrassing. Too, the offending missionary would probably like to get as far as possible from the local scene. But church discipline—a proper New Testament concept—is usually practiced in both the nascent as well as the established national church. No category or class of believer is exempt. Not being permitted to deal with the offense of the "spirited-away" missionary does not build confidence in the new church. Thus, godly leadership in the mission agency is crucial for dealing with this sort of problem. Competent on-the-field leaders will have work to do with the missionary, the family, the on-the-field local church, and national leaders. Leadership in the homeland will also have to relate to the people who are involved there.

Legal and Financial Concerns

The missions program faces both legal and financial concerns that were not extant during the time of the apostle Paul. Despite advances in communications and travel, countries of the world still require visas. In order to guarantee the costs of repatriation, if such becomes necessary, some countries insist that a recognized group pledge financial responsibility for any of their representatives who request residence. This pledge assures the country issuing the visa that the requesting person will not become a financial liability to them. Mission agencies are familiar with those types of procedures and, particularly in countries where the agencies have worked, are a recognized entity whose "word is their bond."

Another legal and financial concern relates to a missionary agency's administrative function. In the United States, not-for-profit religious organizations can request a 501(c)(3) tax-exempt status. Mission agencies and churches can therefore offer donors a receipt for tax-deductible financial donations. Although important, the tax deduction is not the primary financial benefit derived from the mission agency. Mission agencies not only administer the financial support of their missionaries, they also provide financial services to their missionaries and to the groups and individuals who take an interest in and support missions work.

Financial support to missionaries has, however, been misunderstood and has sometimes led to disappointment for both missionaries and for those who donate to mission agencies. Agencies differ as to how missionary support (that is, salary) levels are established and how disbursement is made. In each case, however, the information about the "system" is carefully explained to interested parties (missionaries, missionary candidates, donors, and groups or individuals who are considering making a donation), is painstakingly taught in the candidate procedure, and is often reviewed during the service time of the missionary. Still, interested parties are subject to unpleasant surprises with regard to support levels and to amounts allowable for a tax deduction, primarily because insufficient attention has been paid to the explanations given either in the orientation or the handbook that most agencies provide to their missionaries.

Agencies often determine support levels for missionaries under their direction through a complicated formula but almost always as a result of knowledge gained from experience and the use of multiple resources—both informational and financial. Although it is missionary-friendly, the agency board does not base salaries on emotion but on predetermined policy in the light of such current economic conditions as the cost of living in the host country or the buying power of the foreign currency, factors that vary from country to country and even from rural to urban areas within a given country.

It is important for interested parties to understand that missionaries do not set their own salaries; interested parties must consult with the agency for the correct salary figure. Individual missionaries might request certain items from a donor, items that the missionary considers important, necessary, and even critical. Those items might not, however, be considered as part of the salary and, indeed, might not be items that merit a tax-deductible receipt.

Another area of misunderstanding and disappointment regarding support levels involves the services that mission agencies provide. Most mission agencies recognize their fiduciary responsibility and are careful in the handling of funds. It is usual for a certain percent of a missionary's salary—an amount that is not allowed as a charitable tax deduction to the missionary—be applied to general administrative costs. Those costs are, however, the lowest among not-for-profit entities. On the other hand, the funding thus acquired provides innumerable services to the missionaries and those interested in them. For example, services to mission members include purchasing, shipping, letter service, banking, receipting, bill payment, insurance, emergency services, travel arrangements, doctor appointments, and just about anything else one might imagine. Services rendered to entities in the homeland include information regarding the field, consultation regarding missions, conferences, field activities, visits to the field, receipting, emergency reports, literature, films, videos, speakers, and so on.[13]

The Other Side of the Coin

Some people perceive disadvantages in associating with mission agencies, citing the structures and strictures of organization. Some of these perceptions contribute to what are often called church-mission tensions. That phrase might better be church-mission *dynamic,* because a workable relationship is not difficult to attain. Peters writes,

> To establish and maintain the proper relationship between the local congregation and the sending agency is of utmost importance. Mutual respect, confidence, consistency and loyalty must characterize this relationship.[14]

He continues,

> As long as there is a need for missionaries and such are available and as long as the churches and/or individual men will retain the missionary vision and passion, so long will there be need for missionary sending agencies. However, the missionary, the local congregation, and the missionary society belong organically together and must function in a harmonious cooperative manner to further the work of God, whether they are bound together organizationally or not.[15]

First, it is perceived that organization leads to bureaucracy and a stifling of personal initiative, a grievous condition particularly for the current generation. Some feel that multileveled management of the pyramid organizational structure deprives the individual of participatory management, which is so popular today.[16] Some moderns find it particularly onerous that "final authority" resides in a board or council thousands of miles and several cultures away from where the actual ministry takes place. But this doesn't have to be the case. Input from voices at all levels results in good decisions and good policy. That such sources are "uneven" (i.e., consist of contributions from two extremes and various levels in between; of personnel with limited experience, and thus at times of limited significance and application; of personnel with greater preparation through experience and maturity) means that a supervisory level is required to examine and evaluate them. Obviously, not all suggestions are viable. Humanly speaking, if such "uneven" suggestions were adopted indiscriminately and incorporated into agency principles and practices, policies and plans could quickly evolve that take the mission in a totally different and contrary direction from what was originally intended.[17] On the other hand, imaginative people and their ideas are essential to the life of any organization, certainly to a mission agency. Nonetheless, wisdom hesitates to say, "Adopt all of the ideas that come up!" In fact, wisdom doesn't suggest that all ideas can even be tried, but the wise agency welcomes creativity and innovation, in as much as they contribute to commonly shared goals.

Lately, a feeling has arisen among some people that the agency, putting together the elements of on-field personnel, forces a personnel amalgam that is detrimental to the individual.[18] Although the same would be true in the secular workplace in the land of origin, perhaps the negative elements are exacerbated by the complications of life in a different culture. Granted, membership in a working group brings with it forced social activities and occasions for interpersonal conflict—situations also present in the secular workplace and hardly a reason to avoid association with a mission agency. Biblical ways for dealing with these tensions exist. Indeed, all friendships begin with a meeting of those who did not know each other before. Yet those friendships blossom in shared goals and complimentary gifts and talents, elements that a mission agency seeks to combine. As for conflict, it is neither new nor is it exclusive to missionaries. Paul and Barnabas had a conflict about John Mark in Antioch, of all places, and demonstrated one solution—they separated (Acts 15:36–41).

A sore point with prospective missionary candidates, their friends, and many churches today is associated with agencies known as "faith missions."[19] As opposed to a denominational agency—which receives funding from the denominational budget—faith missions are often independent or nondenominational, and they neither receive dependable allocations nor solicit funds but rather depend upon the Lord to provide.[20] Thus, faith missions often require their missionaries to raise all or part of their own support. Faith missions represent a large portion of the cross-cultural ministry from North America; thus, raising support is widely discussed among interested parties.

The reasons that a missionary might choose or reject becoming involved with either a faith mission or a denominational agency, and the missionary's reaction to the method by which each raises support, range from matters of personal taste to those of efficiency and practicality. [21] For many interested parties, the thought of raising support is distressing. Because of this, they may thus hesitate to work under or donate to any mission agency that requires it.

Some people see the benefits of another option. Many local churches send out a member or members to serve both long- and short-term, or a local church that has been established in another country may request that someone be sent to them to serve either long- or short-term. Some argue that the local church that sends or does the requesting should be responsible for the costs involved in cross-cultural service.

Although it is true that neither the use nor the success of any given funding method proves its correctness, the faith-based missions' more than century-long record of success is hard to discredit.

SEAL OF APPROVAL

Webster summarized the issue well when he quoted both Winter and Peters:

> In assessing the strengths and weaknesses of modern mission agencies, Dr. Ralph Winter of the U.S. Center for World Missions concludes that when it comes to cross-cultural communication of the gospel, "no one has invented a better mechanism for penetrating new social units than the traditional mission society, whether it be Western, African or Asian, whether it be denominational or interdenominational."
>
> Dr. George Peters states a similar conclusion in his book, *A Biblical Theology of Missions:* "There is no question in my mind that our times and culture demand mission organization and mission societies . . . God has set His seal of approval upon mission societies thus far."[22]

CHAPTER 15

THE MISSIONARY'S RESPONSIBILITY TO THE SENDING CHURCH AND MISSION AGENCY

RUSSELL L. PENNEY

THE CHRISTIAN LIFE IS LIVED in submission to a higher authority. As Christians, we live in submission to Christ (1 Cor. 11:3), but we are also called to submit to government authorities (Rom. 13:1; 1 Peter 2:13-15) and our bosses at work (Eph. 6:5; 1 Peter 2:18). Paul tells us, "and be subject to one another in the fear of Christ" (Ephesians 5:21 NASB). Peter and the writer of Hebrews emphasized that, as members of a local body, we are to submit to the spiritual oversight of the elders and the pastor-teacher of the church (1 Peter 5:1-5; Heb. 13:17).

Submission, too, means that missionaries have a responsibility to the local churches that send them as well as to the mission agency that facilitates that sending.

THE BIBLICAL PATTERN OF RESPONSIBILITY

Communication with the Sending Church

Scripture indicates that the first Christian missionaries maintained communication with their sending church, supporters, and mission agency. The Antiochan church took a leading role in sending out missionaries, assuming in essence the role of "sending agent." Paul and Barnabas were the first missionaries set apart by the Holy Spirit and commissioned by the church (13:2-3). Nothing indicates that, during the term of the first missionary journey, the missionaries communicated with their home church. This is not surprising because communication was slow, and the missions trip was short-term. It should not be deduced, however, that the missionaries did not sense a responsibility to communicate with their church. Consider Acts 14:25–28:

> And when they had spoken the word in Perga, they went down to Attalia; and from there they sailed to Antioch, from which they had been commended to the grace of God for the work that they had accomplished. And when they had arrived and gathered the church together, they began to report all things that God had done with them and how He had opened a door of faith to the Gentiles. And they spent a long time with the disciples.

Several implications can be drawn from this passage:

1. The missionaries felt a responsibility to their sending church.
2. They reported the "fruit" of their ministry.
3. They saw God's sovereignty in what they had done.
4. The church was committed to the missionaries.
5. The description of the work was not superficial but described in depth ("all the things that God had done"). Verse 28 says that they spent "a long time" with the disciples.

One gets the impression that the church rejoiced in the missionaries' activities and enjoyed hearing what God was doing among the pagan peoples to whom the missionaries had gone to preach. Thus, early on we see that Paul and his missionary companions felt a responsibility to communicate about their work with their church—the "sending agent."

On his second missionary journey, Paul took Silas (15:40) with him and later chose Timothy to accompany him, too (16:1–3). The trio had great success in their ministry of church-planting through proclamation, conversion, and equipping (making disciples). In Acts 18:22–23, Paul returned to Antioch after his journey, and the Scriptures state, "And when he had landed at Caesarea, he went up and greeted the church, and went down to Antioch. And having spent some time there . . ."

Although the reference is brief, that Paul spent some time there is clear. That he again spent time informing his "sending church" of what God had done through his missionary ministry and expressing his gratitude for their many prayers would be consistent with what occurred in Acts 14:25–28 above. One could wish that Luke had expanded his description of this visit.

Communication with the Mission Agency

Today, the mission agency performs a mediating role in sending out thousands of missionaries. And, in studying Paul's day, we can discern the tentative outline of such a structure. C. Gordon Olsen offers the following insights:

> Mission boards and missions are almost synonymous in the minds of most Christians. Mission boards were formed right at the beginning of the modern missionary movement and are the dominant force in missions today. It is only natural that most Christians would never question their existence. And yet there are a significant number of Christians who seriously question the validity of mission boards—some from a biblical point of view and others from the pragmatic. The author himself was one of them and became an independent missionary for his first term on the field. What are their objections?
>
> Some would suggest that although the organization of the local church is spelled out in the New Testament, there is no such thing as a mission board in the Bible. Believing in the sufficiency of Scripture, they feel that if it is not there, we should not have it. They view the apostle Paul as an independent missionary and feel that mission boards are unscriptural. Others would point to the effectiveness of some independent missionaries and the ineffectiveness of some boards. They would also highlight the internal problems that some boards have struggled with. They might even refer to a board as "something under which bugs hide."[1]

Olsen continues, noting the biblical basis for mission boards:

> Was the apostle Paul really an independent missionary? It is true that the New Testament does not give us the organizational framework of Paul's ministry. However, it is very specific about who Paul's coworkers were. If asked to hazard a guess, most Christians might even venture to say that Paul had as many as a half-dozen coworkers. They would be astonished to find out that the author has identified at least two dozen of Paul's fellow missionaries as mentioned in the New Testament! This seems like the beginnings of a mission board, doesn't it? The apostle Paul quickly took the leadership of this "field-directed mission board."

We know that Barnabas and John Mark were his colleagues on the first journey, and most are aware that Silas, Timothy, and Luke joined Paul on the second journey. By the third journey we find reference to Erastus, Sopater, Aristarchus, Secundus, Gaius of Derbe, Gaius of Macedonia, Tychicus, and Trophimus accompanying Paul (Acts 19:22, 29; 20:4). Epaphras of Colossae, Epaphroditus of Philippi, Demas, Titus, Sosthenes, and Artemas are also mentioned in various places as associated with Paul in his missionary endeavors (2 Cor. 1:1; Phil. 2:25; Col. 4:12; Philem. 23; 2 Tim. 4:10–12, 20; Titus 1:5; 3:12). The exact status of Crescens, Priscilla, Aquila, Apollos, Onesimus and others might be questioned, but probably some of them should be considered as missionaries, not local church pastors or workers. This gives us a team of about two dozen workers. Paul directed his coworkers' comings and goings. He frequently left them to build up a church and then move on. Arthur Glasser points out: "This mobile team was very much on its own. It was economically self-sufficient, although not unwilling to receive funds from local congregations. It recruited, trained and on occasion disciplined its members" [Arthur F. Glasser, "The Apostle Paul and the Missionary Task," in *Perspectives*, eds. Winter and Hawthorne, 107.] Here we clearly have the function of a field-directed mission board without the organizational details.[2]

Olson's arguments are convincing. It is clear that the first "mission board" maintained communication, both written and verbal with its missionaries. The epistles of 1 and 2 Timothy and Titus were written from the "field director" of the mission board to his missionaries. And much of the information in the other epistles was written in response to reports that "missionaries" had relayed to Paul from the field (i.e., Phil. 2:25–30). In Philippians 4:15, Paul recognizes those who were supporting the work financially and expresses gratitude to them.

Thus, it can be seen that, in early Christian missionary activity, lines of communication existed between missionaries, sending churches, field directors, supporters, and workers. In this modern day of easy communication, how much more we should keep our churches, sending agents, colaborers, and supporters informed.

KEEPING YOUR CHURCH, SUPPORTERS, AND MISSION AGENCY INFORMED

Those who support missionaries through prayers, finances, pastoral support, and the handling of administrative needs are invaluable to their ministry. Missionaries could not, in fact, carry out their ministry without this help. Because those who support missionaries are true colaborers, it is essential that individual missionaries keep them current and involved in the ministry, thus recognizing and acknowledging their importance.

Major Methods of Communication

The following list offers a few of the ways to send information to supporters:

1. personal letters
2. prayer/newsletters
3. electronic mail
4. audio tapes
5. telephone calls
6. faxes
7. slide presentations
8. video tapes
9. interviews through digital computer camera (netmeeting)
10. field reports

1. Personal letter

It still means a lot to a supporter when the missionary takes time to write a personal letter communicating his or her gratitude for the support received and specific praises and prayer concerns about the ministry. Every supporter should receive thanks for *every* financial gift that is made.

2. Prayer/newsletter

Because the prayer/newsletter will probably be the main mode of contact while a missionary is on the field, it is imperative that the missionary learn how to write a letter that supporters will read. If all supporters waited with eager anticipation to receive their missionary's letter, it would be nice. This often is not the case. It is important, then, to write a prayer/newsletter that supporters look forward to and will actually read.

The following is a list of suggestions:

1. Include the missionary's personal address and e-mail address on the field.
2. Include the address of the person or agency that handles the missionary's finances.
   - In some cases, this will be the sending church.
   - In other cases, this will be the mission agency.
   - In rare cases, it will be an individual handling the finances from the missionary's home country.

   (**Note:** It is important that the supporter knows to whom checks should be made out and if an accompanying note should designate to whom the support should be credited.)
3. Print the main body of text in not less than 10- to 12-point type.
4. Address the letter to the individual instead of to "Dear Supporter," "Dear Friend," and so on.
5. Write the letter as if you, the missionary, are writing to a friend.
6. Always translate foreign words.
7. Include prayer and praise items in a box or a section that is distinct from the main text. A box serves best in this situation.
8. Leave "white space" on the margins and between the articles.
9. Include pictures whenever possible.
10. For every picture, write a caption that ties it to the text.
11. Use Scripture when it fits, but do not overuse it.
12. Be creative! Creativity is attractive.
13. Be concise. "Snippits" of information are attractive to the reader because they keep the letter from looking overwhelming.
14. Check spelling carefully. Have someone else look it over for grammar and spelling.
15. Sign it personally for a nice touch.
16. Make the supporter feel as though he or she is a part of your ministry (because he or she is). Communicate how the supporter's personal prayers and support are essential to the fruit of the ministry.
17. Communicate personal information. Often, the supporter is concerned not only about the missionary's ministry but also about his or her family and other personal issues.

18. Express gratitude for prayers, letters, formal support, and so on.
19. Limit the letter to no more than one page (front and back).

The publishing of the prayer/newsletter can be handled in several ways. Various computer software programs exist for this. Basic word-processing software (e.g., Microsoft Word, WordPerfect, and Microsoft Works) has many features that allow polished letters to be created without anyone having to buy desktop publishing. Some software programs that are designed specifically for desktop publishing allow the production of professional-looking letters, and these programs often have templates that do much of the work (e.g., Microsoft Publisher). Whatever software is chosen, the above list of essentials should be kept in mind so that the ultimate goal of the newsletter is accomplished—*that supporters read it!*

The missionary's letter can be composed, duplicated, and sent from the field, or it can simply be composed and sent back to the home country for duplication and distribution. If cost is not a concern, a foreign stamp sometimes enhances the attractiveness of the missionary's correspondence.

3. Electronic mail message

Missionaries who have access to a telephone line can take advantage of electronic mail to keep their churches, mission agencies, and individual supporters informed. The commissioning and sending church should be informed regularly of the ministry in which their missionary is involved. Updates on ministry should be bimonthly to monthly.

Particular supporters might also have a special interest in the work. The missionary might send these supporters regularly scheduled personal messages on the progress of the work and the benefit to the national church as a result of the missionary's involvement.

4. Audiotaped message

The advantage of the audiotape is that the people who receive it can hear the missionary's voice with all of the emotions it communicates. The missionary's enthusiasm and excitement, as well as his or her disappointment and concern, come across on a taped message. A tape can be "cut" and sent back to the local church, where it can be duplicated and dispersed to friends and supporters. Sometimes a question-and-answer format most effectively communicates the points that the missionary wants to cover; sometimes narration is best.

5. Telephone call

Telephone calls carry with them many of the advantages of the taped message with the added advantage of being in "real time." Also, the missionary can respond immediately to questions and concerns. The main disadvantage is, of course, the expense.

6. Faxed message

With the faxed message, a missionary can send a perfect facsimile. If the message needs to be sent quickly and the particular format of the text and graphics is important in communicating the message, the fax machine is a valuable tool.

7. Slide presentation

With the advent of inexpensive video cameras, the slide presentation is not often used anymore, although it can still be used effectively. Slides must be interesting and clear, and script must be written and edited to fit perfectly with the order of the slides. A third element for producing an effective slide show is music. This can be added either by the sending or the receiving country.

8. Videotaped presentation

The same elements are needed for the video presentation as for the slide presentation—clear, interesting footage; an engaging, informative script; and good background music. Most video cameras have editing capabilities for putting together an excellent presentation.

9. Live interview using Internet technology

As we saw in chapter 13, new technology allows churches not only to hear their missionaries on the field in "real time" but to see them. Both the church and the missionary need only a personal computer with Internet access and Web Cam. Both computers must have a USB port (now standard on new computers). In addition, the church must have a digital projector. Currently, the quality of the video and the audio can vary depending on the quality of the telephone line. But the technology continually advances and promises to be an asset to missions in the future.

OTHER RESPONSIBILITIES

Missionaries have a responsibility to communicate the results and progress of their ongoing ministry as well as gratitude for prayers and support to their supporters, church, and mission agency. They have a responsibility, too, for making decisions on-field about the direction of the ministry.

Responsibility to Sending Church

Like most ministry principles, the principle of decision-making on the mission field is found in the New Testament. How that principle is applied and interpreted may differ. Chapter 13 of this volume examined the implication of Acts 13:1–2 on the sending of missionaries. And earlier in this chapter we discussed the responsibility of communicating with the sending church. One passage of Scripture seems to deal directly with the decision-making responsibility of missionaries to their sending church. Melvin L. Hodges writes,

> In Acts 15 we see that the sent ones are responsible in a certain sense to those who sent them. In verse 24 the church of Jerusalem writes to the younger churches, disallowing the ministry of certain ones who went out from the church at Jerusalem without being sent: "To whom we gave no such commandment." And then it proceeds to recommend approved workers [v. 25, chosen men (v. 27)]: "We have sent therefore Judas and Silas. . . ." The conclusion is inescapable that the missionaries are responsible to someone in their own homeland for what they teach and what they do.[3]

This passage indicates a general responsibility to the sending church, but the matter addressed relates to doctrine. The gospel itself was being compromised by people who had not been "sent out" (15:1, 24). Those who had been were "sent out" with the approval of the leadership of the church. When they were commissioned, hands were laid on them to show that the church leadership recognized they had been called by God, to separate them from among the congregation to follow God's leading, and to *invest in them authority* to baptize, teach, and establish new congregations in keeping with the doctrine and practice of the church of Jesus Christ (New Testament principles).

Thus, the authority invested in the sent missionary is a doctrinal responsibility as well. If, however, a missionary chooses to depart from the stated doctrinal position of the sending church, this should be communicated to the sending church, mission agency, and supporters. The missionary should, at that point, also consider leaving service as a representative of those who have sent him or her.

Again building on our understanding of the authority invested in missionaries when they are sent and looking at the New Testament pattern of Paul in Acts, we note that once the church sends the missionary, the direction of ministry seems to have been left in the hands of the missionary. The strategies for reaching people with the gospel, planting churches, and training disciples for service and ministry seems to have been left up to Paul. Considering that missionaries on the field are more intimately involved with the culture and the people and are better informed about ministry opportunities, it is likely that certain on-field decisions about ministry strategy are best made by them.

Responsibility to Mission Agency

The missionary must maintain a relationship with the mission agency similar to that with the sending church. Even more responsibility might be involved if a missionary has agreed to certain financial and business requirements (maintaining a certain support base, and so on). As far as decision-making on the field is concerned—since the greater part of responsibility should be entrusted to the missionary, this should prevent churches and mission agencies from sending individuals who are not sufficiently equipped or spiritually mature.

Responsibility to Supporters

In brief, the missionary's responsibility to those who contribute financial and prayer support is similar to that shown to the sending church and mission agency. Missionaries should maintain the doctrinal foundation on which they are sent, express gratitude to supporters for their prayers and finances, and keep these supporters informed about the ministry in which they are colaborers. One last point: Paul made it a practice to pray for his supporters. This is a practice that is well worth following.

HONORING THE RESPONSIBILITY

Career ministry Christians serve under the authority of higher powers, just like most people. Missionaries have a responsibility not only to God, who called them, but to the church that commissions them, the mission agency that supports them, and the financial supporters who sustain them through prayers and gifts. Communication with each of these authorities is a part of the missionary's submission to them. The commissioned missionary has an invested authority, and this also carries with it a doctrinal responsibility. Finally, the missionary has a responsibility not only to keep the sending church, mission agency, and financial supporters informed but to follow Paul's example in thanking supporters and praying for them. In this way, they honor Holy Writ.

CHAPTER 16

SHORT-TERM MISSIONS

JENNIFER COLLINS

PART 1: THE STRENGTHS AND WEAKNESSES OF SHORT-TERM MISSIONS

You've probably received them—by the score: those enthusiastic fund-raising letters from friends and relatives who are about to embark on a short-term missions trip. At first I'm excited about the person's desire to serve, but my excitement is tempered when I sit down to write a check for financial support, and I wonder about the design and goal of the trip. Will my friend receive proper preparation to maximize ministry effectiveness and personal growth? Will he or she come back with judgmental attitudes about missionaries and foreign nationals and their cultures or with sensitivity to cross-cultural differences and his or her own Western biases? Will the field leaders be frustrated with the team's expectations or actions? Will proper debriefing take place after my friend returns home to help him or her sort through the experience for long-term impact? My questions go on and on.

Short-Term Missions: Help or Handicap?

Short-term missions has dramatically changed the face of world missions over the past thirty years. The short-term missionary movement is one of the most powerful forces mobilizing new missionaries today. Members of Southern Baptist churches alone sent more than seventy-five thousand short-termers and eighty-one thousand volunteers in missions during 1996.[1] An explosion has occurred in the number of short-term missionaries with nearly every church, agency, Christian college, and parachurch group sending them out.

Some missions leaders, however, question the validity of short-term missions. They express concerns about the expense, the short-lived results, the self- or vacation-focus of some trips, and the possibility of unprepared teams causing more harm than good. Although a poorly prepared or poorly directed team can be worse than no team at all, short-term missions has enormous potential. It can make worldwide contributions that create long-term impact. To that end, this chapter examines the strengths and weaknesses of short-term missions, and discusses how to improve short-term programs, thereby maximizing ministry effectiveness and participants' personal growth while minimizing weaknesses and problems.

Definition

Short-term missionaries include a wide assortment of people who serve in various capacities for differing lengths of time. For the purposes of this chapter, *short-term missionaries* are defined as "persons who serve in a mission-oriented role that crosses cultural barriers for a period ranging from one week to two years." Short-term missionaries—most often part of a larger team from a church, college, or sending agency—prepare for, travel to, and work together on a specific project such as constructing a church or leading vacation Bible school. These trips generally vary in length from one to six weeks. Because this form of short-term missions most often draws criticism, this chapter concentrates on how to improve their quality and effectiveness.

Biblical Basis

A biblical basis indeed exists for short-term missions. God called Jonah on a short-term mission to Nineveh to warn the Ninevites of His impending judgment (Jonah 3:1–3). Jesus' own ministry included several short-term stays in various places, and He sent out the Twelve (Matt. 10) and the Seventy-two (Luke 10) on short-term preaching and healing missions. God used Philip in a brief encounter to help the Ethiopian eunuch find new life (Acts 8:26–40), and God sent Peter to the household of Cornelius where the apostle remained only a few days (10:19, 48). Paul, the model missionary and church planter, did not stay long-term in any one place.

Undeniably, long-term missions is strategically important, as Robert Coote notes: "In a world where hundreds of millions have yet to hear the name of Christ and additional millions have never heard the gospel presented effectively in their cultured context, there is no substitute for the career missionary."[2] Yet, short-term missions experiences can enhance long-term missions.

Additionally, short-term missions opportunities allow many people who would otherwise be uninvolved to become obedient to Christ's Great

Commission. Although Jesus did not specifically call his disciples to perform short-term missions, He did call us to meet spiritual and physical needs whenever and however we can. And He did not reserve this task for only those who were highly educated and experienced. He sent out the Twelve and the Seventy-two before they fully comprehended the purpose of His incarnation or the kingdom of God. The entire body of Christ constitutes the royal priesthood of believers, the implication of which is that all of Jesus' disciples should be actively fulfilling that which he commanded. First Corinthians 1:20–31 reminds us that God uses the foolish, the weak, the lowly, and even the despised to bring people to salvation.

> Where is the wise man? Where is the scholar? Where is the philoso-pher of this age? Has not God made foolish the wisdom of the world? For since in the wisdom of God the world through its wisdom did not know him, God was pleased through the foolishness of what was preached to save those who believe. (vv. 20–21 NIV)

Short-term experiences can be the catalyst for involving ordinary nonprofessionals in ministry. Such opportunities will open the eyes of previously uninvolved or unconcerned Western Christians to the needs of people from other cultures and distant lands. As eyes are opened, many more individuals will become obedient world Christians who are enthusiastic about supporting and helping to fulfill the Great Commission.

The Strengths of Short-Term Missions

The proven strengths of short-term missions demonstrate that they can be complementary and supplementary to long-term missions. Benefits accrue to the following four categories:

1. the overall missions endeavor
2. the sending churches and communities
3. the hosts and their ministries
4. the participants themselves

Benefits to the Overall Missions Endeavor

The greatest strength of short-term missions is its significant impact on the overall cause of world missions. Many missionaries agree, and they tell me that the benefits make the effort to organize and host short-term teams more than worth it. Contributions to the overall missions endeavor create long-lasting results.

Full-Time Decisions

Short-term experiences sometimes result in full-time missionary work. Few individuals today will, in fact, commit to career missions without some short-term experience.[3] Robertson McQuilkin views short-term missions as a wonderful way for people to get involved in missions and get close enough to God to hear His call. McQuilkin says that as many as 90 percent of career missionaries from North America today have had short-term experience. He comments, "When I discovered where the new wave of baby-boomer missionaries were coming from, I became an advocate of short-term service."[4]

In the study *Baby Boomers and the Future of World Missions,* James Engel and Jerry Jones discovered that baby boomers, the largest segment of our population, crave experience. Therefore, "prior short-term service on the field sharply increases interest in a missionary career" and is more effective for building missions vision and stimulating action than all other means, including missionary speakers, slide presentations, books, or videos. Engel and Jones's survey found that 54 percent of Christian baby boomers are open to considering career missionary service, but the number leaps to 74 percent among those who have participated in on-site mission experiences. "The essential point is that short-termers are more likely than others to become donors, volunteers, and full-time missionaries. Indeed, this may be the premier means of attracting recruits and donors among the baby boomer segment."[5]

The research of STEM Ministries confirms Engel and Jones's findings. STEM's initial study found that more than three of every four short-term participants say that they might return to the mission field, and the study concluded that short-term experiences seem to be instrumental in participants' overwhelmingly positive feelings about a possible return to the field. A recent follow-up study found that former short-term participants who were most inclined to serve long-term or were already serving long-term rated their short-term missions experiences (of fourteen possible factors) as having had the greatest degree of influence on their decision to serve. (The second most influential factor was "meeting/getting to know missionaries.") In addition, repeat short-term trips produce an even greater likelihood of returns to the field on both short- and long-term bases.[6]

I've known college students who were not originally interested in missions careers become so deeply influenced by a short-term experience that they are now serving as long-term missionaries. Nothing else ignites missions participation like *experience*. This has been true in my life. Although I had been interested in missions since I was a child, only after a short-term experience in India did missions became my passion. I began waking up in the middle of the night remembering the scenes of overwhelming need that I had witnessed in India. Memories of the sacrificial service of my new Indian friends flooded my mind. Through my experiences, the Lord called me to examine all my motives and actions in light of the world's spiritual and physical needs that were now so real to me. No other career seemed more desirable than missions mobilization. I was permanently hooked.

Educational psychologists say that people learn best by experiential learning. Edgar Dale's "Cone of Experiential Learning" underscores the importance of getting people beyond the stage of merely observing missions. Dale states that people are likely to remember only 5 to 10 percent of what they learn through verbal or written teaching styles. But when people *experience* something, they retain more than 80 percent of the content.[7]

Once such a lasting impression is made through a short-term experience, it continues to influence a person, often leading to lifelong commitment to world missions participation.

Long-Term Financial and Prayer Support

Beyond recruiting career missionaries, firsthand missions exposure is one of the best means of stimulating missions prayer and giving. Missionaries struggle to communicate the true essence of their ministries to home supporters through slide presentations, stories, or prayer letters. Missions ministries benefit when short-termers gain on-site exposure to the work and catch a vision for the ministry with all of its unique nuances of challenge and reward. STEM Ministries surveyed its participants, looking for long-term, measurable results. Their initial study found that both giving and prayer for missions doubled after people went on a short-term trip. Participants became financial supporters and prayer warriors for ministries they now understood in a way not possible through slides or prayer letters.[8] STEM's follow-up study confirmed these findings, showing that, on average, short-term participants doubled their missions giving and significantly increased time spent in missions-related prayer.[9]

Assistance and Encouragement to Missionaries

Energetic and well-prepared short-termers can stimulate and assist the work of career missionaries when the participants' efforts are coordinated with field priorities. Volunteers can add energetic momentum to an ongoing missions project. For career missionaries who might be lonely, fatigued, or discouraged, a fresh infusion of support can be a tremendous boost. As was mentioned earlier, many participants will continue to pray for, support financially, and write to missionaries after they return from their short-term missions trip. This ongoing affirmation can further ease the missionaries' loneliness and discouragement. Long-term partnerships with the team's church or sending organization may also result, thus providing even more interest, financial support, and prayer, assuring missionaries that they have not been forgotten.

Inspiration to Others

Short-termers can influence others through their example. The sacrifices participants make in order to serve often speak loudly to both friends at home and national Christians on the field. People who observe a volunteer's obedience to God and willingness to give up his or her vacation or break might be motivated to do the same. This influence results in the continuation of missions advancement as even more individuals seek on-site, sacrificial involvement.

Benefits to Sending Churches and Communities

When an individual or church group participates in short-term missions, additional people are mobilized to pray for and support the short-termers, thus paving the way for benefits to accrue throughout home churches and communities.

Increased Missions Vision

Short-term experiences provide inspiration that is incomparable in stimulating and equipping volunteers to share a missions vision with others in their home churches. This shared vision can boost the missions focus, especially for churches that have been too self-focused and lack outreach programs. The team's new enthusiasm for service is often contagious and helps cultivate more focus on others outside the church. This new focus challenges members to get more involved in the needs of the local community and overseas missions. Paul Borthwick says of the impact of short-termers on his church, "Summer missions service teams have been our greatest asset for building missions excitement and commitment at the grassroots."[10]

Spiritual Renewal

Short-termers often return with vivid memories of cross-cultural worship services that strengthened their faith as they felt a unity with Christian brothers and sisters in a foreign land. They might have been jolted out of familiar styles of worship and had their concept of God broadened by the perspective of the host culture. They might have witnessed convicting sacrificial dedication on the part of nationals and missionaries that brought confession and repentance in their own lives. They might have trusted God in new ways and seen dramatic answers to prayer as they've never before experienced. They carry home this newfound excitement about God, which can bring renewal to their entire church as they share.

Service Involvement

Participants frequently come back with an enthusiastic desire to get more involved in service at home, perhaps using newly acquired skills and confidence gained on the field. Short-term missions is a valuable discipleship tool that matures and motivates participants for service, making them more effective church members. Chris Eaton and Kim Hurst have found that short-term volunteers are more likely than other church members to become actively involved in church leadership and service, to become more involved in local community outreach, and to consider evangelism as a higher priority in their own lives.[11]

Understanding of Community

While on the field, short-termers rely daily on others for everything from transportation to meals to obtaining tools and supplies. Perhaps for the first time ever, they have learned to depend on other Christians and have experienced the fullness of the different parts of the body of Christ working together in community (1 Cor. 12:12–36). Participants often learn how the strengths of others can complement their own strengths and compensate for their weaknesses. These discoveries, according to Eaton and Hurst, create excitement. "Community living can be the catalyst by which people learn to appreciate those they never had the time or inclination to notice before. It also affords an arena in which conflict resolution and forgiveness are seen as natural parts of Christian living. A team that has experienced the joys (and perturbations) of community living will bring home a model that affects the whole congregation/ministry."[12]

Benefits to the Hosts and Their Ministries

Tangible service projects provide obvious benefits to the field, but short-termers also bring other, often overlooked benefits to host ministries. It is likely that well-prepared short-termers stimulate lasting effects in one or more of the following areas. (Much of this list comes from Eaton and Hurst's *Vacations with a Purpose*.)[13]

Relationships

Nationals in other countries are usually excited about the fellowship they share with team members. They appreciate making North American friends who will know something about them and who will pray for them and their work. *However, short-termers must be careful not to make promises they can't keep once they leave; otherwise, they can end up greatly disappointing their national friends.*

Culture

Short-termers are not the only ones who have a cross-cultural experience. The nationals usually enjoy the opportunity to learn about North American culture, and they might even find that the visitors shatter their negative stereotypes. The team's behavior might provide amusement and delight, especially if the short-termers invite the nationals to instruct them in their native language and culture. Teaching their new friends often builds the nationals' confidence in relating to different types of people and cultivate in them a desire to learn more about other cultures in God's world.

Ministry Material

The volunteer group might bring new ideas that the host congregation can contextualize and use in ministry. Ideas might include instruction in drama, mime, and puppets; music and song ideas; or VBS programming and activities. Some teams are able to leave materials such as drama scripts, puppets, musical instruments, sound equipment, books, and curricula with the host congregation. The material can be of great use to national churches that are unable to send their staff to training conferences or cannot afford ministry materials.

Affirmation

The national workers are often renewed and rejuvenated simply by the presence of short-termers who come as servants. Whether right or wrong, the hosts might perceive North Americans as rich and powerful and, if so, they are moved when the Americans come and serve in authentic humility. The willingness of North Americans to get involved demonstrates love and affirmation.

Financial

Very often short-termers are the vehicles that God uses to answer the prayers of a national congregation. The team might be able to raise support for needed construction materials that could not otherwise be purchased. After visiting on-site, participants might chip in together or raise further support for a pressing need they have observed. *Caution must be used, however, so that funds are given wisely and appropriately to avoid creating dependency.*

Benefits to Participants

The most direct benefactors of short-term missions are usually the volunteers themselves. Such should not be surprising, as Scripture teaches that the giver is more blessed than the receiver. Personal growth and blessings are usually the by-products of any type of service. This doesn't mean that the field ministry does not also benefit; it simply means that the participants' own growth will be a natural result of their ministry. They will gain more than they can possibly give. Senders should help short-termers find a balance between focusing on their own growth at the expense of the field ministry and on assuming that their contributions to the field are more significant than they really are.

It is realistic, however, to expect that participants will derive personal benefits in several ways.

Spiritual Growth

A short-term experience is almost always an exercise in faith building as participants exit their comfort zones and take risks for the cause of Christ. Short-term projects provide a chance for participants to depend upon God perhaps more than ever before as they confront the unfamiliar. The Holy Spirit seems to have unique access to people's hearts while they are encountering the world's need and being stretched to serve in new ways. God desires that disciples learn to humble themselves and serve as Christ did (Phil. 2:5), and short-term missions experiences are an excellent means for facilitating that learning.

Immediate Involvement

Short-term trips allow individuals to do something for world missions *immediately*, which is especially important for youth, college students, and adults who are considering second careers in missions. Missions speakers, films, and studies often whet the appetite of service-oriented individuals, but then inactivity while such persons get an education or work to pay off debt breeds frustration. A short-term mission, however, provides the opportunity for prospective candidates to actually get involved and use the skills they are developing. A short trip might be the only feasible way that people who have limited vacation time can gain on-site missions experience.

Inclusion of Lay Persons

Short-term missions is redefining our concept of a missionary. Missions opportunities are no longer reserved for only the few who spend years in training. Short-term trips empower ordinary lay people to contribute to missions with their time and talent.[14] Many people discover that, through regular short-term service and ongoing missions mobilization back home, they don't have to be seminary-trained professionals to make an impact.

Leadership Development

Short-term projects often provide excellent ground on which leaders can develop. As participants serve under qualified leaders and field representatives while working together with other team members, they observe and assimilate valuable skills for practical ministry leadership. These leadership skills become even more honed if some aspects of project leadership are delegated to participants. A participant or two may be delegated, for example, to coordinate oversight of a construction project or to develop the VBS curriculum. A few volunteers could organize the donation of medical or building supplies or the planning of evangelistic program materials, such as music and dramas, and then take responsibility for teaching them to the team. Other members could coordinate team devotions, plan for meal preparation and grocery shopping, or track and manage team expenses. Many of these skills are transferable and can also be applied in ministry situations at home.

Vision for Missions and World Evangelism

Short-term experience often wipes away preconceived notions and false ideas. Participants acquire a realistic view of the remaining global task of world evangelization, which instills a more global perspective and a vision for missions. Engel and Jones found that, in general, Christian baby boomers are more interested in domestic causes than in world outreach. Participation in short-term missions, however, drastically changes their scope of interest. Of the persons who had taken a short-term missions trip, 68 percent placed a high priority on world ministry. Only 44 percent of those who had not taken such a step reported the same priority.[15]

Cross-Cultural Understanding

Team members gain cross-cultural experience that allows them to appreciate different cultures and to analyze their own North American cultural values. Participants are often deeply changed as they recognize the consumerism and self-absorption of Western society. Their worldview becomes broadened as they encounter another culture and consider the complexities at work in the lives of the people. This wider perspective often results in a growing interest in other cultures and a decrease in ethnocentric attitudes.

Contentment and Joy

Participants return from short-term missions with new appreciation for the blessings in their lives. The typical North American is consumed with the concerns of our materialistic and accomplishment-oriented culture. This distorted view breeds unhappiness as individuals focus intensely on their own problems and circumstances. But Jesus taught that to lose one's life is to gain it. The best remedy for a self-centered, unhappy life is to get out and serve someone who is less fortunate. Thus, short-term projects can bring a fresh sense of contentment and joy. When a volunteer discovers that the blouse she recently purchased costs more than most nationals earn in a month, she sees her problems in a larger perspective, recognizing that they are not as overwhelming as they once seemed. *Short-termers gain a broader view of what is truly important in life and reap the joy of serving God and others.*

The Potential Weaknesses of Short-Term Missions

It can be seen, then, that the strengths of short-term missions are significant, but short-term missions has potential weaknesses that raise both serious concerns and criticism.

Unrestricted Opportunity

The ease of overseas travel and the number of agencies that are ready to accept short-termers have made it possible for almost anyone to pursue a short-term opportunity. Thus, it has now become "in vogue" to go on a short-term missions trip. People who might not be all that interested in selfless Christian service might organize or join trips because they are "experience junkies" who seek adventure. Individuals and their counterfeit motives can leave the nationals or career missionaries embittered, feeling as if they have been used to host a glorified vacation.[16]

Improper Motives

Besides seeking adventure, some leaders might take young people on a short-term missions trip solely to build group unity. Others, seeking a growth experience for themselves, might give little attention to actually helping the field ministry. Such misplaced motives have engendered criticism because of the effort and money poured into such trips. Observers look at untrained short-termers who have improper motives and see no evidence of a learner/servant mind set; instead, they see individuals who arrive with agendas and expectations and arrogantly pay no attention to the real needs of the people whom they are serving.[17]

One career missionary expressed disappointment with youth groups for whom the trip seemed to be a summer vacation and he had been designated as "camp director." This missionary has received letters from groups previously unknown to him advising that they were coming and "wanted to work with him." But in reality, the groups wanted help and expected the missionary to provide all the tools and service he could at substantial financial cost. In many cases, a thank you from the group was considered payment in full.[18]

Other critics believe that the motive of many short-termers is to ease their evangelical consciences or appease their denominations. The participants then return home, believing that their missions duty has been completed and reasoning that they have served their appropriate "missions time."[19] They are now free from guilt and further duty and can do what they *really* want to do with their lives.

Lack of Preparation

Some teams might show up on the field with proper motives but inadequate preparation. Perhaps they had no chance to meet together beforehand. Such groups might be sincere but lack the cohesiveness that develops through team preparation; they are prone to interpersonal difficulties and lack of focus. They may have little awareness of the need for cross-cultural sensitivity and thus unknowingly offend nationals and give negative impressions of

Christianity. Perhaps they may have unchallenged ethnocentric and judgmental attitudes that greatly diminish their ability to understand the national people and their needs. Some participants might flaunt their money and spend large amounts on souvenirs without any thought as to how their behavior appears to nationals who struggle under difficult economic conditions. Volunteers might present the gospel without any contextualization and cause misunderstandings or offense. Such teams, even when they are sincere, can create more harm than good.

Improper Destinations

Other critics are aware, too, that Western Christians allocate only 1.2 percent of their missions funding and their foreign missionaries to the 1.1 billion people who live in the unevangelized world.[20] They see short-term missions reinforcing this propensity toward the Christianized fields because many agencies choose to send short-termers to well-established ministries.

Inappropriate Projects

Michael J. Anthony, editor of *The Short-term Missions Boom*, notes that not all service projects are created equal. He describes one ten-day trip during which his team did nothing but work long hours digging a trench on a Caribbean island. They did not experience the culture or meet any nationals. Worse yet, he found out later that the trench was filled in and never used. His point is that each project should be evaluated carefully. Some projects are not necessary; other projects do not expose the team to the culture and people, and still other projects are better left to nationals. In the case of the trench, a national worker could have been paid a few dollars a day to dig the ditch, thereby enabling him to feed his family for months.[21]

Team or Authority Difficulties

Some short-term teams are unable to trust the local leaders' ability to plan, coordinate, and direct their project, and participants then end up blaming their hosts when something goes wrong.[22] Participants might not understand and recognize the cultural differences that affect the planning and leadership style of the hosts. On the other hand, teams might have internal strife or improper relationships that seriously detract from the ministry effort. Sometimes participants have difficulty being flexible or submitting to their own team leaders and thereby cause dissension among the team.

Overstated Importance of Assistance

Some short-termers have the notion that unless North Americans do it, the task of world evangelization will not get done. They fail to recognize the quality of much national missions work. They also fail to see that their role in many settings is to encourage, assist, and strengthen the national church. Other short-termers might believe that their work *automatically* enhances the ministry of the missionary or national church. But the delicate world of cross-cultural ministry is based mainly on relationships that require sensitivity, understanding, and especially time, of which short-term teams don't have an abundance.[23]

Quick-Fix Mentality

Robert Yackley, a career missionary in the former Soviet Union, notes that few short-termers stay long enough to make disciples. Although nurturing disciples might not be the stuff of exciting reports or promotional videos, and although it might not even be expedient or cost-effective, it is exactly what Jesus commanded be done.

> Many of the short-term missions and visits have been effective, some even catalytic. Most have been neither. After the hype, when the dust settles, there is generally little left for the indigenous church to build on. . . . We must recognize that the people of these nations are a broken and often despairing people. Their wounds are deep. Their hearts have been severely scarred.[24]

Misguided teams might have hasty agendas to make quick converts and then end up leaving them in the cold with no one to nurture them.

Inappropriate Use of Money and Resources

Critics claim, too, that money for short-term missions is a drain on the financial support given to career missionaries. Others suggest that when it comes to the finances raised to fund short-term missions, it would be better stewardship to send the money to the field instead of sending the workers. They see short-term missions as an inappropriate use of funds that pays little in return toward world evangelization. The cost of sending a team of twenty people to Africa or Asia for two weeks is likely to be more than $1,500 a piece just for airfare, not to mention visas, lodging, food, and local transportation. The total possible expense could be in the range of $40,000 to

$70,000. The costs for on-site leaders also add up as they perform hosting responsibilities and direct attention and resources away from their regular ministry.

False Impressions

Two false impressions might result from short-term missions. First, having large numbers of people going out on short-term projects makes it appear to casual observers that America's missionary task force is stronger than it really is. Second, a short-term experience might not reveal the reality of daily, routine missionary life. Most short-term experiences involve an exciting few weeks of bustling activity. Short-termers, not realizing that such a pace would be impossible to sustain over time, might conclude that field missionaries are lazy because they aren't working at the same intensity.[25] Participants don't, however, struggle day-to-day against myriad obstacles as do field workers.

Lack of Debriefing

Following a short-term experience, participants are sometimes thrust back into their home culture and responsibilities without any assistance in processing their mission encounter. This inattention leaves them bewildered and feeling alone as they reenter North American society and try to make sense of their affluent lifestyle. Gone is the loving community that surrounded them on the field. Gone are the only people who can truly understand what the experience meant. And gone is the exciting sense of purpose they felt on the field. They are left on their own to deal with the feelings of loss, to integrate the experience, and to determine what they have learned and how they should change their lifestyle. The difficulties associated with coming home might be so overwhelming that participants mentally file away the experience, thereby reducing its overall impact.[26]

PART 2: MAXIMIZING FOR LONG-TERM IMPACT

The list of potential weaknesses might lead one to conclude that short-term missions is a terrible idea and that the whole concept should be scrapped. And indeed, a few people do think that. Yet short-term missions is a powerful movement that won't be going away. And, as was mentioned earlier, it has many strengths, not the least of which is its role in recruiting career missionaries. Recent research demonstrates how badly we need such recruitment tools. A survey of Southern Baptist congregations found that foreign missions ranked as the least important among seven suggested ministry areas.[27]

Of the Christian baby boomers whom Engel and Jones surveyed, more than 75 percent believed that the need for missionaries was greater in the United States than overseas. Engel and Jones conclude that the baby boomer generation will not provide either the personnel or the money for traditional world missions in the future; so they encourage mission agencies to offer short-term assignments as a way to turn matters around.[28]

But the potential weaknesses of short-term missions can not be ignored. If programs are carefully examined and the appropriate measures taken, most of the weaknesses associated with promoting, leading, and hosting short-term projects can be mitigated. Too, some criticisms of short-term missions are justified but are based on myth or misinformation. Following are methods to improve short-term programs, and information to challenge the myths.

Before the Experience

Determine the Purpose

Participants should give careful thought to their motives and purpose, that they aren't jumping on the short-term bandwagon just because "everyone else is doing it, and we can't afford to be left in the dust." This thinking might lead to an attitude of "So here we go, ready or not!"—with devastating results. Motives and expectations should be examined, looking for a unifying purpose on which all involved can agree, especially those on the field. Many players are involved in short-term projects; all agendas should be articulated, and everyone on the team should be in agreement.[29] The primary motive should be rooted in love for God and obedience to the Great Commission. Secondary purposes should be balanced between benefits to participants, to the field, and to the overall missions endeavor.

Select Qualified Leaders

Leaders of short-term groups set the tone for the whole experience. It is preferable that leaders have previous short-term missions and travel experience. If not, they must receive training. Leaders should exhibit spiritual personality, emotional stability, physical stamina, and a good-natured, flexible character. They should understand the sensitive nature of cross-cultural ministry and have some knowledge of the host culture and language. And leaders, too, ought to have previous experience with group dynamics and conflict resolution. Being organized, detail-oriented, and having the personal maturity to handle minor and not-so-minor crises are helpful traits as well.

Leaders need to demonstrate a servant leadership style that is able to delegate tasks yet will take ultimate responsibility for outcomes.

If a team has two or more leaders, the division of roles should be clearly defined, giving one leader final responsibility in order to avoid confusion during a crisis. Having two or more leaders is advantageous in that they can share the burden of responsibility, complement each others' strengths, and still provide leadership if one becomes ill. Leaders might, however, have conflicting leadership styles and difficulty sharing responsibility. Misunderstandings can be avoided, however, if a job description is provided that clearly denotes expectations.

Choose Appropriate Ministry and Destination

Organizations such as churches and schools rarely should attempt to initiate field involvement and set up their own short-term programs unless they already know and trust a field missionary who is experienced in handling short-term groups. Such organizations often lack the time required to research the best options for their people and the necessary field relationships to do the task without causing disruption to the on-field work. These types of organizations should instead work with agencies and denominational boards that have successful track records with short-term groups, accepting the advice of qualified boards and agencies concerning opportunities and priorities.[30] Collaborating with experienced entities establishes true partnership between senders, agencies, and host missionaries, and it will make the planning process more manageable as the agency assumes some of the logistical responsibilities.

When selecting a sponsoring agency, participants should look for one that is committed to enabling the local church to accomplish its calling and one that provides training materials to equip volunteers. It is preferable, too, to look for one that is experienced in setting up logistical plans safely, economically, and effectively; that offers service opportunities that will use as many of the gifts and abilities of participants as possible; and that is candid about expectations, costs, and purpose for involvement.[31]

Even when working with an agency, however, participants might find a multitude of possible destinations from which to choose. Because many ministries require people who are committed for the long-term, short-term workers are not helpful on all fields. Participants should evaluate the appropriateness of a short-term destination while remembering that short-termers can accelerate the ministries of on-field career missionaries, even those ministries related to church planting. For example, a team of short-termers can accomplish a door-to-door event promotion for a new church plant faster than a single missionary can. Or, in some settings, volunteers might be able to draw a larger than normal crowd of curious people, giving the new church greater exposure than it would otherwise receive.

Most importantly, participants should ensure that they, as short-term workers, are desired and invited by the hosting leaders. *A short-term project should never be pushed onto unwilling or overtaxed missionaries or national workers.*

When determining the appropriateness of a project, the following questions should be considered:

1. Is this project really needed?
2. Does it reinforce the work of local leaders?
3. Does it stifle local initiative?

The time frame shouldn't interfere with any of the hosts' plans. The goal is to provide assistance and encouragement, not to add stress and become a burden. An additional consideration is the spiritual climate and sensitivity of the destination field in relation to the maturity and capabilities of the team. It is unwise to take a young, inexperienced team to a difficult field, one perhaps where Christians are perceived negatively. The innocent mistakes and cross-cultural insensitivity of young team members might cause irreparable damage.

Because a number of factors need to be considered when choosing a destination, prayer and openness to God's leading should be involved in the selection. Following are some points to consider:

- *The need of the field.* When practical and possible, teams should be sent to areas that are the neediest and most neglected mission fields. One reason, as was mentioned earlier, is that Western Christians are allocating only a small percentage of missions funding and missionaries to the least-evangelized world. Thus, choosing Christianized fields only increases this disproportionate situation. A second reason is that participants who make decisions to become career missionaries often desire to return to the place of their initial overseas experience, which, in the case of Christianized fields, would again increase the imbalance.
- *Stewardship.* Good stewardship should be exercised by carefully

evaluating the cost and time requirements of potential destinations. Attempts should be made to minimize costs and travel time and avoid exotic destinations if equally needy or neglected sites are closer and less expensive.

• *Stability of the country.* To avoid trouble spots, it is prudent to review travel advisories and consider the political and economic stability of the country. One should also consider whether medical care is accessible.

• *Accommodations.* Accommodations and meal arrangements should be evaluated to ensure that they will be safe and conducive to the ministry project. Tents and bucket showers are fine for a construction group, but they might not be adequate for a performing team that must look professional and be neatly dressed every day. Pure drinking water should be available and food carefully prepared to prevent unnecessary and possibly severe sickness. If the team will be preparing its own meals, extra time should be scheduled to allow for this extra effort, or the team might plan to bring their own cook. A suitable facility should be available for debriefing at the end of the trip. It should be confirmed that ground transportation will be safe and insured, and that reliable, experienced, and licensed drivers will be used.

• *On-site leadership.* Field leaders should be able to spend time with the group. To save potential embarrassment and prevent any offense, it is best if someone who knows the ins and outs of the culture can help orient the team. Local leaders will know the history and religious climate of the field and can help participants understand the best strategies for ministry. Local leaders, too, will know how foreign Christians are perceived and can help volunteers avoid reinforcing any negative stereotypes. On-field leaders will also have established a network among local churches and community leaders that will help disseminate information about the credibility of the project and help set up ministry opportunities. Finally, on-site leaders will know how to navigate local bureaucracy in order to reserve transportation, purchase building supplies, secure building permits, and so forth.

• *Type of project.* This is a very important matter. The gifts and abilities of potential participants should be carefully evaluated and service opportunities selected that will make good use of their skills while also benefiting the field ministry. One also needs to consider the host language and whether adequate translators or English speakers will be available to facilitate communication without exhausting the local leaders.

Michael J. Anthony has documented the pros and cons of the two most common types of projects—construction projects and relational ministry projects. The following table addresses construction projects.

Advantages of construction projects	Disadvantages of construction projects
1. Some people will volunteer only for construction-type projects because they lack confidence in their ability to develop interpersonal relationships with people of another culture.	1. They can insulate volunteers from the host culture and possibly foster a task-orientation that views relationships as a distraction from the work.
2. They are measurable and give participants a sense of accomplishment.	2. Inexperienced volunteers can possibly be injured doing something that they are not trained to do.
3. They make it possible for almost anybody to get involved while requiring less time for training.	3. They often add considerable costs (for materials) to the trip.
	4. Such projects might hinder the dignity and economy of the local community as North Americans show up, do all of the work (that local workers needing employment could have done just as well or better), and quickly leave.

The pros of relational ministry projects are as follows:

1. Ministry activities such as evangelism and teaching involve participants in the lives of others, often producing lasting bonds;
2. Such projects allow participants to fulfill the Great Commission, which requires personal involvement in the lives of others;
3. Volunteers gain a deeper understanding of the host culture and an appreciation of the adversities and joys that cross-cultural missionaries encounter.

The cons of relational ministry include the following:

1. Additional preparation and training are required for cross-cultural interpersonal ministry;
2. The potential for interpersonal conflicts and misunderstandings increases.[32]

A project that *combines* constructing a tangible expression of Christ's love with a relational ministry allows a group to experience both sets of advantages, to be stretched in more areas, and to learn to work together in multiple settings. Moreover, when volunteers participate in a combination project, the host community observes the team's tangible service, often becoming more receptive to the group's spiritual message. Finally, work projects alone, although offering advantages, seem to have less lasting impact on participants. If short-term missions is to be maximized for long-term impact, participants must be immersed in the culture to the point where they feel the challenges and needs of the people and want to do something more than merely provide a physical facility. Thus, if a host site requests a work project, perhaps a group of lay persons from the host culture could work alongside the team. The resulting informal but meaningful interaction with nationals will be highly valuable in helping participants understand the national Christians and the difficulties they face. It also makes the activity a cooperative effort rather than a project of the foreign team alone.

My trips to India have included a balance of both types of ministry, thereby benefiting everyone involved. My student groups work on construction projects alongside Indian Christians who are staff and volunteers with our host ministry. The students raise money to cover the travel and living expenses of these nationals who come from all over India to join with our group. Working, resting, talking, and singing together on the work site bonds the two groups quickly and facilitates excellent cross-cultural understanding as casual conversations occur on subjects like the ministry challenges that the Indians face, their family backgrounds, their hopes for the future, and so on. In addition, the nationals tend to develop a sense of pride and self-respect as they make a personal investment in the physical project. The money raised by student groups is also used by our hosts to purchase construction materials and hire local skilled workers such as masons and plumbers. This practice helps strengthen the local economy and provides an opportunity for contact with non-Christian Indians. In addition to construction work, at various events coordinated by our hosts, the teams have given evangelistic programs that included drama, music, puppets, and testimonies. The young people are a drawing card that brings in large numbers of curious Indians who want to see the foreigners, but the programs are a joint effort, with our hosts giving part of the presentation and being available to follow up with seekers and converts.

Clarify Goals and Expectations with Field Leaders

Samuel Melo, who has hosted hundreds of short-term missions trips, recommends making contact with field representatives as soon as the destination is chosen, while keeping in mind that communication with persons in developing countries might require patience. The country's phone service might be less reliable or its postal service slower than that at home.

Once contact is made, the group's expectations and what they hope to accomplish should be clearly stated, the field representative's hopes and expectations should be carefully considered as well.[33] The group's purpose is to serve, so they need to be willing to submit to the desires and priorities of the field leadership. The goal should be to make a notable and encouraging contribution to the host ministry *as defined by local leaders.* If a project or ministry plan isn't a priority on the field, it will bear minimal fruit.

Building a foundation of trust and open communication with field leaders at this early stage is vital. To help eliminate misunderstandings, notes should be taken, follow up phone calls made, letters of confirmation written. Any costs and needs for building materials or other supplies should be discussed in advance.[34] When working directly with national leaders rather than with Western missionaries, it should be kept in mind that cross-cultural miscommunication might be at work in the conversations, so everything needs to be clarified in order to avoid misunderstandings and false assumptions. As Samuel Melo says, "The groups that got the most out of their mission experience were the ones who came prepared and clearly communicated their expectations. It was my joy to help make their dreams come true. . . . Clear and open communication between group leader and the field representative is the essential key to the success of the group."[35]

Ensure Follow-up

If evangelism is involved in the ministry, a way needs to exists for seekers to have their questions answered after the short-term evangelistic effort; otherwise, seekers and converts will be left in the cold. Local ministries should be ready to nurture and disciple new believers and assimilate them into the body of Christ.

Advertise Honestly

When promoting a trip, the description needs to be honest and realistic. Many "ministry" trips are more accurately described as "vision" or "exposure" trips. By realistically advertising the purpose of a trip, visions of grandeur about the significance of participants' service on the field will be minimized. The purpose clearly advertised will also decrease pressure on the host ministries to create ineffective "busy work" ministries for the sake of the guests.[36] For construction projects, the likelihood of project completion during the trip should be determined, and if completion is not the goal, that fact should be made clear so team members will not be disappointed when they must depart, leaving the construction uncompleted.

Any advertising should avoid our culture's tendency to emphasize personal fulfillment over self-sacrifice. And a short-term missions trip can, indeed, be fun, exciting, and fulfilling. If, however, short-term missions is to have long-term results, it must be viewed as not only an exciting adventure but an opportunity for biblical obedience in self-sacrifice and as exposure to needs that will challenge participants to the core. One refreshing advertisement reads, "This is not a summer junket. This is not a fun time. This will drain you in every way. It will build into your heart and life lessons in sacrifice, in giving of yourself to others, and in testimony of God's faithfulness that you would find hard to get any other way."[37] Additionally, potential volunteers need to be confronted with the reality that hundreds of millions of people are lost, and they will not come to a personal faith in Christ unless others are willing to prepare and stay long term to learn the language, identify with the people, and contextualize the gospel. The promotion phase is the time to begin incorporating a view to long-term missions that should permeate the entire experience.

Also important to clarify at the outset are the requirements for team members, including such matters as attendance at training sessions and raising support, amenability to travel conditions and group accommodations, and agreement with the type of ministry so that the participants' expectations move in the appropriate directions. One organizer found that as his church began demanding more of participants and publicizing those requirements (including attendance at seventeen training sessions and a team retreat), applications for trips actually increased and the church was able to be more selective in choosing participants.[38]

Screen Participants

To eliminate many problems related to improper motives and interpersonal difficulties, it is necessary to be selective in choosing participants. Plenty of time should be allowed for selection, especially in assessing the level of maturity and skills required by the particular project. A project application will help in examining applicants' motives, spiritual and emotional maturity, gifts and abilities, and physical health. Applicants should be required, too, to furnish reference letters from church leaders, teachers, or employers, and each letter writer should be contacted. References should be asked about the applicant's character and abilities as they relate to the specific short-term project. If applicants have been on previous short-term trips, it would be prudent to contact the previous team leader to see if any problems occurred. Administering personality profiles or psychological tests in the selection process can help uncover problems that might cause difficulties, especially on longer trips. Tests are also useful for helping team members understand both their own characteristics and those of other members, preparing the way for more effective teamwork and fewer interpersonal conflicts. Interviews are also a helpful screening tool.

Applicants who are emotionally or psychologically unstable should, of course, be rejected, and any applicants with special medical needs must be carefully screened. It is also advisable to be alert for applicants who clearly have unacceptable motives—perhaps they want to escape problems at home, they are seeking an excuse to avoid further missions service, they are going only to be with someone already on the team, or they simply desire an opportunity to travel. Yet if only those applicants with predetermined, lifelong commitments to missions are accepted, many "adventure seekers" will miss the chance to have their hearts turned toward missions. So while it is necessary to exercise caution when selecting short-termers and to talk frankly with them about their motives, it is not necessary to eliminate everyone who desires travel and adventure. And, as the next section explains, the preparation process often moves participants' motives in the right direction.

Prepare Properly

Elizabeth Lightbody, Moody Bible Institute professor and longtime coordinator of short-term projects in the Philippines for SEND International, states, "Short-term ministry is a problem only when people go unprepared. When I worked with short-termers, we gave them good front-end orientation, pastoral care throughout the experience, time to come apart and reflect, on-site visits, and a debriefing before they left the country. As a result, we had fantastic returns. Sixty percent returned to missions, either in the Philippines, some other area of SEND, or with another mission."[39]

It would be ideal if short-term team members could meet together regularly before departure. Six sessions is a minimum, ten to fifteen preferable. If this arrangement is impossible, a few days of preparation and orientation should be built into the beginning of the trip before team members leave the country. Ideal for leading the training is a team leader who knows the group and will have long-term contact with members to help them process the experience afterward.

Paul Borthwick has listed several positive results of proper preparation. First, participants' interest and zeal to serve often increases in direct relation to the amount of effort demanded of them. If participants are required to strive during preparation, they tend to value the experience more. Striving often moves participants from being experience consumers to genuine servants. Second, good preparation improves the response from missionary hosts. They enjoy working with short-termers who come prepared to serve and learn rather than to be entertained. Third, nationals will appreciate the cross-cultural sensitivity of well-trained team members who make a serious effort to adapt to the culture. Finally, preparation increases the long-term impact made in the lives of team members. The improved ministry that results from proper training brings a greater awareness of being used by God. This increased awareness promotes a stronger commitment among participants to seek God's ongoing purposes for their lives.[40]

A preparation program should strive for the following goals:

- to instill a sense of shared purpose and team unity that allows the group to work together effectively
- to help team members understand the host culture and gain cross-cultural sensitivity
- to teach participants the importance of entering the host culture as humble servants and learners
- to prepare volunteers to communicate successfully with nationals
- to develop skill and experience in planned areas of service
- to inform team members of logistics and follow up on their logistical responsibilities
- to promote serious discipleship and prepare participants for the spiritual implications of the experience

To help meet these goals, when planning the training sessions it would be helpful to draw on contacts and resources available in the team's local churches and communities, including church leaders, missionaries on furlough, previous volunteers, and believers from other cultures. Participants can even be required to work on research assignments between sessions. And, if a group displays sufficient maturity, it could play a part in setting policies. When, for example, a mature team researches the economic conditions of the country and the average income of the national congregation, team members could discuss and decide for themselves what approach to spending money in front of nationals would be the best witness.

The training content will depend somewhat on the destination and ministry plan. For training ideas, David C. Forward recommends that the project coordinator contact the field representative and ask what mistakes earlier teams have made and to request the names of contacts on those teams. Then coordinators can ask the team leaders what they wish they had known before they went to that particular field.[41] In general, a training program should include the following:

- *A chance for team members to get to know each other in an environment where bonding can take place and members can learn to work together.* Healthy team relationships transform the group from an assortment of individuals into a cohesive team who can provide effective service toward common goals. Coordinators can help members discover each others' unique gifts, personalities, strengths, and weaknesses, and encourage members to pray for each other and discuss biblical methods for conflict resolution. Coordinators might address, too, the harmful effects of cliques among the team and romances between team members. I agree with Eaton and Hurst: "When relationships between team members are healthy, each person has the optimal chance to absorb all that a trip like this can teach."[42] Positive team relationships also demonstrate to the watching world that participants are Jesus' disciples (John 13:34–35), and they bring glory and praise to God (Rom. 15:5–7).
- *An overview of the country with basic information about history, geography, climate, economy, politics, education, food, current events, ethnic and social groups, and so forth.* Participants will show respect to the missionaries and nationals when the group makes an effort to learn about the country before arrival. One idea is to pair team

members to research various aspects of the country as a team-building exercise and then have them present their findings to the group.

• *An overview of the country's predominant religions, the history of Christianity there, the history of the hosting ministry, tips on contextualizing the gospel, cultural worship styles, and the nationals' perception of Western Christians.* Coordinators can help the group understand the country's religious environment, appreciate the ministry techniques in use, and avoid repeating any past mistakes made by overzealous Christians or insensitive visitors.

• *An opportunity for volunteers to understand their own North American cultural values and biases and the host culture's distinctives.* It would be ideal to bring in a speaker from the host culture or a person who can address issues of culture, stereotypes, and ethnocentrism. The group could also visit an ethnic church or go to an ethnic restaurant. Training should emphasize a servant-learner approach that avoids ethnocentric attitudes of superiority and insensitive cross-cultural mistakes that might alienate nationals. Volunteers should be reminded that they will be the invited guests of local leaders and must be willing to honor the cultural and behavioral guidelines and project techniques (however inefficient they might seem) the hosts give them.

• *Language learning and cross-cultural communication styles.* Because language assimilation can seem like a daunting task to participants, training in this area should be kept as lighthearted and practical as possible. Team members gain confidence by learning a few phrases they can use upon arrival and by risking a few mistakes. Any use of the host language, however limited, will communicate respect and appreciation for the nationals. Nonverbal communication should be discussed as well. Attitudes are communicated nonverbally, especially in settings where participants have limited conversation skills. Training should cover forms of greeting, norms for personal space and touching, common gestures, expected courtesies, the typical level of formality, any subjects that are culturally taboo, and appropriate communication patterns with nationals of the opposite sex.

• *Ministry preparation.* This aspect will vary based on the type of ministry to be performed. It might involve activities such as learning how to teach English to speakers of another language, practicing music and dramas, preparing sermons or VBS material, going over basic construction techniques, or making plans for teaching health and hygiene in remote villages. In all aspects of ministry, the team represents Christ and His love in the foreign culture. And training should not introduce methodology that the local leaders won't be able to replicate; training should empower participants, not create dependency.

- *Logistics.* Training needs to cover all logistics and responsibilities in detail; some participants may have no experience in international travel. Discussed, too, should be expectations for participants' responsibilities such as what to pack, how to obtain vaccines and travel documents, and how to raise support.

- *Spiritual preparation.* Each session should include prayer and devotions or worship because relationship with God is what fuels effective service. Participants must prepare themselves spiritually, seek God's will as they set goals for the trip, and depend upon God as they face the difficulties of fund-raising, language learning, etc. Coordinators should foster in participants an expectant attitude toward God's activity and provision for the project and should encourage participants to open their hearts to the spiritual and social needs of the country and the world. Short-termers might prepare their testimony and learn key tools of evangelism. Each participant ought to be able to clearly explain who Jesus is and why the gospel is important. The team leader's role is more than that of simply preparing the team for cross-cultural ministry. A leader is a discipler and mentor of the spiritual lives of team members and thus an integral part in God's overall plan of developing them into globally minded, mature Christian witnesses.

- *An introduction to the biblical basis for missions and an emphasis on long-term involvement.* God's Word has the power to make a lasting impression, so participants should learn about the biblical basis for missions early on. Jesus' model for ministry is one of complete identification with the people, thus team leaders need to encourage participants to view the short-term trip in part as hands-on training for long-term missions involvement of some kind. As impressive as the large numbers of short-termers are, they will not finish the task of world evangelization by themselves. Participants are to become world Christians who are discovering God's plan for the nations and who are seeking their role in it.

(Note: Several resources listed in appendix 1 include detailed preparation programs with session-by-session curriculum guides.)

Finance the Trip Appropriately

Question: If twenty people from your church are planning to travel to another culture to participate on a short-term mission, how many people are on the team?

Answer: The whole church!

Kim Hurst and Chris Eaton use the above question and answer to illustrate that fund-raising does much more than cover the expenses of a trip; it raises missions awareness and involves the whole church. Hurst and Eaton list the following four purposes for raising support:

1. to raise money to fund the trip (this purpose is obvious!)
2. to raise awareness—when fund-raising is done well, the entire church becomes involved in the plans
3. to build team spirit and cohesiveness—having team members work and pray together as they raise funds is an excellent pre-trip tool for building unity
4. to exercise faith muscles—fund-raising is by nature a faith-building exercise as participants put their trust in God to supply their needs[43]

The above list demonstrates that fund-raising can have positive effects on team members and can involve and influence many people for global missions. Fund-raising also provides an opportunity to mobilize prayer support as team members make their needs known. Team leaders, too, should not overlook the importance of undergirding prayer, and should encourage team members to request prayer support from as many people as possible. Participants who are paying their own way should still send letters requesting prayer support. Church groups might request a commissioning ceremony during the Sunday worship service before departure. This program will increase awareness and prayer support from church leaders and the congregation, emphasize the purpose of the team's mission, and send them out as missionaries representing the body of Christ.[44]

Because the fund-raising process often invites objections and criticism, fund-raising strategy and implementation must be above reproach. Fund-raising policies and how donated money will be used should be frankly communicated. As was mentioned earlier, good stewardship includes choosing an appropriate destination, and participants should send a prompt thank-you note to their supporters and a trip summary report afterward. And if, for instance, Tom is raising funds for his fifth short-term trip, it's probably time for someone to suggest that he find a different way to finance his trip or that he stay home and support someone else's trip.

The process of fund-raising also helps disprove some of the myths about raising money for short-term missions. Although short-term trips do absorb a lot of cash, rarely is it money that was designated for career missionaries and then reassigned. Long-term and short-term missions usually do not compete for the same sources of money, a fact that invalidates the common objection, *Wouldn't it just be better to send the money?* Short-term funds most often come from vacation savings or from donations of family and friends who give *only* because someone they know is going on a trip; participation in the trip is the vehicle for fund-raising.[45] The money given is, in fact, seed money that yields future dividends. Investors in short-term missions become world Christians who then often become investors in long-term missions. What's more, whole churches become involved; it's one thing for church members to hear about needs from distant missionaries but another when their own Suzie goes to Calcutta. I've seen churches and families give more to missions after one of their own returned from a trip and described first-hand the tremendous needs.

Certain costs will, of course, be incurred on the field before the group leaves. Hosts might need to make advance deposits on accommodations or ground transportation and might need to purchase food and building supplies. Advance funds are thus needed to cover these expenses. Wiring money, if possible, through a bank will facilitate this process as well as eliminate having to carry in a lot of cash.

During the Experience

Provide Orientation

It is advisable for the host missionary or national leader to give an orientation session within a day or two of arrival. Local leaders can then discuss the itinerary, the work to be done, cultural information, and guidelines for behavior and dress, and take questions. Team members may wish to record notes and impressions in their journals. Depending on the destination, local leaders could also cover some of the following topics:

- how to shop (if a bartering system is used);
- giving money to beggars or expensive gifts to nationals they befriend;
- picture-taking guidelines;
- appropriate interaction with members of the opposite sex;
- potential risks or dangers.

If the team has prepared program material such as dramas, orientation is a good time to have local leaders review the material and recommend any cultural adjustments.

The team should also have a private time of orientation where the group leader discusses curfews, rooming situations, how to handle conflict, what to do if one becomes sick or separated from the group, and crisis management plans. At this time, team members should be reminded that not following instructions about food and water can devastate the team's health. The private orientation is also a good time to reinforce guidelines given by the host and remind the group that none of them want to do anything to hinder receptivity to the message. The private orientation, too, provides an opportunity to cultivate an attitude of submission to field leadership. The team attitude toward local leaders should be, "We are at your disposal; we have simply come to assist with whatever is important to you."

Encourage Personal and Spiritual Growth

Short-term trips have helped numerous people discover that God can use their gifts to minister to others. Timid, shy persons often become self-confident and willing to take new risks for God. Team leaders can create an environment that fosters growth and gives participants many opportunities to be stretched. Therefore, leaders should not hesitate to talk regularly with individual team members to find out what they are thinking and feeling and what their concerns are, and to remind participants of the value of journaling and of personal quiet times. Leaders can help the group remember their purpose for coming, and encourage them to examine their attitudes daily. Team leaders, too, should then model what they teach. Leaders need to be proactive about respectfully confronting behavior problems such as complaining, inflexibility, judgmental opinions, or exclusive relationships. To facilitate prayer and help participants spend time with all group members, assigning daily prayer partners is a good idea. Another way to promote growth is to ask individuals or small groups to be responsible for each day's group devotions.

Go with the Flow

The group should expect the unexpected; things rarely go exactly as planned and many circumstances are beyond group control. Leaders should emphasize flexibility with the team and then set an example. Problems *will* occur along the way such as illness, transportation breakdowns, or stalled work because of lack of supplies. If, from the outset, leaders have a casual attitude, expecting something might go wrong and that it's all right, both they and their team will have a better experience. The group will then adjust and look for ways to take advantage of problems, such as using extra time to conduct a prayer walk or set up an impromptu ministry with local children while waiting for bus repairs. God can use unexpected circumstances, thus the team should be encouraged to pray that He will do so and to depend upon His guidance rather than upon well-designed plans.

Encourage Cultural Exposure and Participation

Cultural exposure, however, should be planned for and facilitated so that participants truly get a feel for the region and its people. When possible, the group should use public transportation, go to the market, eat the food (if safely prepared), visit homes, attend church services, visit historical sights, and especially interact with the people. The team should be advised ahead of time not to complain, compare, or criticize in front of nationals, and they should be cautioned ahead of time about making promises to write, send gifts, or help individuals unless they are serious about following through. Broken commitments have left many nationals confused and questioning the truthfulness of short-term visitors. The group should be prepared for participation in church services because foreign visitors are often asked to share during worship. The team might prepare a song (in the host language if possible), skit, or testimony beforehand, even if this isn't part of the planned project.

To get participants out into the host culture, they might be given a language assignment—perhaps learning to say, "What do you call this?" in the host language, or given a notebook and asked to talk with nationals until they have learned and recorded twenty-five nouns. This exercise can break down barriers because it forces team members to interact with nationals (in a nonthreatening posture as learners) that puts both parties at ease.

An effort should be made to immerse participants in the culture to the point where they can sense both the adversities and the opportunities in that field. This immersion is what Engel and Jones call *meaningful exposure,* which starts at the grassroots in the field, exposes problems and opportunities, and involves participants in considering solutions. Such a short-term ministry builds long-term vision and continued involvement, in sharp contrast to a project that involves little contact with nationals.[46]

Take a Western Attitude Check

Although short-termers can bring encouragement, motivation, and effective service to a ministry, their efforts are not usually strategically important. Group leaders need, therefore, to help short-termers overcome the idea that their Western intervention is the chief answer to the field ministry's needs, reminding volunteers that God's work will get done even if they hadn't come. It might take longer, but it will get done. Participants are not there because the local leaders aren't capable; they are there as part of the body of Christ, showing love and support for another part of the body. In addition, leaders can help the group recognize that national workers, in contrast to outsiders, are in a superior position to reach their fellow nationals.

Short-termers must also recognize that no quick fixes exist by which to make disciples. Group leaders can remind participants to have servant hearts that are willing to patiently do what needs to be done, rather than count the number of converts. If volunteers are equipped and prepared for spiritual ministry, the trip could be structured to maximize the amount of time participants will be in contact with the same group of nationals. Spending days or weeks together with the same nationals is usually far more effective for genuine spiritual ministry than a "ten-cities-in-ten-days" tour. The more time participants and nationals spend together sharing their lives and hopes, the greater influence the short-termers will have and the more their own lives will be affected.[47]

Build Trust in Field Authority

Leaders can help volunteers overcome any inability to submit to field authority by first setting an example. Then through proper cross-cultural training, leaders can assist participants in respecting and trusting a style of leadership that is different from that to which they are accustomed. Team members should be instructed in how to communicate sensitively with their hosts to avoid misunderstandings, and reminded that the field missionaries and local leaders might not be working at the same intensity level as the team because such a level would be impossible to maintain over the long haul. To help participants gain a better impression of what missionary life is truly like, local leaders could be invited to share information about their daily struggles, the hindrances, and the rewards of their work.

Set Aside Team Time

Because the concept of privacy might be different in the host culture and because the local people most likely will be intrigued by the foreigners and will want to watch them wherever they go, the team might have limited privacy. Thus leaders must find a way for the team to be alone for regular debriefing sessions. The hosts might not fully understand this need, thus the team's time should not be so overscheduled that these meetings are neglected.

During the sessions, the group could discuss experiences, feelings, thoughts, and lessons learned. Leaders can facilitate sharing by asking everyone to answer an open-ended question such as, What one word describes how you are feeling about the culture/the project/the food? What has been the most exciting/challenging/joyful event for you so far? What is God trying to teach you? In what area do you need accountability so you will have no regrets when the trip is over? This is also a time to have devotions, set goals, process spiritual implications, pray, and worship together (although there won't be time for all of this in every meeting). Debriefing is the setting where members can openly question and express their struggles or negative reactions. It should also be a place where participants encourage and support each other, helping to maintain enthusiasm for the project.

Although time alone is important, the group should not miss out on what the hosts can teach them. Invite local leaders to one of the team meetings so that he or she can share his or her testimony, discuss dreams for the future, or answer participants' questions. Especially helpful is having local leaders talk with the team a few days after the initial orientation to answer new questions and explain any cultural apprehensions that have arisen.

Include Recreation and Free Time

The group also needs time to relax, have personal devotions, journal, shop, and sightsee. Unstructured time sometimes has the most significant impact as team members reflect, interact informally among themselves, and encounter nationals in the culture. Participants often submit conflicting requests about what they would like to do with their free time. Some people want to visit points of interest, others request shopping time, still others want to rest. A "wish list," on which all of the various requests are recorded, assures participants that their requests have been heard, but allows all requests to be considered together. The group leader or the participants themselves can then prioritize the list, and then the host can be consulted to see if the top few priorities can be accomplished.

Finish Well

It is advisable to plan a few days' vacation at the end of the experience as a "reward" that the team has earned. This time will provide an essential opportunity for rest and debriefing. In a short while the team members will be returning to their own lives and responsibilities, so this time serves as a buffer to help participants bridge the two worlds. It can ease the stress and difficulty that short-termers experience during reentry and can maximize lessons learned from the entire mission. A few days' vacation gives participants time to think about commitments for life changes while the missions experience is still fresh, and helps participants avoid simply laying down their missions tools, coming home, and falling back into old routines. Participants can spend these last few days in numerous ways. Suggestions for activities include the following:

- Relax and play, and celebrate a job well done.
- Journal and reflect on how to integrate the experience and its spiritual lessons into life at home.
- Use a debriefing curriculum (available in some of the resources listed in appendix 1) to facilitate reflection.
- Consider various aspects of the trip by filling out evaluation forms and then discussing the contents.
- Spend time affirming each others' strengths or taking a spiritual gifts inventory.
- List prayer needs for each other, for the missionaries/local leaders, for the nationals, and for the country as a whole; then spend time praying individually and corporately.
- Review the biblical basis for missions, and seek a role in God's global purposes.
- Write "dear me" letters listing realistic life changes that participants desire to make and that the leader collects and mails back to them later.
- Prepare for the sense of loss and the multitude of other emotions that will be felt upon arrival at home.
- Prepare for the reception by family and friends, some of whom might not be interested in hearing every detail about the trip or who might not know what questions to ask.

- Plan for sharing information about the experience with individuals and perhaps through a group presentation.
- End with a worship and Communion service.

After the Experience

Continue to Debrief

Eaton and Hurst make an excellent point: "We did not expect the individual team members to train themselves or organize their trip, so why should we expect them to follow up on themselves?"[48] Participants may need assistance through the reentry process with continued debriefing. This exercise will help them move successfully through the transition and emotional ups and downs. It is recommended to have at least one group meeting (with no pictures) one week after returning for the sole purpose of sharing thoughts, feelings, and frustrations about the transition back to "regular life." Before the trip, participants may have needed help in overcoming prejudices about the host culture. Now, after the trip, the pendulum has likely swung the other way with participants being so aware of the negative aspects of American culture that they are ready to reject it all and criticize everyone around them. Leaders must help participants find balance, turn judgments into constructive convictions, and affirm the positive aspects of North American culture. Then, a second lighthearted picture party could be planned. Members will appreciate seeing their teammates and having the chance to talk seriously and have fun together.

Continue a Long-Term Emphasis

I like to study the parable of the talents with the team after returning. In many ways, a short-term experience is a valuable gift that God has entrusted to team members. Now they have the opportunity either to bury it or to process and invest it for greater gain in the kingdom of God. Team members are advised to follow through on any promises that they made to people on the field, and are encouraged to find ways in which they can stay involved in missions from home. Some of the teams with whom I've been involved have initiated fund-raising events for the host ministry, sponsored a child in that country, or organized regular prayer meetings with other team members to pray for the mission field. I invite the team to pray about an even greater commitment to missions in the future and challenge them to use any newly developed skills in the local church or community.

Share the Experience with Others

Telling the stories of the trip is another way that the experience can bear fruit. As members share their experiences, other people are influenced, and a ripple effect occurs. Team members should thus be encouraged to find avenues for talking about their experience, and be required to report to those who invested financially and prayerfully in their experience. The team leader might request an opportunity to share during a worship service or special event and then meet with the group to plan for it. A presentation is an ideal way to let the congregation know how their prayers were answered and how their financial support was used to create a meaningful experience.

Some team members might be unsure how to begin describing the trip because it seems impossible to communicate all that happened. Leaders can help their team recognize that people do not want a day-by-day, detail-by-detail account. Rather, participants should be prompted to spend time in prayer in which they seek God's wisdom for selecting what is important to share and relating what will glorify Him the most. They should avoid spending ten minutes of a twenty-minute presentation describing the crazy traffic they encountered (which their listeners will still not fully comprehend), but instead focus on lessons that God taught them and how their life is different because of what they experienced. Because people love stories, participants might think of one person they met and tell a story about that person that gives a window of insight into the experience.

Compile Evaluations

Team leaders would do well to collect and compile team evaluations. Quality evaluation is the key to improvement, so special attention should be given to appraising the trip and noting what should be changed on future projects. But evaluation should be based on more than solely what it accomplished for the team. Field leaders should be asked for their evaluation and suggestions, which should be listened to humbly, with an open mind. A true test of the success of a short-term project is how the host feels about the group after it leaves.

BEARING FRUIT

Some approaches to short-term missions have weaknesses that are valid sources of criticism. But to paint the entire short-term movement with the same brush stroke is unfair. Many well-designed and properly structured programs offer great value. And, like it or not, short-term missions is here to stay. Instead of discounting it, missions leaders should strive to improve short-term programs and channel all of the activity and excitement in directions that will support and complement the work of long-term missions.

As has been noted, with proper motivation and preparation, selection of appropriate projects, healthy partnership with field leaders, and a view toward long-term involvement, short-term missions can make significant contributions to overall missions strategy. Well-trained short-termers can bring enthusiasm, a boost to ongoing work, and truly satisfying results. They can also provide resources and prayer support to long-term missions and help develop a greater missions vision in their home churches. And short-term missions has the capacity to produce, as nothing else can, individuals with a heart for the world and a commitment to career missions. So in organizing short-term programs, the goal of all involved is to "live a life worthy of the Lord, bearing fruit in every good work," that the nations may truly be blessed.

SHORT-TERM MISSIONS REFERENCES

SUGGESTED READING

This appendix lists several resources that provide guidelines for the nuts-and-bolts workings of short-term missions. These resources cover in greater detail many topics that are mentioned in chapter 16 and include practical suggestions for everything from raising support, to choosing travel agencies, to securing liability and medical insurance. Some topics include team leader job descriptions, team member applications, a training and debriefing curriculum, packing lists, tips for traveling, sample itineraries, policy statements, and liability release forms. Some of these resources are hard to find, but Distribution Central (P.O. Box 40519, Pasadena, CA 91114-7519; phone: 626-798-8582; e-mail: Bberry4215@aol.com) carries many of the titles, even those that are out of print.

Aeschliman, Gordon, ed. *The Short-Term Mission Handbook: A Comprehensive Guide for Participants and Leaders.* Evanston, Ill.: Berry, 1993. Includes debriefing curriculum.

Anthony, Michael J., ed. *The Short-Term Missions Boom.* Grand Rapids: Baker, 1994.

Aroney-Sine, Christine. *Survival of the Fittest: Keeping Yourself Healthy in Travel and Service Overseas.* Monrovia, Calif.: MARC, 1994.

Barnett, Betty. *Friend Raising: Building a Missionary Support Team that Lasts.* Seattle: Youth With a Mission, 1996.

Dillon, William P. *People Raising: A Practical Guide to Raising Support.* Chicago: Moody, 1993.

Appendix 1

Eaton, Chris, and Kim Hurst. *Vacations with a Purpose: Leaders Manual.* Elgin, Ill.: David C. Cook, 1993. Includes debriefing curriculum.

Engel, James F., and Jerry D. Jones. *Baby Boomers and the Future of World Missions.* Orange, Calif.: Management Development Associates, 1989.

Forward, David C. *The Essential Guide to the Short-Term Mission Trip.* Chicago: Moody, 1998.

Jordan, Peter. *Reentry: Making the Transition from Missions to Life at Home.* Seattle: YWAM, 1996. Includes debriefing curriculum.

Kohls, Robert L. *Survival Kit for Overseas Living.* Yarmouth, Me.: Intercultural, 1984.

Lingenfelter, Sherwood G., and Marvin K. Mayers. *Ministering Cross-Culturally.* Grand Rapids: Baker, 1986.

McDonough, Daniel P., and Roger P. Peterson. *Can Short-Term Missions Really Create Long-Term Career Missionaries?* Minneapolis: STEM Ministries, 1999.

Mission Today '96: Short-Term Missions: A Special Report. Evanston, Ill.: Berry, 1996.

Peterson, Roger P., and Timothy D. Peterson. *Is Short-Term Missions Really Worth the Time and Money?* Minneapolis: STEM Ministries, 1991.

Short-Term Missions Training: The Ticket to Successful Ministry. Virginia Beach, Va.: Association of International Mission Services (AIMS), 1989.

Stepping Out: A Guide to Short-Term Missions. Seattle: YWAM, 1992. Includes debriefing curriculum.

Tanin, Vicki, Jim Hill, and Ray Howard. *Sending Out Servants: A Church-Based Short-Term Missions Strategy.* Wheaton, Ill.: ACMC, 1992.

VanCise, Martha. *Successful Mission Teams: A Guide for Volunteers.* Birmingham, Ala.: New Hope, 1996.

SUPPORT-RAISING LETTER

April 22, 1999

Mr. and Mrs. Larry Danforth
555 Appleton Trail
Dallas, TX 54321

Dear Larry and Debbie,

In June of this year, Ann and I had the opportunity to travel to a remote
village in southern Bolivia to observe the work that missionaries are doing
with the Guarani, an indigenous people. The missionaries are involved in
church planting and Bible translation work among these precious people.
Because we have been praying for God to direct us in His will for our lives
and ministry, this trip left us very excited. Both we and the missionaries who
are already working there agreed that the skills that God has given Ann and
me could be of great benefit to the work.

After much prayer and seeking the wisdom and counsel of our families, friends,
and church elders, we believe that the Lord is leading us to return to Bolivia
as full-time missionaries. My desire is to teach the people about the Christ
who loves them and died on the cross for them.

We will be returning to Bolivia with Gospel Missionary Union, an interdenominational "faith mission," which means that we must raise our own support for this ministry. We are asking that you prayerfully consider joining us
in our efforts to reach the Guarani for Christ.

Based on the information that the missionaries have provided, we estimate it will cost about $_____ for our initial set-up costs and around $_____ for our monthly needs. A breakdown of these expenses is included in the enclosed information.

We have seen God work in the hearts of His people and, as you can see, we are already halfway to having our expenses covered. We are asking you to pray about whether God wants you to be a part of this ministry. Please let us know if you think He is leading you to be a part of our support team. Your contribution would put us that much closer to getting on the field, reaching the Guarani for Christ, and equipping them to reach others.

Please let us know as soon as possible of your commitment. This can easily be done by dropping me a note in the enclosed envelope. If I do not hear from you within a week, I will call you to see what you are thinking. Thank you for prayerfully considering this Great Commission opportunity.

In the palm of His sovereign hand,

Johnny and Ann Doezel

FINANCIAL NEEDS WORKSHEET

IN JUNE OF THIS YEAR, I had the opportunity to travel to a remote village in southern Bolivia to observe the work that missionaries are doing with the Guarani, an indigenous people. The missionaries are involved in church planting and Bible translation work among these precious people. Because I have been praying for God to direct me in His will for my life and ministry, this trip left me very excited. Both the missionaries who are already working there and I agreed that the skills that God has given me could be of great benefit to the work there.

After much prayer and seeking the wisdom and counsel of my family, friends, and church elders, I believe that the Lord is leading me to return to Bolivia as a full-time missionary. My desire is to teach the people about the Christ who loves them and died on the cross for them.

I will be returning to Bolivia with Gospel Missionary Union, an inter-denominational "faith mission," which means that I will be asked to raise my own financial support. I'm asking that you prayerfully consider joining me in this effort to reach the Guarani for Christ. On the following page is a summary of my estimated financial needs.

FINANCIAL WORKSHEET

Training   _____

Field setup
    Language school   _____
    Household furnishings   _____
    Ministry supplies and equipment   _____
    Vehicle   _____
    Shipping costs   _____
    Visas   _____

Airfare   _____

                TOTAL SET-UP SUPPORT NEEDED $_____

Field expenses
    Rent, utilities, and food   _____
    Medical insurance   _____
    Social Security   _____
    Retirement   _____
    Vehicle insurance, gas, and repairs   _____
    Work fund   _____
    Prayer/support letters and postage   _____
    Conferences   _____

Supporting services   _____

Personal living allowance   _____

                TOTAL MONTHLY SUPPORT NEEDED $_____

Current support update

Set-up support: Current level $_____ Remaining amount $_____
Monthly support: Current level $_____ Remaining amount $_____

HOW YOU CAN HELP THE DOEZEL FAMILY REACH THE GUARANI PEOPLE FOR CHRIST

PRAYER SUPPORT

Paul entreated the believers in Ephesus, "Pray on my behalf, that utterance may be given to me in the opening of my mouth, to make known with boldness the mystery of the gospel, . . . that in proclaiming it I may speak boldly, as I ought to speak" (Eph. 6:19–20 NASB). Please pray that we will speak the life-changing gospel of Jesus Christ boldly and teach the life-changing Word of God joyfully. We will be sending you regular prayer requests from the field.

FINANCIAL SUPPORT

Stapled to this sheet is an explanation of our financial needs and a financial status report. Ninety-five percent of our monthly support must be pledged and one hundred percent of our set-up costs must be donated before we can go to the field. We are letting you know what it will take to sustain us financially while we minister to the Guarani people. (See Romans 15:24 and 1 Corinthians 1:15–16, where the phrase "to be helped on my way" translates the Greek infinitive *propemfthenai,* meaning "to outfit for a trip." In both places, Paul is letting people know about a financial need and asking them to help.)

Those who would like to support this ministry—whether once or monthly—can make their tax-deductible donation check payable to *Guarani for Christ* (address below) and indicate that it is for the ministry of the Doezel family.

You will receive a tax-deductible receipt at the end of the year. Thank you for helping us evangelize and train the Guarani for Christ.

MATERIAL/EMOTIONAL SUPPORT

One of the greatest discouragements a missionary faces on the foreign field is the "out-of-sight-out-of-mind syndrome." Phone calls, e-mail, cards, and letters can be a tremendous encouragement. This may well be a project for a Sunday school class, a women's missionary group, a men's group, and so on. Every week, someone (or several people) could be designated to write, call, or e-mail us in Sucre.

PHYSICAL SUPPORT

Short-term missionaries (both individuals and small teams) are welcome and encouraged. We have much to do, including evangelism, Bible training, and construction projects. We are ready to help you prepare for your trip and will ensure that everything is ready at this end. Please call us if you are interested. It's best if you can do so nine months or more in advance.

Personal Address:
The Doezel Family
Casilla 3999
Sucre, Bolivia

Financial Address:
Guarani for Christ
P. O. Box 879654
Christos, IA 12356

Phone: 011-591-444-4444
Fax: 011-591-555-5555
E-mail: doezel@compunet.com

ENDNOTES

Introduction: A Plea to Return to a Biblical Model

1. Francis Schaeffer, *The Great Evangelical Disaster* (Westchester, Ill.: Crossway, 1984), 64.
2. David J. Hesselgrave, *Scripture and Strategy: The Use of the Bible in Postmodern Church and Mission* (Pasadena, Calif.: William Carey Library, 1994), 9–10.

Chapter 1: The Crisis in Missions

1. Thomas Ice, "Growing Mysticism Versus True Biblical Spirituality," in *Issues 2000: Evangelical Faith and Cultural Trends in the New Millennium*, ed. Mal Couch (Grand Rapids: Kregel, 1999), 53.
2. David F. Wells, *No Place for Truth: Or Whatever Happened to Evangelical Theology?* (Grand Rapids: Eerdmans, 1993), 112–13.
3. David F. Wells, *God in the Wasteland: The Reality of Truth in a World of Fading Dreams* (Grand Rapids: Eerdmans, 1994), 195.
4. Ibid., 196.
5. James F. Engel and Jerry D. Jones, *Baby Boomers and the Future of World Missions* (Orange, Calif.: Management Development Assoc., 1989), 33.
6. Dave Hunt, *A Woman Rides the Beast* (Eugene, Ore.: Harvest House, 1994), 5.
7. Evangelical signers included Pat Robertson; Charles Colson; John White, president of Geneva College (former president of the National Association of Evangelicals); Bill Bright of Campus Crusade; Mark Noll of Wheaton College; Os Guinness; Jesse Miranda of the Assemblies of God; Richard Mouw of Fuller Seminary; J. I. Packer, noted theologian; Herbert Sclossberg; and two of the heads of the Home Mission Board and Christian Life Commission of the Southern Baptist Convention (who later withdrew their names); as well as others.
8. H. J. Schroeder, O.P., gen. ed., *The Canons and Decrees of the Council of Trent* (Rockford, Ill.: Tan Books, 1978), 44.
9. Ibid.
10. Ibid.

11. Fritz Rienecker, *Linguistic Key to the Greek New Testament,* ed. Cleon Rogers (Grand Rapids: Zondervan, 1976, 1980), 357.

12. Austin Flannery, O.P. gen. ed., *Vatican Council II: The Conciliar and Post Conciliar Documents,* rev. ed. (Northport N.Y.: Costello, 1988), 1:378.

13. *The Barna Report: What Americans Believe* (Ventura, Calif.: Regal, 1991), 83–85; cited by John D. Castelein, "Can the Restoration Movement Plea Survive if Belief in Objective Truth Is Abandoned?" *Stone-Campbell Journal* 1 (spring 1998): 27.

14. Paul Copan, *True for You, but Not for Me* (Minneapolis, Minn.: Bethany House, 1998), 11.

Chapter 2: The Sufficiency of Scripture as a Foundation for Missions Theology and Practice

1. C. Peter Wagner, *Confronting the Powers* (Ventura, Calif.: Regal, 1996), 55.

2. Ibid., 43.

3. For a defense of this statement, see John F. Hart, "The Gospel and Spiritual Warfare: A Review of Peter Wagner's Confronting the Powers," *Journal of the Grace Evangelical Society* 10, no. 18 (spring 1997):19–39; and chap. 10, "Demonology and the Mission Field," in this volume.

4. Bernard Ramm, *Protestant Biblical Interpretation* (Boston: W. A. Wilde, 1956), 89–92, as cited by Charles C. Ryrie, *Dispensationalism,* rev. ed. (Chicago: Moody, 1995), 80.

5. Roy B. Zuck, *Basic Bible Interpretation* (Wheaton, Ill.: Victor, 1991), 61–62.

6. Ryrie, *Dispensationalism,* 81.

7. Ibid., 82.

8. David L. Edwards and John R. W. Stott, *Essentials: A Liberal-Evangelical Dialogue* (Downers Grove, Ill.: InterVarsity, 1988); John R. W. Stott, "The Logic of Hell: A Rejoinder," *Evangelical Review of Theology* 18, no. 1 (January 1994): 33–34; Clark H. Pinnock, "The Destruction of the Finally Impenitent," *Criswell Theological Review* 4, no. 2 (spring 1990): 243–59; Ibid. Clark H. Pinnock, *A Wideness in God's Mercy: The Finality of Jesus Christ Is a World of Religions* (Grand Rapids: Zondervan, 1992); Michael Green, *Evangelism through the Local Church* (London: Hodder and Stoughton, 1990); Stephen H. Travis, *I Believe in the Second Coming of Jesus* (Grand Rapids: Eerdmans, 1982); Philip E. Hughes, *The True Image: The Origin and Destiny of Man in Christ* (Grand Rapids: Eerdmans, 1989); Edward W. Fudge, *The Fire That Consumes* (Houston, Tex.: Providential, 1982); John W. Wenham, *The Goodness of God* (Downers Grove, Ill.: InterVarsity, 1974).

9. George Barna, *Generation Next: What You Need to Know about Today's Youth* (Ventura, Calif.: Regal, 1995), 79.

10. *The Barna Report: What Americans Believe* (Ventura, Calif.: Regal, 1991), 83–85; cited by John D. Castelein, "Can the Restoration Movement Plea Survive if Belief in Objective Truth Is Abandoned?" *Stone-Campbell Journal* 1 (spring 1998): 27.

11. Paul Copan, *True for You, but Not for Me* (Minneapolis, Minn.: Bethany House, 1998), 11.
12. Most of these statements are excerpted from Steven McAvoy's chapter on postmodernism in this volume.
13. John F. Hart, "The Gospel and Spiritual Warfare: A Review of Peter Wagner's Confronting the Powers," *Journal of the Grace Evangelical Society,* 10, no. 18 (spring 1997): 25.
14. David J. Hesselgrave, *Scripture and Strategy: The Use of the Bible in Postmodern Church and Mission* (Pasadena, Calif.: William Carey Library, 1994), 9–10.
15. Ruth A. Tucker, *From Jerusalem to Irian Jaya* (Grand Rapids: Zondervan, 1983), 29, 31.
16. Roland Allen, *Missionary Methods: St. Paul's or Ours?* (reprint, Grand Rapids: Eerdmans, 1989), 12.
17. Ibid.
18. Ibid., 16.
19. Ibid., 13.
20. Walter Bruce Davis, *William Carey: Father of Modern Missions* (Chicago: Moody, 1963), 82–83.
21. Ibid., 120.
22. Fritz Rienecker, *Linguistic Key to the Greek New Testament,* ed. Cleon Rogers (Grand Rapids: Zondervan, 1976, 1980), 87.
23. Tucker, *From Jerusalem to Irian Jaya,* 185.
24. David J. Hesselgrave, *Planting Churches Cross-Culturally* (Grand Rapids: Baker, 1980), 142.
25. Allen, *Missionary Methods,* 81.
26. Ibid., 84, referring to Sir William Ramsay's *St. Paul the Traveler.*
27. Ibid., 13.
28. David Sittion, "Mentoring Shapes New Believers into Church Leaders," *Mission Today 96,* 1996, 56.
29. Allen, *Missionary Methods,* 13.
30. Harold Lindsell, *An Evangelical Theology of Missions* (Grand Rapids: Zondervan, 1970), 62.

Chapter 3: The Proper Place of the Study of Missions in Systematic Theology

1. Jean L. McKechnie, ed., *Webster's New Universal Unabridged Dictionary* (Cleveland, Ohio: Simon and Schuster, 1972), 1892.
2. Charles C. Ryrie, *Basic Theology* (Wheaton, Ill.: Victor, 1986), 14.
3. Charles C. Ryrie, *Biblical Theology of the New Testament* (Chicago, Ill.: Moody, 1959), 12. "Biblical theology is that branch of theological science which deals systematically with the historically conditioned progress of the self-revelation of God as deposited in the Bible."
4. Bernard Ramm, *Protestant Biblical Interpretation* (Boston: W. A. Wilde, 1956). A series of comments from Ramm is helpful: "The customary, socially acknowledged designation of a word is the literal meaning of that word" (p. 90). "To interpret literally . . . is nothing more or less than

interpreting words and sentences in their normal, usual customary, proper designation" (p. 91). "Literal interpretation does not mean painful, or wooden, or unbending literal rendition of every word and phrase. The literal meaning of the figurative expression is the proper or natural meaning as understood by students of language" (141).

5. Unless otherwise indicated, all Scripture quotations in this chapter are from the King James Version.

6. Ryrie, *Basic Theology*, 277.

7. Renald E. Showers, *There Really Is a Difference* (Bellmawr, N.J.: Friends of Israel Gospel Ministry, 1990), 20.

8. John Piper, *Let the Nations Be Glad* (Grand Rapids: Baker, 1996), on the doxological purpose of God; *idem, The Pleasures of God: Meditations on God's Delight in Being God* (Portland: Multnomah, 1991), on God's delight in being God.

9. George W. Peters, *A Biblical Theology of Missions* (Chicago: Moody, 1972), 166. The entire section (166–71) addresses this point.

10. Ibid., 169–70.

11. Arnold G. Fruchtenbaum, "Israel and the Church," in *Issues in Dispensationalism*, ed. Wesley R. Willis and John R. Masters (Chicago: Moody, 1994), 114. "National election does not guarantee the salvation of every individual within the nation since only individual election can do that. Nor does national election guarantee the physical salvation of every member of the nation. What national salvation does guarantee is that God's purpose(s) for choosing the nation will be accomplished and that the elect nation will always survive as a distinct entity."

12. Ibid., 115.

13. John F. Walvoord, "Biblical Kingdoms Compared and Contrasted," *Dispensationalism*, ed. Wesley R. Willis and John R. Masters (Chicago: Moody, 1994), 87. "There was no evidence that God required any nations other than Israel to follow Mosaic Law, and He did not judge the other nations for not observing it."

14. See Ryrie, *Basic Theology*, 397–99; and Walvoord, "Biblical Kingdoms Compared and Contrasted," 75–91.

15. Charles C. Ryrie, *So Great Salvation* (Wheaton, Ill.: Victor, 1989), 37–41.

16. Note the attending prohibition: "Then charged he his disciples that they should tell no man that he was Jesus the Christ" (Matt. 16:20) whereas earlier they had done exactly that (John 1:41).

17. Peters, *Biblical Theology of Missions*, 173.

18. Ibid., 172–98. See this source for a comprehensive study of the Great Commission accounts.

19. See Lewis Sperry Chafer, "Contrast Between Israel and the Church," *Systematic Theology* 4 (Dallas: Dallas Seminary Press, 1948), 47–53. See also, Charles C. Ryrie, *Dispensationalism*, rev. ed. (Chicago: Moody, 1995), 123–42.

20. Showers, *There Really Is a Difference*, 183–86.

21. S. Lewis Johnson, "Paul and 'The Israel of God': A Case Study," in *Essays in*

Honor of J. Dwight Pentecost, ed. Stanley D. Tousaint and Charles H. Dyer (Chicago: Moody, 1986), 181, 195. Regarding the phrase *to the Israel of God* in Galatians 6:16, S. Lewis Johnson states, "In spite of overwhelming evidence to the contrary, there remains persistent support for the contention that the term *Israel* may refer properly to Gentile believers in the present age." The article itself is a careful exegesis and reasoned presentation of the proper distinctions with the following conclusion: "If there is an interpretation that totters on a tenuous foundation, it is the view that Paul equates the term 'the Israel of God' with the believing church of Jews and Gentiles. To support it, the general usage of the term *Israel* in Paul, in the New Testament, and in the Scriptures as a whole is ignored. The grammatical and syntactical usage of the conjunction *kai* is strained and distorted—and the rare and uncommon sense accepted when the usual sense is unsatisfactory—only because it does not harmonize with the presuppositions of the exegete. And to compound matters, in the special context of Galatians and the general context of Pauline teaching, especially as highlighted in Romans 11, Paul's primary passages on God's dealings with Israel and then Gentiles are downplayed." Also see Robert L. Saucy, *The Church in God's Program* (Chicago: Moody, 1972), 70–82. Also see Ryrie, *Basic Theology,* 399.

22. Charles C. Ryrie, *So Great Salvation* (Wheaton, Ill.: Victor, 1989), 39.
23. For a contrary position (and what seems a strange mix of sound and fanciful interpretation), see "The Biblical Perspective," in *Perspectives on the World Christian Movement,* ed. Ralph D. Winter and Steven C. Hawthorne (Pasadena: William Carey Library, 1992), A3–A155.

Chapter 4: The Mission of the Church

1. John Piper, *Let the Nations Be Glad: The Supremacy of God in Missions* (Grand Rapids: Baker, 1993), 11.
2. Walter A. Elwell, *Evangelical Dictionary of Theology* (Grand Rapids: Baker, 1989), 312.
3. Loraine Boettner, *The Reformed Doctrine of Predestination* (Phillipsburg, N.J.: Presbyterian and Reformed, 1932), 66.
4. Mal Couch, *What Christianity Is All About* (Ft. Worth: Seminary Publishers, 1991), 3.
5. Ewald M. Plass, *What Luther Says* (St. Louis: Concordia, 1972), 1299.
6. George W. Peters, *A Biblical Theology of Missions* (Chicago: Moody, 1972), 15.
7. Paul Enns, *The Moody Handbook of Theology* (Chicago: Moody, 1989), 366.
8. Robert P. Lightner, *Handbook of Evangelical Theology: A Historical, Biblical, and Contemporary Survey and Review* (Grand Rapids: Kregel, 1995), 235–36.
9. See Cleon Rogers, "The Great Commission," *Bibliotheca Sacra* 130 (July 1973): 258–67; H. E. Dana and Julius R. Mantey, *A Manual Grammar of the Greek New Testament* (New York: Macmillan, 1927), 229; Daniel B. Wallace, *Greek Grammar Beyond the Basics* (Grand Rapids: Zondervan, 1996), 645.

10.   Walter Bauer, *A Greek-English Lexicon of the New Testament and Other Early Christian Literature,* 2d ed., rev. F. W. Gingrich and Frederick Danker, trans. William F. Arndt and F. W. Gingrich (Chicago: Chicago Univ. Press, 1979), 485.

11.   Ibid.

12.   Peters, *Biblical Theology of Missions,* 188.

13.   Ibid., 189.

14.   H. E. Dana and J. R. Mantey, *A Manual Grammar of the Greek New Testament* (New York: Macmillan, 1950), 228.

15.   Louis A. Barbieri Jr., "Matthew," in *The Bible Knowledge Commentary, New Testament,* ed. John F. Walvoord and Roy B. Zuck (Wheaton, Ill.: Victor, 1983), 94.

16.   David J. Hesselgrave, *Planting Churches Cross-Culturally* (Grand Rapids: Baker, 1980), 23–24.

17.   These basic teachings are presented in workbook form for instructing new converts in Russell L. Penney's *Equipping the Saints* series available through Tyndale Theological Seminary, 6800 Brentwood Stair Rd., #105, Ft. Worth, TX 76112. They are entitled *Equipping the Saints, Discipleship Manual; Division I: The Basics;* and *Division II: Basic Bible Knowledge.* You can order by calling 800-886-1415.

18.   Paul G. Culley, "The Motives and Goal of World Missions: II. The Educational Objective," in *Facing Facts in Modern Missions: A Symposium* (Chicago: Moody Bible Institute of Chicago, 1963), 31.

19.   The term *apostolos* is used in the Gospels in reference to the twelve chosen by Christ. They are referred to as *the* twelve apostles (Matt. 10:2; Luke 6:13; 9:1–10; 17:15). These men had some unique qualifications. Müller writes:

> With the exception of Lk. 11:49, Acts 14:14, Luke applies *apostolos* expressly to the Twelve. They had been called by the historical Jesus to their office (Lk. 6:13; cf. 1:17). They had been with him throughout his ministry from the time of John's baptism. The risen Lord had met them in various appearances (Lk. 24:36ff.; Acts 1:3). And so they had the best possible knowledge of what Jesus had said. Before the ascension they had received the promise of the Spirit (Acts 1:4) and the command to evangelize (Acts 1:8). By the event of Pentecost (Acts 2) they were made bearers of the Spirit, the great authorities of early Christianity who, based on Jerusalem, guarded the true tradition which went back to the historical Jesus (D. Müller, "Apostle," in *The New International Dictionary of New Testament Theology,* 4 vols., ed. Colin Brown [Grand Rapids: Zondervan, 1975, 1986], 1:126, 128-9).

> That these conditions were important to maintain is attested to during the choice of a replacement for Judas in that the conditions were stated by Peter: "It is therefore necessary that of the men who have accompanied us all the time that the Lord Jesus went in and out among us—beginning with

the baptism of John, until the day that He was taken up from us—one of these should become a witness with us of His resurrection" (Acts 1:21–22 NASB). Thus, *apostolos* is used in a unique sense of the original twelve apostles chosen by Christ and then to Matthias, who was chosen to replace Judas and who fulfilled these qualifications. Revelation 21:14 shows that the apostles chosen by Christ will have a special place in the New Jerusalem.

Apostolos is also used of Paul. In 2 Corinthians 12:11 Paul states, ". . . for in no respect was I inferior to the most eminent apostles, even though I am a nobody. The signs of a true apostle were performed among you with all perseverance, by signs and wonders and miracles." The signs, wonders, and miracles were specific signs that set Paul apart as an apostle (cf. Rom. 15:19). Paul also stated in 1 Corinthians 9:1, "Am I not free? Am I not an apostle? Have I not seen Jesus our Lord? . . ." (cf. 1 Cor. 15:8). Just as the original twelve apostles had been witnesses of the resurrected Lord, so had Paul, and his witnessing was a proof of his apostleship. Paul not only performed the signs of an apostle and saw the resurrected Lord but also was directly commissioned by the Lord (Acts 22:21; Rom. 1:5; Gal. 1–2; 1 Tim. 2:7).

20. Bauer, *Greek-English Lexicon*, 370–71.
21. Peters, *Biblical Theology of Missions*, 191.
22. Trevor McIlwain, who popularized chronological Bible teaching, is International Coordinator for Church Planting and Evangelism with New Tribes Mission. He is author of the multivolume series *Building on Firm Foundations*. Translations of the material are in progress in Russian, Spanish, Portuguese, Romanian, Chinese, and some tribal languages. Contact New Tribes Mission, 1000 East First Street, Sanford, FL 32771-1487, or by phone at 407-323-3430.
23. Richard N. Longenecker, "The Acts of the Apostles," in *The Expositor's Bible Commentary*, ed. Frank Gaebelein (Grand Rapids: Zondervan, 1981), 257n.
24. Hesselgrave, *Planting Churches Cross-Culturally*, 27.
25. Peters, *Biblical Theology of Missions*, 209.
26. Robert P. Lightner, "The Nature and Purpose of the Church," in *The Fundamentals for the Twenty-First Century*, ed. Mal Couch (Grand Rapids: Kregel, 2000), 337.
27. Ibid., 337–38.
28. Hesselgrave, *Planting Churches Cross-Culturally*, 26.

Chapter 5: The Sovereignty of God in Missions

1. David C. E. Liao, *The Unresponsive: Resistant or Neglected?* (Pasadena, Calif.: William Carey Library, 1972).
2. Edward R. Dayton and David A. Fraser, *Planning Strategies for World Evangelization*, rev. ed. (Grand Rapids: Eerdmans, 1990), 29.
3. Martin Luther, "The Damned Are Self-Condemned," in *What Luther Says: An Anthology*, comp. Ewald M. Plass, 3 vols. (St. Louis: Concordia, 1959), 2:695.
4. Ralph Winter, "Do We Need Heresies on the Mission Field? Can Heresies

Be Silver Linings?" *Mission Frontiers* 18, no. 9-10 (September–October 1996): 6.

5. Christopher Howse, ed., *a.d.: 2000 Years of Christianity*, Part 3: "800–1200" (London: Telegraph Group, 1999), 14.

6. Donald McGavran, *Understanding Church Growth*, rev. ed. (Grand Rapids: Eerdmans, 1970), 223.

7. Peter N. Lundell, "Behind Japan's Resistant Web: Understanding the Problem of Nihonkyo," *Missiology* 23, no. 4 (October 1995): 401–12.

8. Ibid.

9. Nik Repkin, "Why Are the Unreached Unreached?" *Evangelical Missions Quarterly* 32, no. 3 (July 1996): 284–88.

10. Samuel M. Zwemer, The Law of Apostasy in Islam: Answering the Question Why There Are So Few Moslem Converts and Giving Examples of Their Moral Courage and Freedom (New York: Marshall Brothers, 1924).

11. C. Peter Wagner, Confronting the Powers (Ventura, Calif.: Regal, 1996).

12. J. I. Packer, *Evangelism and the Sovereignty of God* (London Inter-Varsity Fellowship, 1961), 27].

13. J. Herbert Kane, Christian Mission in Biblical Perspective (Grand Rapids: Baker, 1976), 102–3.

14. W. H. T. Gairdner, cited by Zwemer, Law of Apostasy in Islam, 14.

15. Obed Borowski, Agriculture in Iron Age Israel (Winona Lake, Ind.: Eisenbrauns, 1987), 57. See also "Harvest," in Dictionary of Biblical Imagery, ed. Leland Ryken, James C. Wilhoit, and Tremper Longman III (Downers Grove, Ill.: InterVarsity, 1998).

Chapter 6: The Destiny of the Unevangelized

1. All Scripture texts are from the *New International Version* (Grand Rapids: International Bible Society, 1984). Italics included in the NIV Scriptures quoted in this chapter have been added by the author.

2. "New Scofield Study System" of the *Scofield Reference Bible*, NIV, note on Exodus 8:2, p. 79.

3. Bruce A. Demarest and Richard J. Harpel, "Don Richardson's 'Redemptive Analogies' and the Biblical Idea of Revelation," *Bibliotheca Sacra*, July–September 1989, 330–40.

4. Ibid., 333.

5. Ibid., 335.

6. Don Richardson, *Eternity in Their Hearts*, 2d ed. (Ventura, Calif.: Regal, 1984), 59.

7. Ibid.

8. Ibid., 41.

Chapter 7: The Challenge of Religious Pluralism

1. Lisa Miller, "The Age of Divine Disunity," subtitled appropriately, "Faith Now Springs from a Hodgepodge of Beliefs," *The Wall Street Journal,* 9 February 1999, B1, 2.

2. Ibid., B1.
3. Ibid. An example of the growing interest between Judaism and Buddhism is a conference named "The Jew and the Lotus" was held in the Philadelphia area in November 1995. See David O'Reilly, "Conference to Examine Jewish Ties to Buddhism," *The Philadelphia Inquirer,* 18 November 1995, B1, 3.
4. The celebration of the opening of the temple is described in Beverly M. Payton, "New Temple Offers an Oasis of Calm," *The Philadelphia Inquirer,* 28 August 1994, BC1–2.
5. A front-page photograph highlighted the celebration with the title "A New Temple Ushers in a Lunar New Year." The photograph was accompanied by an article on a later page: Ralph Cipriano, "Year Dawns on a New Roof," *The Philadelphia Inquirer,* 1 February 1995, B1, 4.
6. Alan Sipress, "Keeping Faith in Growing Numbers," *The Philadelphia Inquirer,* 25 July 1993, A-1, 10. The front-page article was accompanied by a photograph of Muslims at prayer in a local mosque.
7. Ibid., A-1.
8. Mary Otto, "American Muslims' Political Voice Rises," *The Philadelphia Inquirer,* 24 October 1998, A-3.
9. Elsa C. Arnett, "In D.C., a Symbol of Islam's Rising Clout," *The Philadelphia Inquirer,* 2 January 1998, A-26.
10. The corresponding titles and dates for these articles in *The Philadelphia Inquirer* are as follows: Lini S. Kadaba, "Praising Lord Krishna and Spring's Blissful Colors," 8 March 1998, H-1, 5; idem, "Hindu Deity Kali Honored—and Feared," 2 November 1997, H-7; Mary Beth McCauley, "Praying for the Gains of Other People," 4 January 1998, F-15; Saleema Syed, "Even for the College Student, Ramadan Is a Time for Holiness," 4 January 1998, F-15; Naomi Geschwind, "Reform Congregation Tests the Waters with a 'Mikveh,'" 8 November 1998, H-7; "Reflections on Belief in Reincarnation," 3 May 1998, H-5; "Reflecting on Reincarnation," 28 June 1998, H-5; "More on Agnosticism: "Who Else Can I Thank?" 12 October 1997, H-7, F-15; Maggie Galehouse, "Honoring Mothers Near, Far," 13 September 1998, H-7; Frank Wilson, "A Strengthening Link Between East and West," 25 October 1998; and Jim Remsen, "Better Living, Better Dying," 27 December 1998, F-19.
11. "For Ethnic Albanians, Religion Travels with Them to a New Country," *The Philadelphia Inquirer,* Saturday, 15 May 1999, A-2.
12. "Joining the Monastic Life," *The Philadelphia Inquirer,* Wednesday, 26 May 1999, A-2.
13. The quote is from an advertising brochure, "Religions of the World." The author of this 1999 text published by Prentice-Hall is Mary Pat Fisher.
14. Anthony Giddens, *The Consequences of Modernity* (Palo Alto: Stanford University Press, 1991), 6.
15. This description is based on Peter Berger's use of the term *cultural pluralism,* which he saw as one of the key elements of the modern era that contributed

to undermining religious belief and practice. By *cultural pluralism,* Berger referred to "the division of a society into subsocieties with more or less distinct cultural traditions" (*The Heretical Imperative* [Garden City: Doubleday, 1979], 59).

16. Published in 1993 by Harper San Francisco. Kamenetz was a participant in the conference alluded to in endnote 4.

17. Cited in Miller, "The Age of Divine Disunity," *The Wall Street Journal,* 9 February 1999, B1.

18. The *Wall Street Journal* weekend edition, 26 March 1999, cited in endnote 1, lists a sampling of religious Web sites available under the subtitle, "Soul Surfing."

19. "God Goes Online," *The Wall Street Journal* weekend edition, 26 March 1999, W1, 12. The expert cited was Charles Henderson, who is responsible for selecting the sites for Christianity on the Web browser <MiningCo.com.> The article discusses the role of technology in religion. It also raises questions about the changing nature of "religion" as a result of technology and the validity of faith and on-line worship without being physically present with other people.

20. Ibid.

21. David B. Barrett and Todd M. Johnson, "Annual Statistical Table on Global Mission: 1999," *International Bulletin of Missionary Research* 23, no. 1 (January 1999): 25.

22. Ibid. In the *World Christian Encyclopedia: A Comparative Survey of Churches and Religions in the Modern World, a.d. 1900–2000* (New York: Oxford Univ. Press, 1982), 126, Barrett defines *New Religionists* as "followers of the so-called 20th-century New Religions or radical new crisis religions (new Far Eastern or Asiatic indigenous non-Christian syncretistic mass religions embodying major innovations and new religious systems), including Japanese neo-Buddhist and neo-Shinto new religious movements."

23. Renee Schoof, "Growing Group Poses a Dilemma for China," *The Philadelphia Inquirer,* Tuesday, 23 April 1999, A-3.

24. Netland's comments are directed specifically toward explaining why Christian exclusivism has been rejected by outsiders and even by some people inside the church.

25. Ibid., 28–29.

26. Roger Trigg, "Religion and the Threat of Relativism," *Religious Studies* 19 (1983): 297. This article was first called to my attention in Harold A. Netland, *Dissonant Voices: Religious Pluralism and the Question of Truth* (Grand Rapids: Eerdmans, 1991), 29.

27. The sociologist Peter Berger and others called this phenomenon "cultural pluralism" (see his definition in n. 15; cf. Peter Berger, *The Heretical Imperative* [Garden City: Doubleday, 1979], 59).

28. Netland, *Dissonant Voices,* 30.

29. Ibid.

30. Harold A. Netland, "Truth, Authority and Modernity: Shopping for Truth

in a Supermarket of Worldviews," in *Faith and Modernity* (Oxford, U.K.: Regnum Books, 1994), 91. Newbigin's views can be found in *The Gospel in a Pluralist Society* (Grand Rapids: Eerdmans, 1989) and *Truth to Tell* (Grand Rapids: Eerdmans, 1991).

31. Netland, *Dissonant Voices,* 31–32.

32. Ibid., 32.

33. *Webster's Third New International Dictionary of the English Language Unabridged* (Springfield, Mass.: Merriam-Webster, 1993), 1745, defines this kind of society as one "in which members of diverse ethnic, racial, religious, or social groups maintain an autonomous participation in and development of their traditional culture or special interest within the confines of a common civilization."

34. Paul Schrotenboer, "Varieties of Pluralism," *Evangelical Review of Theology* 13, no. 2 (April 1989): 118, originally published in *The Reformed Ecumenical Council Theological Forum* (November 1988).

35. Ibid., italics in original.

36. Peter Berger, Brigitte Berger, and Hansfried Kellner, *The Homeless Mind: Modernization and Consciousness* (Garden City: Doubleday, 1973; reprint, (New York: Vintage Books, 1974), 184.

37. Because of the breadth of this subject and space limitations, I have opted for a brief overview of and response to religious pluralism, along with some suggestions on how the church should respond in light of this challenge. In-depth analyses of religious pluralism are found in D. A. Carson, *The Gagging of God* (Grand Rapids: Zondervan, 1996); Dennis L. Okholm and Timothy R. Phillips, eds., *Four Views on Salvation in a Pluralistic World* (Grand Rapids: Zondervan, 1996); Brad Stetson, *Pluralism and Particularity in Religious Belief* (Westport, Conn.: Praeger, 1994); Alister McGrath, *A Passion for Truth: The Intellectual Coherence of Evangelicalism* (Downers Grove, Ill.: InterVarsity, 1996); Ronald H. Nash, *Is Jesus the Only Savior?* (Grand Rapids: Zondervan, 1994); Netland, *Dissonant Voices;* Millard J. Erickson, *How Shall They Be Saved?* (Grand Rapids: Baker, 1996).

38. John Hick, "A Pluralist View," in *Four Views on Salvation in a Pluralistic World,* ed. Dennis L. Okholm and Timothy Phillips (Grand Rapids: Zondervan, 1995), 39.

39. Ibid., 47.

40. Paul F. Knitter, "Dialogue and Liberation: Foundations for a Pluralist Theology of Religions," *The Drew Gateway* 58, no. 1 (spring 1988), 2.

41. John Hick, "Whatever Path Men Choose Is Mine," in *Christianity and Other Religions* (Philadelphia: Fortress, 1981), 180–82.

42. Schrotenboer, "Varieties of Pluralism," 118.

43. John Hick and Paul F. Knitter, *The Myth of Christian Uniqueness* (Maryknoll, N.Y.: Orbis Books, 1987), ix–xii.

44. Hick, "A Pluralist View," 36, 51–59.

45. John Hick, *Problems of Religious Pluralism* (New York: St. Martin's Press, 1985), 34.

46. Hick, "Whatever Path Men Choose Is Mine," 188.
47. Hick, "A Pluralist View," 36–39.
48. Ibid., 41.
49. Wilfred Cantwell Smith, "An Attempt at Summation," *Christ's Lordship and Religious Pluralism* (Maryknoll, N.Y.: Orbis, 1981), 202. This and the following quote are also cited in Netland, *Dissonant Voices,* 302–03.
50. Paul F. Knitter, *No Other Name?* (Maryknoll, N.Y.: Orbis, 1985), 93. Knitter, like other pluralists, embraces the higher critical methodology described earlier, which challenges the historicity and accuracy of the New Testament documents.
51. Netland, *Dissonant Voices,* 32–33.
52. Ibid., 33.
53. For example, see Gordon D. Kaufman, *Systematic Theology: A Historicist Perspective* (New York: Scribner, 1968).
54. Netland, "Truth Authority and Modernity," 94; italics in original.
55. Ibid., 167. This critique of relativism is based primarily on Netland, *Dissonant Voices.* Dr. Netland was one of my doctoral mentors, and I'm grateful to this godly man for the influence of his careful scholarship on my life and thinking.
56. Ibid., 169. The problems with moral or ethical relativism are beyond the scope of this chapter. For a recent evangelical critique of moral relativism, see Francis J. Beckwith and Gregory Koukl, *Relativism: Feet Firmly Planted in Mid-Air* (Grand Rapids: Baker, 1998).
57. Ibid., 176–77.
58. To argue that conflicting ideas may somehow both be true violates the law of noncontradiction. Some pluralist writers argue that the law of noncontradiction is a form of Western logic that does not apply when discussing religious truth, which is of a higher order.
59. This idea is called "descriptive" or "cultural relativism." It is also a strongly debated topic among—depending on how it is defined—missionaries and cultural anthropologists. See Netland, *Dissonant Voices,* 167–69, for a brief, balanced discussion on cultural relativism. The debate on the limits of cultural relativism is more fully treated in Paul G. Hiebert, *Anthropological Insights for Missionaries* (Grand Rapids: Baker, 1985), 99–104.
60. Ibid., 176. Netland cites Roger Trigg, *Reason and Commitment* (Cambridge University Press: Cambridge, 1973), 123ff., to the effect that "What they [various groups] do in fact accept or reject ought to be a different question from what is worthy of acceptance or rejection."
61. John Hick, "Whatever Path Men Choose Is Mine," 172. The article was first published in an earlier version in *The Modern Churchman* (winter 1974).
62. Gavin D'Costa, *Theology and Religious Pluralism* (London: Basil Blackwell, 1986), 41. D. Z. Phillips carries moral relativism to this very extreme. He states that he would condemn the killing of a child by a neighbor, because our culture says this is wrong. He could not, however, condemn child sacrifice in a remote tribe, because he would not know the moral standards of

the tribe in question. Because truth and morals are relative to a given culture, murder is not the same as child sacrifice (*Faith and Philosophical Enquiry* [London: Shocken Books, 1970], 237; cited in Netland, *Dissonant Voices,* 173).

63. Netland, *Dissonant Voices,* 176–77.
64. Ibid., 177.
65. Eric J. Sharpe, *Understanding Religion* (New York: St. Martin's Press, 1983), 27.
66. Alister E. McGrath, *The Sunnier Side of Doubt* (Grand Rapids: Zondervan, 1990), 21–22.
67. Allan Bloom, *The Closing of the American Mind* (New York: Simon Schuster, 1987), 25–26.
68. Timothy D. Westergren, "Do All Roads Lead to Heaven? An Examination of Unitive Pluralism," in *Through No Fault of Their Own?* ed. William V. Crockett and James G. Sigountos (Grand Rapids: Baker, 1991), 178.
69. Maurice Cranston, "Tolerance," in *The Encyclopedia of Philosophy,* vol. 8, ed. Paul Edwards (New York: Macmillan, 1967), 143. This definition was first called to my attention in Netland, *Dissonant Voices,* 307.
70. S. D. Gaede, *When Tolerance Is No Virtue: Political Correctness, Multiculturalism, and the Future of Truth and Justice* (Downers Grove, Ill.: InterVarsity, 1993), 79.
71. Ibid., 27.
72. Beckwith and Koukl, *Relativism: Feet Firmly Planted in Mid-Air,* 69.
73. Cf. Hick's article, "Jesus and the World Religions," in *The Myth of God Incarnate,* ed. John Hick (London: SCM, 1977), 172. I have found Hick's candidness and honesty to be refreshing and personally challenging. As Carson notes (*The Gagging of God,* 321, n. 25), Hick displays a clarity of thought and intellectual rigor that is atypical of much contemporary pluralist scholarship.
74. See, for example, Carson, *The Gagging of God,* 315–345; I. Howard Marshall, *I Believe in the Historical Jesus* (Grand Rapids: Eerdmans, 1979); Craig Blomberg, *The Historical Reliability of the Gospels* (Downers Grove, Ill.: InterVarsity, 1987); and Millard J. Erickson, *The Word Became Flesh: A Contemporary Incarnational Christology* (Grand Rapids: Baker, 1991).
75. McGrath, *A Passion for Truth,* 229.
76. David F. Wells, *God in the Wasteland: The Reality of Truth in a World of Fading Dreams* (Grand Rapids: Eerdmans, 1994), 131–32.
77. I am indebted to Dr. Jim Lewis for calling this problem to my attention.
78. Sharpe, *Understanding Religion,* 28.
79. Stetson, *Pluralism and Particularity in Religious Belief,* 122.
80. Ibid., 123.
81. Ibid., 118ff.
82. Ibid., 124–5. Stetson ends his defense of exclusivism with a strong statement regarding its tolerance: "I am not convinced that religious exclusivism must necessarily be immoral, and Christian exclusivism in particular is conceptually ordered so as not to issue in the mistreatment of others. For the

Christian exclusivist, one's salvation is completely independent of—and in spite of—one's works or merit, and so any personal pride or personal sense of accomplishment in one's assumed salvation is wholly out of place. Likewise, anything but good will, humanistic concern, and the most fervent hopefulness for the salvation of those presently not trusting in Christ is inconsistent with what ought to be the attitude of those who have been freely forgiven of their sins."

83.   Carson, *The Gagging of God,* 27.
84.   Dennis L. Okholm and Timothy R. Phillips, ed., *More Than One Way? Four Views on Salvation in a Pluralistic World* (Grand Rapids: Zondervan 1995), 19; cf. also Netland, *Dissonant Voices,* 27.
85.   Millard J. Erickson, *How Shall They Be Saved? The Destiny of Those Who Do Not Hear of Jesus* (Grand Rapids: Baker, 1996), 61–62.
86.   Those who would argue the need for conscious faith in Christ include Carson, *The Gagging of God;* Ajith Fernando, *The Supremacy of Christ* (Westchester, Ill.: Crossway, 1995); Ramesh Richard, *The Population of Heaven* (Chicago: Moody), 1994; Ronald H. Nash, *Is Jesus the Only Savior?* (Grand Rapids: Zondervan, 1994); John Piper, *Let the Nations Be Glad! The Supremacy of God in Missions* (Grand Rapids: Baker, 1993). The two foremost evangelical "inclusivists," who suggest that God somehow transmits salvific truth through nature for those who never hear the name of Jesus, are Clark Pinnock, *A Wideness in God's Mercy: The Finality of Jesus Christ in a World of Religions* (Grand Rapids: Zondervan, 1992); John Sanders, *No Other Name: An Investigation into the Destiny of the Unevangelized* (Grand Rapids: Eerdmans, 1992). Alister McGrath refuses to speculate on the destiny of those who never heard, arguing that this decision belongs to God alone, in "A Particularist View: A Post-enlightenment Approach," in *Four Views on Salvation in a Pluralistic World* (Grand Rapids: Zondervan, 1996). The various positions are discussed and critiqued by proponents of the other positions, including religious pluralism, in the last-mentioned preceding text *(Four Views).* See also a similar but more popular approach in John Sanders, ed., *What About Those Who Have Never Heard?* (Downers Grove, Ill.: InterVarsity, 1995). This volume is limited to debate among evangelicals about the destiny of the unevangelized.
87.   Netland, *Dissonant Voices,* 28. Netland writes as an evangelical who defends the exclusivist position. He is here raising the question from the standpoint of the average North American who does not want to make such judgments.
88.   Carson, *The Gagging of God,* 516. He sees this issue as "a test case for assessing the changing face of evangelicalism. . . ."
89.   J. I. Packer, "The Problem of Eternal Punishment," *Crux* 26, no. 3 (September 1990), 22–23. See James Davison Hunter's discussion and analysis regarding the discomfort of evangelicals with the biblical teaching of hell in *Evangelicalism: The Coming Generation* (Chicago: Univ. of Chicago Press, 1987), 33–47. Hunter evaluated the responses of seminarians in a 1982 Evangelical Academy Project. Students indicated sensitivity to the "socially

offensive nature of their views" of salvation and what happens after death. "Virtually half (46%) felt that under most circumstances or even all circumstances, to emphasize to nonbelievers that they will be eternally damned in hell if they do not repent of their sins' was in 'poor taste'" (ibid., 40). Hunter concluded that this data "minimally represents a softening of earlier doctrinal certainties. Of their own salvation, they are confident. It is with regard to the salvation of others that there is ambiguity and doubt. The certainties characteristic of previous generations appear to be giving way to a measure of hesitancy and questioning" (ibid.) When in 1993, eleven years later, evangelical seminarians were asked a similar question as to whether it is "in poor taste when sharing the gospel to emphasize damnation and repentance," 41.9 percent agreed, "either always or under most circumstances" (Wells, *God in the Wasteland*, 198).

90. Ibid., 25.
91. "What Does It Mean to Be Evangelical?" *Christianity Today* 33, no. 9 (16 June 1989): 60, 63.
92. For example, see D. A. Carson, *The Gagging of God*, chap. 13; John Blanchard, *Whatever Happened to Hell?* (Durham, England: Evangelical Press, 1993); Larry Dixon, *The Other Side of the Good News* (Wheaton, Ill.: Victor, 1992); Gary R. Habermas and J. P. Moreland, *Immortality: The Other Side of Death* (Nashville: Nelson, 1992); Jerry L. Walls, *The Logic of Damnation* (Notre Dame, Ind.: Univ. of Notre Dame, 1992); Ajith Fernando, *Crucial Questions About Hell* (Westchester, Ill.: Crossway, 1991); Timothy R. Phillips, "A Christological Reflection," in *Through No Fault of Their Own: The Fate of Those Who Have Never Heard*, ed. William V. Crockett and James G. Sigountos (Grand Rapids: Baker, 1991), 47-59; Leon Morris, "Eternal Punishment," in *Evangelical Dictionary of Theology*, ed. Walter A. Elwell (Grand Rapids: Baker, 1984), 369-370. For a recent discussion of universalism and hell, see Nigel M. de S. Cameron, ed., *Universalism and the Doctrine of Hell* (Grand Rapids: Baker, 1992).
93. See the insightful book by Stephen L. Carter, *The Culture of Disbelief: How American Law and Politics Trivialize Religious Devotion* (New York: Basic Books, 1993).
94. See the comments of Okholm and Phillips, *Four Views on Salvation in a Pluralistic World*, 10-12.
95. Peter Berger, *A Far Glory: The Quest for Faith in an Age of Credulity* (New York: Doubleday, 1993), 41-43.
96. Berger, Berger, and Kellner, *The Homeless Mind*, 165.
97. Os Guinness, *Dining with the Devil* (Grand Rapids: Baker, 1993), 55-59.
98. Wells, *God in the Wasteland*, 195.
99. Ibid., 196.
100. George Barna, *What Americans Believe: An Annual Survey of Values and Religious Views in the United States* (Ventura, Calif.: Regal, 1991), 29.
101. George Barna, *Absolute Confusion: The Barna Report 1993-94* (Ventura, Calif.: Regal, 1993), 80.

102. Josh McDowell and Bob Hostetler, *Right from Wrong* (Dallas, Tex.: Word, 1994), 69.

103. George Barna, *Generation Next: What You Need to Know About Today's Youth* (Ventura, Calif.: Regal, 1995).

104. Ibid., 80.

105. See also the findings of James Davison Hunter, *American Evangelicalism: Conservative Religion and the Quandary of Modernity* (Piscataway, N.J.: Rutgers Univ. Press, 1983); idem, *Evangelicalism: The Coming Generation* (Chicago: Univ. of Chicago Press, 1987). Some of his data are reported later regarding the nature of witness in the New Testament.

106. See, for example, Carl H. Lundquist, *Silent Issues of the Church,* rev. ed. (Wheaton, Ill.: Victor, 1985); Bruce Barron, *The Health and Wealth Gospel* (Downers Grove, Ill.: InterVarsity, 1987); Herbert Schlossberg, *Idols of Destruction: Christian Faith and Its Confrontation with American Society* (Nashville: Nelson, 1983); Michael Scott, ed., *The Agony of Deceit* (Chicago: Moody, 1990); William D. Romanowski, *Pop Culture Wars: Religion and the Role of Entertainment in American Life* (Downers Grove, Ill.: InterVarsity, 1996).

107. For example, see D. A. Carson, "Appendix: When Is Spirituality Spiritual? Reflections on Some Problems of Definition," *The Gagging of God* (Grand Rapids: Zondervan, 1996), 555-69.

108. D. A. Carson, *The Gagging of God,* 42-44. See also the findings noted elsewhere in this chapter from the research of James Davison Hunter and George Barna.

109. See his trilogy: David F. Wells, *No Place or Truth* (Grand Rapids: Eerdmans, 1993); *God in the Wasteland* (Grand Rapids: Eerdmans, 1994); and *Losing Our Virtue: Why the Church Must Recover Its Moral Vision* (Grand Rapids: Eerdmans, 1998).

110. Bruce K. Camp, "Wake Up: You Can Energize Your Church for Missions," *World Christian* 12, no. 2 (June 1999), 26-27.

111. See Carson's chapters 5-7 regarding the Bible's "plotline," as he calls it. Carson develops the biblical plotline in response to the challenge of religious pluralism. Carson has also just published a new volume, *For the Love of God* (Westchester, Ill.: Crossway, 1998), that is designed to develop the plotline of the Bible, titled *For the Love of God* (Westchester, Ill.: Crossway, 1998).

112. Bruce Camp ("Wake Up," 28) suggests the following two resources for small-group study: Paul Borthwick, *Six Dangerous Questions* (Downers Grove, Ill.: InterVarsity, 1996)l; Camp's own study guide, Bruce Camp, *Discovering Our Place in His Plans* (Minneapolis, Minn.: NextStep Resources, 1999).

113. Wells, *No Place for Truth,* 259-60 (italics in original).

114. Hunter, *American Evangelicalism,* 17.

115. Ibid., 86-87.

116. Ibid., 87-91.

117. Wells, *God In the Wasteland,* 27.

118. Wells, *No Place for Truth,* 173.
119. Ibid., 277–78; italics in original.
120. A fine place to start would be with the work of A. A. Trites, *The New Testament Concept of Witness* (Cambridge: Cambridge Univ. Press, 1977). A related and more recent work that I have seen but not read is I. Howard Marshall and David Peterson, eds., *Witness to the Gospel: The Theology of Acts* (Grand Rapids: Eerdmans, 1998).
121. Netland, *Dissonant Voices,* 311.
122. Space does not allow us to discuss how to develop in-depth relationships with people from other faiths. A book that offers some helpful ideas and that was written explicitly for this purpose (although it is no longer in print) is Terry C. Muck, *Those Other Religions in Your Neighborhood: Loving Your Neighbor When You Don't Know How* (Grand Rapids: Zondervan, 1992).
123. Berger, *A Far Glory,* 146–48.
124. Space precludes any development of the relationship that exists between religious pluralism and postmodernism.
125. Nash, *Is Jesus the Only Savior?* 10; Carson, *The Gagging of God,* 10.
126. I am indebted to the following colleagues and friends for offering critiques of this chapter: Drs. Lynn Wallace, Donald and Martha MacCullough, David Stoner, Professor Jean Minto, and Mr. Jason Dexter.

Chapter 8: The Challenge of Postmodernism

1. Truth in missions must be guarded by the sending culture, and 3 John speaks of the receiving culture's responsibility.
2. Unless otherwise noted, all Scripture references and quotations are from the *New American Standard Bible* (La Habre, Calif.: The Lockman Foundation, 1972).
3. Immanuel Kant was a German philosopher, "the embodiment of the Enlightenment" during "a time when thinkers were struggling to free themselves from what they perceived as the bondage of authoritarian thinking, especially ecclesiastical." His three great *Critiques* "were designed to destroy false dependence upon unknowable absolutes and force man back on himself as the source of authority. Metaphysical realities cannot be known; we have only our subjective apprehensions of things." J. D. Douglas, Walter A. Elwell, and Peter Toon, eds., *The Concise Dictionary of the Christian Tradition* (Grand Rapids: Regency Reference Library, Zondervan, 1989), 214.
4. According to Mortimer J. Adler, the long history of religious and philosophical thinking contains "apparently unanimous agreement on the nature of truth." He explained, "just as everyone knows what a liar is, but not as readily whether someone is telling a lie, so the philosophers seem able to agree on what truth is, but not as readily on what is true." Whether the idea of truth is thought to correspond to reality, cohere with reality, or to participate in reality, Adler finds all thinkers concurring that the truth of ideas "depends on their conformity to reality." See Mortimer J. Adler, ed. *The Great Ideas:*

A Syntopicon of Great Books of the Western World, vol. 2 (Chicago: William Benton, 1952), 916; cited by Gordon R. Lewis, *Testing Christianity's Truth Claims* (Chicago: Moody, 1976), 19. Adler wrote this nearly half a century ago. Regardless of whether one accepts his analysis, it may be said that there is no longer agreement as to what truth is. The critical issue today is not what is *true* but what is *truth*.

5. Dennis McCallum, ed., *The Death of Truth* (Minneapolis: Bethany House, 1996), 24.

6. Ibid., 50–51.

7. Gene Edward Veith Jr., *Postmodern Times* (Wheaton, Ill.: Crossway, 1994), 193.

8. Ibid.

9. Allan Bloom, *The Closing of the American Mind* (New York: Simon and Shuster, 1987), 25.

10. *The Barna Report: What Americans Believe* (Ventura, Calif.: Regal, 1991), 83–85; cited by John D. Castelein, "Can the Restoration Movement Plea Survive If Belief in Objective Truth Is Abandoned?" *Stone-Campbell Journal* 1 (spring 1998): 27. Copan reads the Barna Report a little differently. He says that it found 66 percent of American adults didn't believe that absolute truth exists. He also *quotes* the report differently saying, "Specifically, they agreed that there is 'no such thing as absolute truth; two people could define truth in totally conflicting ways, but both could still be correct.'" See Paul Copan, *True for You, but Not for Me* (Minneapolis: Bethany House Publishers, 1998), 11.

11. Copan, *True for You, but Not for Me,* 11.

12. Veith Jr., *Postmodern Times,* 28.

13. Robert E. Fitch, "The Obsolescence of Ethics," *Christianity and Crisis: A Journal of Opinion* 19 (16 November 1959): 163–65; cited by Ravi Zacharias, "Being a Man of the Word," in *A Life of Integrity,* ed. Howard Hendricks (Sisters, Ore.: Multnomah Books, 1997), 60.

14. Carl F. H. Henry, *Carl Henry at His Best* (Portland: Multnomah), 203.

15. Harvey Cox, *Religion in the Secular City* (New York: Touchstone Book, published by Simon and Schuster, 1984), 49.

16. Andrew Delbanco, *The Death of Satan: How Americans Have Lost the Sense of Evil* (New York: Farrar, Straus, and Giroux, 1995), 107; cited by David F. Wells, *Losing Our Virtue* (Grand Rapids: Eerdmans, 1998), 126.

17. Publisher's "blurb" on inside front page of *Finding God at Harvard,* ed. Kelly Monroe (Grand Rapids: Zondervan, 1996).

18. Leith Anderson, "Theological Issues of 21st-Century Ministry," *Bibliotheca Sacra* 151 (April–June 1994): 138–39.

19. Scripture is clear on God and His Word being truth. Paul gives thanks to God for the believers in Thessalonica (and by application, all Christians) because God has chosen them "from the beginning for salvation through sanctification by the Spirit and *faith in the truth*" (2 Thess. 2:13). Whatever else this passage teaches, it tells us that truth is the object of saving faith. It

is not faith alone *(sola fidei)* that saves; it is faith *in the truth* alone *(sola fidei vero)* that saves. Faith of the greatest kind, if placed in Buddha, will not save. "It won't be Oh Buddha that's sittin' on the throne; It won't be ol' Mohammed that's callin' us home; It won't be Hari Krishna that plays that trumpet tune; No, we're goin' to see the Son, not Reverend Moon" (from the song "Oh Buddha" sung by the Imperials, on the album *Heed the Call* published by DaySpring, a division of Word, 1979).

20. Major theories or concepts of the *nature* of truth include the traditionally held "correspondence view," the "pragmatic view," the "coherence view," and the "performative view." See Norman L. Geisler and Paul D. Feinberg, *Introduction to Philosophy* (Grand Rapids: Baker, 1980), 235-51. A more recent modification that has received attention in later inerrancy debates may be called the "intentionality," or "functional," view of truth. See Norman L. Geisler, "The Concept of Truth in the Inerrancy Debate," *Bibliotheca Sacra* 137 (October–December 1980): 328, 337; John S. Feinberg, "Truth, Meaning and Inerrancy in Contemporary Evangelical Thought," *Journal of the Evangelical Theological Society* 26 (March 1983): 17-30.

21. Winfried Corduan, *Handmaid to Theology* (Grand Rapids: Baker, 1981), 10.

22. D. A. Carson, *The Gagging of God* (Grand Rapids: Zondervan, 1996), 182. Carson argues "against Kant, who (as we have seen) insists that one cannot by reason move from the phenomenal realm to the noumenal realm, . . . the apostle Paul is entirely prepared to infer from the created order God's exist-ence, power, and divine nature (Rom. 1:20). Nor is this merely a matter of abstract doctrine for him: it is also a matter of evangelistic strategy and apolo-getic. According to Luke's witness, Paul openly and repeatedly drew such connections when he was evangelizing Gentiles (Acts 14:15-18; 17:24-29)."

23. A. F. Holmes, "Truth," in *The Zondervan Pictorial Encyclopedia of the Bible*, 5 vols., ed. Merrill C. Tenney (Grand Rapids: Zondervan, 1976), 5:827.

24. John S. Feinberg, "Truth: Relationship of Theories of Truth to Hermeneu-tics," in *Hermeneutics, Inerrancy, and the Bible*, ed. Earl D. Radmacher and Robert D. Preus (Grand Rapids: Academie Books), 19.

25. Ibid., 18-19.

26. Walter A. Elwell, ed., *Baker Encyclopedia of the Bible*, 2 vols. (Grand Rapids: Baker, 1988), 2:2108 (emphasis mine).

27. Alister E. McGrath, *Understanding the Trinity* (Grand Rapids: Academie Books, 1988), 29.

28. John V. Dahms, "The Nature of Truth," *Journal of the Evangelical Theologi-cal Society* 28 (December 1985): 456. Dahms adds, "though the author of the Johannine gospel and epistles evinces such an interest in 'truth' and . . . such things to say about it that one may wonder whether he, at least, may not have had such an understanding."

29. Norman L. Geisler, "The Concept of Truth in the Inerrancy Debate," *Bibliotheca Sacra* 137 (October–December 1980): 331.

30. This of course is not to say that the Scriptures were inspired by "dictation."

31. Jack B. Scott, "Amen," in *Theological Wordbook of the Old Testament*, ed.

R. Laird Harris, Gleason L. Archer Jr., and Bruce K. Waltke (Chicago: Moody, 1990), 1:52.

32. R. W. L. Moberly, "Amen," in *New International Dictionary of Old Testament Theology and Exegesis,* ed. William A. VanGemeren (Grand Rapids: Zondervan, 1997): 1:429.

33. Scott, "Amen," in *Theological Wordbook of the Old Testament,* 1:53.

34. Ceslas Spicq, *Theological Lexicon of the New Testament,* 3 vols., trans. and ed. James D. Ernest (Peabody: Hendrickson, 1994), 1:67.

35. A. C. Thiselton, "Truth," in *The New International Dictionary of New Testament Theology,* 3 vols., ed. Colin Brown (Grand Rapids: Zondervan, 1978), 2:875.

36. Ibid.

37. Roger Nicole, "The Biblical Concept of Truth," in *Scripture and Truth,* ed. D. A. Carson and John D. Woodbridge (Grand Rapids: Zondervan, 1983), 293.

38. Thiselton, "Truth," in *The New Dictionary of New Testament Theology,* 3:891.

39. Ibid.

40. James Montgomery Boice, *Witness and Revelation in the Gospel of John* (Greenwood: Attic Press, 1970), 62.

41. See for example, D. M. Crump, "Truth," in *Dictionary of Jesus and the Gospels,* ed. Joel B. Green, Scot McKnight, and I. Howard Marshall (Downers Grove, Ill.: InterVarsity, 1992), 860; Thiselton, "Truth," in *The New International Dictionary of New Testament Theology,* 3:889–890; John Albert Bengel, *New Testament Word Studies,* 2 vols., trans. Charlton T. Lewis and Marvin R. Vincent (reprint, Grand Rapids: Kregel, 1971), 1:552; E. W. Hengstenberg, *Commentary on the Gospel of St. John,* 2 vols. (Edinburgh: T & T Clark, 1865; reprint, Minneapolis: Klock & Klock, 1980), 1:47.

42. D. M. Crump, "Truth," *Dictionary of Jesus and the Gospels,* ed. Joel B. Green, Scot McKnight, and I. Howard Marshall (Downers Grove, Ill.: InterVarsity, 1992), 861.

43. For example, see Rudolf Bultmann, "ἀλήθεια," in *Theological Dictionary of the New Testament,* vol. 1., ed. Gerhard Kittel, trans. and ed. Geoffrey W. Bromiley (Grand Rapids: Eerdmans, 1964), 1:238–249; H. Hubner, "ἀλήθεια," in *Exegetical Dictionary of the New Testament,* 3 vols., ed. Horst Balz and Gerhard Schneider (Grand Rapids: Eerdmans, 1990), 1:57–60.

44. Crump, "Truth," in *Dictionary of Jesus and the Gospels,* 861.

45. Henry Alford, *The Greek Testament,* 4 vols., rev. Everett F. Harrison (Chicago: Moody, 1958), 4:488; R. C. H. Lenski, *The Interpretation of the Epistles of St. Peter, St. John and St. Jude* (Minneapolis: Augsburg, 1966), 493; Donald W. Burdick, *The Letters of John the Apostle* (Chicago: Moody, n.d.) 313; D. Edmond Hiebert, *The Epistles of John* (Greenville: Bob Jones Univ. Press, 1991), 192–193; Stephen S. Smalley, *1, 2, 3 John,* Word Biblical Commentary (Waco: Word, 1984), 231.

46. Besides those passages already mentioned, Scripture gives numerous examples where the correspondence view of truth is used or presupposed. Joshua's

covenant with the Gibeonites was based on a falsehood (Josh. 9:4) by which Joshua was deceived (vv. 1–27). The Gibeonites claimed to be "from a far country" (v. 6), when in fact they were not (vv. 1–4). In Jeremiah's time, the people of Jerusalem are denounced for swearing "falsely" (Jer. 4:2). God says of the people of Judah, "they bend their tongue like their bow; lies and not truth prevail in the land" (9:3); "everyone deceives his neighbor, and does not speak the truth, they have set their tongue to speak lies" (v. 5); "through deceit they refuse to know Me" (v. 6). Ananias and Saphira learned the consequences of lying; their report to the apostles did not correspond to reality (Acts 5:1–11). Paul describes the devolution or fall of humankind, and finds the whole world guilty because "they exchanged the truth of God for a lie" (Rom. 1:25). In worshiping the creature rather than the Creator, they denied reality. Their worship was not true. Examples are multiple where truth is seen as the opposite of lies and falsehood (e.g., Rom. 9:1; 2 Cor. 4:2; 7:14; 11:10–13; 2 Thess. 2:11–12; 1 Tim. 2:7; 2 Tim. 3:13; 1 John 1:6–10). Passages also abound where truth claims are shown to be true or false depending on whether they accurately reflect reality (e.g., Num. 11:23; Deut. 13:2–14; 18:22; 22:20; Ruth 3:12; Josh. 9:15; 1 Kings 22:16; Isa. 48:1–3; Dan. 3:14; 6:12; 9:12–13; 11:2; Mark 5:33; John 1:14; 19:35–36; 2 Cor. 7:14; Titus 1:13–14).

47. See J. T. Reed, "Truth," in *Dictionary of the Later New Testament and Its Developments,* ed. Ralph P. Martin and Peter H. Davids (Downers Grove, Ill.: InterVarsity, 1997), 1186–1187.

48. These implications are also *biblically* supported, either directly or indirectly.

49. Francis A. Schaeffer, *The Complete Works of Francis A. Schaeffer,* 5 vols. (Westchester, Ill.: Crossway, 1982), 1:180.

50. Josh McDowell and Norm Geisler, *Love Is Always Right* (Dallas: Word, 1996), 22.

51. Norman L. Geisler and Ronald M. Brooks, *When Skeptics Ask* (Grand Rapids: Baker, 1990), 265.

52. Carl F. H. Henry, *Christian Countermoves in a Decadent Culture* (Portland: Multnomah, 1986), 110; cited by Erwin W. Lutzer, *Christ Among Other Gods* (Chicago: Moody, 1994), 54.

53. R. Scott Richards, *Myths the World Taught Me* (Nashville: Nelson, 1991), 67.

54. Augustine, *On Christian Doctrine,* trans. D. W. Robertson Jr. (Indianapolis: Bobbs-Merrill, 1958), 54; cited by D. Bruce Lockerbie, "A Call for Christian Humanism," *Bibliotheca Sacra* 143 (July–September 1986): 198.

55. Gordon R. Lewis, "Three Sides to Every Story," in *Interpretation and History,* ed. R. Laird Harris, Swee-Hwa Quek, and J. Robert Vannoy (Singapore: Christian Life Pub., 1986), 209.

56. Frank E. Gaebelein, *The Pattern of God's Truth* (Chicago: Moody, 1968).

57. Norman L. Geisler and Paul D. Feinberg, *Introduction to Philosophy* (Grand Rapids: Baker, 1980), 247.

58. After many years of teaching in Bible college and seminary, Jim Andrews is currently Senior Pastor of Lake Bible Church in Lake Oswego, Oregon.

59. Dorothy L. Sayers, "Creed or Chaos?" in *The Necessity of Systematic Theology*, 2d ed., ed. John Jefferson Davis (Grand Rapids: Baker, 1980), 30. The title of her article from which the quote was taken concisely summarizes her thesis: "Creed or Chaos?" The word *creed* derives from *credere* (Lat., "to believe"), and *credo* (Lat., "I believe"). If truth is not the object of our creed (i.e., what we believe), the alternative is chaos.

60. Josh McDowell and Bob Hostetler, *Right from Wrong* (Dallas: Word, 1994), 81.

61. R. Albert Mohler Jr., "'Evangelical': What's in a Name?" in *The Coming Evangelical Crisis*, ed. John Armstrong (Chicago: Moody, 1996), 39.

62. For an excellent critique of this view, see Norman L. Geisler, "The Concept of Truth in the Inerrancy Debate," *Bibliotheca Sacra* 137 (October–December 1980), 327–339.

63. James Oliver Buswell Jr., *A Systematic Theology of the Christian Religion*, 2 vols. in 1 (Grand Rapids: Zondervan, 1962), 1:19.

64. Norman L. Geisler and Ronald M. Brooks, *When Skeptics Ask* (Grand Rapids: Baker, 1990), 264.

65. Norman L. Geisler, "The Concept of Truth in the Inerrancy Debate," *Bibliotheca Sacra* 137 (October–December 1980): 333.

66. Richard A. Muller, *Dictionary of Latin and Greek Terms* (Grand Rapids: Baker, 1985), 326.

67. Ibid.

68. Ravi Zacharias, *Can Man Live Without God?* (Dallas: Word, 1994), 11.

69. Norman L. Geisler and Ronald M. Brooks, *Come, Let Us Reason* (Grand Rapids: Baker, 1990), 7. For an excellent treatment of this subject see J. P. Moreland, *Love Your God with All Your Mind: The Role of Reason in the Life of the Soul* (Colorado Springs: NavPress, 1997).

70. For discussions on this, see Frederic R. Howe, *Challenge and Response* (Grand Rapids: Zondervan, 1982); Ronald B. Mayers, *Both/And: A Balanced Apologetic* (Chicago: Moody, 1984). See also Ronald B. Mayers, "Both/And: A Biblical Alternative to the Presuppositional/Evidential Debate," in *Evangelical Apologetics*, ed. Michael Bauman, David C. Hall, and Robert C. Newman (Camp Hill, Pa.: Christian Pub., 1996).

71. *Imago Dei* is a Latin term meaning literally "image of God," sometimes *imago divina*, "divine image," and is used by theologians in reference to the likeness or resemblance to God in which man was originally created and which was lost, marred, or vitiated in the fall; *noetic* (from Gk. *noetikos*, "intellectual," and *noein*, "to perceive") relates to the mind or intellect and pertains to the view that knowledge comes through the intellect. See the related articles in this volume by Dr. Thomas Edgar, Dr. Henry Morris, and Dr. Paige Patterson.

72. I am indebted to Dr. Norman Geisler for this discussion. Indeed, the bulk of my discussion in this article is drawn from my class notes from a course on "Prolegomena" (Theology 409) taught by Dr. Geisler at Dallas Theological Seminary in 1981. Whatever value or merit there may be to my discussion I owe to Dr. Geisler. All mistakes of fact, logic, or otherwise are strictly my own.

73. Henry C. Thiessen, *Lectures in Systematic Theology,* rev. Vernon D. Doerksen (Grand Rapids: Eerdmans, 1979), 8.

74. Thomas Aquinas, *The Summa Theologica,* 2 vols., trans. Fathers of the English Dominican Province, rev. Daniel J. Sullivan (Chicago: Encyclopedia Britannica, 1952): 1:11.

75. Thomas C. Oden, *The Living God, Systematic Theology,* vol. 1 (San Francisco: Harper, 1987): 6.

76. Charles Hodge, *Systematic Theology,* 3 vols. (reprint, Grand Rapids: Eerdmans, 1975), 1:49.

77. John H. Gerstner, "Reason and Revelation," *Tenth: An Evangelical Quarterly* 9 (October 1979): 8.

78. William G. T. Shedd, *Dogmatic Theology,* 3 vols. (New York: Charles Scribner's Sons, 1889; reprint, Minneapolis: Klock & Klock, 1979), 1:47.

79. Ibid., 46.

80. Ronald H. Nash, *The Word of God and the Mind of Man* (Grand Rapids: Zondervan, 1982), 131–32.

81. The quotation from Pascal is found in Hank Hanegraff, *Counterfeit Revival* (Dallas: Word, 1997), 11, as cited by David J. MacLeod, "Counterfeit Revival: A Review Article," *The Emmaus Journal* 7 (summer 1998): 71.

82. In 2 Thessalonians 2:13–17, the apostle Paul emphatically associates "comfort" with "faith in the truth," "our gospel," and "the traditions you were taught."

83. C. S. Lewis, *Mere Christianity* (New York: Macmillan, 1952), 39.

84. Joel Belz, "Truth and Power," *World Magazine* 13 (18 July 1998): 4.

85. Benjamin B. Warfield, "Christianity the Truth," *Selected Shorter Writings of Benjamin B. Warfield II,* ed. John E. Meeter (Nutley: Presbyterian and Reformed, 1973), 216.

86. John Charles Ryle, *Knots Untied* (reprint, Cambridge: James Clarke, 1977), 43.

87. Os Guiness, *No God but God* (Chicago: Moody, 1992), 169.

88. Alister E. McGrath, "Doctrine and Ethics," *Journal of the Evangelical Theological Society* 34 (June 1991): 150.

89. Ibid.

90. Rollin T. Chafer, "Orthodoxy and the Truth," in *Truth for Today,* ed. John F. Walvoord (Chicago: Moody, 1963), 9.

Chapter 9: The Necessity of Theological Training for the Missionary

1. Unless otherwise noted, all Scripture references and quotations are from the *New American Standard Bible* (La Habre, Calif.: The Lockman Foundation, 1972).

2. Fritz Rienecker, *A Linguistic Key to the Greek New Testament,* ed. Cleon Rogers (Grand Rapids: Zondervan, 1976, 1980), 622.

3. "Islam," "Buddhism," "Hinduism" *Microsoft® Encarta® 97 Encyclopedia.* © 1993–1996 Microsoft Corporation. All rights reserved.

4. "Christianity, " *Microsoft® Encarta® 97 Encyclopedia.* © 1993–1996 Microsoft Corporation. All rights reserved.

5. "Roman Catholic Church," *Microsoft® Encarta® 97 Encyclopedia.* © 1993–1996 Microsoft Corporation. All rights reserved.

6. "Orthodox Church," *Microsoft® Encarta® 97 Encyclopedia.* © 1993–1996 Microsoft Corporation. All rights reserved.

7. Ronald J. Sider, *Rich Christians in an Age of Hunger* (Downers Grove, Ill.: InterVarsity, 1978), 455–46.

8. United States Census Bureau, "World Population Profile: 1998—Highlights." This information can be seen on the United States Census Bureau Web site at http://www.census.gov/ipc/www.wp98001.html.

9. Ibid. A note here from the USCB states, "The difference between this percentage and the percentage of global population change cited in the preceding paragraph (96%) is international migration from less developed to more developed countries."

10. Ross S. Bennett, ed., *Our World* (Washington, D.C.: National Geographic Society, 1979), 20–22.

11. "Faith in Africa" *Time,* 21 January 1980, 50.

12. Patrick Johnstone, *Operation World* (Grand Rapids: Zondervan, 1993), 117–18.

13. Joon Gon Kim, "New Life in Korea" *Asia Theological News* 5 (November 1979): 19.

14. Lorry Lutz, "A Church-Planting Seminary in Indonesia," *Asia Pulse* 13 (April 1980): 2.

15. C. Peter Wagner, "The Current Scene," *School of World Mission Newsletter* 3 (May 1980): 3.

16. Johnstone, *Operation World,* 65.

17. William R. Read, Victor M. Monterroso, and Harmon A. Johnson, *Latin American Church Growth* (Grand Rapids: Eerdmans, 1969), 219.

18. CAM International, "Annual Report," 1978.

19. Gustavo Gutierrez, *A Theology of Liberation* (Maryknoll, N.Y.: Orbis Books, 1973), 88.

20. Thomas More, *Utopia* (1516; reprint, New York: Simon and Schuster, 1965).

21. Gutierrez, *Theology of Liberation,* 9–10.

22. John S. Mbite, *New Testament Eschatology in an African Background* (London: Oxford Univ. Press, 1971), 185.

23. J. K. Agbeti, "African Theology: What It Is," *Presence* 5 (October 1972): 3.

24. Philip Turner, "The Wisdom of the Fathers and the Gospel of Christ: Some Notes on Christian Adaptation in Africa," *Journal of Religion in Africa* 4 (June 1971): 55.

25. Byang H. Kato, *Theological Pitfalls in Africa* (Kisumu, Kenya: Evangel, 1975), 55.

26. Harvey T. Hoekstra, *The World Council of Churches and the Demise of Evangelism* (Wheaton, Ill.: Tyndale, 1978), 19.

27. Arthur P. Johnston, *The Battle for World Evangelism* (Wheaton, Ill.: Tyndale, 1978), 358.

28. Roger C. Bassham, *Mission Theology: 1948–1975, Years of Worldwide Cre-*

ative Tension Ecumenical, Evangelical, and Roman Catholic (Pasadena, Calif.: William Carey Library, 1979), 331.

29. Clark H. Pinnock, "Hope for Theology and the Church in the Eighties," *Vanguard,* January–February 1980: 27.

30. For information on how to obtain Lausanne "Country Profiles," write MARC, 919 West Huntington Drive, Monrovia, CA 91016.

31. Both the book *Operation World* and the set of cards *Pray for 52 Spiritually Needy Nations* are available from OM Publishing, Box 28, Waynesboro, GA 30830-0028.

32. Wakatama goes so far as to limit the number of schools to one (Pius Wakatama, *Independence for the Third World Church: An African's Perspective on Missionary Work* [Downers Grove, Ill.: InterVarsity, 1976], 64.)

33. Ibid., 80.

34. Lutz, "A Church-Planting Seminary in Indonesia," 2.

Chapter 10: Women on the Mission Field

1. Dana L. Robert, *American Women in Mission* (Macon, Ga.: Mercer Univ. Press, 1997), 5.

2. Ibid., 10.

3. Ibid., 25.

4. Ibid., 37.

5. Ibid.

6. Ruth A. Tucker, *From Jerusalem to Irian Jaya* (Grand Rapids: Zondervan, 1983), 231.

7. Robert, *American Women in Mission,* 229–30.

8. Francis Schaeffer, *The Great Evangelical Disaster* (Westchester, Ill.: Crossway, 1984), 60.

9. Ibid., 44–45.

10. Keith Haywood, letter to author, 7 July, 1999.

11. *The Role of Women in AIM International,* I. C. Report (Pearl River, N.Y.: African Inland Mission International, May 1993), App. D.

12. Raymond C. Ortlund Jr., "Male-Female Equality and Male Headship," in *Recovering Biblical Manhood and Womanhood: A Response to Evangelical Feminism,* ed. John Piper and Wayne Grudem (Wheaton, Ill.: Crossway, 1991), 95.

13. Ibid.

14. Ibid.

15. Ibid., 98.

16. Carl Schultz, "*'ēzer,*" in *Theological Wordbook of the Old Testament,* 2 vols., ed. R. Laird Harris, Gleason L. Archer Jr., and Bruce K. Waltke (Chicago: Moody, 1980), 2:661.

17. Ortlund Jr., "Male-Female Equality and Male Headship," 101–102.

18. Mary A. Kassian, *Women, Creation and the Fall* (Wheaton, Ill.: Crossway, 1990), 18–19.

19. Robert D. Culver, "māshal," in *Theological Wordbook of the Old Testament,*

2 vols., ed. R. Laird Harris, Gleason L. Archer Jr., and Bruce K. Waltke (Chicago: Moody, 1980), 1:534.

20. Vern Sheridan Poythress, "The Church as Family: Why Male Leadership in the Family Requires Male Leadership in the Church," in *Recovering Biblical Manhood and Womanhood: A Response to Evangelical Feminism,* ed. John Piper and Wayne Grudem (Wheaton, Ill.: Crossway, 1991), 233.

21. Ibid., 239.

22. Ibid., 235.

23. Walter Bauer, *A Greek-English Lexicon of the New Testament and Other Early Christian Literature,* 2d ed., rev. F. W. Gingrich and Frederick Danker, trans. William F. Arndt and F. Wilbur Gingrich (Chicago: Univ. of Chicago Press, 1957, 1979), 184.

24. Douglas Moo, "What Does It Mean Not to Teach or Have Authority Over Men?" in *Recovering Biblical Manhood and Womanhood,* ed. John Piper and Wayne Grudem (Wheaton, Ill.: Crossway, 1991), 185.

25. Ibid., 187.

26. John Piper and Wayne Grudem, "An Overview of Central Concerns," in *Recovering Biblical Manhood and Womanhood,* ed. John Piper and Wayne Grudem (Wheaton, Ill.: Crossway, 1991), 71–72.

27. H. Wayne House, *The Role of Women in Ministry Today* (Nashville: Nelson, 1990), 148.

Chapter 11: Demonology and the Mission Field

1. This chapter is dedicated to my good friend, Kenneth Hanna, former department chairman and professor of World Missions at Moody Bible Institute. Ken was originally to write this chapter. When he continued to battle with a recovery from a liver transplant, major intestinal surgery, and finally cancer, the editor asked if I would write this chapter for him. Ken and I have spent many hours together discussing the subject of missions and spiritual warfare, and we have always shared overall agreement on the matter. I deeply regret that he could not write this material from the wealth of his twenty-five years of experience as a missionary in Mexico and Central America with CAM International. Ken died in September 1999.

2. "After healing and words of knowledge, exorcism is an essential ingredient of the Signs and Wonders movement." Timothy Strafford, *Christianity Today,* 8 August 1986, 21.

3. Mark I. Bubeck, *The Adversary: The Christian Versus Demonic Activity* (Chicago: Moody, 1975); C. Fred Dickason, *Demon Possession and the Christian* (Wheaton, Ill.: Crossway, 1988); and Merrill F. Unger, *What Demons Can Do to Saints* (Chicago: Moody, 1977).

4. The intent is not to blame solely evangelical missionaries for this problem; evangelical scholars and theologians are equally guilty.

5. D. E. Aune, "Exorcism," in *International Standard Bible Encyclopedia,* ed. G. W. Bromiley (Grand Rapids: Eerdmans, 1979), 2:243–44.

6. Thomas Ice and Robert Dean Jr., *Overrun by Demons: The Church's Pre-*

occupation with the Demonic (formerly entitled, *A Holy Rebellion: Strategy for Spiritual Warfare*) (Eugene, Ore.: Harvest House, 1990), 30. Now available from Kregel Publications, *What the Bible Teaches About Spiritual Warfare.*

7. John Wimber and Kevin Springer, *Power Healing* (San Francisco: Harper and Row, 1987), 233.

8. Dickason, *Demon Possession,* 192.

9. The counselor is Rita Cabezas, cited with favor by C. Peter Wagner in C. Peter Wagner and F. Douglas Pennoyer, eds., *Wrestling with Dark Angels: Toward a Deeper Understanding of the Supernatural in Spiritual Warfare* (Ventura, Calif.: Regal, 1990), 84.

10. Unger, *What Demons Can Do,* 109.

11. It is interesting to note that immediately after these verses that warn against listening to information gained by spiritistic practices (Deut. 18:9–14), God lays out the promise of the New Moses (i.e., the Messiah), to whom everyone must listen (Deut. 18:15). We either listen to the Word of God and Christ or demons. It cannot be both.

12. For more discussion on epistemology and spiritual warfare, see John F. Hart, "A Review of *Confronting the Powers,*" *Journal of Grace Evangelical Society* 10 (spring 1997): 27–30.

13. For a critique of the "scientizing" of demonology, see the discussion by Robert J. Priest, Thomas Campbell, and Bradford A. Mullen, "Missiological Syncretism: The New Animistic Paradigm," in *Spiritual Powers and Mission: Raising the Issues,* ed. Edward Rommen (Pasadena, Calif.: William Carey Library, 1995), 26–36. The authors interact by collecting data from either demons themselves or from practitioners of other religions.

14. C. Peter Wagner, *Warfare Prayer* (Ventura, Calif.: Regal, 1992), 143–60.

15. Art Moore, "Spiritual Mapping Gains Credibility Among Leaders," *Christianity Today,* 12 January 1998, 55.

16. C. Peter Wagner, *Breaking Strongholds in Your City: How to Use Spiritual Mapping to Make Your Prayers More Strategic, Effective and Targeted* (Ventura, Calif.: Regal, 1993), 12.

17. Ibid.

18. George Otis Jr., *The Last of the Giants* (Grand Rapids: Chosen Books, 1991), 96–100.

19. Wagner brought with him into the United Prayer Track his Spiritual Warfare Network. Wagner, *Breaking Strongholds,* 12; C. Peter Wagner, *Confronting the Powers: How the New Testament Church Experienced the Power of Strategic-Level Warfare* (Ventura, Calif.: Regal, 1996), 30.

20. Wagner, *Confronting the Powers,* 20.

21. Wagner, *Breaking Strongholds,* 12.

22. Wagner attributes the beginning emphasis on "territorial spirits" to a 1988 address at Fuller Seminary by Timothy Warner, former professor of missions at Trinity Evangelical Divinity School. C. Peter Wagner, "Territorial Spirits," *Wrestling with Dark Angels: Toward a Deeper Understanding of the*

Supernatural in Spiritual Warfare, ed. C. Peter Wagner and F. Douglas Pennoyer (Ventura, Calif.: Regal, 1990), 74.

23.   K. Neill Foster with Paul L. King, *Binding and Loosing: Exercising Authority over the Dark Powers* (Camp Hill, Pa.: Christian Pub., 1998), 257.

24.   Priest, Campbell, and Mullen, "Missiological Syncretism," 73.

25.   Ibid. Priest, Campbell, and Mullen favor viewing the princes of Persia and Greece as human agents.

26.   In the case of Saul, even his servants perceived that the evil spirit was sent from God (1 Sam. 16:15). In my view, Saul was an Old Testament believer. The statement that "God changed his heart" (1 Sam. 10:9) is a good, Old Testament description of new birth by faith. But Saul was not demon possessed. The Hebrew is careful to portray each of the incidents when an evil spirit attacked Saul as coming "on" him rather than coming "into" him. Ice and Dean, *Overrun by Demons,* 125.

27.   Cf. the comment of John MacArthur Jr., *How to Meet the Enemy: Arming Yourself for Spiritual Warfare* (Colorado Springs: Chariot Victor, 1992), 31.

28.   Clinton E. Arnold, *Three Crucial Questions About Spiritual Warfare* (Grand Rapids: Baker, 1997), 73–141; Dickason, *Demon Possession* (the entire book is devoted to the subject); Warner, *Spiritual Warfare,* 83–86; Mark I. Bubeck, *The Adversary: The Christian Versus Demon Activity* (Chicago: Moody, 1975), 87–92.

29.   Unger, *What Demons Can Do,* 69. According to a letter written to K. Neill Foster, Unger had a previous background in Foursquare Pentecostalism before becoming dispensational. Foster, *Binding and Loosing,* 65 n. 1. To what degree this played into his conversion to Pentecostal-type views of exorcism and demon possession is not known.

30.   Ibid.

31.   Alex Konya, *Demons: A Biblically Based Perspective* (Schaumburg, Ill.: Regular Baptist Press, 1990), 89.

32.   Dickason, *Demon Possession,* 261–67; cf. also Bubeck, *Adversary,* 41–42. Note that a cessationist view of sign gifts is not essential to dispensationalism (many covenant theologians are cessationists) but is quite natural and consistent with a dispensational handling of Scripture.

33.   Ibid., 264.

34.   Ibid., 263. But consider Konya's evaluation: "It is neither logical nor consistent with the New Testament pattern to separate the ability to cast out demons with the ability to heal miraculously the sick in general." Konya, *Demons,* 81.

35.   For a fuller development of the relationship of Jesus' exorcisms to the kingdom, see Konya, *Demons,* 41–46.

36.   Arnold, *Three Crucial Questions,* 78–81; Timothy M. Warner, *Spiritual Warfare: Victory over the Powers of This Dark World* (Wheaton, Ill.: Crossway, 1991), 79–80; Dickason, *Demon Possession,* 37–38; Unger, *What Demons Can Do,* 86–87; Ed Murphy, *The Handbook for Spiritual Warfare,* revised and updated (Nashville: Nelson, 1996), 49–51; Wimber and Springer, *Power*

Healing, 109–10; Jim Logan, *Reclaiming Surrendered Ground: Protecting Your Family from Spiritual Attacks* (Chicago: Moody, 1995), 31–32.

37. *Webster's Ninth New Collegiate Dictionary* (Springfield, Mass: Merriam-Webster, 1986), 918.

38. A literal translation of the Greek phrase is "to have a demon/spirit." NRSV translates the Greek literally: "He has Beelzebul" (Mark 3:22) or "he has a spirit" (9:17).

39. Dickason, *Demon Possession,* 37; cf. Wimber and Springer, *Power Healing,* 109.

40. Moises Silva, *Biblical Words and Their Meaning* (Grand Rapids: Zondervan, 1983), 44–51; Silva states earlier, "When a discussion depends primarily or solely on the vocabulary, one may conclude either that the writer is not familiar with the contents of Scripture or that Scripture itself says little or nothing on the subject" (p. 22). The Scriptures have much to say about the subject of demon possession.

41. Wimber and Springer, *Power Healing,* 109.

42. Brent Grimsley and Elliot Miller, "Can a Christian Be 'Demonized'?" *Christian Research Journal* 16 (summer 1993): 17.

43. Arnold, *Three Crucial Questions,* 101; and Unger, *What Demons Can Do,* 98.

44. Wimber and Springer, *Power Healing,* 109–10.

45. Unger, *What Demons Can Do,* 106.

46. Ibid., 146, Dickason, *Demon Possession,* 288. To be consistent in their belief, many deliverance counselors would have to suspect that Paul's experience in Romans 7 describes demon possession. He struggled with obsessive (sexual?) lust (vv. 7–8), had a sense of "bondage" to his sins (vv. 14, 23), had a poor self-image (v. 18: "I know that nothing good dwells in me"), and had thoughts that bordered on suicide (v. 24).

47. Arnold, *Three Crucial Questions,* 87; Anderson, *Bondage Breaker,* 174; and Dickason, *Demon Possession,* 45.

48. "There may be degrees of deliverance or freedom from the power of the enemy." Ibid., 343.

49. Warner, *Spiritual Warfare,* 85.

50. That these two Greek words are synonymous is suggested by the parallel passage concerning demon possession in which the two different words are employed (Matt. 17:21 [majority text] with Mark 9:29).

51. Two of the references speak of the unique possession of Judas by Satan whereby he manipulated the betrayer of Christ before the Passion event (Mark 22:3; John 13:27).

52. Hermann Hanse, "ἔχω," in *Theological Dictionary of the New Testament,* ed. Gerhard Kittel, trans. Geoffrey W. Bromiley (Grand Rapids: Eerdmans, 1965), 2:821–22.

53. That *daimonizomai* is equivalent to the phrase, "to have *(echein)* a demon" is confirmed by comparing their parallel use in Luke 8:27, 36 and John 10:20, 21. For Luke and John, the two phrases for *demon possession* are virtually interchangeable.

54. Anderson, *Bondage Breaker*, 175; and cf. Jacques Theron, "A Critical Over-
     view of the Church's Ministry of Deliverance from Evil Spirits," *PNEUMA:
     The Journal for the Society of Pentecostal Studies* 18 (spring 1996): 87.
55. Dickason, *Demon Possession*, 124.
56. Ibid.
57. Even these English translations do not require the understanding that a
     spirit caused the sickness by indwelling the woman.
58. Dickason, *Demon Possession*, 124.
59. One may include "tormented [Gk., *ochleō*] by evil spirits" (Acts 5:16). Be-
     cause the people were miraculously healed by the apostles and because a re-
     lated word *(enochleō)* is used of demonic inhabitation in Luke 6:18, the Acts
     reference appears to be speaking of demon possession. Konya, *Demons*, 23.
60. Walter L. Liefeld ("Luke," in *Expositor's Bible Commentary*, ed. Frank E.
     Gaebelein [Grand Rapids: Zondervan, 1984], 8:971) makes note of Jesus'
     previous methods for healing and casting out demons but rejects the laying
     on of hands as evidence that the woman was demon possessed. Jesus' use of
     laying hands on someone for physical healing is found in Mark 5:23; 6:5;
     8:23, 25; Luke 4:40; cf. Mark 16:18.
61. Even if *spirit of weakness* should be interpreted as a demon, the phrase yields
     no indication that the demon's name was "Weakness" or "Infirmity," as
     some people might suggest.
62. Cf. Luke's use of the unmodified word *spirit* in 9:39 with "I begged your
     disciples to cast it out" (v. 40) and "the demon" (v. 42); in 10:20 with "the
     demons are subject to us" (v. 17); in 11:26 with "seven other spirits more
     evil" (v. 26). Cf. *spirit* in Acts 16:18 with "I command you . . . to come out
     of her!" (v. 18).
63. Unmodified references that could involve angels as well as demons include
     such verses as "thought that they were seeing a spirit" (Luke 24:37); "a
     spirit does not have flesh and bones" (Luke 24:39); "the Sadducees say that
     there is no resurrection, nor an angel, nor a spirit" (Acts 23:8); "suppose a
     spirit or an angel has spoken to him" (Acts 23:9).
64. For Luke, phrases that contain close modifiers include "the spirit of an
     unclean demon" (Luke 4:33); "unclean spirit(s)" (Luke 4:36; 6:18; 8:29;
     9:42; 11:24; Acts 5:16; 8:7); "evil spirit(s)" (Luke 7:21; 8:2; Acts 19:12–13,
     15–16); "having a spirit of divination" (Acts 16:16; NIV, "had a spirit by
     which she predicted the future").
65. When a demon causes some form of illness or physical disease, the Greek
     construction is never a genitive construction, such as "the spirit of . . ." or
     "the demon of . . ." Cf. Greek constructions where demons caused their
     victims to be mute (Matt. 9:33; Luke 11:14) or blind (Matt. 12:22).
66. John Nolland, *Luke 9:21–18:34*, in *Word Biblical Commentary* (Dallas: Word,
     1993), 35b:725–26; for the same view, see Wilkinson, "The Case of the
     Bent Woman," 203–4.
67. David Powlison, *Power Encounters: Reclaiming Spiritual Warfare* (Grand
     Rapids: Baker, 1995), 65-67.

68. Nolland, *Luke 9:21–18:34,* 726.
69. Dickason, *Demon Possession,* 124.
70. John Wilkinson, "The Case of the Bent Woman in Luke 13:10–17," *Evangelical Quarterly* 49 (1977):202.
71. Grimsley and Miller, "Can a Christian Be 'Demonized'?" 18; John A. Martin, "Luke," *Bible Knowledge Commentary, New Testament,* ed. John F. Walvoord and Roy B. Zuck (Wheaton, Ill.: Victor, 1983), 252; and Liefeld, "Luke," 1008.
72. Cf. I. Howard Marshall, *The Gospel of Luke: A Commentary on the Greek Text* (Grand Rapids: Eerdmans, 1978), 698.
73. Bauer, Arndt, Gingrich, and Danker do not include a category for *thugater* ("daughter") that would imply a spiritual condition of faith or salvation. Instead, they list Luke 13:16 along with 1:5 ("daughters of Aaron") as describing a general (biological) relationship. Walter Bauer, "thugater," in *A Greek-English Lexicon of the New Testament and Other Early Christian Literature,* 2d ed., rev. F. W. Gingrich and Frederick Danker, trans. William F. Arndt and F. W. Gingrich (Chicago: Chicago Univ. Press, 1979), 364–65.
74. Liefeld, "Luke," 971.
75. See the preceding discussion under "'Demonized' or 'Demon possession'?"
76. Grimsley and Miller, "Can a Christian Be 'Demonized'?" 18.
77. J. Ramsey Michaels, "Jesus and the Unclean Spirits," in *Demon Possession,* ed. John Warwick Montgomery (Minneapolis: Bethany House, 1976), 53.
78. Arnold, *Three Crucial Questions,* 81.
79. Michaels, "Jesus and the Unclean Spirits," 55.
80. Ibid., 54.
81. Arnold, *Three Crucial Questions,* 88. Cf. also Murphy, *Spiritual Warfare,* 432–33; and Unger, *What Demons Can Do,* 103.
82. Arnold, *Three Crucial Questions,* 88. Arnold also reasons that Ephesians contains extensive spatial language.
83. From his opening chapter, Logan's entire book is developed around this meaning of Ephesians 4:27. Logan, *Reclaiming Surrendered Ground,* 13–14.
84. Arnold, *Three Crucial Questions,* 89.
85. To use the sense of "opportunity" in the Ephesians 4:26–27 context seems quite natural because of the similar use of *topos* in Romans 12:19. Ephesians speaks of man's wrath, and Romans speaks of God's wrath. Believers must give a "place" to or an opportunity for God's wrath (lit., "give place to wrath"). By carrying out our anger and revenge, we fail to give God an opportunity to work and instead give Satan an opportunity to work.
86. Bauer et al., *Greek-English Lexicon,* 823.
87. Grimsley and Miller, "Can a Christian Be 'Demonized'?" 37; and Powlison, *Power Encounters,* 128.
88. Some people have concluded that the question of a Christian's being demon possessed cannot be clearly decided based on the Bible. Dickason, *Demon Possession,* 147. But because this issue bears on the very essence of Christian living and sanctification, and because the Bible is the guidebook on the

demonic realm, that the exegesis and/or theology of the Bible do not give us an answer on the matter would be highly unlikely.

89. To draw lessons about demonic influence from Romans 6, as Arnold does, is pure eisegesis. Anything related to evil spirits is completely absent from—if not avoided in—the entire chapter. Arnold, *Three Crucial Questions*, 90–91.

90. Clinton E. Arnold, *Powers of Darkness: Principalities and Powers in Paul's Letters* (Downers Grove, Ill.: InterVarsity, 1992), 33.

91. It is interesting to note that no mention of demon possession occurs in the entire book of Revelation, even though demons and Satan are dramatically active in the future Tribulation period.

92. Contra Arnold (*Three Crucial Questions*, 92), who speculates, "Because of the background of the people becoming Christians in Ephesus, I am convinced that at least part of Paul's ministry of exorcism in that city was to new believers."

93. Dickason, *Demon Possession*, 154–56, 307–9, 340; On one occasion, Dickason (p. 135) asked a demon in a Christian "if he [i.e., the demon] had used the concept that Christians cannot be inhabited by demons. He replied, 'Oh yes! We use it all the time. It is one of the best tools we have ever promoted.'" Apparently, Dickason believes that this theological truth, which the Holy Spirit did not reveal in the Bible, can be learned with confidence from demonic spirits in "clinical research."

94. This is why Dickason's objection is not valid: "When one states that a genuine believer can never be demonized, he must produce a clear statement from the Bible that says so specifically. If he does not have such a statement, then he is in a predicament." Dickason, *Demon Possession*, 78.

95. I have borrowed this terminology from Zane Hodges, "An Argument from Silence, and All of That: Repentance Reconsidered," *Grace in Focus* 13 (May–June 1998): 1.

96. Konya, *Demons*, 97–98.

97. Warner, *Spiritual Warfare*, 86; and Arnold, *Three Crucial Questions*, 86.

98. Logan, *Reclaiming Surrendered Ground*, 77–84.

99. Unger, *What Demons Can Do*, 105.

100. Murphy, *Spiritual Warfare*, 438–39, 449–62. "Of the six major doors through which demons attach themselves to the lives of human beings, the door of child abuse is perhaps the most common . . ." Ibid., 449.

101. Dysfunctional home life, demonic transference through sexual relations, and sexual sins are found in Murphy, *Spiritual Warfare*, 440–44.

102. Unger, *What Demons Can Do*, 75.

103. Dickason, *Demon Possession*, 232.

104. "Scripture, however, never says a word about the cause of demonization." Powlison, *Power Encounters*, 41. "In fact, there is *no* direct teaching *anywhere* in the New Testament concerning how to determine demon possession" (italics original). Konya, *Demons*, 99.

105. Anderson, *Bondage Breaker*, 21; Logan, *Reclaiming Surrendered Ground*, 31; and Dickason, *Demon Possession*, 81.

106. Ice and Dean, *Overrun by Demons,* 119; cf. Powlison, *Power Encounters,* 41.

107. Warner, *Spiritual Warfare,* 51, 58; Dickason, *Demon Possession,* 256, 267, 273, 300; Anderson, *Bondage Breaker,* 64–67; Murphy, *Spiritual Warfare,* 394; and Foster, *Binding and Loosing,* 114–16.

108. Wagner, *Confronting the Powers,* 138, 159; and Arnold, *Three Crucial Questions,* 105–6.

109. Dickason, *Demon Possession,* 273.

110. Ibid., 256.

111. Warner, *Spiritual Warfare,* 58.

112. Hart, "Review of *Confronting the Powers,*" 35.

113. Arnold, *Three Crucial Questions,* 40, 122; Anderson, *Bondage Breaker,* 64–67; Murphy, *Spiritual Warfare,* 394; Foster, *Binding and Loosing,* 114–16; and Dickason, *Demon Possession,* 247–48.

114. Howard Clark Kee, "The Terminology of Mark's Exorcism Stories," *New Testament Studies* 14 (January 1968): 235–39.

115. For similar treatments of Jesus' rebuke of demons, see Konya, *Demons,* 44–45; and Powlison, *Power Encounters,* 86–87.

116. Ice and Dean, *Overrun by Demons,* 168.

117. That the celestial beings of 2 Peter 2:11 are fallen angels, see Edwin A. Blum, "Second Peter," in *Expositor's Bible Commentary,* ed. Frank E. Gaebelein (Grand Rapids: Zondervan, 1996), 74.

118. The New Living Translation (NLT) takes the Greek phrase *krisin blasphemias* as containing an objective genitive, "did not dare accuse Satan of blasphemy." The NRSV seems to take the genitive similarly: "he did not dare to bring a condemnation of slander against him." But the parallel passage in 2 Peter 2:11 has an adjectival construction, *blasphēmon krisin* ("slanderous judgment").

119. Dickason, *Demon Possession,* 256.

120. Bauer et al., *Greek-English Lexicon,* 303, give "punish" as a possible meaning for *epitimao* in Jude 9. The noun form *(epitimia)* of the word "rebuke" has "punishment" as its only definition. Ibid.

121. Michael Green, *The Second Epistle of Peter and the Epistle of Jude,* in Tyndale New Testament Commentaries, vol. 18, ed. R. V. G. Tasker (Grand Rapids: Eerdmans, 1968), 170.

122. Konya, *Demons,* 82.

123. I argue for a broader interpretation of *salvation* for Romans 1:16 in an upcoming article, "Why Confess Christ? The Use and Abuse of Romans 10:9-10," in the fall 1999 issue of the *Journal of the Grace Evangelical Society.*

124. Priest, "Missiological Syncretism," 24–25.

125. Understand, it is not to be denied that evangelism and church planting are certainly strategies of offense and an advance in our battle with Satan. *Attack* here refers to offensive-type spiritual warfare (power encounters, casting out demons, rebuking demons, praying against territorial spirits, etc.).

126. *Delivered from the Powers of Darkness,* dir. John R. Cross, writ. Mary Lonetti with Stephen Lonetti, 35 min. Destination Summit, 1997, videocassette.
127. Konya, *Demons,* 112; and Powlison, *Power Encounters,* 101.
128. An unfortunate by-product of this teaching is that Christians are subtly discouraged from adopting children who for various reasons are "unadoptable." Cf. the dangers of adoption suggested in Logan, *Reclaiming Surrendered Ground,* 110–11; Murphy, *Spiritual Warfare,* 438. Such cautions about adoption conflict with Christ's model and teaching on compassion for the needy.
129. For a more comprehensive discussion of the superstitious worldview behind these teachings, see Priest et al., "Missiological Syncretism," 56–64.

Chapter 12: Financial Support of the Missionary

1. S. Aalen, *"time,"* in *The New International Dictionary of New Testament Theology,* ed. Colin Brown (Grand Rapids: Zondervan 1976, 1986), 50.
2. Fritz Rienecker, *Linguistic Key to the Greek New Testament,* ed. Cleon Rogers (Grand Rapids: Zondervan, 1976, 1980), 453.
3. Walter Bauer, *A Greek-English Lexicon of the New Testament and Other Early Christian Literature,* 2d ed., rev. F. W. Gingrich and Frederick Danker, trans. William F. Arndt and F. W. Gingrich (Chicago: Chicago Univ. Press, 1979), 709.
4. Ibid.
5. See Albert T. Platt, chapter 14, "The Role of the Mission Agency," in this volume.
6. J. Herbert Kane, *Life and Work on the Mission Field* (Grand Rapids: Baker, 1980), 66.
7. Ibid., 67.
8. Ibid., 71.

Chapter 13: The Responsibility of the Local Church

1. Tom Telford, *Missions in the 21st Century: Getting Your Church in the Game* (Wheaton, Ill.: Harold Shaw, 1998), 148. Telford questions whether the percentage is even this high. He states, "To be perfectly frank, I think there may be far fewer than 10 percent of churches with missions programs. Some churches say they have missions programs because they send a token 5 percent of their budget to some denominational or church agency, and then wash their hands of further responsibility. Sorry, but that's not missions."
2. Robert P. Lightner, "The Nature of the Church," in *The Fundamentals for the Twenty-First Century,* ed. Mal Couch (Grand Rapids: Kregel, 2000), 337–38.
3. Harold R. Cook, *Christian Missions,* rev. ed. (Chicago: Moody Bible Institute of Chicago, 1971), 222.
4. Cook, whose book was published in 1971, shows how effective the missions conferences were formerly in challenging young people to missions. He states, "A 1967–68 survey of 253 new missionaries in three Spanish language schools

in Latin America showed that about 40 percent were decisively influenced by their church's missionary conference to dedicate their lives to missions. No other gathering was even a third as effective."

5. Ibid., 238 n.
6. John Piper, *Let the Nations Be Glad: The Supremacy of God in Missions* (Grand Rapids: Baker, 1993), 56.
7. Ibid., 57.
8. Ibid., 45.
9. Fritz Rienecker, *Linguistic Key to the Greek New Testament*, ed. Cleon Rogers (Grand Rapids: Zondervan, 1976, 1980), 453.
10. Walter Bauer, *A Greek-English Lexicon of the New Testament and Other Early Christian Literature*, 2d ed., rev. F. W. Gingrich and Frederick Danker, trans. William F. Arndt and F. W. Gingrich (Chicago: Chicago Univ. Press, 1979), 709.
11. Telford, *Missions in the 21st Century*, 159.
12. Bauer, *Greek-English Lexicon*, 722.
13. Telford, *Missions in the 21st Century*, 42–43.
14. Cook, *Christian Missions*, 120–21.
15. David J. Hesselgrave, *Planting Churches Cross Culturally* (Grand Rapids: Baker, 1980), 142.
16. Ibid.
17. Ibid., 66.
18. Steven McAvoy, "The Laying on of Hands in the Old Testament and the Gospels," Appendix I in *A Bible Handbook to the Acts of the Apostles*, ed. Mal Couch (Grand Rapids: Kregel, 1999), 406.
19. George W. Peters, *A Biblical Theology of Missions* (Chicago: Moody, 1972), 221–22.
20. Bauer, *Greek-English Lexicon*, 96.
21. Peter Jordan, *Re-Entry* (Seattle, Wash.: YWAM, 1992), 77.
22. Ibid., 78–79.
23. Peter Jordan's *Re-Entry* is highly recommended. It was very helpful to my wife and me when we returned from our service in Eastern Europe.
24. Lightner, "The Nature of the Church."

Chapter 14: The Role of the Mission Agency

1. Warren W. Webster, "The Messenger and Mission Structures," in *Perspectives on the World Christian Movement: A Reader*, ed. Ralph D. Winter and Steven C. Hawthorne (Pasadena: William Carey Library, 1992), D-239.
2. Perhaps the most significant example of such an element is Sunday school, although one could add specialized young people's ministries, the use of media, baptisteries, sound amplification, etc. In general, however, simply because something cannot be demonstrated in the New Testament does not necessitate disallowing such in the ministry that is the Lord's work.
3. That nothing in Scripture indicates that the church at Antioch accepted financial responsibility for Paul and Barnabas should not be construed as

approval for financial noninvolvement in missionary activity on the part of a local church. The situation in Acts 13 is new for both the church and the chosen teachers, who were not likely to have been on the church payroll before the Holy Spirit revealed the plan. Apparently pay, support, money, or even "needs" were not a part of the Spirit's directive at that time. But other assemblies of believers along the way did contribute (cf. Phil. 4:16).

4. W. E. Vine, Merrill F. Unger, and William White Jr., *An Expository Dictionary of Biblical Words* (Nashville: Nelson, 1984), 1015.

5. Webster, "The Messenger and Mission Structures," 240.

6. ". . . on the one hand, the structure we call the New Testament Church is a prototype of all subsequent Christian fellowships. . . . On the other hand, Paul's missionary band can be considered a prototype of all subsequent missionary endeavors organized out of committed, experienced workers who affiliated themselves as a second decision beyond membership in the first structure." Ralph D. Winter, "The Two Structures of God's Redemptive Mission," in *Perspectives on the World Christian Movement: A Reader,* ed. Ralph D. Winter and Steven C. Hawthorne (Pasadena Calif.: William Carey Library, 1992), B-46. See also in the aforementioned publication and, supporting this same thesis, the article by Arthur F. Glasser, "The Apostle Paul and the Missionary Task," A-128.

7. George W. Peters, *A Biblical Theology of Missions* (Chicago: Moody, 1972), 224. Worthy of note is Peter's dealing with four important organizational principles found in Scripture (224–26).

8. C. Peter Wagner, *On the Crest of the Wave, Becoming a World Christian* (Glendale, Calif.: Regal, 1983), 73–74.

9. Charles C. Ryrie, unpublished class notes, Dallas Theological Seminary, Dallas, Tex.

10. See Peters, *Biblical Theology of Missions,* 159ff.

11. As in the case of the local church, fidelity to the Word of God depends on the leadership. A doctrinal statement is only as strong as those who hold it. Thus, in the case of a mission agency, only when care is exercised in the choice of board members can there be any hope for an ongoing theological soundness. (The same is true for membership at the missionary level.) Board leadership for any part of God's work should be entrusted to the godly, those who are well taught in the Word, those who are keeping themselves unspotted from the world. No one should be vested with board membership simply because of personality, professional title, training, ability, or wealth.

12. An unfortunate tendency exists among new missionary recruits to disparage what is in place in favor of something new. Equally unfortunate is that often the "new" is very much a cultural "import," one that comes with great enthusiasm but too little cultural examination in regard to propriety.

13. Missionaries who are displeased that the agency takes out a certain (usually minor) amount from their support for administrative costs are, after benefiting from these services on the field for a term, usually pleased to relinquish that small amount.

14. Peters, *Biblical Theology of Missions,* 229.
15. Ibid.
16. Agency organizational structure, be it of the pyramid variety or some other, should not bring about a departure from the biblical concept of servant leadership.
17. Such an influence on practices has been attempted during meetings of missionaries on the field (usually annual conferences) where a newly arrived missionary, quite sure that everyone has mismanaged matters until that time, forcefully suggests "the right way" and is seen as being more "revolutionary" than "reformer." Such attempts demonstrate little or no insight into the whys and wherefores but strong opinions that come from "this-is-the-way-we-did-it-in-such-and-such-a-church." An older missionary offered to my wife sage advice during a conference of missionaries: "Have Al keep quiet and listen!" Several years later, when a brand new missionary tried to impose his will concerning a matter about which he knew very little, that same older missionary who had offered the earlier advice commented to my wife, "Now aren't you glad Al kept quiet back then?"
18. A reaction against forced work relationships might have contributed to the phenomenon of whole teams joining a mission with the desire to be sent to the same field to work together. Somewhere along the line, the term *team* has undergone a semantic change and now seems to have the meaning "group." In keeping with the use of the word in athletics, *team* implies people of different skills who complement one another. A place certainly exists for that kind of "team" on the mission field, and whereas "groups" can also be productive, missions should put together people whose skills complement one another to best accomplish the task.
19. The term *faith missions* was probably born in the Hudson Taylor/China Inland Mission emphasis on trusting God and the nonsolicitation of funds.
20. "Generally speaking denominational missions get their support from the denominational budget and thus pay their missionaries a regular salary. They do not require their missionaries to 'raise their support.' This is not true of most Baptist missions, however, which function more like interdenominational missions in not having a denominational budget to draw from." G. Gordon Olson, *What in the World Is God Doing?* (Cedar Knolls, N.J.: Global Gospel, 1989), 257.
21. "How many of us who serve in pastoral ministry would like to pursue this process? Would we like to submit our families to the difficulties of support raising and maintenance? Would we view the disruption of our children's lives and education as necessary elements of our work? How many masters would we like to serve? Missionaries contend with sending churches, supporting churches, parachurch agencies, nationals and each is part of the puzzle of international ministry." Patrick Howell, "Returning to the Biblical Paradigm in Modern Missions," in *Voice,* January–February 1999, 23.
22. Webster, "The Messenger and Mission Structures," C-244.

Chapter 15: The Missionary's Responsibility to the Sending Church and Mission Agency

1. C. Gordon Olson, *What in the World Is God Doing?* (Cedar Knolls; N.J.: Global Gospel Pub., 1988, 1989), 253–54.
2. Ibid., 254
3. Melvin L. Hodges, "The Relationship of the Missionary to the Home (Sending) Church," in *Facing Facts in Modern Missions: A Symposium* (Chicago: Moody Bible Institute of Chicago, 1963), 55.

Chapter 16: Short-Term Missions

1. David C. Forward, *The Essential Guide to the Short-Term Mission Trip* (Chicago: Moody, 1998), 14.
2. Robert Coote, "Good News, Bad News: North American Protestant Overseas Personnel Statistics in Twenty-Five Year Perspective," *International Bulletin of Mission Research* 19 (January 1995): 6.
3. Robert J. Yackley, "When the Saints Go Marching In," *Evangelical Missions Quarterly,* July 1994, 306.
4. Robertson McQuilkin, "Six Inflammatory Questions—Part 2," *Evangelical Missions Quarterly,* July 1994, 260.
5. James F. Engel and Jerry D. Jones, *Baby Boomers and the Future of World Missions* (Orange, Calif.: Management Development Assoc., 1989), 32–39.
6. Roger P. Peterson and Timothy D. Peterson, *Is Short-Term Missions Really Worth the Time and Money?* (Minneapolis: STEM, 1991), 24.
7. Michael J. Anthony, ed., *The Short-Term Missions Boom* (Grand Rapids: Baker, 1994), 34.
8. Peterson and Peterson, *Is Short-Term Missions Really Worth the Time and Money?* 21–22.
9. Ibid., 9.
10. Anthony, *Short-Term Missions Boom,* 51.
11. Chris Eaton and Kim Hurst, *Vacations with a Purpose: Leader's Manual* (Elgin, Ill.: David C. Cook, 1993), 27–28.
12. Ibid., 30.
13. Ibid., 36–38.
14. Seth Barnes, "The Changing Face of the Missionary Force," *Evangelical Missions Quarterly* (October 1992): 376.
15. Engel and Jones, *Baby Boomers and the Future of World Missions,* 22.
16. Paul Borthwick, "Are Short-Termers Ready to Minister?" in *Mission Today '96: Short-Term Missions: A Special Report* (Evanston, Ill.: Berry, 1996), 178.
17. Dennis K. Massaro, "Who Really Benefits from Short-Terms?" in *Mission Today '96: Short-Term Missions: A Special Report* (Evanston, Ill.: Berry, 1996), 151.
18. Glen Howard, "Summer Teams" (letter to the editor), *Evangelical Missions Quarterly,* July 1994, 10.
19. Borthwick, "Are Short-Termers Ready to Minister?" 178.
20. John A. Siewert and Edna G. Valdez, eds., *Mission Handbook 1998–2000: A*

Guide to U.S. and Canadian Christian Ministries Overseas (Monrovia, Calif.: MARC, 1997), 43.

21. Borthwick, "Are Short-Termers Ready to Minister?" 54.
22. Andrew Atkins, "Work Teams? No, 'Taste and See' Teams," *Evangelical Missions Quarterly,* October 1991, 385.
23. Ibid., 385–86.
24. Yackley, "When the Saints Go Marching In," 304–5.
25. William D. Taylor, "Flying with Two Wings," in *Mission Today '96: Short-Term Missions: A Special Report* (Evanston, Ill.: Berry, 1996), 167.
26. Eaton and Hurst, *Vacations with a Purpose,* 159–61.
27. Davis Duggins, "Hiding from the Harvest?" *Moody,* November–December 1996, 14.
28. Engel and Jones, *Baby Boomers and the Future of World Missions,* 33.
29. Massaro, "Who Really Benefits from Short-Terms?" 150.
30. Engel and Jones, *Baby Boomers and the Future of World Missions,* 40.
31. Anthony, *Short-Term Missions Boom,* 113–17.
32. Ibid., 56–60.
33. Ibid., 122.
34. Ibid., 121–23.
35. Ibid., 130.
36. Yackley, "When the Saints Go Marching In," 306.
37. John Beerly, *Summer Missions Programs in Haiti* (Caronport, Sask.: Briercrest Bible College, 1991).
38. Larry Ragan, *Training Short-Term Teams* (Atlanta, Ga.: Produced by ACMC), audiocassette.
39. Elizabeth Lightbody, "More Than a Vacation," *Moody,* November–December 1996, 25.
40. Borthwick, "Are Short-Termers Ready to Minister?" 180,182.
41. Forward, *The Essential Guide to the Short-Term Mission Trip,* 129.
42. Eaton and Hurst, *Vacations with a Purpose,* 87.
43. Anthony, *Short-Term Missions Boom,* 74–76.
44. Forward, *The Essential Guide to the Short-Term Mission Trip,* 115–16.
45. Anthony, *Short-Term Missions Boom,* 83.
46. Engel and Jones, *Baby Boomers and the Future of World Missions,* 39–40.
47. Yackley, "When the Saints Go Marching In," 306–7.
48. Eaton and Hurst, *Vacations with a Purpose,* 159.